PUTTING
MICROSOFT® WORKS
TO WORK

PUTTING MICROSOFT® WORKS TO WORK

12 READY-TO-USE MODELS FOR THE IBM® PC, PS/2™ AND COMPATIBLES

Douglas Cobb
The Cobb Group

PUBLISHED BY
Microsoft Press
A Division of Microsoft Corporation
16011 NE 36th Way, Box 97017, Redmond, Washington 98073-9717

Library of Congress Cataloging in Publication Data

Cobb, Douglas Ford.
Putting Microsoft Works to work.
Includes index.
1. Microsoft Works (Computer program)   2. IBM microcomputers—
Programming.   3. Business—Data processing.   I. Title.
HF5548.4.M53M62   1988   650'.028'55369   87-35244
ISBN 1-55615-107-1

Printed and bound in the United States of America.

  23456789   MLML   21098

Distributed to the book trade in the United States
by Harper & Row.

Distributed to the book trade in Canada by General
Publishing Company, Ltd.

Distributed to the book trade outside the United States
and Canada by Penguin Books Ltd.

Penguin Books Ltd., Harmondsworth, Middlesex, England
Penguin Books Australia Ltd., Ringwood, Victoria, Australia
Penguin Books N.Z. Ltd., 182-190 Wairau Road, Auckland 10, New Zealand

British Cataloging in Publication Data available

Acquisitions editor: Claudette Moore
Project editor: Eric Stroo
Technical editors: Mike Halvorson
                  Gerald Joyce
Production editor: Evan Konecky

To my friends Ken, John, Austin, and Roger,
who have made so much difference in my life.

CONTENTS

Acknowledgments

Lots of people worked exceptionally hard to make this book possible. I would like to thank them here:

The dedicated individuals at Microsoft Press, who carefully edited, proofread, and produced the book.

Eric Schlene, for his technical editing. Bruce Jacobsen and Robert Orndorff of Microsoft, for supplying us with software and for answering our questions. Gena Cobb, for her support. The Bear, who puts it all in perspective. Barbara Wells, Brenda Bankston, Shannon Portman, Sandy Jetter, Kevin Fuqua, Denise Rogers, Jo McGill, Grand Britt, Donald "Lubba Man" Fields, Tracey Milliner, Tom Cottingham, Julie Tirpak, Franny Corrigan, Patty Flynn, Steve Cobb, Judy Myhnier, Mark Crane, Maureen Pawley, Elayne Noltemeyer, Chris Brown, Linda Baughman, Alan McGuffey, and Linda Watkins, who make my job the best job around.

PREFACE

Microsoft Works is one of the most exciting programs ever for the IBM PC and compatibles. Works is an integrated program that offers all the tools most people need—a word processor, a spreadsheet with charting, a database manager, and data communications—at a price most people can afford. Works is no-compromise software at a no-nonsense price: a great tool for the new generation of computers and computer users.

Works offers amazing performance that is unprecedented in inexpensive software. Unlike most other integrated programs, Works doesn't demand that you settle for less than the best. Each Works environment is the equal of many stand-alone programs.

The heart of the program is its powerful word processor, which offers all the tools you need to create professional-quality memos, letters, and reports. Works includes a full-featured spreadsheet that is completely compatible with the industry standard, Lotus 1-2-3. The charting capabilities in Works allow you to create presentation-quality charts from the numbers in your Works spreadsheets. Works' form-based database manager lets you store, sort, and query lists of information and then report on that information using its powerful report generator. The communications component makes it easy to communicate with other computers. And because Works integrates all these capabilities into a single program, you can easily share information among the different parts of the program.

About This Book

Putting Microsoft Works to Work is a book of templates—creative, ready-to-use applications of the Works tools. In this book, you'll find 12 templates, some fairly simple, others quite complex. Some are designed to be used at home, some at work. All the templates are practical tools that will help you put Works to work for you.

I've written this book with two purposes in mind.

First, I've written it to offer you a set of ready-to-use templates for Works—templates that you can use to manage your business and personal affairs. For instance, you can use the Checkbook Register and Balancer in Chapter 3 to manage and balance your checkbook and the Simple General Ledger in Chapter 4 to account for your receipts and expenditures.

Second, I've written it to help you learn how to use Works. The book offers detailed instructions for building each template, including step-by-step instructions for such procedures as making entries in cells, copying values, labels, and formulas, formatting cells, changing column widths, creating charts, defining database forms and database reports, and creating mail-merge documents. By building and using the templates in this book, you'll learn how to use Works.

Chapter 1 explains a few basic concepts that you'll need to understand before you begin to create and use the templates. In this chapter, you learn how to choose commands from menus, navigate in dialog boxes, and highlight ranges. In addition, you learn in general terms how to open and save and print files. If you are brand new to Works, you'll probably want to start with this chapter. If you're already familiar with Works, you can begin with any one of the chapters that explain the templates.

Chapters 2 through 13 each have three basic sections. The first section in each chapter, "About the Template," is an overview of the template, which explains its general layout and operation. The second section, "Creating the Template," offers detailed, step-by-step instructions for building the template from scratch. By following the instructions in this section to the letter, you'll be able to create any of the templates in this book in just a few hours. (In some cases, you'll need only a few minutes.) The third section, "Using the Template," explains the process of using the template. This section in each chapter offers a detailed example that explains the ins and outs of using the template.

The Cash Flow Tracker in **Chapter 2** will help you plan your cash balances more accurately. To use this template, you record your beginning cash balance and your anticipated cash receipts and disbursements for the coming year. When you're finished, Works computes estimated cash balances for each week of the year. You can use this template at home to track your personal cash flow or at work to manage your business cash flow. This spreadsheet demonstrates several interesting techniques, including a macro that lets you add rows to the spreadsheet with just a few keystrokes.

The Checkbook Register and Balancer in **Chapter 3** lets you manage your checking account in Works. To use this template, you enter each check you write and each deposit you make in the template's check register. The spreadsheet uses formulas to compute the balance of your account after every check and deposit. At the end of the month, when you need to balance the checkbook, you just code the checks and deposits that have not cleared the bank. The spreadsheet then makes the selections and performs the math for you.

The Simple General Ledger in **Chapter 4** is a simple accounting system you can use to keep track of your income and expenses. The Simple General Ledger lets you set up the system of accounts that you want to use to classify your income and expenses. After you set up this system, you enter your checks and deposits and give each one an account code. The Simple General Ledger uses these codes—and the account numbers you've defined—to "post" each check and deposit to an account. This template demonstrates a number of clever Works techniques, such as a procedure for using the Copy command to copy information from one spreadsheet to another.

Chapter 5 tells you how to create an amortization table using the Loan Amortization Calculator. This template can handle any combination of principal balance, term (as long as 360 months), and interest rate, and it can handle common special situations, such as additional monthly principal payments and variable interest rates. The template can also help you analyze a loan. For example, it computes the total amount you will have to pay to amortize a loan and the amount of interest you will pay across the life of the loan. You can also use it to analyze the status of the loan at any point in its life. You can use this template at home to track your house mortgage and car loan and at work to manage your business debt.

If you are running a small business or managing a product in a larger business, you'll want to use the Breakeven Analysis template in **Chapter 6**. This simple template computes the breakeven point for a product, given the selling price and the variable and fixed costs for the product. The template also includes a breakeven chart that illustrates the relationship between unit sales and revenues, costs, and profits.

If you perform financial analysis, you'll want to consider the Ratio Analysis template in **Chapter 7**. To use this template, you enter the balance sheet and income statement for the company you want to analyze in the appropriate cells in the spreadsheet. When you're finished, the template computes a number of key financial ratios for the company: the Current Ratio, the Quick Ratio, the Debt/Equity Ratio, and so on.

The Mailing-List Manager in **Chapter 8** provides the basic tools you'll need to begin managing your mailing list in Works. Although the Mailing-List Manager is one of the simplest applications in this book, it is also one of the most useful. You can use it at home to store the names and addresses of your friends and acquaintances, or you can use it at work to hold the names of your employees, customers, sales prospects, and so on. As you build the template, you'll learn how to create, query, and sort databases, and to create merge documents in Works.

Companies and individuals who bill by the hour will be interested in the Time Tracker in **Chapter 9**. This easy-to-build template provides the basic tools you'll need to track time in Works. In addition, as you build the template, you'll learn how to create, query, and sort databases and how to create and use database reports in Works.

The Accounts Receivable Tracker in **Chapter 10** can be used by small businesses to manage accounts receivable. This template consists of a Works database in which you record each invoice your company writes and a series of report definitions. To use the template, you simply enter the information for each invoice in the AR database. Then, as you receive payments, you post them to the database as well. The template contains formulas that compute the outstanding balance and the age of each invoice. The template's reports let you view the data in the AR database in a variety of forms. The template even includes a report that prints account statements.

If you run a business, you ought to consider building and using the Profit and Loss Forecast in **Chapter 11**. This template makes it easy to build a profit plan—a forecast of income and expenses—for your business. Although it is fairly complicated, it is also extremely useful and flexible enough to be used by a business of almost any size.

The Business Cash Flow Forecast in **Chapter 12** makes it easy to forecast cash balances for your business one year into the future. You enter your estimates for sales, cost of goods sold, operating expenses, fixed asset purchases and sales, and debt service; then, the template computes cash collection and disbursements and net cash receipts. The template includes a cleverly devised formula that borrows short-term debt when cash balances fall below a minimum level that you set and then repays that debt when excess cash becomes available. This template is flexible enough to be used by small companies and by multi-million dollar businesses.

The template in **Chapter 13**, the Personal Financial Plan, uses Works as the basis for a one-year personal income statement and balance sheet projection. The Personal Financial Plan is an ideal tool for creating a personal budget for the coming year. It can help you avoid the embarrassment of an overdrawn checking account or an unpaid bill. It might even keep you from missing an opportunity to make a terrific investment.

Who Should Use This Book?

Putting Microsoft Works to Work can be used by anyone who uses Microsoft Works. Beginning users will appreciate the book's step-by-step instructions and thorough, careful explanations. If you are new to Works, *Putting Microsoft Works to Work* will help you come up to speed quickly. Advanced users will enjoy the tricks and techniques that are explained in each chapter. If you've been working with Works for a while, this book will help you move up to the next level of expertise.

Although the templates in the book are generally arranged in order of increasing complexity, you don't have to start at the beginning. Each template stands on its own, so you can begin anywhere.

There's More

If you don't want to build the templates in this book from scratch, you can buy them in finished form on disk from Microsoft Press. (See the following offer.) If you order the templates on disk, you can skip or skim the section of each chapter that describes the template creation and proceed to "Using the Template."

Special Offer

Companion Disk To
PUTTING MICROSOFT WORKS TO WORK

Microsoft Press has created the Companion Disk to PUTTING MICROSOFT WORKS TO WORK. You can choose the set of two 5.25-inch disks or the single 3.5-inch disk; either way, you'll get all twelve templates presented in this book. You'll also save yourself the valuable time that's required to type in the templates and the frustration of finding those inevitable typing errors. The Companion Disk to PUTTING MICROSOFT WORKS TO WORK is a handy—and valuable—resource tool.

If you have questions about the files on the disk, you can send your written queries or comments to Doug Cobb, c/o The Cobb Group, 301 North Hurstbourne Lane, Louisville, KY, 40222.

The Companion Disk to PUTTING MICROSOFT WORKS TO WORK is only available directly from Microsoft Press. To order, use the special bound-in card at the back of the book. If the card has already been used, send $15.95 (plus $2.50 per disk for domestic postage and handling, $4.00 per disk for foreign orders) to: Microsoft Press, Attn: Companion Disk Offer, 13221 SE 26th, Suite L, Bellevue, WA, 98005. Please specify 5.25-inch or 3.5-inch format. Payment must be in U.S. funds. You may pay by check or money order (payable to Microsoft Press) or by American Express, VISA, or MasterCard; please include both your credit card number and the expiration date. All orders are shipped UPS (no P.O. boxes please); allow 4 weeks for delivery.

Works Basics

4 disks
"WORKS"

Works combines four distinct document types—word processing, spreadsheeting, database management, and communications—into a single software package. The four types of documents are, of course, different—each one is designed for a different kind of work—but because they are combined in a single program, many skills apply equally to every one: selecting commands from menus, for example, negotiating dialog boxes, or saving and opening documents. These skills and others are explained in this chapter. After you master them, you can begin to create the templates presented in the chapters that follow.

THE SETUP PROGRAM

Before you begin to use Works, use the setup program on the Setup/Utilities disk to install Works for your computer. The setup program has two functions. First, it creates a working copy of Works, either on a floppy disk or on your hard disk. Second, it configures Works to take advantage of your particular equipment.

To complete the setup program, begin by booting your computer and making A: the active drive. To do this, place an MS-DOS disk in the A drive and turn on your computer. After a few moments, your computer will boot and display an *A>* prompt. Next, place the Setup/Utilities disk in drive A, type *setup*, and press Enter.

The next screen presents a few instructions for using the setup program and offers three choices: *Create a new program disk*, *Modify a program disk*, and *Exit the program*. To install Works for the first time, choose *Create a new program disk*. Then, continue with the setup program, making selections and swapping disks when prompted to do so. To complete the process, you will need to identify the type of equipment you are using—your computer, your graphics card, and any printers. If you are installing Works on a hard disk, you have another decision: The setup program lets you place the Help files or the Spell files or both sets of files on your disk, provided that it contains sufficient free space. When prompted to do so, choose one of the available options.

How?

When you finish the entire process, the screen displays the message *You have successfully completed Microsoft WORKS setup.* Press any key to leave the setup program and return to MS-DOS. Once back at the system prompt, you can proceed to load Works.

STARTING WORKS

Before you can use Works, you must load it into your computer. The way you do this depends on whether you set up Works on a hard disk or on a floppy disk.

Loading Works from a Floppy Disk

If you set up Works on a floppy disk, load the program from drive A. If your computer is off, insert an MS-DOS disk into drive A and turn on your computer. After a few moments, your computer boots and displays the prompt A>. If your computer is on but not at an MS-DOS prompt, exit whatever program you are running. If you see a prompt other than A> at this point, type *a:* and press Enter to make A: the active drive. When you are at the A> prompt, insert your Works disk (that is, the copy that you made with the setup program) in drive A, close the door of that drive, type *works*, and press Enter.

Loading Works from a Hard Disk

If you set up Works on a hard disk, load the program from that disk. If your computer is off, turn it on. After a few moments, it boots and displays the prompt C>. If your computer is on but not at an MS-DOS prompt, exit whatever program you are running. If you see a prompt other than C> at this point, type *c:* and press Enter to make C: the active drive.

When C: is the current drive, make current the directory that contains your Works program files—in most cases, C:\WORKS. To make C:\WORKS the current directory, type *cd c:\works* and press Enter. Then, load Works simply by typing *works* and pressing Enter.

When Works is loaded, your screen will look like Figure 1-1. The structure in the middle of this screen is the New dialog box, which lets you create a new Works document. The four options in the box—Word Processing, Spreadsheet, Database, and Communications—correspond to the four possible types of Works documents.

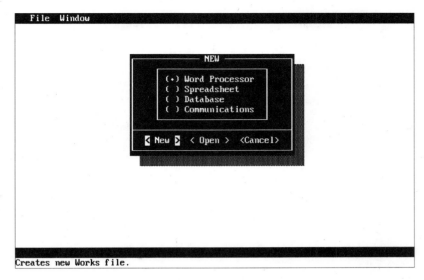

Figure 1-1. *The initial screen after you load Works.*

Creating a Works Document

To create a new Works document, choose the type of document you want to create from the list in the New dialog box, and then choose New. To choose the type of document you want to create, you can use the Up Arrow and Down Arrow keys to move the dot to the document type, or you can type the first letter of the option: *s* or *S* for Spreadsheet, *d* or *D* for Database, and so on. If you have a mouse, you can choose a document type by pointing to it and clicking the left button on the mouse. Works then moves the dot to that option.

Next, choose the New button at the bottom of the box to tell Works to create a document of the type you specified. You can choose the New button in any of four ways. First, because New is the default button (indicated by the bold angle brackets), you can choose it by pressing Enter. Second, you can type *n* or *N*, the first letter in New. Third, you can press the Tab key to move the cursor to the New button, and then press Enter. If you have a mouse, you can point to the New button and click.

The other buttons at the bottom of the New dialog box instruct Works to perform different tasks. If you choose Open, Works displays a dialog box from which you can open an existing Works document. If you choose Cancel, Works closes the New dialog box without creating or opening a document.

A TOUR OF THE SCREEN

The different types of Works documents are designed for specific work. For example, Spreadsheet documents consist of a grid of rows and columns; Word Processor documents have a ruler at the top; and Database documents can be viewed either as a grid or through a form.

Despite the differences among document types, they share a number of common structural features. Figure 1-2 points out these features: the Menu bar, the Status line, the Message line, and the Work area.

The strip at the top of the document is its *Menu bar*. It displays the names of the various menus that are available in that type of document. For example, as you can see in Figure 1-2, Word Processor documents have seven menus: File, Edit, Print, Select, Format, Options, and Window. Each menu in any document contains a number of commands. These commands let you manipulate the information in the current document. To use a command, you must pull down the menu on which it appears. You'll learn how to gain access to the Menu bar and select commands from menus later in this chapter.

The second line from the bottom of the screen is the Status line. Works displays information about the current document—including the name of the document—on this line. Exactly what else appears on the Status line depends on the document type. In a Word Processor document, for example, the Status line displays, among other

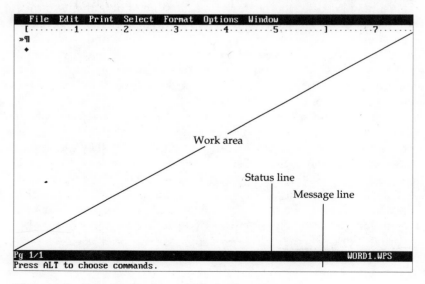

Figure 1-2. Common features of Works documents.

things, the number of the current page and the format characteristics of the currently highlighted text. In a Spreadsheet document, Works displays the address of the currently selected cell or block of cells.

The line at the bottom of the screen is the Message line. Works uses this line to display prompts and instructions, primarily explanations of what particular commands do and what you need to do to complete them.

You enter and edit information in the Work area, the area of the screen below the Menu bar and above the Status line. In a Word Processor document, the Work area is a series of ruled pages; in a spreadsheet, a grid of cells; in a database, either a custom-designed form or a grid of cells; and in a Communications document, a display of information sent to it by a remote computer.

If you installed Works for use with a mouse and activated the mouse before or as you loaded Works, your documents look slightly different from the one shown in the previous figure. In particular, they have a scroll bar along the right edge, and, in most cases, another along the bottom edge of the Work area. For example, Figure 1-3 shows a Word Processor document that contains these structures. Scroll bars let you use your mouse to move around within a Works document. The vertical scroll bar (the one at the right edge of the screen) lets you move up and down within the document. The horizontal scroll bar (the one at the bottom of the Work area) lets you move right and left across a document.

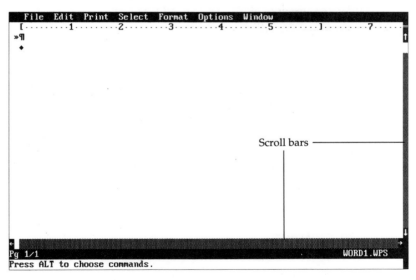

Figure 1-3. *Works screen with scroll bars.*

THE WORKS KEYBOARD

Works lets you take full advantage of the keyboard of your IBM or compatible computer. Let's look briefly at the ways you can use your keyboard with Works.

Moving the Cursor

You can use a number of keys and key combinations to move around in Works documents. Although the precise effect of each key or key combination depends to some extent on the document type, the basic effect is the same throughout Works. The table in Figure 1-4 lists the keys and key combinations you use in Works to move the cursor and explains the function of each (in the various document types).

Key	Moves cursor...
Down Arrow	Down one cell (SS), line (WP), record (DB list), or field (DB form)
Left Arrow	Left one cell (SS), character (WP), or field (DB)
Right Arrow	Right one cell (SS), character (WP), or field (DB)
Up Arrow	Up one cell (SS), line (WP), record (DB list), or field (DB form)
End	Right to end of current row (SS), line (WP), or record (DB)
Home	Left to beginning of current row (SS), line (WP), or record (DB)
PgDn	Down one screen (SS, WP, and DB)
PgUp	Up one screen (SS and WP)
Tab	Right one column or field (SS and DB)
Shift-Tab	Left one column or field (SS and DB)
Ctrl-Down Arrow	Down to end of current block (SS) or end of paragraph (WP)
Ctrl-Left Arrow	Left to end of current block (SS) or left one word (WP)
Ctrl-Right Arrow	Right to end of current block (SS) or right one word (WP)
Ctrl-Up Arrow	Up to end of current block (SS) or beginning of paragraph (WP)
Ctrl-End	Down and right to end of document
Ctrl-Home	Up and left to beginning of document
Ctrl-PgDn	Right one screen (SS), down to end of paragraph (WP), or down to next record (DB form)
Ctrl-PgUp	Left one screen (SS), up to beginning of paragraph (WP), or up to previous record (DB form)

Figure 1-4. Cursor movement keys in Works.

Function Keys

Works uses the special function keys on your keyboard for a variety of purposes, as explained in Figure 1-5. The special function keys—[F1], [F2], and so on—are located at the left edge or at the top of your keyboard. Notice that some keys have different purposes in different types of documents and that some keys are active only in certain types of documents. Also notice that Works uses the Shift and Ctrl keys with several function keys.

Key	Name	Purpose
[F1]	Help	Access Help
[F2]	Edit	Edit current cell
[F3]	Move	Execute Move command
Shift-[F3]	Copy	Execute Copy command
[F4]	Reference	Create absolute and mixed references
[F5]	Go To	Move cursor to new location
[F6]	Window	Move cursor to next window
Shift-[F6]	Prev Window	Move cursor to previous window
[F7]	Repeat Search	Look for next occurrence of search string
Shift-[F7]	Repeat Command	Repeat previous command
[F8]	Extend	Highlight a range of cells or characters
Shift-[F8]	Highlight Column	Highlight a column of cells
	Shrink	Reduce size of highlight (WP only)
Ctrl-[F8]	Highlight Row	Highlight a row of cells
Shift-Ctrl-[F8]	Highlight Spreadsheet	Highlight entire spreadsheet
[F9]	Calc	Calculate spreadsheet
	View Form	View database form
[F10]	Exit Define	Exit form, report, or chart define
Shift-[F10]	View	View chart or report on screen

Figure 1-5. Function keys in Works.

Other Keys

A few other keys are especially important in Works. The Enter key lets you store entries in a spreadsheet or database, execute certain commands (such as the Copy command in a Spreadsheet document), and end paragraphs in the Word Processor. You'll use it quite often as you build the templates.

The Esc key lets you unhighlight a range of cells or characters, back out of a menu that you entered accidentally, or cancel a command.

As you'll learn in a few pages, the Alt key activates the Menu bar. When you press this key, Works highlights the key letter in each menu name. You can then pull down a menu by pressing one of those keys.

Works offers special Control-key combinations that serve as shortcuts for various commands. For example, pressing Ctrl-B in a Word Processor document is equivalent to selecting the Bold command from the Format menu. Pressing Ctrl-' in a Spreadsheet or Database document copies into the current cell the contents of the cell directly above it. You'll learn more about such special keys as we use them to create the templates.

WORKING WITH MENUS AND COMMANDS

As mentioned earlier, the top line of every Works document is the Menu bar. Each word on the bar represents a menu, which contains commands that let you manipulate the information in the document.

Each document type has a unique set of menus, although many elements are identical. Some menus appear in more than one document type, and in some cases, menus with the same names contain exactly the same commands. For example, all documents have a File menu that contains eight commands: New, Open, Save, Save As, Save All, Close, DOS, and Exit.

Although each type of Works document has its own set of menus, you use the same techniques to select a command from any menu. Selecting a command from a menu is a three-step process: Get access to the Menu bar, pull down the menu that contains the command you want to select, and select that command.

Getting Access to the Menu Bar

To get access to the Menu bar in any Works document, press the Alt key. Works highlights the first item on the Menu bar (which is always the menu name *File*) and boldfaces one letter in each menu name. The Message line displays the prompt *Type highlighted letter of menu or use arrow keys and press Enter.*

Pulling Down a Menu

After you get access to the Menu bar, select and pull down the menu that contains the command you want to issue. You can do so in two ways. First, you can use the Right and Left Arrow keys to move the highlight to the name of the menu you want to open, and then press Enter or the Up or Down Arrow key. For example, to open the Edit menu from a spreadsheet, press Alt, press the Right Arrow key once, and then press Enter. Figure 1-6 shows the result.

The alternative is to type the letter of the menu name that appears in bold type after you get access to the Menu bar. To open the Edit menu, for example, type *e* or *E*; to open the Format menu, type *t* or *T*; and so forth. In fact, you need not release the Alt key before you type the letter that identifies the menu name. To open the Print menu, for example, you can hold down the Alt key and type *p* or *P*.

Figure 1-6. *Edit menu in Word Processor document.*

Selecting a Command from a Menu

Pulling down a Works menu reveals the commands in that menu. As you can see in Figure 1-6, the Edit menu in a word processor document contains eight commands: Undo, Move, Copy, Copy Special, Delete, Insert Special, Insert Field, and Insert Chart. Like many menus, this one is divided into sections that group the commands according to their functions.

When you first pull down a menu, Works highlights the topmost command on that menu. To issue the first command, therefore, simply press Enter. To select another command, you can use the Up and Down Arrow keys to highlight the command you want to issue, and then press Enter. If you press the Down Arrow key while the last (bottommost) command in a menu is highlighted, Works moves the highlight to the first (topmost) command in that menu. If you press the Up Arrow key while the highlight is on the first command in a menu, Works moves the highlight to the last command. While Works highlights a command on an open menu, the Message line displays a brief explanation of the command.

An easier approach to choosing a command is to type the highlighted key letter of that command. For example, type *f* or *F* to select Fill Down from the Edit menu shown in Figure 1-6. Notice that the key letter of a command is not always the first letter in the name of that command.

When you type the key letter for a command, Works executes that command immediately; it does not move the highlight to that command and wait for you to press Enter. Until you are more comfortable with Works menus, therefore, select commands by highlighting the command and pressing Enter so that you can avoid issuing commands unintentionally.

Holding down the Alt key does not affect the choice of a command—Works issues the command whose key letter you type. Consequently, you can hold down the Alt key during the entire process of issuing a command, if you wish.

In some cases, you may want to close a menu without selecting a command. Press the Alt key to close the menu, but keep the Menu bar active. Press the Esc key to close the open menu and deactivate the Menu bar.

Using a Mouse

If you installed Works for use with a mouse, you can pull down menus and select commands by clicking or dragging. You can also use the keystroke methods described above, of course, either alone or in conjunction with the mouse techniques.

Clicking

One way to issue a command with a mouse is to position the mouse pointer on the menu name, click the left button on your mouse to open the menu, and then point to and click on the name of a command. Works executes the command—exactly as it does if you highlight the command and press Enter.

Dragging

An alternative to clicking is to pull down a menu and select a command by dragging. To do this, point to the name of the menu that contains the command you want to issue. Now, hold down the left button on your mouse, drag the mouse pointer to the command, and release the button. As the pointer touches each command, the Message line displays the brief explanation of that command. When you release the button, Works performs the highlighted command.

Inactive Commands

In certain situations, some commands on some Works menus are inactive: You are not able to issue them. The key letters for such commands do not appear boldfaced in the menu. For example, the Delete and Insert commands in Figure 1-6 on the previous page are inactive. These commands remain inactive until you take some necessary action—such as highlighting a block of text.

Types of Commands

You can divide Works commands into four functional groups: commands that execute immediately, toggle commands, commands that require an action, and commands that require additional information. Some have characteristics of two different types. For example, the Copy Special command on the Spreadsheet Edit menu requires you to perform an action *and* to supply more information.

Commands that execute immediately

When you issue certain commands, Works performs the indicated action immediately. Many (but not all) commands that execute immediately require that you first select what the command will act upon. For example, you must highlight the cells that you want to erase before you issue the Clear command in a spreadsheet.

Toggle commands

Some Works commands are "toggle" switches that turn a particular setting or characteristic on and off. Each time you choose a toggle command, Works changes the status of the command to the opposite of the status indicated by the menu. For example, the Manual Calculation command on the Spreadsheet's Options menu toggles the spreadsheet between automatic and manual recalculation. If a setting is on, a dot appears on the menu to the left of the command. If the setting is off, the area to the left of the command is blank.

Commands that require an action

Many Works commands require an action after you issue them. When you issue such a command, Works displays a prompt on the Message line that tells you what you need to do. In most cases, you need to specify a destination and then press Enter. For example, after you issue the Copy command in a Word Processor document, Works displays the message *Select new location and press ENTER or press ESC to cancel.* After you move the cursor to a destination and press Enter, Works copies the text you marked to the destination you specified.

Commands that require more information

Most Works commands require you to supply more information. The names of these commands are followed by an ellipsis—a series of three dots. For example, the New command on the File menu appears as *New...*, and the Print command appears as *Print...* on the Print menu.

Whenever a command requires more information, Works displays a dialog box—a window that contains choices, spaces in which to enter information, and so forth. When you pull down the File menu and select the Open command, for example, you see a dialog box like the one shown in Figure 1-7 on the following page.

The simplest dialog boxes contain only a few choices. For example, the dialog box that Works presents when you issue the DOS command requires only that you select one of two buttons: <OK> or <Cancel>. As you'll learn, however, most dialog boxes contain more choices. Works lets you work in the dialog box until you choose one of the buttons at the bottom of the box. One button (usually the one labeled OK) instructs Works to invoke the command using the settings (if any) that you specified in the dialog box. Another button (usually the one labeled Cancel) cancels the command and any revisions to the settings.

Figure 1-7.

Working with Dialog Boxes

Using a dialog box is a two-step process. First, you supply the information that the dialog box requests. Then, you use one of the buttons at the bottom of the box to tell Works what action to take.

Dialog boxes can contain five different elements: text boxes, check boxes, option boxes, list boxes, and buttons. (All dialog boxes contain buttons.) For example, the dialog box shown in Figure 1-7 contains a text box, two list boxes, an option box, and two buttons.

Moving between elements

When Works displays a dialog box, the cursor is in the first element—the one closest to the upper left corner. To edit an element in a dialog box, you must move the cursor to that element in one of three ways. First, you can use the Tab and Shift-Tab keys. Pressing the Tab key moves the cursor to the next element in the dialog box. The Shift-Tab combination moves the cursor to the previous element.

The effect of moving the cursor to an element in a dialog box depends on the type of element you move it to. In a text box, Works highlights the contents of the box. If the box is blank, Works places the cursor at the beginning of the box. In a list box, Works moves the cursor to the element that is currently selected. If no element is selected, Works places the cursor on the top item in the list but does not select it. In an option box, Works places the cursor on the currently selected option. In a check box, Works places the cursor in that box but does not change its state. When you move the cursor to a button, Works simply positions the cursor on that button.

Using the Alt key and key letters: You can also move to an element in a dialog box by holding down the Alt key and typing the boldfaced letter of that element. In a list box or a text box, Works responds precisely as it does when you tab to that element. In a check box, Works moves the cursor to that box and toggles the setting to its opposite state. If the setting is off, for example, Works turns it on.

Within an option box each option has its own key letter. When you hold down the Alt key and type the key letter of one of the options, Works moves the cursor to that option and selects it. Because you can select only one option at a time, this action negates the selection of any other option in the box.

If a button has a key letter, you can hold down the Alt key and type the key letter. Works not only moves the cursor to that button but also performs the action that the button commands.

Using a mouse: If you installed Works for use with a mouse, you can use your mouse to move among the elements in a dialog box. Simply point to an area in that element and click the left button on your mouse. When you do this, Works moves the cursor to the element on which you clicked. If you click on a check box, Works changes the state of that box. If you click on a button, Works performs the action that the button commands. If you click on an option box, Works selects the option on which you clicked. If you click on a text box, Works positions the cursor on the letter (if any) on which you clicked.

Using the elements in a dialog box

In this section, we'll explain how to alter the settings in each type of element within a Works dialog box.

Check boxes: Check boxes are "toggle" elements—they are either on or off. An X in a check box indicates that the setting controlled by that box is on. If the box is empty, the setting is off. While the cursor is positioned in a check box, you can turn it on or off by pressing the Spacebar.

You also can use the direction keys to activate and deactivate check boxes. Press the Up or Down Arrow keys to turn on a check box. If the setting is already on, it remains on. Press the Right or Left Arrow keys to turn a check box off. If the setting is already off, it remains off.

Of course, you can also hold down the Alt key and type the key letter of the check box in which the cursor is currently positioned, or you can point to that box with your mouse and click. In either case, Works changes the state of the box and keeps the cursor in place.

Figure 1-8 on the following page shows the Print dialog box in a Word Processor document. The Print Specific Pages check box is turned on, and the page range *1–3* is specified to be printed.

Option boxes: Option boxes present a fixed number of mutually exclusive choices. Within any option box, one option is always selected, and only one option can be selected at a time. You can select another option in that box in a number of ways. First, you can use the direction keys to move the cursor from option to option.

Figure 1-8.

Because Works selects the option on which the cursor is positioned, moving the cursor selects a new option. You can also type the key letter of that option (it's not necessary to hold down the Alt key), or you can point the mouse to that option and click.

List boxes: List boxes present a variable number of choices. As in an option box, only one option can be selected at a time. Unlike the options in an option box, however, the items in a list box are not fixed; different items may appear in the box at different times. For example, Works uses list boxes to present the names of the files on a disk. The list of filenames changes as you add or delete files from the disk or if you place a new disk in the drive. Works always arranges the items in any list box in ascending alphabetical order.

You can use various techniques to select an item in a list box. First, you can use the Up and Down Arrow keys to move the cursor through the list one item at a time. In a list box, the cursor does not "wrap" from one end of the list to another.

When you use the Tab or Shift-Tab keys or an Alt-key combination to enter a list box, Works positions the cursor on the first item in that box but does not select it. The first time you press an arrow key, Works selects that item—it doesn't move to the second item in the list, as you might expect. After the first time, however, pressing the arrow keys does let you select other files in the list.

Frequently, a list contains more items than Works can display in the box at one time. In those cases, part of the list remains hidden beyond the top or bottom border of the box, or both. To look at the hidden items, you can use the Up and Down Arrow keys to scroll the list.

You also can use the End, Home, PgUp, and PgDn keys to select items in a list box. The End key selects the final item in the list; the Home key selects the first item. The PgDn or PgUp key shifts the list down or up by one new boxful of items.

To move the cursor to the beginning of a particular group of entries in a list, type the first letter of the entries in that group. Works then moves the cursor to the first item in the list that begins with that letter. If no item in the list begins with the letter you type, Works does nothing.

Works displays a scroll bar at the right edge of every list box. The position of the scroll box (the black rectangle) within this bar indicates the position of the current boxful of items within the entire list.

If you installed Works for use with a mouse, you can use various alternative techniques to select items within a list box. If the item you want to select is visible within the box, select it simply by pointing to it and clicking the left button on your mouse. If the item you want to select is not visible, use any of the techniques described above to bring it into view or use the mouse to manipulate the scroll bar at the right edge of the list box. Using your mouse, you can click on the arrow at the bottom or top of the bar to scroll a new item into the list box. Or you can click elsewhere on the scroll bar, above or below the scroll box, to display a new boxful of records. You can also drag the scroll box within the scroll bar to display the corresponding portion of the list.

Text boxes: Works uses text boxes to request information that it cannot solicit in any other way. Generally, you specify information in a text box by typing, but the precise technique depends on whether you use a mouse, and whether the box already contains an entry.

When you move the cursor to an empty text box by tabbing or by using a key letter, Works places the cursor at the beginning of that box. If the box contains an entry, Works highlights the entry. You can then make a new entry, replace an existing entry, or edit an existing entry.

If the box is empty, whatever you type simply appears in the box. If the box contains an entry, you can replace or edit it. If you type while the entire entry is highlighted (as it is when you first move to the box), Works replaces that entry with whatever you type. If you want to edit the entry instead of replacing it, you must first remove the highlight. Press the Home key to remove the highlight and place the cursor on the first character in the entry. Press the Left Arrow key to place the cursor on the final character. Press either the Right Arrow or End key to place the cursor on the space following the final character.

After you remove the highlight from the entry, you can use the same four cursor movement keys to move around within the entry. As you would expect, pressing the Left Arrow key moves the cursor one character to the left, and pressing the Right Arrow key moves the cursor one character to the right. Pressing the Home key moves the cursor to the first character in the entry, and pressing the End key moves the cursor to the right of the last character.

While the cursor is on a character in the entry, Works inserts whatever you type to the left of that character. You can also use the Delete key to delete the character at the cursor or the Backspace key to delete the character to the left of the cursor.

To delete a group of adjacent characters, first highlight the series of characters you want to delete. To do so, move the cursor to the character at either end of the group, hold down the Shift key, and press the Right Arrow, Left Arrow, Home, or End key to expand the highlight. Then press either the Delete or Backspace key.

If you installed Works for use with a mouse, you can use some additional techniques to position the cursor and select characters in a text box. When you point to a text box and click, Works positions the cursor on the character to which you were pointing. If the box is empty, Works positions the cursor at the left edge of the box. If you click to the right of the last character in the box, Works positions the cursor immediately to the right of the entry. Then use the Delete or Backspace key to delete a character, or type characters you want to insert.

To highlight a group of characters within a text box using your mouse, simply point to the character at either end of the group, hold down the left button on your mouse, drag to the opposite end of the group, and release the button. Then, use the Delete or Backspace key to delete the selected characters, or type to replace them.

The width of a text box does not limit the number of characters you can type into it. If you type more characters in a text box than the box can contain, Works scrolls the existing text to the left to accommodate the new characters.

Buttons: Every Works dialog box contains at least one button. Buttons appear at the bottom of the dialog box, enclosed in angle brackets (<>). When you select a button, Works acts immediately—usually to execute or to cancel the command that produced that dialog box.

You can choose buttons in a dialog box in various ways. First, you can use the Tab key or the Shift-Tab key combination to move the cursor to the button you want to choose, and then press Enter. If you have a mouse, you can choose buttons simply by pointing to them and clicking.

One button in every dialog box is the default, or preselected, button. Unlike the angle brackets for other buttons, those for the default button are bold. To choose a default button, you don't need to move the cursor to it; simply press Enter while the cursor is anywhere in the dialog box (except on another button). In dialog boxes that contain an OK button, that button is always the default.

To choose a button with a key letter, hold down the Alt key and type that letter (lowercase or uppercase). Every Works dialog box has a Cancel button. Because this button never has a key letter, you cannot use an Alt-key combination to choose it. Instead, move the cursor to the Cancel button and press Enter, click on the button with your mouse, or press the Esc key. Works cancels the command and closes the dialog box.

Highlighting

Many Works commands require you to highlight, or select, the range of entries or characters you want to work with. To do this, you move the cursor to the cell or character at either end or at any corner of the range you want to highlight. Then, you press the Extend key ([F8]) and use the direction keys to point to the opposite end or corner of the range.

For example, suppose you want to highlight a block of cells that extends from cell A1 down to cell A5 and across the spreadsheet through column D. To do this, move the cursor to cell A1, press [F8] to enter the Extend mode, and then press the Right and Down Arrow keys to move the cursor down to cell D5. The selected area, which we designate by naming opposite corners—range A1:D5—appears in Figure 1-9.

If you have a mouse, you can highlight a range of cells or characters by dragging. Simply use the mouse to point to the cell or character at either end of the range you want to highlight, press the left mouse button, and hold it down as you drag the mouse pointer to the other end of the range.

You can use any of the cursor movement keys to move the cursor and highlight. For example, if you press the End key while Works is in the Extend mode, you highlight to the end of the current line or row.

If you highlight a range incorrectly, you can unhighlight it by pressing the Esc key twice. The first time you press it, Works leaves the Extend mode; the second time, Works unhighlights the range and returns the cursor to its original location.

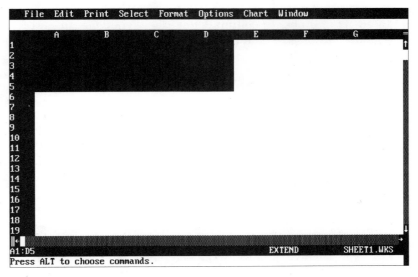

Figure 1-9. Spreadsheet with range A1:D5 highlighted.

Each Works environment has special tricks for highlighting. In the Word Processor, pressing the Extend key multiple times expands the highlighted area in increasingly larger increments. The first time you press [F8] in a Word Processor document, Works enters the Extend mode. If you press [F8] again, Works highlights the entire word on which the cursor was positioned. Press [F8] again, and Works highlights the current paragraph. Press [F8] yet again, and Works highlights the entire document. Pressing Shift-[F8] at any time shrinks the highlighted area one step.

In spreadsheets or databases, the Select menu lets you highlight entire rows and columns or entire records and fields. When you position the cursor in a row of a spreadsheet and select Row from the Select menu, Works highlights all the cells in that row. In a similar manner, choosing Column from the Select menu highlights all the cells in the current column. If you highlight cells in several rows and select the Row command, Works highlights all the cells in those rows. Likewise, you can highlight a series of columns by highlighting a cell in each column and then selecting the Column command. To use the shortcut keys, you can press Shift-[F8] to highlight a column, instead of choosing Column from the Select menu. Similarly, pressing Ctrl-[F8] is the same as choosing Row from the Select menu.

To highlight the entire spreadsheet, you first use the Row or Column command to highlight one row or column. Then, you simply select the other option (Row if you selected Column the first time, Column if you selected Row the first time). You can also press Shift-Ctrl-[F8] to select the entire spreadsheet.

If you have a mouse, you can highlight rows or columns in a spreadsheet by clicking on the row number or the column letter. To highlight several rows or columns, point to the row number or column letter where you want to start highlighting, press the mouse button and hold it down, and drag the mouse pointer to the last row or column you want to highlight.

In a Database document, a row contains a record, and a column contains the entries for a field. As you might expect, then, the Field and Record commands on the Select menu in a database work exactly like the Column and Row commands in a spreadsheet. You can also use the Shift-[F8] and Ctrl-[F8] keys to select fields and records. If you have a mouse, you can use it to select fields and records in the same way you use it to select columns and rows in a spreadsheet.

FILE MANAGEMENT

Although the four Works environments produce different kinds of documents—Spreadsheet, Database, Word Processor, and Communications—the commands you use to create, open, save, and close documents are essentially the same for all. You'll find many of the commands you need on the File menu: the New command lets you create new documents of any type, the Save and Save As commands let you save documents, and the Close command lets you close an open document. Other commands on the Window menu let you manage documents when you have more than one document open at a time.

Creating a New Document

Choose New from the File menu to create a new Works document. When you select this command, Works displays the New dialog box shown in Figure 1-10, the same dialog box that you see when you load Works.

Choose the type of document you want to create, and then press Enter or choose the New button to create a new document of that type. To create a new Spreadsheet document, for example, pull down the File menu, select the New command, choose the Spreadsheet option from the New dialog box, and then press Enter or choose OK. Works then displays a new Spreadsheet document like the one shown in Figure 1-11 on the following page.

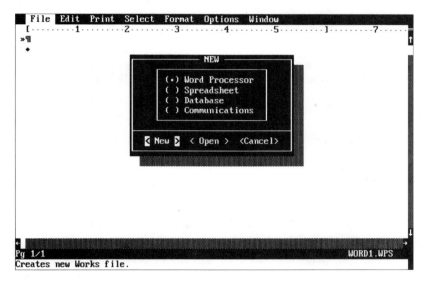

Figure 1-10.

Default document names

Every Works document has a name, which appears at the right edge of the Status line. Works assigns a name to every new document.

Works assigns Spreadsheet documents default names that begin with SHEET and end with the extension .WKS. Word Processor documents have default names that begin with WORD and end with the extension .WPS. Database documents have default names that begin with DATA and end with the extension .WDB. Communications documents have names that begin with the letters COMM and end with the extension .WCM.

The default name of a document also includes a number to the left of the extension that distinguishes the document from other documents in the current directory with default names of that type. For example, Works assigns the name WORD2.WKS

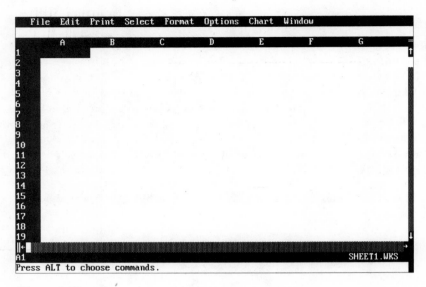

Figure 1-11.

to the second Word Processor document you create during a session. The name *SHEET1.WKS* in the Status line indicates that that document in Figure 1-11 was the first spreadsheet created during the current Works session.

The Open and Cancel buttons

The New dialog box contains two other buttons, labeled Open and Cancel. Choose the Open button to close the New dialog box and display the Open dialog box, which lets you open an existing document (one that you previously saved to disk). This dialog box is the same one that Works displays when you select Open from the File menu. We'll explore the Open command later in this chapter. Choose the Cancel button to close the New dialog box without creating a new document.

Saving Documents

The work you do in any Works document resides in your computer's random access memory (RAM) until you save the document to disk. As a result, your computer can get access to the information in the document quickly. However, if your computer loses power for any reason, any information stored in RAM is lost. Consequently, RAM is suitable only for temporary storage of your work.

Fortunately, Works lets you store "permanent" copies of your work in files on disk. Unless you delete the file in which you've stored a document or damage the disk on which that file is stored, the document is saved permanently. In this section, you'll learn how to use a variety of commands to save your Works documents.

Saving a document for the first time

You can use either the Save or Save As command on the File menu to save a new document for the first time. When you issue either command from within a document that you have not yet saved, Works displays a Save As dialog box, such as the one shown in Figure 1-12.

When you choose OK in the Save As dialog box, Works saves the current document under the name specified in the File Name text box, in the format specified in the Format option box. Works saves the file in the default directory unless the File Name text box also contains drive/directory information.

Specifying a filename: The File Name text box, the first element in the Save As dialog box, lets you specify the name of the file to which you want Works to save the current document. The Save As command always enters and highlights a suggested filename. If you have not saved the current document previously, the suggested filename is the default name for the document, such as *SHEET1.WKS* or *DATA2.WDB*. The dialog box shown in Figure 1-12, for example, is the result of issuing the Save As command from within the new Spreadsheet document shown in Figure 1-11. If you have saved a document previously, the suggested filename is the name under which you last saved it. To save the document under the suggested name, press Enter or choose OK.

To specify a new name for a file, either replace the existing name or edit it. For example, you might save a Spreadsheet document that contains your 1987 budget under the name BUDGET87.WKS.

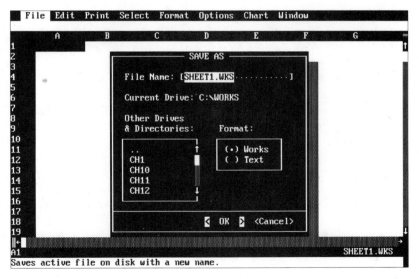

Figure 1-12.

Filename rules: Because Works operates within MS-DOS, the filenames you assign must abide by the restrictions it imposes. First, the filename can have no more than eight characters, with a three-character filename extension. For example, CUSTOMER.WKS is a valid name, but CUSTOMERS.WKS is not.

In addition, you cannot use any of the following characters in a filename: blank space, asterisk (*), question mark (?), slash (/), backslash (\), period (.) (other than to separate a filename from an extension), double quotation mark ("), semicolon (;), colon (:), left bracket ([), right bracket (]), vertical line (¦), comma (,), greater than (>), less than (<), plus (+), and equal sign (=). For example, TEST.WKS is a valid filename, but TEST?.WKS is not.

The filename you specify can have an extension of no more than three letters. When you save a file, Works includes any extension you specified as part of the filename. If you do not include either a period or an extension, Works adds the standard extension for the type of document you are saving: .WKS for Spreadsheet documents, .WPS for Word Processor documents, .WDB for Database documents, and .WCM for Communications documents. If you end a filename with a period but no extension, Works saves the file without an extension. For example, if the File Name text box contains *TEMP.* as the filename, and you choose OK, Works simply uses the name TEMP when it saves the document.

The extension you specify for a file does not have any effect on the form in which Works saves that file: If the document is a spreadsheet, Works saves it as a spreadsheet, even if you assign it an incorrect standard extension, such as .WPS, or a nonstandard extension, such as .SSC. Using improper standard extensions and nonstandard extensions does, however, make it more difficult to locate and reopen a file after you save it. To list files with nonstandard extensions in Works, you must use some special techniques.

Saving the file: After you specify a filename, you can save the current document to that file by choosing OK. If you change the suggested filename, the new name appears as the name of the document when you reopen the file. For example, if you save a Spreadsheet document named SHEET1.WKS to a file named BUDGET.WKS, the name of the document, which appears on the Status line, changes on the screen to BUDGET.WKS as well.

After you save a document to disk, it remains on the screen so that you can continue working in it. Later in this chapter, you'll learn how to use the Close command to both save and remove the document.

If you specify an invalid filename and then choose OK, Works displays an Error alert box that contains the message *Illegal file name.* and an OK button. When you choose this button, Works returns you to the Save As dialog box and highlights the illegal portion of the filename. You can change the name and then choose OK again.

Changing the default directory: Because Works saves documents to the default directory—usually A:\ or C:\WORKS—you can route a file to any directory simply by making that directory the default directory.

To change the default directory, make a choice from the Other Drives & Directories list box. At any time, this box contains a list of the disk drives available on your computer (usually shown as *[-A-]* and *[-B-]* if your computer has two floppy drives, and as *[-A-]* and *[-C-]* if your computer has a floppy drive and a hard disk). The box also lists any subdirectories of the default directory. If the default directory is not at the root level, Works also includes the choice .. (for the parent directory).

To change the default directory, move the highlight to the name of the drive or directory that you want to make current, and then choose OK. (If you have a mouse, you can double-click on the drive or directory name instead.) Works places the name of the new current directory to the right of the Current Drive prompt and replaces the entry in the File Name text box with the name of the drive/directory you chose.

For example, suppose that C:\WORKS is the current directory, and you want to save the current document in the C:\WORKS\FILES subdirectory. To do this, move the highlight in the Other Drives & Directories list box to FILES and choose OK. Works makes C:\WORKS\FILES the new default directory and displays any subdirectories it contains in the Other Drives & Directories list box.

You also can specify a new default directory by typing its name (or symbols that lead Works to it from the current directory) in the File Name text box and then choosing OK. For example, suppose that C:\WORKS is the current directory, and you want to save the current document in the C:\WORKS\FILES subdirectory. To do this, type *C:\WORKS\FILES* in the File Name text box and choose OK.

If you change the default directory, the drive/directory information in the File Name text box is no longer necessary. Simply type the filename, which replaces the highlighted drive/directory information.

If you did not change the default directory, you can simply type the directory name (preceded by the drive name, if different from the default), followed by the filename, in the File Name text box. For example, suppose that C:\WORKS is the current directory, and you want to save the current document to a file named MYFILE.WPS in the \WKSFILES directory of the disk in drive A. To do this, type *A:\WKSFILES\MYFILE.WPS* in the File Name text box and press Enter or choose OK.

After you specify a filename, choose OK to save the current document to the specified file in the indicated directory. Works changes the name of the document to match the name of the file.

Specifying the file type: The Format option box in the Save As dialog box lets you specify the format in which you want Works to save the document. The type of document you are saving determines the number of options displayed. You can save a Word Processor document in one of three formats—Works, Text, and Plain; Spreadsheet and Database documents in one of two formats—Works or Text; and Communications documents only in Works format (no options displayed).

The Works option commands Works to save a complete, working copy of the current document. Word Processor documents retain their formats, alignments, fonts, paragraph spacing, and so forth; Spreadsheet documents retain their formulas, functions, formats, range names, and other structures; Database documents maintain their forms and any report definitions you have established; Communications documents maintain all their settings.

The Works format is the default selection in every Format option box because you'll nearly always want to save your documents in Works files.

The Text option commands Works to save the information from the current document as an ASCII text file. Choose the Text option when you want to share the information in a Works document with another program. In Text format, the document lacks the special attributes that are saved using Works format. Each paragraph of a Word Processor document is saved on a single line of the file. Each is separated from the next paragraph by a single carriage return. Spreadsheets and databases are saved in comma-delimited form, with formulas and functions converted to their current values.

Whenever you save a Word Processor document in Text format, Works displays the dialog box shown in Figure 1-13. Choose Yes to save the document in the Text format; choose No or Cancel to cancel the Save As command.

The Plain option, which is available only for Word Processor documents, is very similar to the Text option. However, the Plain option adds a carriage return at the end of each line of the document—that is, at each point where Works wraps text from one line to another, and at each end-of-line marker. Like the Text format, the Plain format is useful when you want to share information with another program.

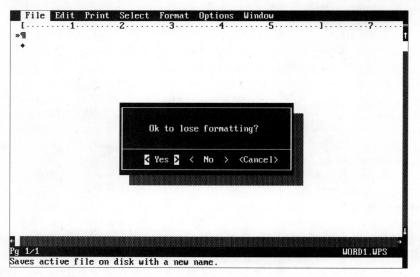

Figure 1-13.

Whenever you command Works to save a Word Processor document in Plain format, it displays the dialog box shown in the preceding figure. Choose Yes to save the document in the Text format; choose No or Cancel to cancel the Save As command.

A note: When you save a file in an alternative format (Text or Plain), use an extension or a filename (or both) other than the one you plan to use when you save the file in Works format. For example, you might specify the extension *.TXT* for Text format or *.PLN* for Plain format. The use of a different filename or extension prevents Works from overwriting the alternatively-formatted version of the file with a Works-formatted version when you resave the document. (Works changes the name of the open document only when you save that document in the Works format—it does not change the document name when you save the file in an alternative format.)

Overwriting an existing file

If the directory and name you specify match the directory and name of an existing file, Works doesn't save the document immediately. Instead, it presents a dialog box with the prompt *Overwrite existing file?* Choose Yes (the default button) to save the current document on top of the existing file, destroying the original contents of that file. Choose No to return to the Save As dialog box and specify a different name.

Canceling a save

If you decide not to save a new document after issuing the Save or Save As command, choose Cancel at the bottom of the Save As dialog box or press the Esc key. Works closes the dialog box and returns you to your former position within the document you were saving.

Resaving a document

After you save a document for the first time, you will probably save it again and again. In most cases, you'll use the Save command to save the document to the same file. The current document overwrites the old version of the document.

Interestingly, Works actually resaves the document only if you made a change since you last saved it. If not, Works simply closes the Save menu and returns to the document.

After you use the Save command to resave a document, the document remains on the screen—exactly as it does when you save it for the first time. You can continue your work where you left off. Because it's so convenient to save your work, do so after every major change you make to a document or every 15 minutes, whichever comes first. That way, you'll never lose a lot of work if your computer fails for one reason or another.

The Backup option: Whenever you issue the Save command, Works copies the previous version of a file into a special subdirectory named BACKUP, located one level below the directory in which the original version of the file is stored. If that subdirectory does not exist, Works creates it. This automatic backup can protect you from disaster. For example, suppose that you create a Spreadsheet document and save it under the name BUDGET.WKS. After making some changes to that spread-sheet, you use the Save command to save the updated version of the document to disk. If you discover that you accidentally deleted a portion of your document before you last saved it, you can recover an intact version from the BACKUP subdirectory. Simply use the Open command to bring it back into Works.

Making backup copies of your files each time you save does, however, require both time and disk space. To turn off the automatic backup feature, select Settings from the Window menu and then select the Backup check box. Figure 1-14 shows the Settings dialog box with the Backup option turned on.

Resaving a file under a new name: Although you will usually want to save each new version of a document so that it overwrites the existing version, you might prefer, at times, to save a document without overwriting the previous version. For example, as you are developing and refining a spreadsheet, you might want to keep previous versions as an "audit trail" of your work.

To do this, you choose Save As from within a previously saved document and then use the Save As dialog box to resave your document under a new name, in a new directory, or both. Simply edit or replace the filename and replace or override the default directory.

The Close command

The Close command lets you save any current changes to a document and then removes the document from memory. Unlike the Save and Save As commands, which save the current document and leave it open, the Close command closes it.

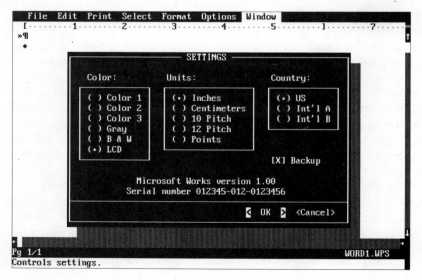

Figure 1-14.

Closing a previously saved document: If you issue the Close command from within a previously saved document, and you made changes to the document during the current session, Works displays a dialog box that asks if you want to save your changes. Choose Yes (the default button) to save the document on top of the previous version—as if you had issued the Save command—and then close the document. Choose No to close the file without first saving the current changes. If you choose Cancel, Works cancels the Close command, leaves the document in memory, and returns you to your previous position in it.

If you issue the Close command from within a previously saved document, but you have made no changes since you last saved it, Works simply closes the document.

Closing a new document: When you issue the Close command from within a new (not yet saved) document to which you have made changes, Works presents the dialog box described in the preceding paragraphs. Choose Cancel to cancel the Close command and leave the document open. Choose No to close the document without saving it. Choose Yes to display a Save As dialog box, which lets you specify a name, directory, and format for the file. Then, press Enter or choose OK from the Save As dialog box to save the document to the indicated directory and then close it. Choose Cancel from the Save As dialog box to cancel the Close command and to leave the document open.

Disk-full errors

If you store your files on floppy disks, you're likely to encounter a disk-full problem at one time or another. If the disk becomes full as you're saving a file, Works displays an alert box with the message *Disk is full.* When you choose OK to acknowledge this message, Works removes the alert box from the screen. Insert a disk that has enough room for the file. Then, reissue the Save command to display the Save As dialog box (if it is not already displayed), and choose OK from the box to save the file under its current filename.

Although you usually encounter disk-full errors when you save to a floppy disk, you might also encounter them when you save to a hard disk. If that happens, save the document to a file on a floppy disk or select DOS from the File menu and delete some files from the hard disk. (The files in the BACKUP subdirectory are a good place to start deleting.) Then, return to Works and try to save your document again.

Opening Files

After you save a document to a file and remove it from memory, the Open command lets you bring it back into Works. When you issue this command, an Open dialog box appears, like the one shown in Figure 1-15 on the following page. As you can see, it contains six elements that allow you to specify the file you want to open: a File Name text box, a Files list box, an Other Drives & Directories list box, a List Which Files option box, an OK button, and a Cancel button.

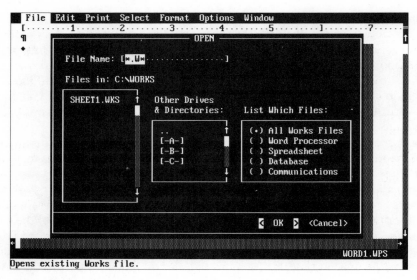

Figure 1-15.

To open a file in Works, you first select Open from the File menu. Then, select the type of file you want to open from the List Which Files option box. After you press Enter or choose OK, Works displays only files of that type in the Files list box. Second, move to the Other Drives & Directories list box and select the drive/directory that contains the file you want to open. After you press Enter or choose OK, the Files list box contains only files in the specified directory. Next, select the file you want to open from the list in the Files list box, and press Enter or choose OK again to open the file.

Choosing the file type

The first step in opening a file is choosing a file type from the List Which Files option box. If you choose All Works Files (the default), Works looks for all files whose extensions begin with the letter W. This includes all files with standard Works extensions: .WPS (Word Processor), .WKS (Spreadsheet), .WDB (Database), and .WCM (Communications). If you choose Spreadsheet, Works looks for files whose extensions begin with the letters WK (to include not only files with the standard Works extension for spreadsheets, but also files from Lotus 1-2-3 releases 1A and 2).

When you choose an option, Works immediately replaces the entry (if any) in the File Name text box with an entry that specifies the chosen file type. If you choose the Spreadsheet option, for example, Works places the entry *.WK* in the File Name box.

If you choose OK after selecting a file type, Works updates the file list so that it includes only files of the selected type within the current directory.

Choosing a drive/directory

The current directory is the one whose name appears to the right of the words *Files in:* under the File Name text box. For example, the Open dialog box shown in Figure 1-15 indicates that C:\WORKS is the current directory.

The box below the current directory lists only files in that directory. If the current directory contains the file you want to open, simply select its name from the list and press Enter or choose OK. If not, use the Other Drives & Directories list box to change the current directory.

To choose a directory, simply highlight its name. Works immediately inserts that name in the File Name box. If you then press Enter or choose OK, Works changes the current directory to the one you selected and updates the list of filenames to include only those that match the pattern specified in the File Name text box.

Opening the file

Next, choose the file you want to open from the Files list box. Select a file as you would from any other list box: Use the cursor movement keys or your mouse to highlight the filename. To move directly to the part of the list that contains the filename, type the first letter of that name.

When the File Name text box contains the name of the file you want to open, simply press Enter or choose OK. Works reads the document stored in the specified file into memory and then displays the document exactly as it appeared when you last saved it.

Because each Works document occupies the whole screen, the newly opened document obscures any other document that is currently open. Later in this chapter, you'll learn how to display different documents in memory; that is, how to switch among the various documents that you can open within Works.

Alternative approaches

To open a file, you can also type the directory and filename directly in the File Name text box. For example, suppose C:\WORKS is the current directory, and you want to open a file named BUDGET.WKS that is stored at the root level of the disk in drive A. Type *A:\BUDGET.WKS* and press Enter or choose OK to open the file from the A drive. Note, however, that C:\WORKS remains the default directory—Works still lists files for C:\WORKS when you choose the Open command.

You can also command Works to open a file when you load the program. At the MS-DOS prompt, type *works*, followed by a space, and then type the name of the file you want to open and press Enter. (If the file is in a directory other than the one that contains your Works program files, include the directory in the filename.) For example, to open the file named BUDGET.WKS, which is stored in a different directory, C:\WORKS\FILES, you would type *WORKS FILES\BUDGET.WKS*, and press Enter.

Opening a non-Works file

Although you will usually open Works-formatted files, you can open other types of files as well. When you attempt to open a non-Works file, Works displays a dialog box with a series of options, as shown in Figure 1-16. Choose the type of document into which you want Works to load the file and press Enter or choose OK.

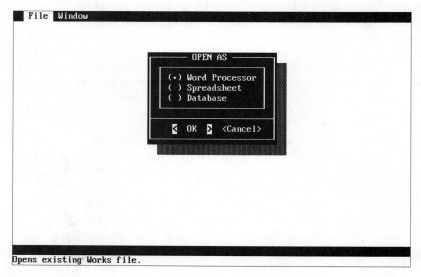

Figure 1-16.

WORKING WITH MULTIPLE DOCUMENTS

Works lets you have as many as eight documents open at one time. After you open the first document, use the New command to create a new document or the Open command to open an existing document.

You can think of your open documents arranged in a stack, much like a stack of playing cards. You might have a number of cards (documents) in the stack, but only one—the card (document) at the top—is visible. Each time you create a new document or open an existing one, Works places it on the top of the stack.

For example, suppose you load Works and create a new Word Processor document named WORD1.WPS. Because this is the only open document, it is the visible, or active, one. After you create this document, suppose you open a spreadsheet named BUDGET.WKS. Works places the newly opened document at the top of the stack, obscuring WORD1.WPS, which now occupies the second position in the stack. Next, suppose you create a new spreadsheet, which Works names SHEET1.WKS. When you do this, Works places SHEET1.WKS at the top of the stack, obscuring BUDGET.WKS (now second in the stack) and WORD1.WPS (now third).

Window Management

To work with a document that is hidden in the stack, use the Window menu to bring it to the top, or make it active. The Window menu includes a list of the documents that are currently open.

Figure 1-17 shows what your Window menu would look like if you followed the steps outlined in the previous example. Notice that the documents appear in the order that you opened or created them: WORD1.WPS, then BUDGET.WKS, and then SHEET1.WKS.

As you can see, Works displays a number to the left of each document name at the bottom of the Window menu. These numbers are the "key characters" of those selections. When you select the name of a document from the list, Works brings that document to the top of the stack and makes it the active document. While the document is active, you can work within it—enter and edit information, issue commands, and so forth.

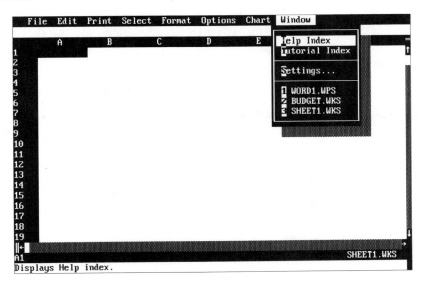

Figure 1-17.

Saving and Closing

As previously mentioned, the Save command lets you save an individual document—the active document. Works offers another command on the File menu, Save All, that lets you save multiple documents. When you select this command, Works resaves every open document that you have saved previously in the Works format.

Like the Save command, the Save All command saves only those documents that you have changed since you last saved them. Unlike the Save command, however, the

Save All command does not give you a chance to save new documents—those that you have not previously saved in the Works format. Those documents remain open. To save documents that you have not previously saved, use the Save or Save As command on each one.

Works does not give you a single command that closes more than one document at a time. You have to close each one individually. As you close each document, Works makes the next one in the stack active and removes the name of the closed document from the list on the Window menu.

PRINTING

The commands that make it possible to print a Works document are located on the Print menu. Figure 1-18 shows a typical Print menu (in this case, the Print menu from a Word Processor document). Although the Print menu for each environment has unique commands, the menus all have three commands that control the basic printing process: Print, Layout, and Select Text Printer.

The process of printing a document has three steps. First, you use the Layout command to set the margins, page dimensions, and headers and footers for the printed document. Second, you use the Select Text Printer command to specify the printer on which you want to print and the port to which that printer is connected. Third, you issue the Print command, which instructs Works to print the document.

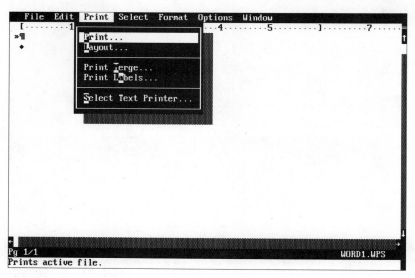

Figure 1-18.

Specifying Print Settings: The Layout Command

The Layout command on the Print menu lets you define the settings that control the layout of a printed document. When you select the Layout command, Works displays the Layout dialog box shown in Figure 1-19.

The margin settings

The four text boxes in the upper left corner of the Layout dialog box let you control the margins—the amount of white space that Works leaves at the top, bottom, left, and right edges of the printed page.

The default values of these four margin settings, shown in Figure 1-19, are appropriate for most documents. However, you can alter them easily. To do so, move the cursor to the setting you want to alter and then either edit or replace it. To change the top margin from 1 inch to 2 inches, for example, move the cursor to the Top Margin text box and type 2. If you don't include a unit of measure, Works assumes that the units are inches.

The page dimension settings

The Page Length and Page Width text boxes let you specify the dimensions of the paper on which you want to print. The default values for these settings, 11 inches and 8.5 inches, are shown in Figure 1-19.

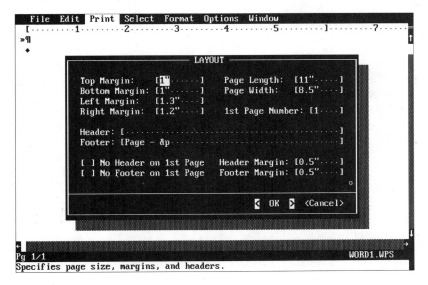

Figure 1-19.

Like the default margin settings, the default page dimension settings are appropriate for printing most documents. But if you need to change a setting, simply move the cursor to the corresponding text box and either edit or replace the existing entry. If you don't include a unit of measure, Works assumes that you mean inches.

The 1st Page Number setting

Works has the ability to print a page number on each page of a printed document. The 1st Page Number text box lets you control the number Works prints on the first page. In most cases, you'll want Works to start with the number 1; that's why the default value of this setting is *1*. In some cases, however, you might want the printed document to start with another number. For example, suppose you're about to print a Word Processor document that contains Chapter 2 of a book you are writing. If Chapter 1 was 26 pages long, you want Works to begin numbering Chapter 2 with 27—not 1. To instruct Works to do this, you would enter the value *27* in the 1st Page Number text box.

Headers and footers

The remaining settings in the Layout dialog box control the printing of headers and footers. A header is a line of information that appears at the top of each page; a footer is a line of text that appears at the bottom. Headers and footers often contain information such as the title of a report, the number of a chapter, the print date, and the page number. Works allows you to specify both the contents of headers and footers and the amount of space they occupy on the page.

Specifying the contents of headers and footers: To specify a header for a document, simply move the cursor to the Header text box and type what you want Works to print in the header. To print the phrase *Amalgamated Widgets FY 1988 Budget* at the top of each page, for example, type that phrase in the Header box. To have the phrase *Top Secret* at the bottom of each page, type that phrase in the Footer box.

As you can see in Figure 1-19, Works does not supply a default header. Works does supply a default footer, however. This footer consists of the word *Page* - and the special code *&p* and commands Works to print consecutive page numbers on the pages of the document, beginning with the number in the 1st Page Number text box. Other special codes, listed in your *Microsoft Works Reference*, let you print the date, the time, or the document name or control the alignment of header and footer text.

Positioning the header and footer: You also control whether Works prints the header or the footer (or neither) on the first page and how much space it devotes to the header and footer. Two check boxes, labeled No Header on 1st Page and No Footer on 1st Page, control these options. An X in a box indicates that the option is on: Works does not print the element on the first page.

The entries in the Header Margin and Footer Margin text boxes control the location at which Works prints the header and footer, relative to the top and bottom of the page. For example, a header margin of *0.5"* tells Works to leave one-half inch of white space between the top of the page and the line on which it prints the header.

The header must fall within the top margin and the footer within the bottom margin of the page. That means that the value you specify for the header margin cannot exceed the value you specify for the top margin. If it does, Works displays an alert box that warns you that the header or footer overlaps the top or bottom margin. In most cases, you should specify values for your header and footer margins that are about one-half the values you specify for your top and bottom margins, respectively. That way, Works prints the header midway between the top of the page and the first line of text, and it prints the footer midway between the last line of text and the bottom of the page.

Leaving the Layout box: After you customize the entries in the Layout dialog box, choose OK at the bottom of the box to store the settings and remove the box from the screen. If you choose Cancel instead, Works removes the Layout box and ignores changes to its settings.

The settings you specify in a Layout dialog box apply only to the document from which you issued the Layout command. When you save a document, Works saves its Layout settings with it. Consequently, you don't need to redefine the Layout settings each time you print a document unless you need to change them.

Selecting a Printer: The Select Text Printer Command

The Select Text Printer command lets you convey information about your printer. When you choose Select Text Printer from the Print menu, Works displays a dialog box like the one shown in Figure 1-20.

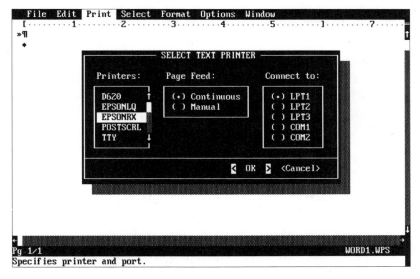

Figure 1-20.

Choosing a printer

The Printers list box displays alphabetically the names of any text printers that you selected in the Works setup process. If you selected only one printer during the setup process, then the name of that printer is the only one in the list box. To specify the printer you want to use, highlight its name.

Choosing a connection

Next, tell Works the port to which that printer is connected. To do this, choose the port from the Connect option box. The first three options—LPT1, LPT2, and LPT3—identify parallel ports, and the last two—COM1 and COM2—identify serial ports. If your printer is a parallel printer (most are), connect it to one of your computer's parallel ports and select the name of that port from the box. If you're not sure which port your printer is attached to, try printing with LPT1 selected. If you have a serial printer (such as an HP LaserJet), connect it to one of your computer's serial ports and select the name of that port from the option box. If you don't know which serial port is which, try printing with COM1 selected.

Choosing Manual or Automatic Page Feed

The Page Feed option box, in the center of the dialog box, lets you specify whether Works should pause for you to insert a new sheet of paper after it prints each page. If you are printing on continuous-feed (form-feed) paper, choose Continuous. That way, Works advances to the next form and continues printing as soon as it finishes a page. If you are printing on single sheets of paper (cut-sheets), choose Manual instead. While the Manual setting is active, Works pauses when it reaches the end of each page and prompts you to insert another sheet. Insert a new sheet of paper and choose OK to instruct Works to print the next page.

Saving the Select Text Printer settings

Unlike the Layout settings, which apply only to the current document, the settings in the Select Text Printer dialog box apply to every document you print, until you change them again. Works saves the settings in the WORKS.INI file—the same file in which it saves other universal Works settings. Note, however, that Works does not save these settings in the WORKS.INI file at the same time that you change them—it waits until you exit Works.

Printing the Document: The Print Command

After you specify the settings and choose a printer, you are ready to print the current document. To do this, select the Print command—the first command on any Print menu. Works displays a Print dialog box like the one shown in Figure 1-21. You can use this box to define a specific print job: the number of copies, the particular pages to print, and the destination (whether it be a printer or a file). When you choose the OK button at the bottom of this box, Works prints the current document.

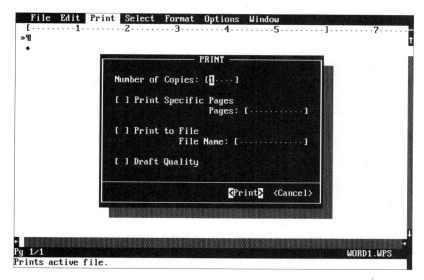

Figure 1-21.

The first five elements in the Print dialog box are the same for all document types: a Number of Copies text box, a Print Specific Pages check box and its related Pages text box, and a Print to File check box and its related File Name text box. The sixth element in the Print dialog box varies with the environment. If you are printing a Word Processor document, the last check box lets you specify draft-quality printing. If you are printing a Spreadsheet document, the last check box lets you specify whether you want Works to include the spreadsheet's row numbers and column labels in the printout. If you are printing a Database document, the last check box lets you specify whether you want Works to print record numbers and field labels for the database.

Specifying the number of copies

The Number of Copies text box lets you specify the number of copies you want Works to print (1 to 9999). The default value in this box, *1*, tells Works to print only a single copy. To print more than one copy of your document, replace or edit this entry. When Works prints multiple copies of a document, it prints one complete copy before it begins the next.

Printing specific pages

Use the Print Specific Pages check box and the related Pages text box to tell Works to print only certain pages of a report. If the Print Specific Pages check box contains an X (meaning that it is on), Works prints only the pages specified in the Pages text box.

To print specific pages of a document, first turn on the Print Specific Pages check box. Then, move the cursor to the Pages text box and enter the numbers of the pages that you want Works to print. You must perform these two tasks in that order.

The Pages text box gives you a lot of flexibility in selecting the pages you want to print. To print a single page, simply enter the number of that page in the box. To print several non-adjacent pages, separate the page numbers with commas. To print pages 1, 3, 5, and 7, for example, enter *1, 3, 5, 7* in the Pages box. To print a group of adjacent pages, separate the numbers of the first and last pages in the group with either a hyphen (-) or a colon (:). For example, to print pages 3, 4, 5, 6, and 7, you can enter either *3-7* or *3:7* in the text box. You can even combine references to individual pages and ranges of adjacent pages. For example, the entry *1, 3, 5-9, 26* instructs Works to print pages 1, 3, 5, 6, 7, 8, 9, and 26.

In many cases, you'll want Works to start printing at a page other than the first page of a document and continue printing through the end of the document. To do this, enter a range in the Pages box that begins with the first page you want to print and ends with a page number greater than (or equal to) the final page of the document.

Printing to a file

The Print to File check box and the File Name text box let you print a document to a file rather than to your printer. If the Print to File check box contains an X, Works saves the document to the file named in the File Name text box. Works saves the file in exactly the same form as it would have printed the file, including headers, footers, margins, tabs, print attributes, and so forth.

To print to a file, first turn on the Print to File check box. Then, move the cursor to the File Name text box and enter the name of the file to which you want to save the document. Like any filename, the filename you specify can contain a maximum of eight characters, plus an extension of no more than three characters.

Works saves the file to the current default directory unless you include drive/ directory information in the text box. For more information on how a File Name text box works, including an explanation of default directories, see the section of this chapter entitled "Saving a document for the first time."

After you print a document to disk, you can print it to a printer using the MS-DOS PRINT or TYPE commands. For instructions on using these commands to print a file, see your MS-DOS reference manual or a good book on MS-DOS.

Printing

When you are ready to print the document, connect the printer to the specified port, turn it on, align the paper, and press Enter or choose Print at the bottom of the Print dialog box.

To pause or stop the printing process before the entire job is done, press the Esc key. When you do this, Works stops sending information to the printer and presents a dialog box. (If your printer has a buffer, it doesn't stop printing immediately. Instead, it continues to print until it empties the buffer.) If you then choose OK, Works resumes printing where it left off. If you choose Cancel, however, Works advances the paper to the top of the next page and then cancels the Print command.

Saving the Print settings

Works does not save the settings in the Print dialog box. As soon as you choose OK or Cancel, it resets the Number of Copies setting to 1, turns off the Print to File setting, and clears the File Name text box. You have to respecify these settings each time you print. (Works does retain the settings in the Print Specific Pages check box and in the Pages text box for the duration of the current Works session.)

LEAVING WORKS

When you finish using Works and want to quit completely, select Exit from the File menu. If you saved all your open documents since you last changed them, Works takes you directly to the MS-DOS environment. If you didn't save them, Works asks if you want to save your changes to each document. After you select the Exit command, Works stores information about your work in a file named WORKS.INI. Be sure you leave this file alone so Works can use it the next time you start the program.

CONCLUSION

This chapter explains a number of "universal" Works skills—techniques that you can use in every Works environment. In the rest of this book, you'll use these techniques as you build and learn to use Works templates. The directions in each of those sections assume that you have a fairly good mastery of these basic skills. For example, you won't find detailed instructions for issuing a command, choosing an item from a list box, opening a file, or printing a document. If at any time you need a refresher on any of these basic skills, please refer back to the appropriate sections of this chapter.

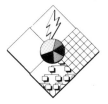

The Cash Flow Tracker

Have you ever bounced a check? Although we don't like to admit it, most of us have overdrawn our accounts at one time or another. Most of us have also left too much money idle in our checking accounts instead of investing it in money market or other interest-bearing accounts.

Fortunately, bounced checks and excessive checking account balances are easy to prevent. All you have to do is plan your cash receipts and disbursements carefully so that the balance in your checking account is always greater than zero—but not too much greater. Doing this kind of planning on paper is tedious and time-consuming. Doing it with Microsoft Works is quick and easy.

With the Cash Flow Tracker you can plan cash receipts and disbursements for the coming year and avoid the embarrassment of bounced checks and the expense of lost interest. Although the Cash Flow Tracker is one of the simplest templates in this book, it is also one of the most useful. You can use it at home or in your business. The template is flexible enough to be used by multimillion-dollar businesses and by low-budget startup ventures.

ABOUT THE TEMPLATE

Figure 2-1 on the following page shows the Cash Flow Tracker as it looks when you first create it. Figure 2-2 beginning on page 43 shows the spreadsheet with some sample information. As you can see, the spreadsheet has only one area, the cash flow table. As shown in Figure 2-3 on page 45, the top part of this table appears on the screen whenever you load the Cash Flow Tracker. Column A contains the date of the first day of each week in the coming year. In columns B, C, D, and E you record the description and amount of each receipt and disbursement you anticipate in the coming year. The formulas in column F compute the running cash balance after each receipt or disbursement.

	A	B	C	D	E	F
1	===				
2			Cash Flow Tracker			
3	===				
4	Week		Receipts		Disbursements	
5	Beginning	Description	Amount	Description	Amount	Balance
6	-------	--------------	--------	--------------	--------	--------
7		Beginning Balance				$0.00
8	12/27/87					$0.00
9	1/3/88					$0.00
10	1/10/88					$0.00
11	1/17/88					$0.00
12	1/24/88					$0.00
13	1/31/88					$0.00
14	2/7/88					$0.00
15	2/14/88					$0.00
16	2/21/88					$0.00
17	2/28/88					$0.00
18	3/6/88					$0.00
19	3/13/88					$0.00
20	3/20/88					$0.00
21	3/27/88					$0.00
22	4/3/88					$0.00
23	4/10/88					$0.00
24	4/17/88					$0.00
25	4/24/88					$0.00
26	5/1/88					$0.00
27	5/8/88					$0.00
28	5/15/88					$0.00
29	5/22/88					$0.00
30	5/29/88					$0.00
31	6/5/88					$0.00
32	6/12/88					$0.00
33	6/19/88					$0.00
34	6/26/88					$0.00
35	7/3/88					$0.00
36	7/10/88					$0.00
37	7/17/88					$0.00
38	7/24/88					$0.00
39						$0.00
						$0.00
	9/25/88					
48	10/2/88					
49	10/9/88					$0.00
50	10/16/88					$0.00
51	10/23/88					$0.00
52	10/30/88					$0.00
53	11/6/88					$0.00
54	11/13/88					$0.00
55	11/20/88					$0.00
56	11/27/88					$0.00
57	12/4/88					$0.00
58	12/11/88					$0.00
59	12/18/88					$0.00
60	12/25/88					$0.00

Figure 2-1.

	A	B	C	D	E	F
1	===					
2	CASH FLOW TRACKER					
3	===					
4	Week		Receipts		Disbursements	
5	Beginning	Description	Amount	Description	Amount	Balance
6	-------	-------------	--------	-------------	--------	--------
7		Beginning Balance				$4,572.98
8	12/27/87	Paycheck	$1,145.62	Mortgage	$745.94	$4,972.66
9				Car Payment	$155.00	$4,817.66
10				Student Loan	$115.00	$4,702.66
11				Credit Cards	$100.00	$4,602.66
12				Other Bills	$375.00	$4,227.66
13				Cash Expenses	$175.00	$4,052.66
14	1/3/88			Cash Expenses	$175.00	$3,877.66
15	1/10/88	Paycheck	$1,145.62	Cash Expenses	$175.00	$4,848.28
16	1/17/88	Dividend Check	$375.00	Cash Expenses	$175.00	$5,048.28
17	1/24/88	Paycheck	$1,145.62	Cash Expenses	$175.00	$6,018.90
18	1/31/88			Mortgage	$745.94	$5,272.97
19				Car Payment	$155.00	$5,117.97
20				Student Loan	$115.00	$5,002.97
21				Credit Cards	$100.00	$4,902.97
22				Other Bills	$375.00	$4,527.97
23				Cash Expenses	$175.00	$4,352.97
24	2/7/88			Cash Expenses	$175.00	$4,177.97
25	2/14/88	Paycheck	$1,145.62	Cash Expenses	$175.00	$5,148.59
26	2/21/88			Cash Expenses	$175.00	$4,973.59
27	2/28/88	Paycheck	$1,145.62	Mortgage	$745.94	$5,373.27
28				Car Payment	$155.00	$5,218.27
29				Student Loan	$115.00	$5,103.27
30				Credit Cards	$100.00	$5,003.27
31				Other Bills	$375.00	$4,628.27
32				Cash Expenses	$175.00	$4,453.27
33	3/6/88			Cash Expenses	$175.00	$4,278.27
34	3/13/88	Paycheck	$1,145.62	Cash Expenses	$175.00	$5,248.89
35	3/20/88			Cash Expenses	$175.00	$5,073.89
36	3/27/88	Paycheck	$1,145.62	Mortgage	$745.94	$5,473.58
37				Car Payment	$155.00	$5,318.58
38				Student Loan	$115.00	$5,203.58
39				Credit Cards	$100.00	$5,103.58
40				Other Bills	$375.00	$4,728.58
41	4/3/88	Dividend Check	$350.00	Cash Expenses	$175.00	$4,903.58
42	4/10/88	Paycheck	$1,145.62	IRA Contribution	$2,000.00	$4,049.20
43				Cash Expenses	$175.00	$3,874.20
44	4/17/88			Cash Expenses	$175.00	$3,699.20
45	4/24/88	Paycheck	$1,145.62	Mortgage	$745.94	$4,098.88
46				Car Payment	$155.00	$3,943.88
47				Student Loan	$115.00	$3,828.88
48				Credit Cards	$100.00	$3,728.88
49				Other Bills	$375.00	$3,353.88
50				Cash Expenses	$175.00	$3,178.88
51	5/1/88			Cash Expenses	$175.00	$3,003.88
52	5/8/88	Paycheck	$1,145.62	Cash Expenses	$175.00	$3,974.50
53	5/15/88			Cash Expenses	$175.00	$3,799.50

Figure 2-2.   (continued)

Figure 2-2. Continued.

	A	B	C	D	E	F
54	5/22/88	Fed Tax Refund	$475.00	Cash Expenses	$175.00	$4,099.50
55	5/29/88	Paycheck	$1,145.62	Mortgage	$745.94	$4,499.18
56				Car Payment	$155.00	$4,344.18
57				Student Loan	$115.00	$4,229.18
58				Credit Cards	$100.00	$4,129.18
59				Other Bills	$375.00	$3,754.18
60				Cash Expenses	$175.00	$3,579.18
61	6/5/88			Cash Expenses	$175.00	$3,404.18
62	6/12/88	Paycheck	$1,145.62	Cash Expenses	$175.00	$4,374.80
63	6/19/88			Cash Expenses	$175.00	$4,199.80
64	6/26/88	Paycheck	$1,145.62	Mortgage	$745.94	$4,599.49
65				Car Payment	$155.00	$4,444.49
66				Student Loan	$115.00	$4,329.49
67				Credit Cards	$100.00	$4,229.49
68				Other Bills	$375.00	$3,854.49
69				Cash Expenses	$175.00	$3,679.49
70	7/3/88	Dividend Check	$375.00	Cash Expenses	$175.00	$3,879.49
71				Vacation	$2,500.00	$1,379.49
72	7/10/88	Paycheck	$1,145.62	Cash Expenses	$175.00	$2,350.11
73	7/17/88			Cash Expenses	$175.00	$2,175.11
74	7/24/88	Paycheck	$1,145.62	Cash Expenses	$175.00	$3,145.73
75	7/31/88			Mortgage	$745.94	$2,399.79
76				Car Payment	$155.00	$2,244.79
77				Student Loan	$115.00	$2,129.79
78				Credit Cards	$100.00	$2,029.79
79				Other Bills	$375.00	$1,654.79
80				Cash Expenses	$175.00	$1,479.79
81	8/7/88			Cash Expenses	$175.00	$1,304.79
82	8/14/88	Paycheck	$1,145.62	Cash Expenses	$175.00	$2,275.41
83	8/21/88			Cash Expenses	$175.00	$2,100.41
84	8/28/88	Paycheck	$1,145.62	Mortgage	$745.94	$2,500.10
85				Car Payment	$155.00	$2,345.10
86				Student Loan	$115.00	$2,230.10
87				Credit Cards	$100.00	$2,130.10
88				Other Bills	$375.00	$1,755.10
89				Cash Expenses	$175.00	$1,580.10
90	9/4/88			Cash Expenses	$175.00	$1,405.10
91	9/11/88	Paycheck	$1,145.62	Reseed Lawn	$1,400.00	$1,150.72
92				Cash Expenses	$175.00	$975.72
93	9/18/88			Cash Expenses	$175.00	$800.72
94	9/25/88	Paycheck	$1,145.62	Mortgage	$745.94	$1,200.40
95		Sell Stock	$2,500.00	Car Payment	$155.00	$3,545.40
96				Student Loan	$115.00	$3,430.40
97				Credit Cards	$100.00	$3,330.40
98				Other Bills	$375.00	$2,955.40
99				Cash Expenses	$175.00	$2,780.40
100	10/2/88			Cash Expenses	$175.00	$2,605.40
101	10/9/88	Paycheck	$1,145.62	Buy Sofa	$800.00	$2,951.02
102	10/16/88	Dividend Check	$375.00	Cash Expenses	$175.00	$3,151.02
103	10/23/88			Cash Expenses	$175.00	$2,976.02
104	10/30/88	Paycheck	$1,145.62	Mortgage	$745.94	$3,375.71

(continued)

Figure 2-2. Continued.

	A	B	C	D	E	F
105				Car Payment	$155.00	$3,220.71
106				Student Loan	$115.00	$3,105.71
107				Credit Cards	$100.00	$3,005.71
108				Other Bills	$375.00	$2,630.71
109				Cash Expenses	$175.00	$2,455.71
110	11/6/88			Cash Expenses	$175.00	$2,280.71
111	11/13/88	Paycheck	$1,145.62	Cash Expenses	$175.00	$3,251.33
112	11/20/88			Cash Expenses	$175.00	$3,076.33
113	11/27/88	Paycheck	$1,145.62	Mortgage	$745.94	$3,476.01
114				Car Payment	$155.00	$3,321.01
115				Student Loan	$115.00	$3,206.01
116				Credit Cards	$100.00	$3,106.01
117				Other Bills	$375.00	$2,731.01
118				Cash Expenses	$175.00	$2,556.01
119	12/4/88			Xmas Presents	$400.00	$2,156.01
120				Cash Expenses	$175.00	$1,981.01
121	12/11/88	Paycheck	$1,145.62	Cash Expenses	$175.00	$2,951.63
122	12/18/88			Cash Expenses	$175.00	$2,776.63
123	12/25/88	Paycheck	$1,145.62	Mortgage	$745.94	$3,176.31
124				Car Payment	$155.00	$3,021.31
125				Student Loan	$115.00	$2,906.31
126				Credit Cards	$100.00	$2,806.31
127				Other	$375.00	$2,431.31
128				Cash Expenses	$175.00	$2,256.31

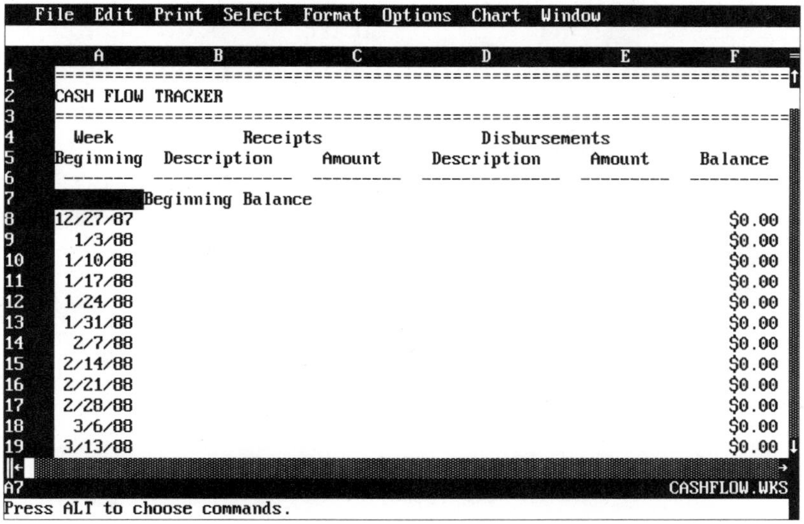

Figure 2-3.

CREATING THE TEMPLATE

To create the Cash Flow Tracker, first open a new spreadsheet: Selecting the New command from the File menu, choose the Spreadsheet option, and choose New. Then, select Manual Calculation from the Options menu. When Works operates in manual calculation mode, it does not recalculate the entire spreadsheet after each entry. This mode saves you time when you are entering a large spreadsheet such as the Cash Flow Tracker.

Next, change the default format for the spreadsheet from General to Dollar with two decimal places. To change the default format for a spreadsheet, highlight the entire spreadsheet and then choose the appropriate format command from the Format menu. To begin, press Shift-Ctrl-[F8] to highlight every cell in the spreadsheet. (Hold down the Shift and Ctrl keys and press [F8].) Now, select Dollar from the Format menu. When the Dollar dialog box appears, press Enter or choose OK to accept the default number of decimal places, 2.

Next, you need to change some column widths in the spreadsheet. To change the width of a column, select a cell in that column, select Width from the Format menu, type the new column width, and press Enter or choose OK. The table in Figure 2-4 shows the new widths for each column in the Cash Flow Tracker.

Now, you're ready to begin making entries. First, enter the header labels shown in Figure 2-1 (page 42) in rows 1, 2, and 3. The double lines in rows 1 and 3 are composed of equal signs (=) spanning columns A through F. To create these double lines, enter a label made up of equal signs in each cell in row 1 and then copy that series of labels to row 3. In each cell in row 1, type a quotation mark (") followed by the proper number of equal signs (corresponding to the column width). In cell A1, for example, type a quotation mark followed by a string of nine equal signs ("=========).

Next, you need to enter the labels *Week, Receipts,* and *Disbursements* in cells A4, B4, and D4. Notice in Figure 2-1 that the label *Receipts* is centered between columns B and C and that the label *Disbursements* is centered between columns D and E. To achieve this effect, you have to type a number of leading spaces when you enter these labels. For example, to enter the label *Receipts* in cell B4, move the cursor to cell

Column	Width
A	9
B	16
C	11
D	16
E	11
F	11

Figure 2-4. *Column Widths for the Cash Flow Tracker.*

B4, press the Spacebar 10 times, type *Receipts,* and press Enter. To enter the label *Disbursements* in cell D4, move the cursor to cell D4, press the Spacebar seven times, type *Disbursements,* and press Enter.

Next, move the cursor to row 5 and enter the labels *Beginning, Description, Amount, Description, Amount,* and *Balance* in cells A5 through F5. Then, move down to row 6 and enter dashed lines in cells A6 through F6. To create each line, move the cursor to the appropriate cell, type a quotation mark, and type the correct number of hyphens (-). Make each line two characters shorter than the column in which it is entered. For example, make the label in cell A6 7 characters long and the label in cell B6 14 characters long.

When all these labels are in place, center them: Highlight the range A4:F6, select Style from the Format menu, and choose Center from the Style dialog box.

After you create the column labels, freeze rows 1 through 6 on the screen. This ensures that the column labels remain visible—even when the cursor is way down in the spreadsheet. To freeze rows 1 through 6, move the cursor to cell A7, choose Row from the Select menu, and select Freeze Titles from the Options menu.

Creating the Table

Now you're ready to create the table itself. First, move the cursor to cell B7 and enter the label *Beginning Balance.* Now, move the cursor to cell A8 and enter the date of the first day (Sunday) of the current week. For example, if you are creating this application on Tuesday, February 2, 1988, enter *1/31/88*—the date of the first day of the current week—in cell A8. In Figure 2-1, we entered the date *12/27/87*—the first day in the first week in the year 1988.

Next, move the cursor to cell A9 and enter the formula

=A8+7

This formula sets the value of cell A9 equal to the value in cell A8 plus 7. Because the date in cell A8 represents a Sunday, and because a week consists of seven days, this formula returns the serial date value of the Sunday following the one represented by the date in cell A8. Because you assigned cell A9 Dollar format with two decimal places, however, the result of the formula is displayed as a series of number signs (#########). To display this value in date form, select Time/Date from the Format menu, choose Month, Day, Year (with Short date form) from the Time/Date dialog box, and press Enter or choose OK.

After you enter the formula in cell A9 and format that cell, copy the formula and format to the range A10:A60. To do this, highlight the range A9:A60 and select Fill Down from the Edit menu. Next, press the Calc key ([F9]) to recalculate these formulas. The result is a series of dates, each seven days greater than the one preceding. The last date is almost exactly one year after the first date.

Now you're ready to define the formulas in column F. To begin, move the cursor to cell F8 and enter the formula

`=F7+C8-E8`

This formula computes the cash balance as of the end of the first week. It simply adds the current week's cash receipts (in cell C8) to the beginning balance (in cell F7) and then subtracts the current week's cash disbursements (in cell E8) from that total. Because you have not yet entered any disbursements or receipts in the spreadsheet, the value in cell F8 matches the beginning balance in cell F7.

Next, copy the formula from cell F8 into the range F9:F61. To do so, highlight the range F8:F61 and select Fill Down from the Edit menu. Then, press the Calc key ([F9]) to recalculate these formulas. The result is a series of dollar values. Because you have not yet entered any disbursements or receipts, all the values in column F are identical to the beginning balance in cell F7. Finally, press Ctrl-Home to return the cursor to the upper left corner of the table.

Saving the Template

That's all there is to it—the Cash Flow Tracker is built. Before you do anything else, save the spreadsheet. To do so, select Save As from the File menu. Then, if you want to save the file in a directory other than the current one, choose that directory from the Other Drives & Directories list box and then choose OK. Next, type a name (such as *CASHFLOW.WKS*) and press Enter or choose OK to save the file. To save the file in the current directory, simply type a filename and press Enter or choose OK.

USING THE TEMPLATE

To put the Cash Flow Tracker to work, you must first open the spreadsheet. (If you just created the template, you can skip this step.) To do this, choose Open from the File menu. Then, if the file you want to open is not in the current directory, first select the directory that contains the file from the Other Drives & Directories box and then choose OK. Then, choose the filename from the list of files and press Enter or choose OK to open the file.

Moving the Cursor

As you can see in Figure 2-1 on page 42, the first 13 rows of the cash flow table appear on the home screen. To look at a different part of the spreadsheet, use your mouse or the cursor movement keys to move the cursor to the appropriate cell. For example, to view the next screenful of information, press the PgDn key. To move directly to the bottom of the table, move the cursor to column F (which contains an uninterrupted series of entries), and press Ctrl-Down Arrow. To return to the top of the table from any position, move the cursor to column F and press Ctrl-Up Arrow.

To move to a specific row in the spreadsheet, press the GoTo key, type *A* followed by the number of the row, and press Enter or choose OK. For example, to move to row 50, press the GoTo key, type *A50*, and press Enter or choose OK.

If you used the Freeze Titles option on the Options menu to "freeze" rows 1 through 6, those rows stay in view as you move the cursor through the application. For the same reason, you cannot use the arrow keys to move the cursor into any of these rows. When you press Ctrl-Home, the cursor moves to cell A7 instead of cell A1.

Entering the Receipts and Disbursements

First, if you have not done so already, move the cursor to cell F7 and enter the beginning balance for the forecast—the balance in your checkbook at the beginning of the first week in the forecast. If, for example, the balance in your checkbook on 12/27/87 was $4,572.98, enter that number in cell F7.

Now you're ready to enter cash receipts and disbursements. Exactly how you go about doing this probably depends on whether you are tracking personal cash flow or business cash flow. If you are monitoring your personal cash flow, begin by entering your predictable cash receipts—salary and wages, rental income, and so on— in columns B and C, and your predictable disbursements—rent or mortgage payment, car payment, other loan payments, normal cash expenses, and so on—in columns D and E. To keep the cash flow table simple and understandable, you can probably summarize your smaller cash disbursements (and perhaps smaller receipts as well) into one comprehensive amount.

When the predictable receipts and disbursements are in place, post your other receipts and disbursements—dividends, interest, tax refunds, tax payments, gifts, vacation expenses, and so on. These irregular items are actually the core of the application, because they can lead to large changes in your cash flow balances. Think carefully about these items so that you don't forget any major ones.

If you are tracking business cash flow, the job of posting receipts and disbursements is a bit tricky. Typically, a business can predict expenses accurately but cannot predict cash receipts confidently. For this reason, begin by posting predictable cash disbursements such as salaries, payroll taxes, rent, loan payments, and so on. To keep things simple, summarize your smaller cash disbursements into one comprehensive amount.

When the disbursements are in place, post your estimated weekly cash receipts to the spreadsheet. Instead of posting specific invoices or receipts, you'll probably want to enter a description in column D, such as *Regular Weekly Receipts*, and a summary amount in column E. When the predictable cash receipts and disbursements are in place, post unpredictable or irregular receipts or disbursements—purchases or sales of assets, tax bills, and so on.

Timing of Receipts and Disbursements

The Cash Flow Tracker tracks cash balances on a weekly basis. The dates in column A are the first dates in each week of the coming year. Of course, most receipts and disbursements do not occur on the exact dates that appear in column A. Instead, they occur between those dates. However, think of each date in column A as a week that begins with that date and ends on the day before the next date in the column. When you post receipts and disbursements, post them into the row that represents the week in which the disbursement or receipt will occur, in other words, in the row that contains the beginning date for the week in which the receipt or disbursement is to occur.

Posting Receipts

To post a cash receipt, move the cursor to column B in the row that represents the week in which the receipt occurs and type the description of the receipt; then move to column C and enter the amount of the receipt. For example, suppose you expect to receive a paycheck on January 2, 1988. The net amount of the check will be $1,145.62. Because this receipt occurs in the week beginning 12/27/87, post it to row 8 on the sample spreadsheet. Move the cursor to cell B8 and type a label such as *Paycheck*. Then, move the cursor to cell C8 and enter the number *1145.62*. Figure 2-5 shows the result.

```
 File  Edit  Print  Select  Format  Options  Chart  Window
1145.62
           A          B            C           D            E          F
1  ========================================================================
2  CASH FLOW TRACKER
3  ========================================================================
4     Week              Receipts               Disbursements
5  Beginning  Description     Amount      Description     Amount     Balance
6  ----------------------     ----------  ----------------------     ---------
7              Beginning Balance                                     $4,572.98
8  12/27/87 Paycheck          $1,145.62                              $4,572.98
9     1/3/88                                                         $4,572.98
10    1/10/88                                                        $4,572.98
11    1/17/88                                                        $4,572.98
12    1/24/88                                                        $4,572.98
13    1/31/88                                                        $4,572.98
14    2/7/88                                                         $4,572.98
15    2/14/88                                                        $4,572.98
16    2/21/88                                                        $4,572.98
17    2/28/88                                                        $4,572.98
18    3/6/88                                                         $4,572.98
19    3/13/88                                                        $4,572.98
C8                              CALC                      CASHFLOW.WKS
Press ALT to choose commands.
```

Figure 2-5.

Note the letters *CALC* on the Status line in Figure 2-5. This is an indication that formulas have not been recalculated to reflect recent entries in the spreadsheet. Because you chose manual recalculation, the new receipts you post do not immediately update the running cash balance. To update the balance, press the Calc key ([F9]). Figure 2-6 shows the recalculated spreadsheet.

```
 File  Edit  Print  Select  Format  Options  Chart  Window
1145.62
          A            B              C            D          E           F        =
1  ============================================================================↑
2  CASH FLOW TRACKER
3  ============================================================================
4     Week            Receipts                  Disbursements
5  Beginning  Description      Amount     Description    Amount     Balance
6  ---------  ---------------  ---------  -------------  ---------  ---------
7             Beginning Balance                                     $4,572.98
8  12/27/87  Paycheck          $1,145.62                            $5,718.60
9   1/3/88                                                          $5,718.60
10  1/10/88                                                         $5,718.60
11  1/17/88                                                         $5,718.60
12  1/24/88                                                         $5,718.60
13  1/31/88                                                         $5,718.60
14   2/7/88                                                         $5,718.60
15  2/14/88                                                         $5,718.60
16  2/21/88                                                         $5,718.60
17  2/28/88                                                         $5,718.60
18   3/6/88                                                         $5,718.60
19  3/13/88                                                         $5,718.60 ↓
‖←                                                                        →
C8                                                            CASHFLOW.WKS
Press ALT to choose commands.
```

Figure 2-6.

Posting Disbursements

To post a cash disbursement, move the cursor to column D in the row that represents the week in which the disbursement will occur and type the description of the disbursement. Then, move to column E and enter the amount of the disbursement. For example, suppose you have to make your monthly mortgage payment on January 2, 1988. The amount is $745.94. Because this disbursement occurs in the week beginning 12/27/87, post it to row 8. Move the cursor to cell D8 and type a label such as *Mortgage Payment*. Then, move the cursor to cell E8 and enter the number *745.94*. Figure 2-7 on the following page shows the two new entries. To update the balance, press the Calc key ([F9]). Figure 2-8 on the following page shows the recalculated spreadsheet.

```
 File  Edit  Print  Select  Format  Options  Chart  Window
745.94
          A           B           C           D           E           F
       ==================================================================
1
2      CASH FLOW TRACKER
3      ==================================================================
4         Week           Receipts              Disbursements
5      Beginning  Description   Amount    Description   Amount     Balance
6      ---------  -----------   ------    -----------   ------     -------
7                 Beginning Balance                                $4,572.98
8      12/27/87 Paycheck     $1,145.62 Mortgage        $745.94  $5,718.60
9         1/3/88                                                  $5,718.60
10        1/10/88                                                 $5,718.60
11        1/17/88                                                 $5,718.60
12        1/24/88                                                 $5,718.60
13        1/31/88                                                 $5,718.60
14        2/7/88                                                  $5,718.60
15        2/14/88                                                 $5,718.60
16        2/21/88                                                 $5,718.60
17        2/28/88                                                 $5,718.60
18        3/6/88                                                  $5,718.60
19        3/13/88                                                 $5,718.60
E8                              CALC                          CASHFLOW.WKS
Press ALT to choose commands.
```

Figure 2-7.

```
 File  Edit  Print  Select  Format  Options  Chart  Window
745.94
          A           B           C           D           E           F
       ==================================================================
1
2      CASH FLOW TRACKER
3      ==================================================================
4         Week           Receipts              Disbursements
5      Beginning  Description   Amount    Description   Amount     Balance
6      ---------  -----------   ------    -----------   ------     -------
7                 Beginning Balance                                $4,572.98
8      12/27/87 Paycheck     $1,145.62 Mortgage        $745.94  $4,972.66
9         1/3/88                                                  $4,972.66
10        1/10/88                                                 $4,972.66
11        1/17/88                                                 $4,972.66
12        1/24/88                                                 $4,972.66
13        1/31/88                                                 $4,972.66
14        2/7/88                                                  $4,972.66
15        2/14/88                                                 $4,972.66
16        2/21/88                                                 $4,972.66
17        2/28/88                                                 $4,972.66
18        3/6/88                                                  $4,972.66
19        3/13/88                                                 $4,972.66
E8                                                           CASHFLOW.WKS
Press ALT to choose commands.
```

Figure 2-8.

Adding Rows

In some weeks, you'll have only a single receipt or disbursement. In those cases, simply post the receipt or disbursement and move to the next week. In other weeks, you'll have to add a row to the spreadsheet to accommodate numerous receipts and disbursements. For example, suppose a car payment is due on January 2, 1988. The amount of the payment is $155. Because this disbursement occurs in the week beginning 12/27/87, you should post it to row 8. But because row 8 already contains a disbursement, you need to insert an extra row below row 8. Move the cursor to any cell in row 9 and press Ctrl-[F8] to select the row. Then, choose Insert from the Edit menu to insert a new row 9 in the spreadsheet, select the range F8:F10, and choose Fill Down from the Edit menu to copy the appropriate formula to cells F9 and F10. The "Modifications" section of this chapter tells you how you can build a macro that lets you insert a new row with a few keystrokes.

At this point, you can post the disbursement to the spreadsheet in the usual way: Type the description for the disbursement (*Car Payment*) in cell D9 and enter the amount of the disbursement (*155*) in cell E9. Then, to update the balance, press the Calc key ([F9]). Figure 2-9 shows the spreadsheet after the row and the new expenditure are added.

```
 File   Edit   Print   Select   Format   Options   Chart   Window
155
            A            B            C            D            E          F         =
1  =========================================================================
2  CASH FLOW TRACKER
3  =========================================================================
4     Week           Receipts              Disbursements
5  Beginning  Description     Amount    Description     Amount     Balance
6  ---------  -----------     ------    -----------     ------     -------
7             Beginning Balance                                    $4,572.98
8  12/27/87 Paycheck       $1,145.62 Mortgage           $745.94  $4,972.66
9                                    Car Payment         $155.00  $4,817.66
10    1/3/88                                                      $4,817.66
11   1/10/88                                                      $4,817.66
12   1/17/88                                                      $4,817.66
13   1/24/88                                                      $4,817.66
14   1/31/88                                                      $4,817.66
15    2/7/88                                                      $4,817.66
16   2/14/88                                                      $4,817.66
17   2/21/88                                                      $4,817.66
18   2/28/88                                                      $4,817.66
19    3/6/88                                                      $4,817.66
‖←█                                                          →
E9                                                          CASHFLOW.WKS
Press ALT to choose commands.
```

Figure 2-9.

You may wonder why it is necessary to copy the formula in column F to both the newly inserted row and the row beneath that row. Remember that each formula in column F references the preceding cell in column F. For example, the formula that computes the balance in cell F10

=F9+C10-E10

references cell F9, the preceding cell in column F. If you insert a new row between rows 9 and 10, this formula, which would now be in cell F11, changes to

=F9+C11-E11

Notice that the formula still references cell F9, the cell in column F two rows above the formula, when it should be referencing cell F10, the previous cell in column F. To correct this error, the macro copies the formula from the cell two rows above this row (cell F9 in the example) to both the newly inserted row (row 10 in the example) and the row below that row (row 11 in the example). Copying the formula to both cells not only fills the newly inserted row but also corrects the formula in column F of the row below the inserted row.

Recurring Receipts and Disbursements

Some receipts and disbursements occur at regular intervals throughout the year. For instance, most mortgage companies require a payment on the first or last day of each month. Similarly, most of us are paid weekly, biweekly, semimonthly, or monthly. Regardless of the interval, the amount of the transaction is usually the same.

You can use the Copy command to enter repeating receipts and disbursements easily. Simply enter the description and amount of the first occurrence of the receipt or disbursement into the appropriate cells and then copy those entries to the row representing the week in which the disbursement or receipt will occur again.

To copy a receipt or disbursement, highlight the cells that contain the description and amount of the receipt or disbursement, select the Copy command from the Edit menu, highlight the cells in which you want to place the copy, and press Enter. Works duplicates the contents of the first set of highlighted cells into the destination cells. The destination cells remain highlighted after the copy is complete. To create the second copy, select the Copy command again, highlight the next pair of destination cells, and press Enter. You can repeat these steps until you post all occurrences of the receipt or disbursement.

For example, suppose you must make a payment of $745.94 on your mortgage on the first of each month. Rather than entering each payment individually, enter the disbursement once and then duplicate it. To begin, enter the first occurrence of the disbursement in cells D8 and E8 as you did earlier. Once the first entry is in place, move the cursor to cell D8 and highlight the range D8:E8, as shown in Figure 2-10. Then, select Copy from the Edit menu and then point to cell D14. (Notice that row 14 represents the week in which the first day of the next month falls.) Next, press Enter to copy the selected entries from cells D8:E8. Finally, press the Calc key ([F9]) to update the balance, as shown in Figure 2-11.

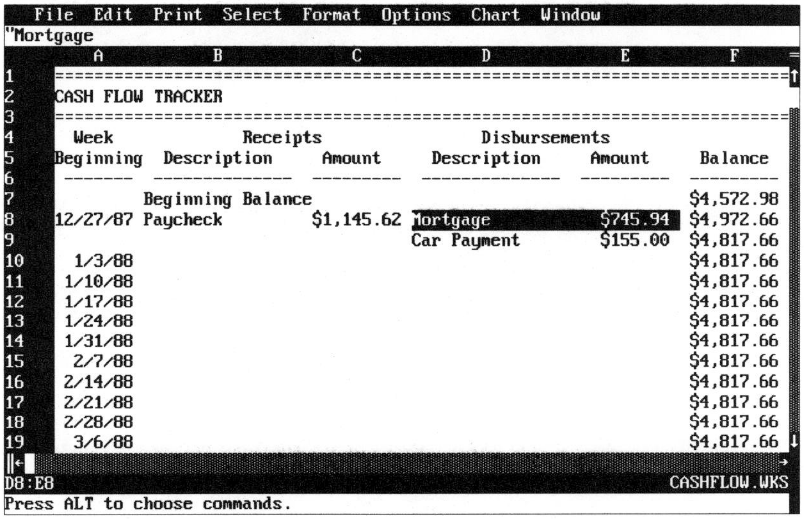

Figure 2-10.

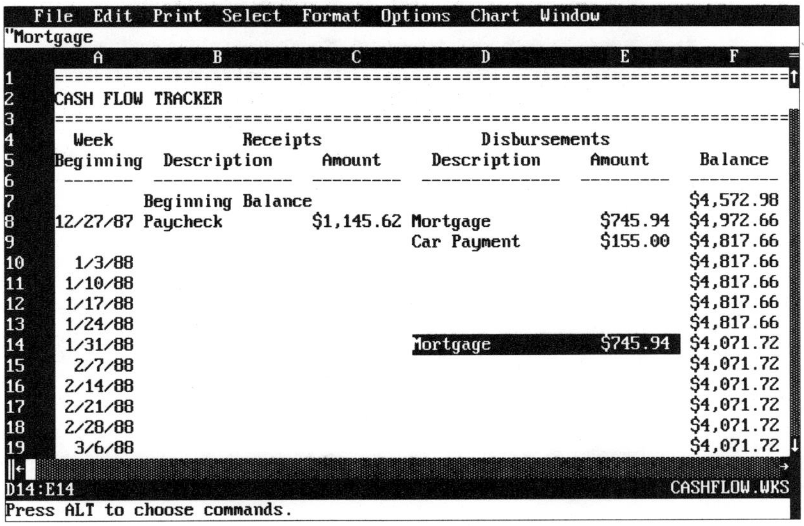

Figure 2-11.

Notice that cells D14 and E14 remain highlighted in Figure 2-11. To copy the mortgage disbursement again, choose Copy from the Edit menu, select cell D18, and press Enter. You can repeat these steps as many times as necessary. Of course, if you have two or more entries that occur on the same week of each month, you will want to insert several new rows—one row for each additional expense or receipt you need to post.

Highlighting Unusual Items

After you enter the predictable receipts and disbursements, enter the irregular items—sales of assets, expenditures for gifts, vacations, taxes, and so on. After you enter these unusual items, press [F9] to recalculate. Then, you might use the bold style to draw attention to them. To assign the bold style to a receipt or disbursement, select the cells that contain the description and amount of the item, choose Style from the Format menu, choose Bold, and press Enter or choose OK. Works assigns the bold style to the selected cells. Their contents appear in bold type on the screen and, if your printer can print bold characters, in printed copy.

For example, suppose you expect to deposit $2,000 into your IRA during the week beginning April 10, 1988. Figure 2-12 shows this disbursement in cells D24 and E24 of the Cash Flow Tracker. To assign the bold style to these cells, select the range D24:E24, choose Style from the Format menu, choose Bold, and press Enter or choose OK. Then press the Home key to return the cursor to column A. Figure 2-13 shows the result.

```
 File  Edit  Print  Select  Format  Options  Chart  Window
=A23+7
         A           B            C           D           E          F
1    ============================================================
2    CASH FLOW TRACKER
3    ============================================================
4    Week        Receipts              Disbursements
5    Beginning  Description    Amount   Description    Amount   Balance
6    ---------- -------------- --------- -------------- --------- ----------
15    2/7/88                                                    $4,071.72
16    2/14/88                                                   $4,071.72
17    2/21/88                                                   $4,071.72
18    2/28/88                                                   $4,071.72
19    3/6/88                                                    $4,071.72
20    3/13/88                                                   $4,071.72
21    3/20/88                                                   $4,071.72
22    3/27/88                                                   $4,071.72
23    4/3/88                                                    $4,071.72
24    4/10/88                         IRA Contribution $2,000.00 $4,071.72
25    4/17/88                                                   $4,071.72
26    4/24/88                                                   $4,071.72
27    5/1/88                                                    $4,071.72
 +
A24                              CALC                    CASHFLOW.WKS
Press ALT to choose commands.
```

Figure 2-12.

```
 File  Edit  Print  Select  Format  Options  Chart  Window
=A23+7
          A           B            C            D            E          F       =
1  ============================================================================
2  CASH FLOW TRACKER
3  ============================================================================
4     Week              Receipts              Disbursements
5  Beginning   Description    Amount    Description    Amount     Balance
6  ---------   ---------------  ----------   ---------------  ----------   ----------
15   2/7/88                                                            $4,071.72
16   2/14/88                                                           $4,071.72
17   2/21/88                                                           $4,071.72
18   2/28/88                                                           $4,071.72
19   3/6/88                                                            $4,071.72
20   3/13/88                                                           $4,071.72
21   3/20/88                                                           $4,071.72
22   3/27/88                                                           $4,071.72
23   4/3/88                                                            $4,071.72
24   4/10/88                               IRA Contribution $2,000.00  $4,071.72
25   4/17/88                                                           $4,071.72
26   4/24/88                                                           $4,071.72
27   5/1/88                                                            $4,071.72
A24                      CALC                              CASHFLOW.WKS
Press ALT to choose commands.
```

Figure 2-13.

Charting the Cash Balances

You can use Works' Chart environment to create a chart from the series of cash balances in column F of the Cash Flow Tracker. Charting the cash balances makes it easy to review the cash flow trends across the entire year at a glance and to find excessive or insufficient cash balances.

To create a chart based on the cash balances in column F, first highlight the cells in column F that contain cash balances. In the original version of the spreadsheet, this is the range F7:F60. As you add rows to the spreadsheet, however, this range grows. In Figure 2-2, beginning on page 43, for example, the sample entries extend through row 128. To select all the cells that contain cash balances with the keyboard, move the cursor to cell F7, press the Extend key ([F8]), and then press Ctrl-Down Arrow. If you have a mouse, click on cell F7 and then use the scroll bars to display the last cell in column F that contains an entry. When that cell is on the screen, press Shift and click that cell.

Now, you can create a chart to depict the highlighted column of values. Select New from the Chart menu to create a new Chart document, as shown in Figure 2-14 on the following page. Then, to look at the chart you defined, choose View from the Chart menu. Figure 2-15 on the following page shows the chart.

```
 Chart  Print  Data  Format  Options  Window
4572.98
      A          B            C           D             E         F        =
1  =========================================================================== ↑
2  CASH FLOW TRACKER
3  ===========================================================================
4            Week        Receipts              Disbursements
5  Beginning  Description  Amount    Description      Amount    Balance
6  ---------  -----------  --------- ---------------  --------  --------
116                                  Credit Cards     $100.00   $3,106.01
117                                  Other Bills      $375.00   $2,731.01
118                                  Cash Expenses    $175.00   $2,556.01
119  12/4/88                         Xmas Presents    $400.00   $2,156.01
120                                  Cash Expenses    $175.00   $1,981.01
121  12/11/88  Paycheck   $1,145.62  Cash Expenses    $175.00   $2,951.63
122  12/18/88                        Cash Expenses    $175.00   $2,776.63
123  12/25/88  Paycheck   $1,145.62  Mortgage         $745.94   $3,176.31
124                                  Car Payment      $155.00   $3,021.31
125                                  Student Loan     $115.00   $2,906.31
126                                  Credit Cards     $100.00   $2,806.31
127                                  Other            $375.00   $2,431.31
128                                  Cash Expenses    $175.00   $2,256.31 ↓
F7:F128                    CHART                        CASHFLOW.WKS
Press ALT to choose commands or F10 to exit Chart screen.
```

Figure 2-14.

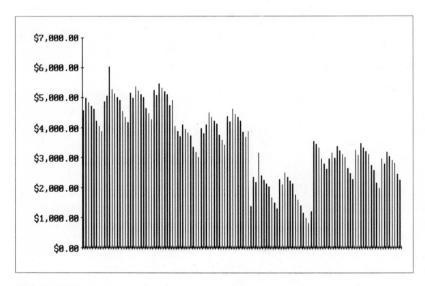

Figure 2-15.

As you can see, Works created a bar chart from the data you highlighted. However, you might prefer to view the information in the form of a line chart or an area line chart. To change the form of the chart, press the Esc key or click your mouse to return to the Chart design screen and choose the desired chart type

from the Format menu. For example, to change the chart to a line chart, choose
Line from the Format menu. To view the new chart, choose View from the Chart
menu. Figure 2-16 shows the chart as a line chart.

After you create the chart and change its type, you might want to add titles and
other enhancements to it. To add a title, first press the Esc key or click with your
mouse to return to the Chart design screen. Then, choose the Titles option from the
Data menu to display the dialog box shown in Figure 2-17 on the following page.
Now you can type a chart title, a chart subtitle, x-axis and y-axis titles, and a right
y-axis title for the chart. To create a title, simply choose the appropriate blank in the
dialog box and type the title. After you finish one title, choose the next blank and
type the next title. Don't press Enter to end a title; pressing Enter returns you to the
Chart design screen. If you press Enter by mistake, choose the Titles command again.

For example, to define a sample chart title, type *John Doe Family* on the Chart title
line. Then, to define a subtitle, press Tab to move the cursor to the Subtitle box and
type *1988 Cash Flow Estimate*. Notice that the Subtitle text box is shorter than the entry
1988 Cash Flow Estimate. As you type, the insertion point will reach the right edge of
the box. At that point, the text begins to shift one character to the right with each keystroke, which allows you to enter text that is longer than the text entry box itself.

To define the x-axis title, press the Tab key to move the cursor to the X-Axis text
box and type *Weeks (1 to 52)*. Finally, to define the left y-axis title, press Tab to move
the cursor to the Y-Axis text box and type *Cash Balance*. When you're finished, press
Enter to return to the Chart document and then choose View from the Chart menu to
look at the chart shown in Figure 2-18 on the following page.

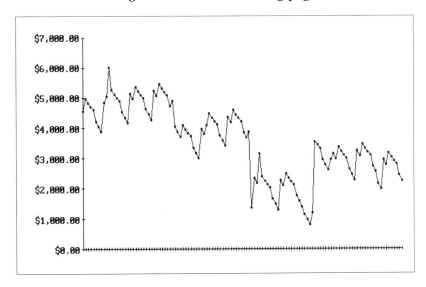

Figure 2-16.

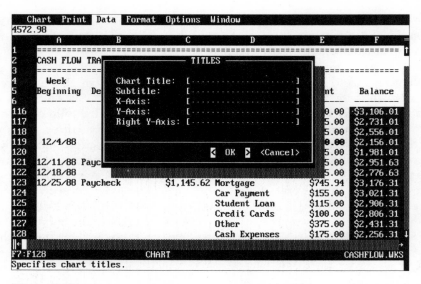

Figure 2-17.

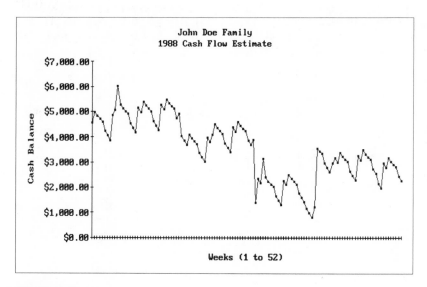

Figure 2-18.

Next, you might want to remove the data point markers from the line chart. To
do so, press the Esc key or click to return to the Chart design screen and choose Data
Format from the Format menu. When you see the Data Format dialog box (as in

Figure 2-19), move to the list of options under Markers and choose the None option. Then, press Enter or choose Format or Format All to end the command and return to the chart document. Choose View from the Chart menu to see the chart shown in Figure 2-20.

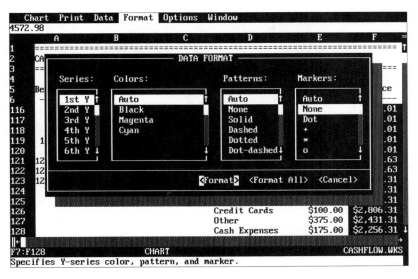

Figure 2-19.

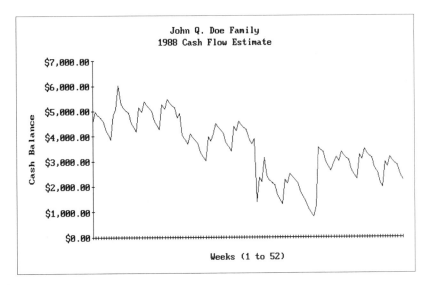

Figure 2-20.

When you created the chart shown in Figure 2-20, for example, Works gave it the name CHART1. Although these default names are perfectly adequate, you may want to give your charts names that describe their purpose. For example, you might give CHART1 the name CASHBAL. To do so, press the Esc key or click with your mouse to return to the chart design screen. Then, pull down the Chart menu, select Charts, and highlight the name CHART1 (the current name of the chart). Then, type CASHBAL in the Name text box and choose Rename.

To return to the spreadsheet, select Exit Chart from the Chart menu. Press any cursor movement key to deactivate the extended cursor.

Printing and Saving

After you set up your cash flow table, save that spreadsheet to a new file. To do this, select Save As from the File menu. Then, if you want to save the file in a directory other than the current one, choose that directory from the Other Drives & Directories list box and then choose OK. Next, type a new name for the spreadsheet and press Enter or choose OK.

Be sure to save your filled-in Cash Flow Tracker spreadsheets under a name other than the name you used for the original, empty template. If you save a filled-in spreadsheet under the same name as the original template, the filled-in version replaces the original version. Choose a name for your file that clearly identifies its contents.

To print the Cash Flow Tracker, first choose Layout from the Print menu and change any print settings you want to change. For example, if you have a wide-carriage printer and plan to print this spreadsheet onto 11-by-14-inch paper, you might want to change the Page Width setting from 8.5" to 14". You might also want to change the Top, Bottom, Left, and Right margins and define a header and footer. Next, you can use the Font command on the Print menu to select the font you want Works to use to print the report. To squeeze the entire report onto one page, choose a relatively compressed font (such as Elite) and a small point size (such as 6 or 8).

After you adjust the settings, select Print from the Print menu, adjust any of the settings in the Print dialog box, and choose the Print button to print the worksheet.

To print only a portion of the Cash Flow Tracker, first use the Set Print Area command on the Print menu to define the range to print. To print only the first month of transactions, for example, first highlight the range A8:F14 and then choose Set Print Area from the Print menu. Next, use the Layout and Font commands to make any needed adjustments to the Works print settings. Finally, select Print from the Print menu and choose the Print button to print the selected range. Because the Freeze Titles command is active, Works first prints the frozen rows, and then it prints the selected area.

Printing the Chart

You can also use Works to print the chart that you created. To do this, first make the chart you want to print active by choosing its name from the Chart menu. Then, use choose Layout from the Print menu and change any print settings. Finally, select Print Chart from the Print menu and choose the Print button to begin printing.

Interpreting the Results

After you enter your receipts and disbursements in the Cash Flow Tracker, chart the cash flow balances in column F, and save and print the spreadsheet, take a few minutes to analyze the results. Look at your chart: Does your cash balance dip to near or below $0.00 at any point? If so, you have a problem you can solve in several ways. First, you can change the timing of certain receipts or disbursements to eliminate the cash shortfall. For instance, you could delay a major expenditure for a few weeks or find a way to receive a major cash inflow in advance. To change the timing of a receipt or disbursement, reenter the description and amount of the receipt or disbursement in the new location and then use the Clear command to erase the existing description and amount.

For example, Figure 2-21 on the following page shows a section of a sample cash flow table. Notice that the cash balance at the end of the week that begins on 10/2/88 is $105.40. Suppose that this table represents your cash flow projection and that you're not comfortable with a balance that low. You can solve this problem by delaying a disbursement or by accelerating a receipt. Suppose your solution is to move the sale of stock for $2,500 that is currently projected for the week beginning 10/23/88 to the week beginning 9/25/88. To do this, move the cursor to cell B95 and type the description *Sell Stock*; then, move to cell C95 and enter the projected amount of the sale, *2500*. When the new entry is in place, move the cursor to cell B103, highlight the range B103:C103, and select Clear from the Edit menu. Finally, press the Calc key ([F9]) to recalculate the spreadsheet. Figure 2-22 on the following page shows the result. Notice that the low cash balance is eliminated.

Do not use the Move command to move a receipt or disbursement to a new location. Using the Move command to move a value from one cell to another changes any formulas that refer to the original cell so that they refer to the new location. In this case, such changes to the formulas will produce incorrect results.

Instead of changing the timing of a receipt or disbursement, you can eliminate one or more major disbursements from the table (and from your plans). For example, to remedy the shortfall shown in Figure 2-21, simply erase the disbursement for a sofa ($800) from row 101. To erase an entry, highlight the cells that contain the description and amount and use the Clear command on the Edit menu to erase them. Then, press the Calc key ([F9]) to update the running cash balances. Does the cash shortfall still exist? If so, you'll need to take further action. If not, you're in great shape.

```
 File  Edit  Print  Select  Format  Options  Chart  Window
=F99+C100-E100
      A          B          C          D           E         F
    =================================================================
1   CASH FLOW TRACKER
2
3   =================================================================
4      Week              Receipts          Disbursements
5   Beginning  Description   Amount    Description     Amount   Balance
6   ---------- ------------- --------- --------------- -------- -------
93    9/18/88                          Cash Expenses    $175.00   $800.72
94    9/25/88  Paycheck     $1,145.62  Mortgage         $745.94 $1,200.40
95                                     Car Payment      $155.00 $1,045.40
96                                     Student Loan     $115.00   $930.40
97                                     Credit Cards     $100.00   $830.40
98                                     Other Bills      $375.00   $455.40
99                                     Cash Expenses    $175.00   $280.40
100   10/2/88                          Cash Expenses    $175.00   $105.40
101   10/9/88  Paycheck     $1,145.62  Buy Sofa         $800.00   $451.02
102  10/16/88  Dividend Check $375.00  Cash Expenses    $175.00   $651.02
103  10/23/88  Sell Stock   $2,500.00  Cash Expenses    $175.00 $2,976.02
104  10/30/88  Paycheck     $1,145.62  Mortgage         $745.94 $3,375.71
105                                     Car Payment      $155.00 $3,220.71
F100                                                      CASHFLOW.WKS
Press ALT to choose commands.
```

Figure 2-21.

```
 File  Edit  Print  Select  Format  Options  Chart  Window
      A          B          C          D           E         F
    =================================================================
1   CASH FLOW TRACKER
2
3   =================================================================
4      Week              Receipts          Disbursements
5   Beginning  Description   Amount    Description     Amount   Balance
6   ---------- ------------- --------- --------------- -------- -------
93    9/18/88                          Cash Expenses    $175.00   $800.72
94    9/25/88  Paycheck     $1,145.62  Mortgage         $745.94 $1,200.40
95              Sell Stock   $2,500.00  Car Payment      $155.00 $3,545.40
96                                     Student Loan     $115.00 $3,430.40
97                                     Credit Cards     $100.00 $3,330.40
98                                     Other Bills      $375.00 $2,955.40
99                                     Cash Expenses    $175.00 $2,780.40
100   10/2/88                          Cash Expenses    $175.00 $2,605.40
101   10/9/88  Paycheck     $1,145.62  Buy Sofa         $800.00 $2,951.02
102  10/16/88  Dividend Check $375.00  Cash Expenses    $175.00 $3,151.02
103  10/23/88                          Cash Expenses    $175.00 $2,976.02
104  10/30/88  Paycheck     $1,145.62  Mortgage         $745.94 $3,375.71
105                                     Car Payment      $155.00 $3,220.71
B103:C103                                                 CASHFLOW.WKS
Press ALT to choose commands.
```

Figure 2-22.

Similarly, you can overcome cash shortfalls by adding new cash receipts. You might sell some stock or another investment or arrange for a loan. Post these new receipts to the spreadsheet exactly as you posted every other receipt: Enter the description in column B of the appropriate row and the amount in column C.

What if the table shows that you have excessively high cash balances? Consider "disbursing" some cash to make an investment. Or consider purchasing something that you thought you could not afford. When you decide what you want to do, record the new disbursement as you would any other.

Updating the Table

After you set up the Cash Flow Tracker and check it for excessive or insufficient cash balances, save the spreadsheet and forget it for a while. Every so often, however, you should open the spreadsheet and update your estimates. Have your normal weekly receipts and disbursements kept pace with your estimates? Have you actually received all the cash you expected to receive from unusual sources? Have you incurred all the irregular disbursements you expected? Have you received any windfalls or paid out any cash that you did not predict? If necessary, update your estimates. You can do this by actually changing individual receipts and disbursements and by adding and deleting receipts and disbursements (the preferred method), or you can add a single "plug" entry that updates the cash balance.

After you bring the Cash Flow Tracker into line with your actual receipts and disbursements, check the accuracy of your remaining estimates. If your weekly receipts or disbursements run consistently above or below your estimates, update the remaining estimates. Similarly, if you become aware of any unplanned receipts or disbursements, add those to the table.

When the spreadsheet is up-to-date, insert a "placemark" in it to show when it was last updated. Assign the range name NOW (or any other name, for that matter) to the cell that contains the date on which the current week begins. To do this, move the cursor to the cell in column A that contains the date on which the current week begins. Then, select Name from the Edit menu, type the name *NOW*, and either press Enter or choose OK. Now, save the updated spreadsheet.

Entering this placemark makes it easier to find your place when you update the spreadsheet. The next time you open the file, press [F5] or choose GoTo from the Select menu, type *NOW* or choose Now from the Names list box, and press Enter or choose OK. Works moves the cursor to the cell with the name NOW, and you can begin updating.

MODIFICATIONS

A few modifications might make the basic Cash Flow Tracker more useful to you. If you need more or less detail in your cash flow forecast, you can change the reporting period from weekly to daily or monthly. To do so, change the formulas in column A so that they create the interval you desire. If you want a daily reporting period, change the interval to 1. For a monthly period, the interval differs from month to month (31 days in January, 28 in February, and so on). If you want a daily forecast, you can create a separate spreadsheet for each month. Otherwise, your spreadsheet can get awfully large.

If your spreadsheet becomes too crowded, you're probably trying to report receipts and disbursements in too much detail. Go back and summarize your transactions to eliminate the smaller amounts. If you know in advance that you'll have a great number of receipts and disbursements, think of ways to summarize those transactions before you start.

Because you will probably need to add rows frequently, a useful way to improve the template is to write a macro that lets you add new rows to the spreadsheet with a few keystrokes. Figure 2-23 shows the completed macro, which issues the commands to insert a row in the table and to copy the correct formula in the cell in column F in this new row.

You don't need to create this macro until you decide to add a row to the spreadsheet for the first time. When that time comes, you can insert the row you need to add and create the macro all at once using the macro recorder. To use this feature, a program called MS-Key must be loaded. If you have not already loaded the program, close any open documents and choose Exit from the File menu to exit Works. Then, type *mskey* at the system prompt and press Enter. To return to Works, type *Works* and press Enter.

To begin recording, first move the cursor to column A and position it in the row below which you want to add a new row. When the cursor is in place, press Alt-/ to activate the MS-Key menu bar. Now, pull down the Macro menu and select Record to begin recording your keystrokes. When you select this command, a dialog box appears that instructs you to press the key or key combination to which you want to link this macro. Press Alt-i to tell Works that you want it to "play back" the macro you are about to record whenever you press Alt-i.

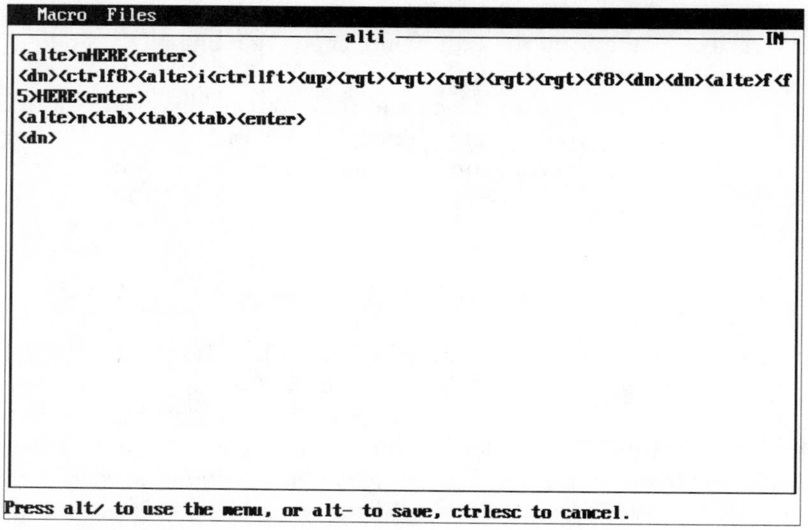

```
Macro  Files
─────────────────────── alti ───────────────────────────────────IN─
<alte>nHERE<enter>
<dn><ctrlf8><alte>i<ctrllft><up><rgt><rgt><rgt><rgt><rgt><f8><dn><dn><alte>f<f
5>HERE<enter>
<alte>n<tab><tab><tab><enter>
<dn>




























Press alt/ to use the menu, or alt- to save, ctrlesc to cancel.
```

Figure 2-23.

Now that MS-Key is recording your keystrokes, you can build the macro simply by performing the procedures that incorporate a new row into the spreadsheet. Because Works lets you perform many procedures in a variety of ways (choosing a command, for example), two macros can appear different but accomplish precisely the same result. If you want your macro to match the one shown in Figure 2-23, perform the steps exactly as you are instructed. Note that the macro recorder does not record mouse operations, so be sure to use keyboard techniques.

If you make a mistake, press Alt-/, pull down the Macro menu, and choose the Cancel command. Then, press Alt-/ again, choose Record from the Macro menu, press Alt-i, and start recording again from the beginning.

To begin, press Alt-e to display the Edit menu, and press *n* to choose the Name command. Now, type *HERE* and press Enter to assign the range name HERE to the current cell. Next, press the Down Arrow key to move the cursor to the next row and press Ctrl-[F8] to highlight the current row. Then, press Alt-e and press *i* to choose Insert from the Edit menu. Works inserts a blank row into the spreadsheet.

Now you need to "patch up" the formulas in column F to fill in the gap made by the addition of the new row. To do so, first press Ctrl-Left Arrow, press the Up Arrow key, and then press the Right Arrow key five times. This step returns the cursor to the row it was in when you began recording and places it in column F. Next, press the Extend key ([F8]) and press the Down Arrow key twice to highlight the current cell and the two cells below it. Finally, press Alt-e and press *f* to choose Fill Down from the Edit menu. Works copies the formula from the first of the three cells to the two cells below.

Now, press the Go To key ([F5]), type *HERE*, and press Enter. When you do this, Works moves the cursor back to its original location. Next, press Alt-e and then press *n* to choose Name from the Edit menu, and type *HERE*. Now, press the Tab key three times and press Enter to choose the Delete button. Works then removes the HERE range. Finally, press the Down Arrow key to move the cursor down to the new row.

The last step is to stop recording keystrokes. To do this, press Alt-/ to activate the MS-Key menu bar and select the End command from the Macro menu to stop recording. That's it! The macro is now in memory. To save the macro for later use, first press Alt-/ and pull down the File menu. Then, choose Save, type a filename (such as *CASHFLOW.KEY*), and press Enter to save the macros currently in memory to the indicated file.

To use the macro in subsequent *Works* sessions, load MS-Key before you load Works. Then, after you open your Cash Flow Tracker spreadsheet, press Alt-/ and choose Open from the File menu. Type the filename (for example, *CASHFLOW.KEY*) and press Enter to read the macro into memory. Then, press the Esc key to display the Menu bar for your spreadsheet.

CONCLUSION

The Cash Flow Tracker is a simple but useful spreadsheet. Almost any individual or business can use it to forecast cash balances and to schedule cash receipts and disbursements. Even if you don't use this template, however, you can employ some of the tricks and techniques you learned in building it in your own spreadsheets. Borrow from or modify the template in any way you wish. Just use your imagination!

Checkbook Register and Balancer

Be honest: Do you look forward to balancing your checkbook each month? If you're like most of us, the answer is no. Balancing the checkbook is a tedious—and sometimes terrifying—process that most of us would just as soon avoid. It doesn't have to be that way, though. The mathematical and logical capabilities of Microsoft Works can cut dramatically the time and effort required to balance your checkbook.

The Checkbook Register and Balancer lets you use Works to manage your checking account. Instead of recording each check you write and each deposit you make on a paper check register, you record them on the spreadsheet. The formulas in the spreadsheet compute the balance of your account after every check and deposit. At the end of the month, when you need to balance the checkbook, you merely code the checks and deposits that have not cleared the bank. The spreadsheet then makes the selections and performs the math for you—the whole process is a snap.

Although this template is easy to build and use, it illustrates some clever Works techniques. For instance, it demonstrates a neat way to use the MAX function to create an interruptible series of values. It also explains an easy way to create running totals, and it shows you how to use IF functions to make selections from a column of coded values.

ABOUT THE TEMPLATE

Figure 3-1 on the following pages shows the Checkbook Register and Balancer after you create the template. Figure 3-2 on the following pages shows the spreadsheet with some sample data. As you can see, the template has three major areas, labeled CHECK REGISTER, RECONCILIATION, and OUTSTANDING ITEMS. The Check Register occupies columns A through G.

	A	B	C	D	E	F	G	H	I	J	K
1	===										
2	CHECKBOOK REGISTER AND BALANCER							CHECKBOOK REGISTER AND BALANCER			
3	===										
4	CHECK REGISTER							RECONCILIATION			
5	===										
6											
7	Check					Running					
8	Number	Date	Payee-Payor	Notation	Amount	Balance	Out?				
9	Beginning Balance					$0.00		Balance Per Bank			
10	1000					$0.00		Outstanding Items			
11	1001					$0.00					
12	1002					$0.00		Reconciled Bank Balance			
13	1003					$0.00		Book Balance			
14	1004					$0.00					
15	1005					$0.00		Unreconciled Difference			
16	1006					$0.00					
17	1007					$0.00					
18	1008					$0.00					
19	1009					$0.00					
20	1010					$0.00					
~~	1011										
391						$0.00					
392	1382					$0.00					
393	1383					$0.00					
394	1384					$0.00					
395	1385					$0.00					
396	1386					$0.00					
397	1387					$0.00					
398	1388					$0.00					
399	1389					$0.00					
400	1390					$0.00					

Figure 3-1.

	A	B	C	D	E	F	G	H	I	J	K
1	===										
2	CHECKBOOK REGISTER AND BALANCER							CHECKBOOK REGISTER AND BALANCER			
3	===										
4	CHECK REGISTER							RECONCILIATION			
5	===										
6											
7	Check					Running					
8	Number	Date	Payee-Payor	Notation	Amount	Balance	Out?				
9	Beginning Balance					$6,479.25		Balance Per Bank			
10	1000	4/1/87	Cleaners	Shirt Laundry	($7.50)	$6,471.75		Outstanding Items			
11	1001	4/1/87	Hardware Store	Paint Brushes	($12.35)	$6,459.40					
12	D	4/2/87	Brother-in-Law	Repay $25 loan	$25.00	$6,484.40		Reconciled Bank Balance			
13	1002	4/2/87	Bookstore	"Iacocca"	($8.95)	$6,475.45		Book Balance			
14	1003	4/3/87	Local S&L	Mortgage	($600.00)	$5,875.45					
15	CW	4/3/87	Cash	Cash Machine	($200.00)	$5,675.45		Unreconciled Difference			
16	1004	4/4/87	GMAC	Car Payment	($205.00)	$5,470.45					
17	1005	4/4/87	First Bank	MasterCard Bill	($127.35)	$5,343.10					
18	1006	4/4/87	ELSI	Student Loan	($115.00)	$5,228.10					
19	1007	4/4/87	Power Company	Electric Bill	($135.00)	$5,093.10					
20	1008	4/4/87	Water Company	Water Bill	($35.00)	$5,058.10					
~~	1009	4/4/87	SCB	Telephone Bill	($56.00)	$5,...					
			...C Corp.	Pay 3/15-3/31							
65	1047	5/30...			(...00)	$5,569.85	1				
66	1048	5/30/87	SCB	Telephone Bill	($56.00)	$5,513.85	1				
67	D	5/31/87	ABC Corp.	Pay 5/15-5/31	$1,500.00	$7,013.85	1				
68	1049	6/1/87	Storer	Cable TV	($35.15)	$6,978.70	1				
69	A	6/2/87	First Bank	Service Charge	($7.00)	$6,971.70					
70	DW	6/2/87	USA Fitness	Health Club	($55.00)	$6,916.70					
71	1050					$6,916.70					
72	1051					$6,916.70					
73	1052					$6,916.70					

Figure 3-2.

```
          L         M         N         O         P         Q         R         S         T         U         V
=====================================================================================================================
                                        CHECKBOOK REGISTER AND BALANCER
=====================================================================================================================
For Period Ending              OUTSTANDING ITEMS
=====================================================================================================================
                                        Items
                                        Coded                PREVIOUSLY OUTSTANDING ITEMS
                                        Outstanding          Number   Date      Amount
                                        $0.00
           $0.00                        $0.00
        ---------                       $0.00
           $0.00                        $0.00
           $0.00                        $0.00
        ---------                       $0.00
           $0.00                        $0.00
        =========                       $0.00
                                        $0.00
                                        $0.00
                                        $0.00
                                        $0.00
                                        $0 00
```
```
                                        --.00
                                        $0.00
                                        $0.00
                                        $0.00
                                        $0.00
                                        $0.00
                                        $0.00
                                        $0.00
```

```
          L         M         N         O         P         Q         R         S         T         U         V
=====================================================================================================================
                                        CHECKBOOK REGISTER AND BALANCER
=====================================================================================================================
For Period Ending              5/31/87 OUTSTANDING ITEMS
=====================================================================================================================
                                        Items
                                        Coded                PREVIOUSLY OUTSTANDING ITEMS
                                        Outstanding          Number   Date      Amount
       $6,924.20                        $0.00
         ($7.50)                        $0.00
        ---------                       $0.00
       $6,916.70                        $0.00
       $6,916.70                        $0.00
        ---------                       $0.00
           $0.00                        $0.00
        =========                       $0.00
                                        $0.00
                                        $0.00
                                        $0.00
                                        $0 00
```
```
                                        ---
                                       ($35.00)
                                       ($56.00)
                                      $1,500.00
                                       ($35.15)
                                        $0.00
                                        $0.00
                                        $0.00
                                        $0.00
                                        $0.00
```

The top part of the Check Register, shown in Figure 3-3, appears when you first load the spreadsheet. In this area, you enter the basic information about each check you write: check number, date, payee, notation, and amount. You also record the date and amount of each deposit in this area. The formulas in column F compute the running balance in your checking account.

Column G allows you to identify outstanding checks and deposits—those that have not cleared the bank. Use this section once a month when you balance your checkbook. To code a check or deposit as outstanding, enter the number 1 in column G next to that check or deposit. The spreadsheet then sums the amounts of the outstanding checks and deposits and uses the sum to help reconcile the checkbook balance of your account with the bank balance.

The Reconciliation area, shown in Figure 3-4, occupies the range H1:N19. Use this section once a month to reconcile the checkbook balance for your account with the bank balance. First, code the outstanding checks by entering the number 1 in the appropriate cells of column G. Then, enter the date as of which you are balancing the checkbook in cell N4 and the bank balance as of that date in cell L9. When all these numbers are in place, recalculate the worksheet. The formulas in cells L10, L12, and L13 compute the total of the outstanding items, the reconciled bank balance, and the book balance. The formula in cell L15 subtracts the book balance from the reconciled bank balance to arrive at the unreconciled difference between the bank and book balances. After you balance the checkbook, this number will be $0.00.

```
 File   Edit   Print   Select   Format   Options   Chart   Window
"  Beginning Balance
         A         B          C              D           E          F          G      =
1    ===============================================================================
2    CHECKBOOK REGISTER AND BALANCER
3    ===============================================================================
4    CHECK REGISTER
5    ===============================================================================
6
7    Check                                                        Running
8    Number    Date     Payee-Payor    Notation       Amount      Balance    Out?
9       Beginning Balance                                         $6,479.25
10    1000     4/1/87 Cleaners         Shirt Laundry    ($7.50)   $6,471.75
11    1001     4/1/87 Hardware Store   Paint Brushes   ($12.35)   $6,459.40
12       D     4/2/87 Brother-in-Law   Repay $25 loan   $25.00    $6,484.40
13    1002     4/2/87 Bookstore        "Iacocca"        ($8.95)   $6,475.45
14    1003     4/3/87 Local S&L        Mortgage       ($600.00)   $5,875.45
15      CW     4/3/87 Cash             Cash Machine   ($200.00)   $5,675.45
16    1004     4/4/87 GMAC             Car Payment    ($205.00)   $5,470.45
17    1005     4/4/87 First Bank       MasterCard Bill($127.35)   $5,343.10
18    1006     4/4/87 ELSI             Student Loan   ($115.00)   $5,228.10
19    1007     4/4/87 Power Company    Electric Bill  ($135.00)   $5,093.10
 ||←
A9                                                                CR1000.WKS
Press ALT to choose commands.
```

Figure 3-3.

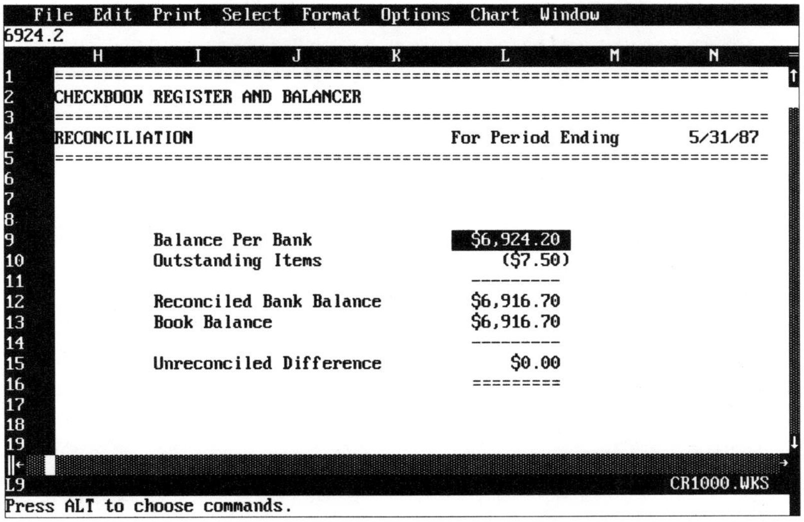

```
 File  Edit  Print  Select  Format  Options  Chart  Window
6924.2
        H       I       J       K       L       M       N
1    ========================================================
2    CHECKBOOK REGISTER AND BALANCER
3    ========================================================
4    RECONCILIATION                    For Period Ending    5/31/87
5    ========================================================
6
7
8
9          Balance Per Bank              $6,924.20
10         Outstanding Items               ($7.50)
11                                       ----------
12         Reconciled Bank Balance       $6,916.70
13         Book Balance                  $6,916.70
14                                       ----------
15         Unreconciled Difference          $0.00
16                                       =========
17
18
19
L9                                                  CR1000.WKS
Press ALT to choose commands.
```

Figure 3-4.

The Outstanding Items area of this template occupies columns O through U. The formulas in column O use the IF function to test the values in column G for items that have been coded as outstanding and to post the amount of each outstanding item to column O. The table in columns Q, R, and S helps you make a transition from your paper checkbook register to your spreadsheet. Use it to record checks and deposits that were outstanding the last time you balanced your checkbook before you created the template.

CREATING THE TEMPLATE

To create the Checkbook Register and Balancer, first use the New command on the File menu to display the New dialog box if it is not on your screen already. Then, choose Spreadsheet and press Enter, or select the New button to create a new blank spreadsheet. Now, select Manual Calculation from the Options menu to put Works in manual recalculation mode. This mode lets you avoid delays as you create the template because Works does not recalculate the entire spreadsheet after every entry.

Next, you need to change the widths of some columns in the spreadsheet. To change the width of a column, move the cursor to a cell in that column, select Width from the Format menu, type the new column width, and press Enter or choose OK. The table in Figure 3-5 on the following page shows the new widths for each column in the template that are different from the default width of 10.

Column	Width
A	6
B	9
C	15
D	15
F	12
G	5
L	12
O	12
Q	6
R	9
S	12

Figure 3-5. Column widths for the Checkbook Register and Balancer.

The Check Register

Now you're ready to start making entries. To begin, enter the header labels for this area in rows 1, 2, 3, 4, and 5. The double lines in rows 1, 3, and 5, which are composed of equal signs (=), span columns A through G. To create these double lines, enter a label made up of a series of equal signs (=) in each cell in row 1, and then copy that series of labels from row 1 to row 3 and row 5. To enter each label in row 1, type a quotation mark (") followed by the proper number of equal signs (corresponding to the column width). For example, to enter the label in cell A1, move the cursor to cell A1, type a quotation mark, and then type a string of six equal signs ("======). If you forget the quotation mark, Works will try to interpret the entry as a formula and will display the message *Error: Missing Operand*.

To copy the labels from row 1, highlight the range A1:G1, select Copy from the Edit menu, highlight cell A3, and press Enter. Then, select Copy from the Edit menu again, highlight cell A5, and press Enter.

The entries in cells A2 and A4 are simple labels. To enter them, move the cursor to cell A2 and type *CHECKBOOK REGISTER AND BALANCER*; then, move to cell A4 and type *CHECK REGISTER*.

Next, enter the labels *Check* and *Running* in cells A7 and F7 and the labels *Number*, *Date*, *Payee-Payor*, *Notation*, *Amount*, *Balance*, and *Out?* in cells A8 through G8. These labels identify the contents of the columns that make up the Checkbook Register area of the template.

To center all these labels, highlight the range A7:F8, select Style from the Format menu, choose Center from the Style dialog box, and press Enter or choose OK.

The Beginning Balance

After you enter the headers, move the cursor to cell A9, type a space, and type the label *Beginning Balance*. Then, move across to cell F9 and enter the value *0*. Before you begin to use the spreadsheet, you will enter the actual beginning balance in cell F9. Finally, assign Dollar format with two decimal places to cell F9. To do so, move the cursor to that cell, select Dollar from the Format menu, and then choose OK or press Enter. (Because the default number of decimal places is 2, you need not change that setting.)

The Check Number column

Next, move to cell A10 and enter the number of the first check you want to include in the register. If you don't know this number, leave this cell blank or enter a dummy number. (For instance, Figure 3-3 on page 72 shows the number 1000.) When you begin to use the spreadsheet, however, be sure to enter the correct number in cell A10.

Now move to cell A11 and enter the formula

=MAX ($A$10 : A10) +1

This formula—which at first may seem unnecessarily complex—uses the MAX function to compute the next check number in the series. The formula sets the value of cell A11 equal to the largest value in the range A10:A10, plus 1. For instance, because cell A10 in Figure 3-1 on page 70 contains the value 1000, cell A11 contains the value 1001.

Next, copy the formula in cell A11 down column A. To do this, highlight the range A11:A400 and select Fill Down from the Copy menu. (To highlight the range quickly, move the cursor to cell A11, press the Extend key ([F8]), press the Go To key ([F5]), type *A400* in the Reference text box, and press Enter or choose OK.) Then, press the Calc key ([F9]) to recalculate the spreadsheet.

Now, let's go back and figure out what these formulas mean. Notice that you used an absolute reference ($A$10) to define one anchor of the range A10:A10 in the formula in cell A11 and a relative reference (A10) to define the other anchor. Because you defined the range reference in this way, the range "grew" as you copied the formula down column A. For example, the formula in cell A12 in your spreadsheet is now *=MAX($A$10:A11)+1*. Similarly, the formula in cell A13 is *=MAX($A$10:A12)+1*, and the formula in cell A400 is *=MAX($A$10:A399)+1*. As you can see, when Works copied this formula, it held the absolute anchor of the range ($A$10) constant but adjusted the relative anchor to reflect the position of each copy of the formula. As a result, each formula returns the value that is one greater than the largest value in the preceding cells in column A.

This little trick—using an absolute reference for one anchor of a range and a relative reference for the other anchor—comes in handy whenever you need to expand a range. If you use your imagination, you're likely to find ways to use this trick in your own spreadsheets.

Now that you understand how these formulas work, you may be wondering why we used them. Why didn't we simply enter the formula =A10+1 in cell A11 and then copy that formula down column A? Here's the answer. As you use the checkbook register, you record both checks and deposits. You indicate deposits by entering a *D* in the appropriate cell in column A. Had we used the formula =A10+1 to create the series of formulas in column A, then these label entries (for deposits) would have caused the formulas beneath them in column A to return *ERR*. The MAX function, however, can handle the deposit entries; it simply assigns the value 0 to the Ds in column A and correctly computes the number of the next check in the series.

While you have the range A11:A400 highlighted, select Style from the Format menu, choose the Right option, and choose OK. This command sets the default format for label entries in column A to right aligned. From this point on, each label entry you make in column A will be right aligned.

Next, assign Dollar format with two decimal places to column E (the Amount column). To do this, highlight the range E11:E400, select Dollar from the Format menu, and press Enter or choose OK to accept the default number of decimal places.

The Running Balance column

To create the formulas in the Running Balance column, move the cursor to cell F10 and enter the formula

```
=F9+E10
```

This formula defines the running balance after the first check or deposit to equal the beginning balance (cell F9) plus the amount of that check or deposit (cell E10).

After you enter the formula in cell F10, assign the cell Dollar format with two decimal places. To do so, move the cursor to cell F10, select Dollar from the Format menu, and choose OK or press Enter.

Now, copy the contents of cell F10 to the range F11:F400. To do this, highlight the range F10:F400 and select Fill Down from the Edit menu. The result of this command is a series of formulas in column F, each of which refers to the preceding formula in column F and the value in column E in the current row. After you make the copy, press the Calc key ([F9]) to recalculate the spreadsheet. Because you have not entered any checks in the register, all the formulas in column F return the same result.

The Reconciliation Area

Now you're ready to define the Reconciliation area. To display the appropriate part of the spreadsheet, press Ctrl-PgDn or, if you have a mouse, click once on the horizontal scroll bar. Doing either of these things brings columns H through N into view. Then, enter the header labels for this area in rows 1, 2, 3, 4, and 5. The double lines in rows 1, 3, and 5, which are composed of equal signs (=), span columns H through N. To enter the labels in cells H2 and H4, move the cursor to cell H2 and type *CHECKBOOK REGISTER AND BALANCER*; then, move to cell H4 and type *RECONCILIATION*.

Now, move to cell L4 and enter the label *For Period Ending*. In cells I9, I10, I12, I13, and I15, enter the labels *Balance Per Bank*, *Outstanding Items*, *Reconciled Bank Balance*, *Book Balance*, and *Unreconciled Difference*. These labels identify the contents of the cells in the Reconciliation area.

Next, highlight the range L10:L15, select Dollar from the Format menu, and press Enter or choose OK to accept the default number of decimal places. This command assigns Dollar format with two decimal places to the range L10:L15.

Next, move to cell L10 and enter the formula

`=SUM(O9:O400)+SUM(S9:S400)`

When you use the spreadsheet, this formula computes the total value of outstanding items by totaling the values in columns O and S. (Because you have not entered any checks in the Check Register, this formula returns 0 for now.) Note that the formulas you will enter in column O use the IF function to test for outstanding items and post the amount of each outstanding item to column O. In column S, you record any checks or deposits that were outstanding the last time you balanced your checkbook (by hand). The sum of all these items is the total amount of checks and deposits outstanding.

Next, enter a label consisting of two spaces followed by nine hyphens (---------) in cell L11. To enter this label, move the cursor to cell L11, press the Spacebar twice, type nine hyphens, and press Enter. Now, use the Copy command to duplicate the label in cell L14. To do this, move the cursor to cell L11, select Copy from the Edit menu, move the cursor to cell L14, and press Enter.

Now, move the cursor to cell L12 and enter the formula

`=L9+L10`

This formula sums the balance per bank (cell L9) and the outstanding items (cell L10) to compute the reconciled bank balance. (Because you have not entered any checks in the Check Register, this formula returns 0 for now.) The reconciled bank balance is the bank balance less any outstanding checks and plus any outstanding deposits. Unless you need to make additional adjustments, or unless your bank statement contains an error, the reconciled bank balance equals your checkbook balance.

Next, move to cell L13 and enter the formula

`=F400`

This formula, which refers to the last entry in the Running Balance column, computes the current Check Register balance. Now, move to cell L15 and enter the formula

`=L12-L13`

This formula computes the unreconciled difference between the bank balance and the checkbook balance by subtracting the checkbook balance (cell L13) from the reconciled bank balance (cell L12). The result of this formula is 0 if the register balance equals the reconciled bank balance. (Because you have not entered any checks in the Check Register, both of these formulas return 0 for now.)

Finally, enter a label consisting of two spaces followed by nine equal signs (=========) in cell L16. To enter this label, move the cursor to cell L16, press the Spacebar twice, type nine equal signs, and press Enter.

The Outstanding Items Area

Now you're ready to create the formulas in the Outstanding Items area. To display the appropriate part of the spreadsheet, press Ctrl-PgDn or, if you have a mouse, click once on the horizontal scroll bar. Doing either of these things brings columns O through U into view.

When these columns are in view, enter the header labels for this section in rows 1, 2, 3, 4, and 5. The double lines in rows 1, 3, and 5 are composed of equal signs (=) that span columns O through U. To enter the labels in cells O2 and O4, move the cursor to cell O2 and type *CHECKBOOK REGISTER AND BALANCER*, and then move to cell O4 and type *OUTSTANDING ITEMS*. Next, enter the labels *Items*, *Coded*, and *Outstanding* in cells O6, O7, and O8. Finally, highlight the range O6:O8 and select Style from the Format menu. When the Style dialog box appears, choose Right and press Enter to realign the entries in these cells flush right.

Now, you're ready to enter the formulas in column O. These formulas use the codes you enter in column G to determine which checks and deposits are outstanding. The spreadsheet uses these formulas to "post," or enter, any outstanding checks and deposits to the Outstanding Items column. To begin, move the cursor to cell O9 and enter the value *0*. Then, move to cell O10 and enter the formula

```
=IF(G10=1,E10,0)
```

This formula says: If the code in cell G10 equals 1, then return the value from cell E10 (the amount of the current check or deposit); otherwise, return 0. The spreadsheet posts the value from column E in row 10 to cell O10 if you entered the code 1 in cell G10, and it posts a 0 to that cell if cell G10 is blank or contains a value other than 1.

After you enter the formula in cell O10, give that cell and cell O9 Dollar format with two decimal places: Highlight the two cells, select Dollar from the Format menu, and press Enter or choose OK.

Next, copy the contents of cell O10 into the range O11:O400. To do so, highlight the range O10:O400 and select Fill Down from the Edit menu. The result is a series of formulas in column O, each of which tests the value in the corresponding cell in column G and posts the appropriate value to column O. To recalculate the spreadsheet, press the Calc key ([F9]). Because you have not entered any checks in the register, all the formulas in column O return 0.

Next, set up the table that stores previously outstanding items. You use it only once—when you first set up the checkbook register—but it is a critical part of the template. In this table, you enter the number, date, and amount of any checks or deposits that were outstanding the last time you balanced your checkbook (before you began to use the spreadsheet).

To begin, enter the label *PREVIOUSLY OUTSTANDING ITEMS* in cell Q7 and the labels *Number, Date,* and *Amount* in cells Q8, R8, and S8. To center the three labels in row 8, highlight the range Q8:S8, select Style from the Format menu, choose Center from the Style dialog box, and press Enter or choose OK.

Next, format the cells below these labels in columns Q, R, and S. First, select the range Q9:Q400, select Style from the Format menu, choose the Right option, and press Enter or choose OK. This command right-aligns the entries in column Q. Next, highlight the range R9:R400, select Time/Date from the Format menu, choose the Month, Day, Year option (with the Short date form), and press Enter or choose OK. This command assigns the date format MM/DD/YY to the cells in column R. Finally, highlight the range S9:S400, select Dollar from the Format menu, and press Enter or choose OK to assign column S Dollar format with two decimal places.

Freezing Rows 1 Through 8

The last step in creating this template is to freeze rows 1 through 8. This ensures that the header information in these rows is visible—even when the cursor is way down in the spreadsheet. To freeze rows 1 through 8, move the cursor to cell A9 and then select Freeze Titles from the Options menu to lock rows 1 through 8.

Saving the Template

That's it—the template is finished. Before you do anything else, save the spreadsheet. To do so, select Save As from the File menu. Then, if you want to save the file in a directory other than the current one, choose that directory from the Other Drives & Directories list box and choose OK. Next, type a filename (such as *CHKBK.WKS*), and press Enter or choose OK to save the file. If you want to save the file in the current directory, simply type a filename and press Enter or choose OK.

USING THE TEMPLATE

Now that you've created the Checkbook Register and Balancer, you're ready to put it to work. First, open the spreadsheet. (If you just created the template, skip this step.) To begin, choose Open from the File menu. Then, if the file you want to open is not in the current directory, select the directory that contains the file from the Other Drives & Directories box and choose OK. Then, type the name of the file in the File Name text box or choose the filename from the list box. Press Enter or choose OK to open the file. If the file you want to open is in the current directory, simply type or highlight the filename and then press Enter or choose OK.

Moving the Cursor

As Figure 3-3 on page 72 shows, the first 11 rows of the Check Register appear on the home screen (the screen that appears when you press Ctrl-Home). To look at a different part of the register, use your mouse or the cursor movement keys to move the cursor to the appropriate cell. For example, to view the next screenful of information, press PgDn. To move directly to the bottom of the table, simply move the cursor to column A or column F (columns that contain an uninterrupted series of entries) and press Ctrl-Down Arrow. To return to the top of the table from any position, move the cursor to column A or column F and press Ctrl-Up Arrow.

To move to a specific row in the spreadsheet, press the Go To key ([F5]), type *A* followed by the number of the row, and press Enter or choose OK. For example, to move to row 50, you would press [F5], type *A50*, and press Enter or choose OK.

If you used the Freeze Titles option on the Options menu to freeze rows 1 through 8, those rows stay in view as you move the cursor through the spreadsheet. Notice that you cannot use the arrow keys to move the cursor into any of the frozen rows. When you press Ctrl-Home, the cursor moves to cell A9 instead of to cell A1.

To display the Reconciliation area, first press Ctrl-Home to move the cursor to cell A9, then press Ctrl-PgDn to bring that part of the spreadsheet into view. If you have a mouse, press Ctrl-Home to move the cursor to cell A9, and then click once on the horizontal scroll bar. Either method displays columns H through N.

To view the Outstanding Items area, first press Ctrl-Home to move the cursor to cell A9, then press Ctrl-PgDn twice to display that part of the spreadsheet. If you have a mouse, press Ctrl-Home to move the cursor to cell A9, and then click twice on the horizontal scroll bar. Either method displays columns O through U.

Setting Up the Spreadsheet

Before you can use the spreadsheet, you have to enter some figures to set it up. First, you need to post the beginning checkbook balance to cell F9. Then, you need to record the number, date, and amount of any outstanding checks and deposits in the Outstanding Items area. Although you'll probably enter only a handful of items in this table, it can contain as many as 400.

Posting the Beginning Balance

The first step in using this spreadsheet is to post the correct beginning balance to cell F9. Enter the balance of your checking account as of the last time you balanced your checkbook. This number is probably different from the balance according to your bank statement, because it reflects payments and deposits that occurred between the time the bank printed your statement and the time you actually balanced the checkbook. Don't enter any of the outstanding checks or deposits in the register— merely enter the correct book balance of your account when you last balanced the checkbook. For example, to post the beginning balance $6,479.25 to the spreadsheet, move the cursor to cell F9 and type *6479.25*.

Entering Previously Outstanding Items

Next, enter the number, date, and amount of any checks or deposits that were outstanding when you last balanced the checkbook in the Previously Outstanding Items table. These items are critical to computing the proper beginning balance for the account. First, move the cursor to cell Q9 and enter the number, date, and amount of the first outstanding item in cells Q9, R9, and S9. Then, enter the number, date, and amount of the second outstanding item in cells Q10, R10, and S10; of the third item in cells Q11, R11, and S11; and so on. Enter the amounts of outstanding checks as negative numbers. To record outstanding deposits, enter a *D* in column Q and enter the amount as a positive number.

For example, suppose that when you last balanced your checkbook, the four checks and one deposit shown in the table in Figure 3-6 were outstanding. To enter these items, move the cursor to cell Q9, type *972* (the number of the first outstanding check), move to cell R9, type *2/28/87* (the date of the first outstanding check), and then move to cell S9 and type *–67.55* (the amount of the first outstanding check). Be sure to type the amount of the check as a negative number.

Now, move the cursor to cell Q10, type the number of the second check, and enter the rest of the information for that check in row 10. (Note that the spreadsheet uses parentheses to identify the number you entered in cell Q9 as a negative number.) To enter the outstanding deposit, move the cursor to cell Q11, type *D*, move to cell R11, type *3/28/87*, and then move to cell S11 and type *115*. Move the cursor to cell Q12, type the number of the third check, and enter the rest of the information for that check in row 12. Do likewise for the fourth check in row 13. Figure 3-7 on the following page shows these items in the spreadsheet.

Number	Date	Amount
972	2/28/87	($67.55)
984	3/18/87	($45.25)
D	3/28/87	$115.00
998	3/30/87	($17.50)
999	3/31/87	($50.00)

Figure 3-6. Sample data: previously outstanding items.

Entering old checks and deposits

When you first start using the spreadsheet, go back and enter all the checks you have written and deposits you have made since you last balanced your checkbook. After you enter these checks and deposits in the register, simply record each payment or deposit as it occurs.

Posting checks and deposits: To post a check to the spreadsheet, move the cursor to column B in the first empty row in the Check Register and enter the information

```
     File  Edit  Print  Select  Format  Options  Chart  Window
 -50
              O        P       Q       R        S         T        U
 1   =====================================================================
 2   CHECKBOOK REGISTER AND BALANCER
 3   =====================================================================
 4   OUTSTANDING ITEMS
 5   =====================================================================
 6         Items
 7         Coded              PREVIOUSLY OUTSTANDING ITEMS
 8   Outstanding        Number  Date       Amount
 9         $0.00          972  2/28/87      ($67.55)
10         $0.00          984  3/18/87      ($45.25)
11         $0.00            D  3/28/87      $115.00
12         $0.00          998  3/30/87      ($17.50)
13         $0.00          999  3/31/87      ($50.00)
14         $0.00
15         $0.00
16         $0.00
17         $0.00
18         $0.00
19         $0.00
 S13                            CALC                        CHKBK.WKS
 Press ALT to choose commands.
```

Figure 3-7.

for that check: the date in column B, the payee in column C, a notation (if any) in column D, and the amount (as a negative number) in column E.

Provided that the check number for the check you are recording is in sequence (that is, its number is one greater than the number of the previous check in the register), you need not enter a check number in column A. For instance, if the last check you wrote was check 1000, and the next check is check 1001, you need not enter the number of the new check. If for some reason the number of the next check is out of sequence, enter the check number in the appropriate cell in column A.

Posting deposits is much like posting checks. To post a deposit, move the cursor to column A in the first empty row and type *D*. Then, move across that row entering the information for the deposit: the date in column B, the payor in column C, a notation (if any) in column D, and the amount (as a positive number) in column E.

An example: Suppose that you're setting up the checkbook register for the first time. Since you last balanced your checkbook, you've written the three checks and made the one deposit shown in the table in Figure 3-8. To begin using the register, enter each item in the register. To do this, move the cursor to cell A10, type *1000* (the number of the first check); move to cell B10, type *4/1/87* (the date of the first check); move to C10, type *Cleaners* (the payee of the first check); move to D10, type *Shirt Laundry* (the notation of the first check); move to E10, and type *−7.5* (the amount of the first check). Be sure to enter the amount of the check as a negative number.

Now, move the cursor to cell B11, type *4/1/87*, and then move across row 11 entering the payee, notation, and amount of the second check. Because the number of the second check (1001) is in sequence, you need not enter the check number in cell A11.

Number	Date	Payee/Payor	Notation	Amount
1000	4/1/87	Cleaners	Shirt Laundry	($7.50)
1001	4/1/87	Hardware Store	Paint Brushes	($12.35)
D	4/2/87	Brother-in-Law	Repay $25 loan	$25.00
1002	4/2/87	Bookstore	"Iacocca"	($8.95)

Figure 3-8. Sample data: old checks and deposits.

To enter the deposit, move the cursor to cell A12 and type *D*. Move to cell B12, type *4/2/87*; move to cell C12, type *Brother-in-Law*; move to cell D12, type *Repay $25 Loan*; move to cell E12, and type *25*.

Finally, move the cursor to cell B13, type *4/2/87*, and then move across row 13, entering the payee, notation, and amount of the third check. To enter the notation *"Iacocca"*, move the cursor to cell D13 and type *""Iacocca"*. Because the number of the second check (1002) is in sequence, you need not enter the check number in cell A13. This is true even though the previous item in the register is a deposit. When you recalculate the spreadsheet, the formulas in column A compute the correct number.

Because you chose manual recalculation, the spreadsheet does not update the running balance and the check numbers immediately as you post new checks and deposits. To recalculate the spreadsheet, press the Calc key ([F9]). Figure 3-9 shows the updated Check Register.

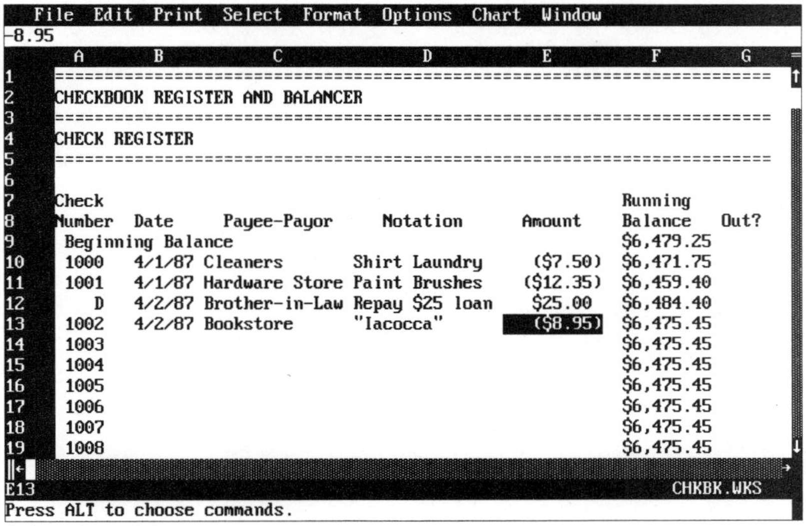

Figure 3-9.

Saving the register

After you set up the Check Register and record previously outstanding items, save that spreadsheet to a new file. To do so, select Save As from the File menu. Then, if you want to save the file in a directory other than the current one, choose that directory from the Other Drives & Directories list box and choose OK. Next, type a new name for the spreadsheet, and press Enter or choose OK to save the file. If you want to save the file in the current directory, simply type a filename and press Enter or choose OK. Choose a name for the file that clearly identifies its contents. For example, if the first check in the new register was check number 1000, type a name such as *CR1000* (for Check Register 1000).

Save your filled-in spreadsheets under a name other than the name you used for the original, empty Checkbook Register and Balancer. If you save a filled-in spreadsheet under the same name as the template, the filled-in version replaces the template.

Entering New Checks and Deposits

After you enter all the transactions you've made since you last balanced the checkbook, and record any previously outstanding items, the spreadsheet is "up to date." From this point on, you simply post each check or deposit as you write it.

Suppose the next check you write is number 1003, written for $600.00 to the Local S&L on April 3, 1987, for your monthly mortgage payment. Enter the date, *4/3/87*, in cell B14, the payee, *Local S&L*, in cell C14, the notation, *Mortgage*, in cell D14, and the amount, *−600*, in cell E14. Because the check number is in sequence, you can skip column A. Now, recalculate the spreadsheet to update the running balance and the check number. Figure 3-10 shows the spreadsheet with this check in place.

```
  File  Edit  Print  Select  Format  Options  Chart  Window
-600
        A        B          C            D            E           F         G
1   ======================================================================
2   CHECKBOOK REGISTER AND BALANCER
3   ======================================================================
4   CHECK REGISTER
5   ======================================================================
6
7   Check                                                      Running
8   Number  Date    Payee-Payor      Notation      Amount     Balance   Out?
9       Beginning Balance                                     $6,479.25
10   1000   4/1/87  Cleaners        Shirt Laundry  ($7.50)    $6,471.75
11   1001   4/1/87  Hardware Store  Paint Brushes  ($12.35)   $6,459.40
12    D     4/2/87  Brother-in-Law  Repay $25 loan  $25.00    $6,484.40
13   1002   4/2/87  Bookstore       "Iacocca"      ($8.95)    $6,475.45
14   1003   4/3/87  Local S&L       Mortgage       ($600.00)  $6,475.45
15   1004                                                     $6,475.45
16   1005                                                     $6,475.45
17   1006                                                     $6,475.45
18   1007                                                     $6,475.45
19   1008                                                     $6,475.45
E14                               CALC                        CR1000.WKS
Press ALT to choose commands.
```

Figure 3-10.

Entering Special Items

Although most items you enter in the Check Register are deposits or checks, from time to time you will probably need to post special items, such as cash machine withdrawals or direct withdrawals. For the most part, you post these special items the same way you post other items. However, instead of entering a check number or a D (for deposit) in the Check Number column for these special items, enter a code for each item to identify it. For example, use the code CW to designate cash machine withdrawals, the code DW to designate direct withdrawals (such as loan payments that are automatically deducted from your account), and the code A to designate account adjustments (such as bank fees or service charges).

For example, suppose that on April 3, 1987, you withdraw $200 at a cash machine. To record this check, move the cursor to cell A15, type *CW* (for Cash Withdrawal); move to cell B15, type *4/3/87*; move to cell C15, type *Cash*; move to cell D15, type *Cash Machine*; move to cell E15, and type *–200*. Then, recalculate the spreadsheet to update the running balance as shown in Figure 3-11.

```
 File  Edit  Print  Select  Format  Options  Chart  Window
-200
        A       B        C           D           E         F        G
1    ===========================================================================
2    CHECKBOOK REGISTER AND BALANCER
3    ===========================================================================
4    CHECK REGISTER
5    ===========================================================================
6
7    Check                                              Running
8    Number  Date      Payee-Payor   Notation   Amount  Balance   Out?
9    Beginning Balance                                   $6,479.25
10   1000    4/1/87  Cleaners       Shirt Laundry  ($7.50)  $6,471.75
11   1001    4/1/87  Hardware Store Paint Brushes  ($12.35)  $6,459.40
12   D       4/2/87  Brother-in-Law Repay $25 loan  $25.00  $6,484.40
13   1002    4/2/87  Bookstore      "Iacocca"       ($8.95)  $6,475.45
14   1003    4/3/87  Local S&L      Mortgage     ($600.00)  $5,875.45
15   CW      4/3/87  Cash           Cash Machine ($200.00)  $5,675.45
16   1004                                                    $5,675.45
17   1005                                                    $5,675.45
18   1006                                                    $5,675.45
19   1007                                                    $5,675.45
E15                                                    CR1000.WKS
Press ALT to choose commands.
```

Figure 3-11.

Printing the Register

To print the Check Register, begin by using the Set Print Area command on the Print menu to define the cells to print. To print the entire Check Register, highlight the range A9:G400. After you select the appropriate range, select Set Print Area from the Print menu.

Instead of printing the entire Check Register, you might want to print only the section that contains your checks and deposits for the past month. In that event, highlight only the cells in columns A through G in the rows that contain the checks you want to print and then select Set Print Area from the Print menu.

Next, choose Layout from the Print menu and change print settings as necessary. If you have a wide-carriage printer and plan to print this spreadsheet onto 11-by-14-inch paper, you might want to change the Page Width setting from 8.5" to 14". You might also want to change the Top, Bottom, Left, and Right margins, and define a header and a footer. Next, use the Font command on the Print menu to select the font you want Works to use to print the report.

After you adjust all the settings, select Print from the Print menu to display the Print dialog box. Adjust any settings in that dialog box and then choose Print to print the spreadsheet. Works then prints the selected range, plus the appropriate columns from the Titles area at the top of the spreadsheet.

Balancing the Checkbook

So far, we've considered only the way you record your checks. Now let's consider how you can use the spreadsheet to balance your checkbook each month. The process has four steps. First, enter the account balance from the statement in cell L9 and the "as of" date for the reconciliation in cell N4. Second, determine which checks and deposits recorded in the Check Register have cleared the bank and which are still outstanding. Third, "decode" any items that were previously coded as outstanding (that have subsequently cleared), and then code any new items that are outstanding. Fourth, post any credits or debits that appear on the bank statement but are not recorded in your register. These items include bank fees and service charges, unrecorded cash machine withdrawals, and unrecorded direct withdrawals.

After you complete these four steps, recalculate the spreadsheet to update the formulas in the Reconciliation area. If everything is working properly, cell L15 contains the value $0.00, indicating that no unreconciled difference exists between the bank statement and your register: The checkbook is balanced. If cell L15 contains a value other than $0.00, you need to figure out what is wrong.

An example: Balancing for the first time

Let's walk through an example so that you can see how the whole process works. Assume that you entered the checks and deposits shown in Figure 3-12 on page 88 and then recalculated, and that the bank statement indicated an account balance of $6,482.46. Assume further that checks 998, 1000, 1010, 1015, 1025, 1026, 1027, 1028, 1029, 1030, 1031, and 1032 and the deposit for $1,500 made on May 2, 1987, are outstanding. Finally, assume that the statement reflects two unrecorded items: a service charge of $8 and a direct withdrawal of $55 drawn by USA Fitness Center, your health club, on April 4, 1987, for monthly dues.

Posting the date and bank balance: To begin, post the account balance from the bank statement to cell L9 in the Reconciliation area. To do so, move the cursor to cell L9 and enter the number *6482.46.* Next, enter the "as of" date for the reconciliation, the date on which you actually perform it. In this case, assume that you perform the reconciliation on May 3, 1987. To enter this date in cell N4, press the Go To key ([F5]), type *N4* in the Reference text box, and press Enter. Then, type *5/3/87.*

Erasing previously outstanding items: After you post the account balance to cell L9, move the cursor to the Outstanding Items area of the spreadsheet. Remove any items that have now cleared the bank from the table of previously outstanding items. To remove an item, simply highlight the number, date, and amount of the item and choose Clear from the Edit menu. The spreadsheet removes any items you erase from its calculation of total outstanding items.

In the example, all the previously outstanding items but check 998 have cleared the bank. In other words, only check 998 is still outstanding, so you can remove all the other items from the table. To do so, first highlight the range Q9:S11 and then select Clear from the Edit menu. This step erases checks 972 and 984 and the one deposit. Next, highlight the range Q13:S13 and select the Clear command again to erase check 999. Figure 3-13 on page 89 shows the result.

Decoding old outstanding items: Now, "decode" any checks or deposits that you coded as outstanding the last time you balanced the checkbook. To decode an item, simply remove the code—the number 1—that appears next to that item in column G. To do this, either highlight the cell that contains the code and select Clear from the Edit menu, or replace the code with any number other than the number 1. In general, the first method is preferred.

Because in this example we are balancing the checkbook for the first time, we have no items to decode, and we can skip this step. You have to perform this step, however, each time you balance the checkbook after the first time. You'll learn how to do so later in this chapter.

Coding new outstanding items: After you decode the items that are no longer outstanding, you need to code any newly outstanding items. To code a check or deposit as outstanding, simply enter the number *1* next to that item in column G. The formulas in column O use these codes to determine which items are outstanding, and the formula in cell L9 computes the total of the outstanding items by summing the values posted in column O.

To begin coding the outstanding items in the example, move the cursor to the top of column G. Next, move the cursor down that column, one row at a time, entering *1* in each row that contains an outstanding item. For instance, to code the first outstanding item in the example, check 1000, move the cursor to cell G10 and enter the number *1.* To code the next outstanding item, check 1010, move the cursor to cell G23 and enter the number *1.* Continue in this way—moving the cursor down column G and entering *1* next to each outstanding check or deposit—until they are all coded. Figure 3-14 shows some of these codes in column G.

	A	B	C	D	E	F	G
1	==						
2	CHECKBOOK REGISTER AND BALANCER						
3	==						
4	CHECK REGISTER						
5	==						
6							
7	Check					Running	
8	Number	Date	Payee-Payor	Notation	Amount	Balance	Out?
9	Beginning Balance					$6,479.25	
10	1000	4/1/87	Cleaners	Shirt Laundry	($7.50)	$6,471.75	
11	1001	4/1/87	Hardware Store	Paint Brushes	($12.35)	$6,459.40	
12	D	4/2/87	Brother-in-Law	Repay $25 loan	$25.00	$6,484.40	
13	1002	4/2/87	Bookstore	"Iacocca"	($8.95)	$6,475.45	
14	1003	4/3/87	Local S&L	Mortgage	($600.00)	$5,875.45	
15	CW	4/3/87	Cash	Cash Machine	($200.00)	$5,675.45	
16	1004	4/4/87	GMAC	Car Payment	($205.00)	$5,470.45	
17	1005	4/4/87	First Bank	MasterCard Bill	($127.35)	$5,343.10	
18	1006	4/4/87	ELSI	Student Loan	($115.00)	$5,228.10	
19	1007	4/4/87	Power Company	Electric Bill	($135.00)	$5,093.10	
20	1008	4/4/87	Water Company	Water Bill	($35.00)	$5,058.10	
21	1009	4/4/87	SCB	Telephone Bill	($56.00)	$5,002.10	
22	D	4/4/87	ABC Corp.	Pay 3/15-3/31	$1,500.00	$6,502.10	
23	1010	4/5/87	Carpet World	Carpet Cleaning	($36.00)	$6,466.10	
24	1011	4/7/87	Storer	Cable TV	($35.15)	$6,430.95	
25	1012	4/8/87	LS Ayres	Cosmetics	($25.73)	$6,405.22	
26	1013	4/11/87	Heleringers	Sofa	($551.45)	$5,853.77	
27	1014	4/13/87	Kroger	Groceries	($75.56)	$5,778.21	
28	1015	4/14/87	IRS	Taxes	($879.00)	$4,899.21	
29	1016	4/19/87	Dr. Chen	Office Visit	($30.00)	$4,869.21	
30	1017	4/19/87	Johnson Drugs	Prescription	($12.50)	$4,856.71	
31	D	4/21/87	ABC Corp.	Pay 4/1-4/15	$1,500.00	$6,356.71	
32	1018	4/23/87	Maxie's	Clothing	($245.00)	$6,111.71	
33	1019	4/25/87	Jane Smith	Babysitter	($8.00)	$6,103.71	
34	1020	4/26/87	Kroger	Groceries	($62.50)	$6,041.21	
35	1021	4/27/87	Jim Jones	Newspaper	($9.00)	$6,032.21	
36	1022	4/27/87	Dime Store	House Supplies	($36.75)	$5,995.46	
37	1023	4/29/87	Lazarus	Clothing	($75.00)	$5,920.46	
38	1024	4/30/87	Joe Davis	Painting	($315.00)	$5,605.46	
39	1025	5/1/87	Local S&L	Mortgage	($600.00)	$5,005.46	
40	1026	5/1/87	USA Fitness	Health Club	($55.00)	$4,950.46	
41	1027	5/1/87	GMAC	Car Payment	($205.00)	$4,745.46	
42	1028	5/1/87	First Bank	MasterCard Bill	($27.50)	$4,717.96	
43	1029	5/1/87	ELSI	Student Loan	($115.00)	$4,602.96	
44	1030	5/1/87	Power Company	Electric Bill	($95.00)	$4,507.96	
45	1031	5/1/87	Water Company	Water Bill	($35.00)	$4,472.96	
46	1032	5/1/87	SCB	Telephone Bill	($26.00)	$4,446.96	
47	D	5/2/87	ABC Corp.	Pay 4/15-4/30	$1,500.00	$5,946.96	
48	1033					$5,946.96	
49	1034					$5,946.96	
50	1035					$5,946.96	

Figure 3-12.

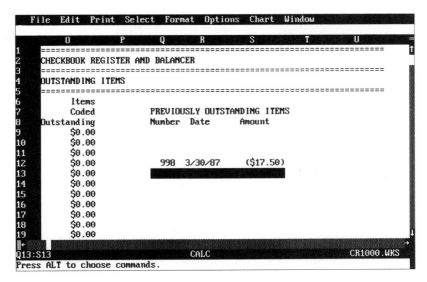

Figure 3-13.

```
 File  Edit  Print  Select  Format  Options  Chart  Window
1
       A       B         C            D          E          F       G
1    ===============================================================
2    CHECKBOOK REGISTER AND BALANCER
3    ===============================================================
4    CHECK REGISTER
5    ===============================================================
6
7    Check                                            Running
8    Number  Date     Payee-Payor    Notation    Amount    Balance  Out?
37    1023   4/29/87 Lazarus        Clothing     ($75.00)  $5,920.46
38    1024   4/30/87 Joe Davis      Painting    ($315.00)  $5,605.46
39    1025   5/1/87  Local S&L      Mortgage    ($600.00)  $5,005.46     1
40    1026   5/1/87  USA Fitness    Health Club  ($55.00)  $4,950.46     1
41    1027   5/1/87  GMAC           Car Payment ($205.00)  $4,745.46     1
42    1028   5/1/87  First Bank     MasterCard Bill ($27.50) $4,717.96   1
43    1029   5/1/87  ELSI           Student Loan ($115.00) $4,602.96     1
44    1030   5/1/87  Power Company  Electric Bill ($95.00) $4,507.96     1
45    1031   5/1/87  Water Company  Water Bill   ($35.00)  $4,472.96     1
46    1032   5/1/87  SCB            Telephone Bill ($26.00) $4,446.96    1
47     D     5/2/87  ABC Corp.      Pay 4/15-4/30 $1,500.00 $5,946.96    1
G47                             CALC                    CR1000.WKS
Press ALT to choose commands.
```

Figure 3-14.

Posting adjustments: The last step in balancing the checkbook is to enter any unrecorded credits or debits. These may include such items as bank fees and service charges, unrecorded cash machine withdrawals, and unrecorded direct withdrawals. Post these items to the register exactly as you post any other special item: Move the cursor to the first blank row in the register, enter a code that identifies the item in column A, and then enter the date, payee/payor, notation, and amount in columns B through E.

In the example, we have two unrecorded debits: a service charge of $8.00 and a direct withdrawal of $55.00. To post these items to the register, move the cursor to cell A48 (the first blank row in the register) and type *A* (for Adjustment). Then, move to cell B48, type *5/2/87*; move to cell C48, type *First Bank*; move to cell D48, type *Service Charge*; move to cell E48, and type *–8*. Next, move the cursor to cell A49 and type the identifier *DW* (for Direct Withdrawal). Then, move to cell B49, type *5/2/87*; move to cell C49, type *USA Fitness*; move to cell D49, type *Health Club*; move to cell E49, and type *–55*. Figure 3-15 shows these two adjustments in the register.

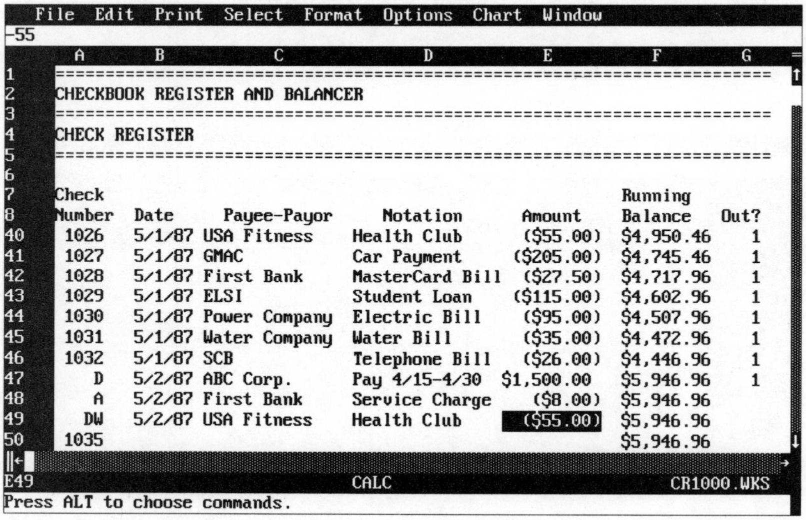

Figure 3-15.

Does it balance? After you post the account balance to cell L9, decode any old outstanding items, code any new outstanding items, and post any unrecorded credits or debits to the register, you're ready to recalculate the spreadsheet. To do this, press the Calc key ([F9]) or select Calculate Now from the Options menu. Recalculating the spreadsheet updates the formulas in the Reconciliation area, as shown in Figure 3-16.

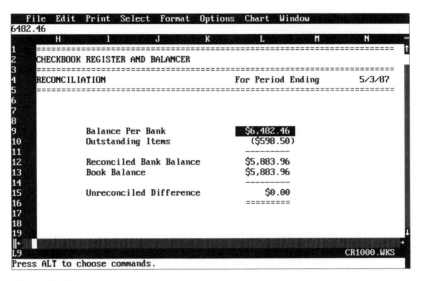

Figure 3-16.

If everything is working properly, the formula in cell L15 returns the value 0. (Notice that cell L15 in Figure 3-16 contains the value $0.00.) A value of $0.00 in cell L15 indicates that no unreconciled difference exists between the bank statement and your register: You balanced your checkbook successfully.

If the formula in cell L15 returns a value other than 0, you need to figure out what is wrong. Typically, any difference between the bank balance and the balance in your Check Register is due to your failure to record reconciling items properly: You forgot to decode previously outstanding checks, to code new outstanding checks, or to post additional credits or debits. If the value in cell L15 is not $0.00, check carefully for any unrecorded reconciling items and post any such items you find to the spreadsheet. Once these items have been recorded, recalculate the spreadsheet and check again to see if the checkbook is balanced.

If the value in cell L15 is still not $0.00, review your records for any checks or deposits you failed to enter in the register. If you find any items that you forgot to record, enter those items as adjustments in the next available row of the register. Then, recalculate the spreadsheet and check the value in cell L15.

If the checkbook is still out of balance, check once more for errors you might have made and then look for an error in the bank statement itself. Bank errors, though rare, do happen. If you find an error, compare the amount of the error to the value in cell L15. If the two amounts agree—and it's likely that they will—then you've found the error. You should, of course, notify your bank immediately so that it can adjust your account.

Saving and printing the reconciliation

After you balance the checkbook, save the spreadsheet by selecting Save from the File menu. This command stores the current version of the spreadsheet under the name you selected when you last saved it and replaces the previous version with the new version.

Next, you might want to print a copy of the Reconciliation area and a copy of the Check Register. To do this, you'll first need to use the Set Print Area command on the Print menu to define the cells to print before you begin. For example, if you want to print only the Reconciliation area, highlight the range H9:N16. To print the Check Register, highlight the range A9:G400 (or as many rows as contain entries). After you select the appropriate range, select Set Print Area from the Print menu.

Next, choose Layout from the Print menu and change print settings as necessary. Then, select Print from the Print menu to display the Print dialog box. Adjust any settings in that dialog box and then choose the Print button to print the spreadsheet. Works then prints the selected range, plus the appropriate columns from the Titles area at the top of the spreadsheet.

Instead of printing the entire Check Register, you might want to print only the section that contains your checks and deposits for the past month. In that event, highlight only the cells in columns A through G in the rows that contain the checks you want to print, and then select Set Print Area from the Print menu.

Of course, you can also print the entire spreadsheet if you wish. To print the whole spreadsheet, you can skip the Set Print Area command altogether if you have not already defined a smaller print area. If you have already defined a print area, highlight the entire spreadsheet and then select the Set Print Area command to redefine the print area to include the entire worksheet.

Balancing for the second time

For the most part, you follow the same steps each time you reconcile your checking account. As we mentioned, though, the first time you balance your checkbook with this spreadsheet is slightly different from every subsequent time. As you noticed in the first example, the Check Register contains no outstanding items the first time you balance the checkbook. Each time you balance the checkbook subsequently, examine the register for outstanding items from prior months and decode any checks that have cleared the bank or deposits that have been credited.

To see how this process works, let's extend the preceding example by supposing that another month has passed. In the meantime, you entered the checks and deposits shown in Figure 3-17 on page 94. Your new bank statement indicates an account balance of $6,924.20. Assume that checks 1015, 1029, 1035, 1042, 1043, 1044, 1045, 1046, and 1047 and the deposit for $1,500 made on June 3, 1987, are outstanding, and that the statement reflects two unrecorded items: a service charge of $7.00 and a direct withdrawal of $55.00 drawn by USA Fitness Center.

To begin, move the cursor to cell N4 by pressing [F5], typing *N4*, and pressing Enter. Enter the date *5/31/87*. Then, post the account balance from the bank statement to cell L9 in the Reconciliation area. To do this, move the cursor to cell L9 and enter the number *6924.20*.

Now, move the cursor to the Outstanding Items area of the spreadsheet and remove any newly cleared entries from the table of previously outstanding items. In the example, the only remaining item, check 998, has now cleared the bank. To remove this item, highlight the range Q12:S12 and select Clear from the Edit menu.

Next, decode any checks or deposits that you coded as outstanding when you last balanced the checkbook. To decode an item, simply remove the code—the number 1—that appears next to that item in column G. Highlight the cell that contains the code and select Clear from the Edit menu.

In the first example, checks 1000, 1010, 1015, 1025, 1026, 1027, 1028, 1029, 1030, 1031, and 1032 and the deposit for $1,500 made on May 2, 1987, were outstanding. Except for checks 1015 and 1029, all these items have now cleared. To decode all the checks and the one deposit that cleared, first highlight the range G10:G27 and select Clear from the Edit menu. Then, highlight the range G29:G42 and select Clear again. Finally, highlight the range G44:G49 and select Clear one last time. That's all there is to it— you decoded the newly cleared items.

Now, you need to code any newly outstanding items. To do so for the items in the example, move the cursor to cell G52 and type *1*. (Row 52 contains check 1035, which is outstanding.) Next, move the cursor down that column, one row at a time, entering *1* in each row that contains an outstanding item. For instance, to code the next outstanding item in the example, check 1042, move the cursor to cell G62 and enter the number *1*. To code the next outstanding item, check 1043, move the cursor to cell G63 and enter the number *1*. Continue in this way—moving the cursor down column G and entering *1* next to each outstanding check or deposit—until all the outstanding checks and deposits are coded.

The last step in balancing the checkbook is to enter any unrecorded credits or debits. In the example, there are two unrecorded items: a service charge of $7.00 and a direct withdrawal of $55.00. To post these items to the register, move the cursor to cell A69 (because row 69 is the first blank row in the register) and type *A* (for Adjustment). Then, move to cell B69, type *6/2/87*; move to cell C69, type *First Bank*; move to cell D69, type *Service Charge*; move to cell E69, and type *–7*. Next, move the cursor down to cell A70 and type the identifier *DW* (for Direct Withdrawal). Now, move to cell B70, type *6/4/87*; move to cell C70, type *USA Fitness*; move to cell D70, type *Health Club*; move to cell E70, and type *–55*.

After you perform the steps for balancing your account, recalculate the spreadsheet by pressing the Calc key ([F9]) or selecting Calculate Now from the Options menu. Works updates the formulas in the Reconciliation area, as shown in Figure 3-18 on page 95. Because the value in cell L15 is $0.00, you know that the checkbook is balanced.

	A	B	C	D	E	F	G
1	===
2	CHECKBOOK REGISTER AND BALANCER
3	===
4	CHECK REGISTER
5	===
6							
7	Check					Running	
8	Number	Date	Payee-Payor	Notation	Amount	Balance	Out?
9	Beginning Balance					$6,479.25	
10	1000	4/1/87	Cleaners	Shirt Laundry	($7.50)	$6,471.75	1
11	1001	4/1/87	Hardware Store	Paint Brushes	($12.35)	$6,459.40	
12	D	4/2/87	Brother-in-Law	Repay $25 loan	$25.00	$6,484.40	
13	1002	4/2/87	Bookstore	"Iacocca"	($8.95)	$6,475.45	
14	1003	4/3/87	Local S&L	Mortgage	($600.00)	$5,875.45	
15	CW	4/3/87	Cash	Cash Machine	($200.00)	$5,675.45	
16	1004	4/4/87	GMAC	Car Payment	($205.00)	$5,470.45	
17	1005	4/4/87	First Bank	MasterCard Bill	($127.35)	$5,343.10	
18	1006	4/4/87	ELSI	Student Loan	($115.00)	$5,228.10	
19	1007	4/4/87	Power Company	Electric Bill	($135.00)	$5,093.10	
20	1008	4/4/87	Water Company	Water Bill	($35.00)	$5,058.10	
21	1009	4/4/87	SCB	Telephone Bill	($56.00)	$5,002.10	
22	D	4/4/87	ABC Corp.	Pay 3/15-3/31	$1,500.00	$6,502.10	
23	1010	4/5/87	Carpet World	Carpet Cleaning	($36.00)	$6,466.10	1
24	1011	4/7/87	Storer	Cable TV	($35.15)	$6,430.95	
25	1012	4/8/87	LS Ayres	Cosmetics	($25.73)	$6,405.22	
26	1013	4/11/87	Heleringers	Sofa	($551.45)	$5,853.77	
27	1014	4/13/87	Kroger	Groceries	($75.56)	$5,778.21	
28	1015	4/14/87	IRS	Taxes	($879.00)	$4,899.21	1
29	1016	4/19/87	Dr. Chen	Office Visit	($30.00)	$4,869.21	
30	1017	4/19/87	Johnson Drugs	Prescription	($12.50)	$4,856.71	
31	D	4/21/87	ABC Corp.	Pay 4/1-4/15	$1,500.00	$6,356.71	
32	1018	4/23/87	Maxie's	Clothing	($245.00)	$6,111.71	
33	1019	4/25/87	Jane Smith	Babysitter	($8.00)	$6,103.71	
34	1020	4/26/87	Kroger	Groceries	($62.50)	$6,041.21	
35	1021	4/27/87	Jim Jones	Newspaper	($9.00)	$6,032.21	
36	1022	4/27/87	Dime Store	House Supplies	($36.75)	$5,995.46	
37	1023	4/29/87	Lazarus	Clothing	($75.00)	$5,920.46	
38	1024	4/30/87	Joe Davis	Painting	($315.00)	$5,605.46	
39				Mortgage	($600.00)	$5,005.46	1
	1042	5/30/87	Local S&L	Club	($55.00)	$4,950.46	1
60	1043	5/30/87	Cash	Car Paym...			
61	1044	5/30/87	GMAC	Car Payment	($205.00)	$5,883.96	
62	1045	5/30/87	First Bank	MasterCard Bill	($127.35)	$5,883.96	
63	1046	5/30/87	ELSI	Student Loan	($115.00)	$5,883.96	
64	1047	5/30/87	Power Company	Electric Bill	($135.00)	$5,883.96	
65	1048	5/30/87	Water Company	Water Bill	($35.00)	$5,883.96	
66	1049	5/30/87	SCB	Telephone Bill	($56.00)	$5,883.96	
67	D	5/31/87	ABC Corp.	Pay 5/15-5/31	$1,500.00	$5,883.96	
68	1051	6/1/87	Storer	Cable TV	($35.15)	$5,883.96	
69	1052					$5,883.96	
70	1053					$5,883.96	
71	1054					$5,883.96	
72	1055					$5,883.96	

Figure 3-17.

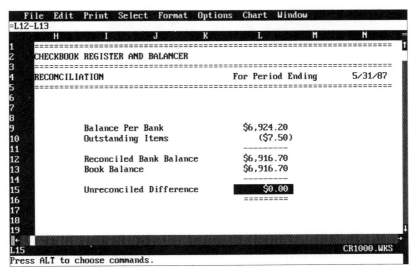

```
 File  Edit  Print  Select  Format  Options  Chart  Window
=L12-L13
         H        I        J        K        L        M        N
1  ===================================================================
2  CHECKBOOK REGISTER AND BALANCER
3  ===================================================================
4  RECONCILIATION                          For Period Ending      5/31/87
5  ===================================================================
6
7
8
9           Balance Per Bank                 $6,924.20
10          Outstanding Items                  ($7.50)
11                                           ----------
12          Reconciled Bank Balance          $6,916.70
13          Book Balance                     $6,916.70
14                                           ----------
15          Unreconciled Difference            $0.00
16                                           =========
17
18
19
L15                                                        CR1000.WKS
Press ALT to choose commands.
```

Figure 3-18.

After you balance the checkbook, choose Save to save the spreadsheet. Next, print a copy of the Reconciliation area and a copy of the Check Register.

Adding Checks

The basic Checkbook Register and Balancer holds nearly 400 transactions. To store more than the maximum number of transactions, you need to add rows to the spreadsheet.

Because several formulas in the template reference cells in row 400, be sure to add any new rows above row 400. If you try to add rows below row 400, the spreadsheet will not work properly. This is an important rule—don't forget it.

To add rows, first determine how many additional rows you want. Then, highlight row 400 and a block of additional rows below row 400. The total number of rows you highlight should match the number of rows you want to add. Next, select Insert from the Edit menu to insert the number of rows you selected above row 400. The spreadsheet moves the entries in row 400 down to a lower row; the formulas that originally referenced row 400 now refer to the new location of those entries.

Now, copy the formulas in cells A399, F399, and G399 to the newly inserted rows. To do so, highlight a range that includes these three cells and all the new rows you added to the spreadsheet. For instance, if you added five rows to the register in the first step, highlight the range A399:G404. If you added only one row, highlight the range A399:A400. After you highlight the appropriate range, simply select Fill Down from the Edit menu. This command copies the formulas from cells A399, F399, and O399 (along with the formats you assigned to those cells and to columns B and E) into the new rows. That's it—you're ready to post more transactions to the register.

Sharing Data with the Simple General Ledger

The data stored in the Checkbook Register and Balancer is valuable: It tells you how you are spending your money. To take full advantage of this information, however, you need to create the Simple General Ledger presented in the next chapter. Then, you can copy information from the Checkbook Register to the Ledger, and the Ledger can post each check or deposit to an account. You'll learn how to do that in the next chapter.

CONCLUSION

As much as we despise the task, we have to balance our checkbooks from time to time. Balancing the checkbook is a tedious and difficult task for most of us. Thanks to Microsoft Works, however, it doesn't have to be that way. As you have seen in this chapter, Works's Spreadsheet environment provides the perfect tool for managing your checkbook. The Checkbook Register and Balancer you built in this chapter is more than adequate for most individuals as well as for many small businesses.

Even if you don't use this spreadsheet, you can employ some of the tricks and techniques you learned in building it. Use these techniques, including the series-building technique and the posting technique, to create better spreadsheets.

A Simple General Ledger

The preceding chapter introduced a Works spreadsheet, the Check Register and Balancer, that lets you manage and balance your checking account. As useful as that spreadsheet is, it is not complete—it lacks a way to classify your checks and deposits into different income and expense accounts. In this chapter, we'll create another spreadsheet, the Simple General Ledger, that overcomes that limitation.

The Simple General Ledger is a simple accounting system for keeping track of your income and expenses. It lets you set up a system of accounts to classify your income and expenses. After you set up this system, you can enter your checks and deposits and code each one to a particular account. The spreadsheet then uses these codes—and the account numbers you previously defined—to post, or enter, each check and deposit to the appropriate account.

The Simple General Ledger takes advantage of a few neat Works techniques. It demonstrates a clever way to use the IF function to post values into columns. It also illustrates the use of mixed references to create a formula that can be copied into all the cells in a rectangular range. In addition, you'll see how to copy information from one spreadsheet to another.

ABOUT THE TEMPLATE

Figure 4-1 beginning on page 98 shows the Simple General Ledger as it will look after you create it, and Figure 4-2 beginning on page 98 shows the spreadsheet with sample data. As the figures show, the Simple General Ledger has two areas, labeled CHECK REGISTER and ACCOUNT POSTING. The Check Register occupies columns A through F. The top of the Check Register, shown in Figure 4-3 on page 100, appears when you first load the template. In these columns, you enter the basic information about each check you write: the check number, date, payee, notation, and

	A	B	C	D	E	F	G	H	I	J	K	L
1	==
2	SIMPLE GENERAL LEDGER						SIMPLE GENERAL LEDGER
3	==
4	CHECK REGISTER						ACCOUNT POSTING		For Period Ending
5	==
6							INCOME		EXPENSES		Furniture/
7	Check						Taxable	Tax Free	Housing	Utilities	Imprvmnts	Food
8	Number	Date	Payee/Payor	Notation	Amount	Accnt	1	2	10	11	12	13
9							$0.00	$0.00	$0.00	$0.00	$0.00	$0.00
10							$0.00	$0.00	$0.00	$0.00	$0.00	$0.00
11							$0.00	$0.00	$0.00	$0.00	$0.00	$0.00
12							$0.00	$0.00	$0.00	$0.00	$0.00	$0.00
13							$0.00	$0.00	$0.00	$0.00	$0.00	$0.00
14							$0.00	$0.00	$0.00	$0.00	$0.00	$0.00
15							$0.00	$0.00	$0.00	$0.00	$0.00	$0.00
16							$0.00	$0.00	$0.00	$0.00	$0.00	$0.00
17							$0.00	$0.00	$0.00	$0.00	$0.00	$0.00
18							$0.00	$0.00	$0.00	$0.00	$0.00	$0.00
19							$0.00	$0.00				
							$0.00	$0.00				
									$0.00	$0.00	$0.00	$0.00
104							$0.00	$0.00	$0.00	$0.00	$0.00	$0.00
105							$0.00	$0.00	$0.00	$0.00	$0.00	$0.00
106							$0.00	$0.00	$0.00	$0.00	$0.00	$0.00
107							$0.00	$0.00	$0.00	$0.00	$0.00	$0.00
108							$0.00	$0.00	$0.00	$0.00	$0.00	$0.00
109							--------	--------	--------	--------	--------	--------
110						$0.00	$0.00	$0.00	$0.00	$0.00	$0.00	$0.00
111						========	========	========	========	========	========	========

Figure 4-1.

	A	B	C	D	E	F	G	H	I	J	K	L
1	==
2	SIMPLE GENERAL LEDGER						SIMPLE GENERAL LEDGER
3	==
4	CHECK REGISTER						ACCOUNT POSTING		For Period Ending			4/30/87
5	==
6							INCOME		EXPENSES		Furniture/
7	Check						Taxable	Tax Free	Housing	Utilities	Imprvmnts	Food
8	Number	Date	Payee/Payor	Notation	Amount	Accnt	1	2	10	11	12	13
9	1000	4/1/87	Cleaners	Shirt Laundry	($7.50)	15	$0.00	$0.00	$0.00	$0.00	$0.00	$0.00
10	1001	4/1/87	Hardware Store	Paint Brushes	($12.35)	12	$0.00	$0.00	$0.00	$0.00	($12.35)	$0.00
11	D	4/2/87	Brother-in-Law	Repay $25 loan	$25.00	2	$0.00	$25.00	$0.00	$0.00	$0.00	$0.00
12	1002	4/2/87	Bookstore	"Iacocca"	($8.95)	18	$0.00	$0.00	$0.00	$0.00	$0.00	$0.00
13	1003	4/3/87	Local S&L	Mortgage	($600.00)	10	$0.00	$0.00	($600.00)	$0.00	$0.00	$0.00
14	CW	4/3/87	Cash	Cash Machine	($200.00)	25	$0.00	$0.00	$0.00	$0.00	$0.00	$0.00
15	1004	4/4/87	GMAC	Car Payment	($205.00)	20	$0.00	$0.00	$0.00	$0.00	$0.00	$0.00
16	1005	4/4/87	First Bank	MasterCard Bill	($127.35)	22	$0.00	$0.00	$0.00	$0.00	$0.00	$0.00
17	1006	4/4/87	ELSI	Student Loan	($115.00)	23	$0.00	$0.00	$0.00	$0.00	$0.00	$0.00
18	1007	4/4/87	Power Company	Electric Bill	($135.00)	11	$0.00	$0.00	$0.00	($135.00)	$0.00	$0.00
19	1008	4/4/87	Water Company	Water Bill	($35.00)	11	$0.00	$0.00	$0.00	($35.00)	$0.00	$0.00
20	1009	4/4/87	SCB	Telephone Bill	($56.00)	11	$0.00	$0.00	$0.00	($56.00)	$0.00	$0.00
21	D	4/4/87	ABC Corp.	Pay 3/15-3/31	$1,500.00	1	$1,500.00	$0.00	$0.00	$0.00	$0.00	$0.00
22	1010	4/5/87	Carpet World	Carpet Cleaning	($36.00)	10	$0.00	$0.00	($36.00)	$0.00	$0.00	$0.00
23	1011	4/7/87	Storer	Cable TV	($35.15)	25	$0.00	$0.00	$0.00	$0.00	$0.00	$0.00
24	1012	4/8/87	LS Ayres	Cosmetics	($25.73)	17	$0.00	$0.00	$0.00	$0.00	$0.00	$0.00
25	1013	4/11/87	Heleringers	Sofa	($551.45)	12	$0.00	$0.00	$0.00	$0.00	($551.45)	$0.00
26	1014	4/13/87	Kroger	Groceries	($75.56)		$0.00	$0.00	$0.00	$0.00	$0.00	($70.00)
27	1015	4/14/87	IRS	Taxes	($879.00)	24	$0.00	$0.00	$0.00	$0.00	$0.00	$0.00
28	1016	4/19/87	Dr. Chen	Office Visit	($30.00)	19	$0.00	$0.00	$0.00	$0.00	$0.00	$0.00
29	1017	4/19/87	Johnson Drugs	Prescription	($12.50)	19	$0.00	$0.00	$0.00	$0.00	$0.00	$0.00
30	D	4/21/87	ABC Corp.	Pay 4/1-4/15	$1,500.00	1	$1,500.00	$0.00	$0.00	$0.00	$0.00	$0.00
31	1018	4/23/87	Maxie's	Clothing	($245.00)	14	$0.00	$0.00				
	1019	4/25/87	Jane Smith	Babysitter	($8.00)	18	$0.00					
102								$0.00	$0.00	$0.00	$0.00	$0.00
103								$0.00	$0.00	$0.00	$0.00	$0.00
104							$0.00	$0.00	$0.00	$0.00	$0.00	$0.00
105							$0.00	$0.00	$0.00	$0.00	$0.00	$0.00
106							$0.00	$0.00	$0.00	$0.00	$0.00	$0.00
107							$0.00	$0.00	$0.00	$0.00	$0.00	$0.00
108							$0.00	$0.00	$0.00	$0.00	$0.00	$0.00
109							--------	--------	--------	--------	--------	--------
110						($873.79)	$3,000.00	$25.00	($636.00)	($226.00)	($878.80)	($207.50)
111						========	========	========	========	========	========	========

Figure 4-2.

	M	N	O	P	Q	R	S	T	U	V	W	X

Clothing	Cleaning/ Laundry	Household Supplies	Personal Expenses	Entrtnmnt	Medical	Autos		Credit Cards	Debt	Taxes	Other
14	15	16	17	18	19	20	21	22	23	24	25
$0.00	$0.00	$0.00	$0.00	$0.00	$0.00	$0.00	$0.00	$0.00	$0.00	$0.00	$0.00
$0.00	$0.00	$0.00	$0.00	$0.00	$0.00	$0.00	$0.00	$0.00	$0.00	$0.00	$0.00
$0.00	$0.00	$0.00	$0.00	$0.00	$0.00	$0.00	$0.00	$0.00	$0.00	$0.00	$0.00
$0.00	$0.00	$0.00	$0.00	$0.00	$0.00	$0.00	$0.00	$0.00	$0.00	$0.00	$0.00
$0.00	$0.00	$0.00	$0.00	$0.00	$0.00	$0.00	$0.00	$0.00	$0.00	$0.00	$0.00
$0.00	$0.00	$0.00	$0.00	$0.00	$0.00	$0.00	$0.00	$0.00	$0.00	$0.00	$0.00
$0.00	$0.00	$0.00	$0.00	$0.00	$0.00	$0.00	$0.00	$0.00	$0.00	$0.00	$0.00
$0.00	$0.00	$0.00	$0.00	$0.00	$0.00	$0.00				$0.00	$0.00
$0.00	$0.00	$0.00	$0.00	$0.00							
$0.00	$0.00	$0.00	$0.00					$0.00		$0.00	$0.00
$0.00	$0.00	$0.00	$0.00			$0.00	$0.00	$0.00	$0.00		
			$0.00		$0.00	$0.00	$0.00	$0.00	$0.00	$0.00	
$0.00	$0.00	$0.00	$0.00	$0.00	$0.00	$0.00	$0.00	$0.00	$0.00	$0.00	$0.00
$0.00	$0.00	$0.00	$0.00	$0.00	$0.00	$0.00	$0.00	$0.00	$0.00	$0.00	$0.00
--------	--------	--------	--------	--------	--------	--------	--------	--------	--------	--------	--------
$0.00	$0.00	$0.00	$0.00	$0.00	$0.00	$0.00	$0.00	$0.00	$0.00	$0.00	$0.00
========	========	========	========	========	========	========	========	========	========	========	========

	M	N	O	P	Q	R	S	T	U	V	W	X

Clothing	Cleaning/ Laundry	Household Supplies	Personal Expenses	Entrtnmnt	Medical	Autos		Credit Cards	Debt	Taxes	Other
14	15	16	17	18	19	20	21	22	23	24	25
$0.00	($7.50)	$0.00	$0.00	$0.00	$0.00	$0.00	$0.00	$0.00	$0.00	$0.00	$0.00
$0.00	$0.00	$0.00	$0.00	$0.00	$0.00	$0.00	$0.00	$0.00	$0.00	$0.00	$0.00
$0.00	$0.00	$0.00	$0.00	$0.00	$0.00	$0.00	$0.00	$0.00	$0.00	$0.00	$0.00
$0.00	$0.00	$0.00	$0.00	($8.95)	$0.00	$0.00	$0.00	$0.00	$0.00	$0.00	$0.00
$0.00	$0.00	$0.00	$0.00	$0.00	$0.00	$0.00	$0.00	$0.00	$0.00	$0.00	$0.00
$0.00	$0.00	$0.00	$0.00	$0.00	$0.00	$0.00	$0.00	$0.00	$0.00	$0.00	($200.00)
$0.00	$0.00	$0.00	$0.00	$0.00	$0.00	($205.00)	$0.00	$0.00	$0.00	$0.00	$0.00
$0.00	$0.00	$0.00	$0.00	$0.00	$0.00	$0.00	$0.00	($127.35)	$0.00	$0.00	$0.00
$0.00	$0.00	$0.00	$0.00	$0.00	$0.00	$0.00	$0.00	$0.00	($115.00)	$0.00	$0.00
$0.00	$0.00	$0.00	$0.00	$0.00	$0.00	$0.00	$0.00	$0.00	$0.00	$0.00	$0.00
$0.00	$0.00	$0.00	$0.00	$0.00	$0.00	$0.00	$0.00	$0.00	$0.00	$0.00	$0.00
$0.00	$0.00	$0.00	$0.00	$0.00	$0.00	$0.00	$0.00	$0.00	$0.00	$0.00	$0.00
$0.00	$0.00	$0.00	$0.00	$0.00	$0.00	$0.00	$0.00	$0.00	$0.00	$0.00	($35.15)
$0.00	$0.00	$0.00	($25.73)	$0.00	$0.00	$0.00	$0.00	$0.00	$0.00	$0.00	$0.00
$0.00	$0.00	$0.00	$0.00	$0.00	$0.00	$0.00	$0.00	$0.00	$0.00	$0.00	$0.00
$0.00	$0.00	($5.56)	$0.00	$0.00	$0.00	$0.00	$0.00	$0.00	$0.00	$0.00	$0.00
$0.00	$0.00	$0.00	$0.00	$0.00	$0.00	$0.00	$0.00	$0.00	$0.00	($879.00)	$0.00
$0.00	$0.00	$0.00	$0.00	$0.00	($30.00)	$0.00	$0.00	$0.00	$0.00	$0.00	$0.00
$0.00	$0.00	$0.00	$0.00	$0.00	($12.50)	$0.00					$0.00
($245.00)	$0.00	$0.00	$0.00	$0.00	$0.00						
$0.00	$0.00	$0.00	$0.00					$0.00	$0.00	$0.00	
			$0.00			$0.00	$0.00	$0.00	$0.00	$0.00	$0.00
$0.00	$0.00	$0.00	$0.00	$0.00	$0.00	$0.00	$0.00	$0.00	$0.00	$0.00	$0.00
$0.00	$0.00	$0.00	$0.00	$0.00	$0.00	$0.00	$0.00	$0.00	$0.00	$0.00	$0.00
$0.00	$0.00	$0.00	$0.00	$0.00	$0.00	$0.00	$0.00	$0.00	$0.00	$0.00	$0.00
$0.00	$0.00	$0.00	$0.00	$0.00	$0.00	$0.00	$0.00	$0.00	$0.00	$0.00	$0.00
--------	--------	--------	--------	--------	--------	--------	--------	--------	--------	--------	--------
($245.00)	($7.50)	($42.31)	($25.73)	($25.95)	($42.50)	($205.00)	$0.00	($127.35)	($115.00)	($879.00)	($235.15)
========	========	========	========	========	========	========	========	========	========	========	========

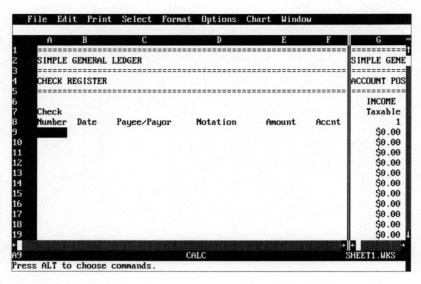

Figure 4-3.

amount. You also record the date and amount of each deposit in this section. The
Simple General Ledger lets you either enter the information about each transaction
directly or use the Copy command to transfer the transactions from the Check Register and Balancer. In Column F, you enter the codes that let you post each check and
deposit to an account.

The Account Posting area occupies columns G through X. Each column in this
area represents an account—Taxable Income, Nontaxable Income, Housing Expenses, Utilities Expenses, and so on—and each account has a number. The cells in
this area contain formulas that use the account codes in column F and the account
numbers in row 8 to post the amount of each check from column E to an account.

CREATING THE TEMPLATE

First, use the New command on the File menu to create a blank spreadsheet.
When the new spreadsheet appears on the screen, select Manual Calculation from the
Options menu. Selecting this command prevents Works from recalculating the entire
spreadsheet after every entry and so speeds up the creation of the template.

Next, change the widths of some of the columns in the spreadsheet. To do so,
position the cursor in a column, select Width from the Format menu, type the new
column width, and press Enter or choose OK. The table in Figure 4-4 shows the new
widths for each column in the Simple General Ledger that you need to change from
the default width of 10. Note that you can change the widths of columns G through X
all at once: Highlight the range G1:X1, choose Width from the Format menu, type *11*,
and press Enter or choose OK.

Column	Width
A	6
B	8
C	15
D	15
E	11
F	7
G through X	11

Figure 4-4. *Column widths for the Simple General Ledger*

The Check Register

Now you're ready to begin making entries. Enter the header labels for this section in rows 1, 2, 3, 4, and 5. The double lines in rows 1, 3, and 5 are composed of equal signs (=) spanning columns A through F. To create these double lines, enter a label made up of equal signs in each cell in row 1, and then copy that series of labels from row 1 to rows 3 and 5. In each cell in row 1, type a quotation mark (") followed by the proper number of equal signs (corresponding to the column width). For example, to enter the label in cell A1, move the cursor to cell A1, type a quotation mark, and then type a string of six equal signs ("======). If you forget the quotation mark, Works will try to interpret the entry as a formula and will display the message *Error: Missing Operand.* After you enter a label in each cell in row 1, highlight the range A1:F1, select Copy from the Edit menu, highlight cell A3, and press Enter or choose OK. Then select Copy again, highlight cell A5, and press Enter or choose OK.

The entries in cells A2 and A4 are simple labels. To enter them, move the cursor to cell A2 and type *SIMPLE GENERAL LEDGER*; then, move to cell A4 and type *CHECK REGISTER.*

Next, identify the columns that make up the Check Register. Enter the label *Check* in cell A7 and the labels *Number, Date, Payee/Payor, Notation, Amount,* and *Accnt* in cells A8 through F8. To center the labels, highlight the range A7:F8, select Style from the Format menu, choose Center from the Style dialog box, and press Enter or choose OK.

Next, change the format of columns B and E in the Check Register. To begin, highlight the range B9:B108. You can do this quickly using the Go To key ([F5]): Move the cursor to cell B9 and press the Extend key ([F8]); then, press [F5], type *B108,* and press Enter. Now, select Time/Date from the Format menu, choose Month, Day, Year from the Show box (with Short date form), and press Enter or choose OK.

To assign Dollar format with two decimal places to column E, highlight the range E9:E108, select Dollar from the Format menu, and press Enter or choose OK.

Now, enter a formula in cell E110 that sums the values in the Amount column (column E). To begin, enter a label consisting of two spaces followed by eight hyphens (--------) in cell E109. Then, move to cell E110 and enter the formula

=SUM(E9:E109)

This formula simply sums the values in the range E9:E109. Now, select Dollar from the Format menu and press Enter (or choose OK) to assign Dollar format with two decimal places to cell E110. Finally, move the cursor to cell E111 and enter a label consisting of two spaces followed by eight equal signs (========).

The Account Posting Area

Now you are ready to define the Account Posting area. To display this part of the spreadsheet, press Ctrl-Home, Ctrl-PgDn, and the Left Arrow key. If you have a mouse, press Ctrl-Home and click once on the horizontal scroll bar, and then press the Left Arrow key.

Now, enter the header labels for this section in rows 1, 2, 3, 4, and 5. The double lines in rows 1, 3, and 5 are composed of equal signs (=) that span columns G through X. To create these double lines, enter a label made up of a quotation mark (") followed by a number of equal signs (corresponding to the width of the column) in each cell in row 1, and then copy that series of labels to rows 3 and 5. Next, enter the label *SIMPLE GENERAL LEDGER* in cell G2 and the label *ACCOUNT POSTING* in cell G4. Then, move to cell I4 and enter the label *For Period Ending*. Now, move the cursor to cell G6, type three spaces, and type the word *INCOME*. Then move the cursor to cell I6, type three spaces, and type *EXPENSES*.

Account Descriptions and Numbers

Now you need to enter the account numbers and descriptions for each of the accounts in columns G through X. Use row 8 for the account numbers and rows 6 and 7 for the descriptions. The spreadsheet uses the account numbers you supply to post each transaction to the appropriate column. The account descriptions identify the contents of each column.

Before you enter the account numbers and descriptions, take a minute to figure out exactly how you want your financial data to be organized. What accounts do you want the ledger to include? If you plan to use the Simple General Ledger at home, you might want to use many of the accounts shown in Figure 4-2 beginning on page 98: Taxable Income, Nontaxable Income, Housing, Utilities, Furniture/Improvements, Food, and so on. If you plan to use the template in a business, you probably need different accounts, including Rent, Payroll, Payroll Taxes, Supplies, Travel and Entertainment, and so on. Create accounts only for expenditures that occur frequently or that are extremely important to track. You merely waste an account if you allocate a column to a type of expenditure that occurs only every third month or so. Include an account labeled *Other* in the Expenses section to hold expenses that don't fit elsewhere.

After you decide which accounts to include in your system, enter a description of each in rows 6 and 7. Next, assign each account a number. Use any numbering system you want, as long as each account has a unique number. You might adopt the account-numbering system we used in the sample spreadsheet: We gave the two income accounts in columns G and H the numbers 1 and 2, and the expense accounts in columns I through X the numbers 10 through 25. Next, right-align the labels in the ranges K6:X6 and G7:X7. To do this, you must first highlight the range K6:X6, select Style from the Format menu, choose the Right alignment option, and press Enter or choose OK. Now, highlight the range G7:X7 and repeat the Style command to align the second row.

The Posting Formulas

Now you're ready to create the formulas that actually post the transactions. To begin, move the cursor to cell G9 and enter the formula

`=IF($F9=G$8,$E9,0)`

This complex-looking formula compares the value in cell F9 to the value in cell G8. If the two values are equal, the IF function returns the value from cell E9. Otherwise, it returns the value 0. In other words, this formula compares the account code (which you enter in cell F9) for the transaction in row 9 to the number for the account in column G (which you've just entered in cell G8). If the numbers match, the function returns the amount of the transaction from cell E9. The effect of the formula is to post, or enter, the value from cell E9 to column G. If the account code for this transaction (cell F9) does not match the account number for this column (cell G8), the function returns 0.

After you enter this formula in cell G9, assign it the Dollar format with two decimal places. To do so, choose Dollar from the Format menu and then press Enter or choose OK to accept the default number of decimal places, 2.

Now, copy this formula to the other cells in the Account Posting area. First, select the range G9:X9 and choose Fill Right from the Edit menu to copy the formula from cell G9 to the range H9:X9. Next, highlight the range G9:X108 and choose Fill Down from the Edit menu. This command copies the formulas from row 9 to rows 10 through 108 in columns G through X. When you finish, each cell in the range G9:X108 contains a formula.

You may wonder why we used the references $F9, G$8, and $E9 in the original formula in cell G9 (=IF($F9=G$8,$E9,0). These references are called mixed references—partly relative and partly absolute. When you copied this formula to the other cells in the Account Posting area, Works adjusted these references in some interesting ways. For example, cell H9 contains the formula

```
=IF($F9=H$8,$E9,0)
```

Notice that the reference to cell G8 in the original formula changed to H8 in this formula, but that the other references did not change. The modified formula serves exactly the same purpose as the original: It compares the account code for the transaction in row 9 (cell F9) to the account number for the account in column H (cell H8). If the numbers are equal, the function returns the amount of the transaction from cell E9. Otherwise, it returns 0.

Similarly, cell G10 contains the formula

```
=IF($F10=G$8,$E10,0)
```

Notice that the references to cells F9 and E9 in the original formula have changed to F10 and E10 in this formula. As you would expect, the modified formula operates exactly like those in cells G9 and H9.

Like the formulas in cells G9, H9, and G10, each formula in the range G9:X108 refers to a cell in column F, a cell in row 8, and a cell in column E. Each of these formulas tests an account code in column F against an account number in row 8 and, if those numbers agree, posts a value from column E to that account. Later in the chapter, you'll see an example of this process.

The Totals

Now, enter a set of formulas in row 110 that sum the values in each account. To begin, move the cursor to cell G109 and enter a label consisting of two spaces followed by eight hyphens in that cell. Then, in cell G110, enter the formula

```
=SUM(G9:G109)
```

This formula simply sums the values in the range G9:G109. Finally, move the cursor to cell G111 and enter a label consisting of two spaces followed by eight equal signs.

Now, give cell G110 Dollar format with two decimal places. To do so, select Dollar from the Format menu and press Enter or choose OK to accept the default number of decimal places, 2.

Because the rest of the formulas in row 110 are equivalent to the one in cell G110, you can simply copy the formula in cell G110. Highlight the range G109:X111 and then select Fill Right from the Edit menu to copy the contents of cells G109, G110, and G111 to columns H through X. Because the formula in cell G110 contains relative references, those references change as the formula is copied. After the copy, for instance, cell H110 contains the formula *=SUM(H9:H109)*, and cell I110 the formula *=SUM(I9:I109)*.

Freezing Rows 1 Through 8

The next step is to "freeze" rows 1 through 8. This ensures that the appropriate column labels remain visible even when the cursor is way down in the spreadsheet. To freeze rows 1 through 8, move the cursor to cell A9 and select Freeze Titles from the Options menu.

Splitting the Screen

Your last step is to split the screen vertically into two windows just to the right of column F. Splitting the screen at this spot lets you see the entire Check Register and one column of the Account Posting area (one account) on the screen at the same time.

The technique you use to split the screen depends on whether you use a mouse. If you use a mouse, press Ctrl-Home to move the cursor to cell A9, point to the double-line window marker in the lower left corner of the screen, press your mouse button, and drag to the right. As you drag your mouse, a double-line window divider appears on the screen. Continue to drag this line until it is immediately to the right of column F. When you release the button, Works splits the screen at the position of the divider. You want column F to appear in one window and column G to be visible in the other window. If you can't see column F in the left-hand window, move the divider slightly to the right. If you can't see the full width of column G in the right-hand window, drag the divider slightly to the left.

If you aren't using a mouse, you must use the arrow keys to split the screen. First, press Ctrl-Home to move the cursor to cell A9. Then, select Split from the Options menu to display both a vertical and a horizontal double-line divider. Press the Right Arrow key to move the vertical divider to the right until it is immediately to the right of column F, and then press Enter. Works splits the window at the position of the divider. You want column F to appear in the left-hand window and column G to be visible in the other window. To adjust the position of the divider, select the Split command again and move the divider slightly to the right or to the left.

Saving the Template

That's all there is to it. Before you do anything else, save the completed template. To do so, select Save As from the File menu. Then, if you want to save the file in a directory other than the current directory, choose that directory from the Other Drives & Directories box and choose OK. Next, type a name (such as *POSTING.WKS*), and press Enter or choose OK to save the file. If you want to save the file in the current directory, simply type a name and press Enter or choose OK.

USING THE TEMPLATE

After you create the Simple General Ledger, you're ready to put it to work. You'll probably use the Simple General Ledger once a month to post your checks. If your volume of transactions is light, you might use the spreadsheet only once a year. More than likely, you'll use the spreadsheet heavily when you first create it to post the checks you've already written in the current year.

To begin, open the Simple General Ledger. (If you just created the template, skip this step.) To do so, choose Open from the File menu. Then, if the file you want to open is in the current directory, either type the filename under which you saved the spreadsheet (for example, *POSTING.WKS*), or highlight the name of the template in the list, and press Enter or choose OK to open the file. If the file you want to open is not in the current directory, select the directory that contains the file from the Other Drives & Directories list box and choose OK. Then, either type the filename or choose it from the list and choose OK.

Moving the Cursor

As shown in Figure 4-3 on page 100, the first 11 rows of the Check Register appear on the home screen. To look at a different part of the register, use your mouse or the cursor movement keys to move to the appropriate cell. For example, press the PgDn key to look at the next screenful of information; to display the preceding screenful, press the PgUp key. If you have a mouse, use the vertical scroll bar to move up and down in the Check Register.

To move to a specific row, press the Go To key ([F5]), type A followed by the number of the row, and press Enter or choose OK. For example, to move to row 50, press [F5], type *A50*, and press Enter or choose OK.

If you used the Freeze Titles option to freeze rows 1 through 8, the headings in those rows stay in view as you move the cursor through the spreadsheet. You cannot use the arrow keys to move the cursor into any of these rows. When you press Ctrl-Home, the cursor moves to cell A9 instead of to cell A1.

To see the Account Posting area, first press Ctrl-Home to move the cursor to cell A9. Then, press Ctrl-PgDn or, if you are using a mouse, click once on the horizontal scroll bar. Either method displays columns G through K in the left-hand window. To view the next screen of the Account Posting area, press Ctrl-PgDn or click on the horizontal scroll bar again. To move back to the left, press Ctrl-PgUp or click to the left of the scroll box on the horizontal scroll bar.

After you split the screen, you can use the Window key ([F6]) to move the cursor from one window to another. If you are using a mouse, simply clicking in a cell moves the cursor to the window that contains that cell. If you move the cursor to the right-hand window, press the Left and Right Arrow keys to scroll through the Account Posting area. As you move the cursor, one account after another appears in the right-hand window. (If you are using a mouse, the horizontal scroll bar in the right-hand window lets you scroll to the left or right.)

Posting Checks

After you load the spreadsheet, enter each check, deposit, and other transaction for the past month or year in the Check Register. In column F enter a code for each transaction, and then recalculate the spreadsheet. You can post your transactions to the Check Register in two different ways. You can enter your transactions manually, or if you are using the Checkbook Register and Balancer to manage your checking account, you can import the information about your transactions from the Check Register of that spreadsheet into the Simple General Ledger.

The Manual Method

If you're not using the Checkbook Register and Balancer, you'll have to enter your transactions manually. As you might expect, the process is fairly simple: You merely enter the check number, date, payee/payer, notation, and amount of each check in columns A, B, C, D, and E. Enter deposits and other additions as positive numbers; enter checks and other withdrawals as negative numbers.

For example, suppose the first check you want to enter is check 1000, written on April 1, 1987, for $7.50 to The Cleaners for shirt laundry. Enter the number, *1000*, in cell A9, the date, *4/1/87*, in cell B9, the payee, *Cleaners*, in cell C9, the notation, *Shirt Laundry*, in cell D9, and the amount, *−7.5*, in cell E9.

When you post transactions other than checks (such as deposits, cash machine withdrawals, or service charges), enter an identifying letter code instead of a number in column A. For instance, you might enter a *D* in column A to identify a deposit. When you enter a cash machine withdrawal, you might enter the code *CW* in column A.

The Import Method

If you are using the Checkbook Register and Balancer to manage your checking account, you can import the information about your transactions from the Check Register of that spreadsheet into the Simple General Ledger. To do this, you'll use the Copy Special command, which allows you to copy only the values contained in a cell or range and not the formulas that compute those values. First, open the Checkbook Register and Balancer file that contains the transaction records you want to import, and then open an empty Simple General Ledger spreadsheet. Next, highlight the cells in the Check Register that contain the transactions you want to import and select Copy Special from the Edit menu. Now, select the name of the open Simple General Ledger spreadsheet from the Window menu. When that spreadsheet appears, move the cursor to cell A9 and press Enter. When you do this, Works displays the Copy Special dialog box. Choose the Values Only option and then press Enter or choose OK to copy the highlighted information from the Check Register into the Simple General Ledger.

Let's look at an example. Suppose you set up the Checkbook Register and Balancer and entered the checks shown in Figure 4-5. You saved this spreadsheet as CHECKS87.WKS. You want to import all the transactions for April 1987 into the Simple General Ledger. We assume you saved the empty Simple General Ledger in a file named POSTING.WKS. To begin, open both the CHECKS87 and the POSTING spreadsheets. Next, highlight the range A10:E38 in the CHECKS87 spreadsheet and select the Copy Special command from the Edit menu. Now, select POSTING.WKS from the Window menu.

	A	B	C	D	E	F	G
1	==
2	CHECKBOOK REGISTER AND BALANCER
3	==
4	CHECK REGISTER
5	==
6							
7	Check					Running	
8	Number	Date	Payee-Payor	Notation	Amount	Balance	Out?
9	Beginning Balance					$6,479.25	
10	1000	4/1/87	Cleaners	Shirt Laundry	($7.50)	$6,471.75	
11	1001	4/1/87	Hardware Store	Paint Brushes	($12.35)	$6,459.40	
12	D	4/2/87	Brother-in-Law	Repay $25 loan	$25.00	$6,484.40	
13	1002	4/2/87	Bookstore	"Iacocca"	($8.95)	$6,475.45	
14	1003	4/3/87	Local S&L	Mortgage	($600.00)	$5,875.45	
15	CW	4/3/87	Cash	Cash Machine	($200.00)	$5,675.45	
16	1004	4/4/87	GMAC	Car Payment	($205.00)	$5,470.45	
17	1005	4/4/87	First Bank	MasterCard Bill	($127.35)	$5,343.10	
18	1006	4/4/87	ELSI	Student Loan	($115.00)	$5,228.10	
19	1007	4/4/87	Power Company	Electric Bill	($135.00)	$5,093.10	
20	1008	4/4/87	Water Company	Water Bill	($35.00)	$5,058.10	
21	1009	4/4/87	SCB	Telephone Bill	($56.00)	$5,002.10	
22	D	4/4/87	ABC Corp.	Pay 3/15-3/31	$1,500.00	$6,502.10	
23	1010	4/5/87	Carpet World	Carpet Cleaning	($36.00)	$6,466.10	
24	1011	4/7/87	Storer	Cable TV	($35.15)	$6,430.95	
25	1012	4/8/87	LS Ayres	Cosmetics	($25.73)	$6,405.22	
26	1013	4/11/87	Heleringers	Sofa	($551.45)	$5,853.77	
27	1014	4/13/87	Kroger	Groceries	($75.56)	$5,778.21	
28	1015	4/14/87	IRS	Taxes	($879.00)	$4,899.21	1
29	1016	4/19/87	Dr. Chen	Office Visit	($30.00)	$4,869.21	
30	1017	4/19/87	Johnson Drugs	Prescription	($12.50)	$4,856.71	
31	D	4/21/87	ABC Corp.	Pay 4/1-4/15	$1,500.00	$6,356.71	
32	1018	4/23/87	Maxie's	Clothing	($245.00)	$6,111.71	
33	1019	4/25/87	Jane Smith	Babysitter	($8.00)	$6,103.71	
34	1020	4/26/87	Kroger	Groceries	($62.50)	$6,041.21	
35	1021	4/27/87	Jim Jones	Newspaper	($9.00)	$6,032.21	
36	1022	4/27/87	Dime Store	House Supplies	($36.75)	$5,995.46	
37	1023	4/29/87	Lazarus	Clothing	($75.00)	$5,920.46	
38	1024	4/30/87	Joe Davis	Painting	($315.00)	$5,605.46	

Figure 4-5.

Next, highlight cell A9 and press Enter. When the Copy Special dialog box appears, choose the Values Only option and then press Enter or choose OK. Figure 4-6 shows the POSTING spreadsheet after it imports the data.

```
 File  Edit  Print  Select  Format  Options  Chart  Window
1000
      A        B        C            D            E        F  ||    G
1  ================================================================  =========
2  SIMPLE GENERAL LEDGER                                           SIMPLE GENE
3  ================================================================  =========
4  CHECK REGISTER                                                   ACCOUNT POS
5  ================================================================  =========
6                                                                     INCOME
7  Check                                                              Taxable
8  Number  Date    Payee/Payor    Notation      Amount    Accnt        1
9   1000  4/1/87 Cleaners      Shirt Laundry    ($7.50)              $0.00
10  1001  4/1/87 Hardware Store Paint Brushes   ($12.35)             $0.00
11   D    4/2/87 Brother-in-Law Repay $25 loan  $25.00               $0.00
12  1002  4/2/87 Bookstore      "Iacocca"        ($8.95)             $0.00
13  1003  4/3/87 Local S&L      Mortgage        ($600.00)            $0.00
14   CW   4/3/87 Cash           Cash Machine    ($200.00)            $0.00
15  1004  4/4/87 GMAC           Car Payment     ($205.00)            $0.00
16  1005  4/4/87 First Bank     MasterCard Bill ($127.35)            $0.00
17  1006  4/4/87 ELSI           Student Loan    ($115.00)            $0.00
18  1007  4/4/87 Power Company  Electric Bill   ($135.00)            $0.00
19  1008  4/4/87 Water Company  Water Bill      ($35.00)             $0.00
A9:E37                            CALC                            POSTING.WKS
Press ALT to choose commands.
```

Figure 4-6.

Limitations

The Simple General Ledger enables you to post as many as 100 transactions at one time, probably enough to let you do monthly postings. If you need to post more than 100 checks at a time using this template, you have two choices. One option is to use the Insert command on the Edit menu to add a few rows to the spreadsheet. You'll learn how to do that later in this chapter. The other option is to post your first 100 transactions to one Simple General Ledger spreadsheet, the next 100 to a second spreadsheet, and so on. If you write far more than 100 checks a month, however, you are likely to need a more sophisticated program to manage and post your disbursements.

Entering Account Numbers

After you enter or import your transactions, assign an account code to each one. To do so, simply move the cursor to column F of the row that contains the transaction and enter the number of the account to which you want to post that transaction.

For example, to post the first transaction in Figure 4-6 on page 109 to account 15, move the cursor to cell F9 and enter the value *15*. Figure 4-7 shows the result.

```
   File  Edit  Print  Select  Format  Options  Chart  Window
15
         A       B          C             D    ·      E        F  ||    G
1   ===========================================================  ||========
2   SIMPLE GENERAL LEDGER                                        ||SIMPLE GENE
3   ===========================================================  ||========
4   CHECK REGISTER                                               ||ACCOUNT POS
5   ===========================================================  ||========
6   Check                                                        ||INCOME
7   Number  Date    Payee/Payor     Notation      Amount   Accnt ||Taxable
8                                                               ||      1
9    1000  4/1/87  Cleaners       Shirt Laundry   ($7.50)    15 ||   $0.00
10   1001  4/1/87  Hardware Store Paint Brushes   ($12.35)      ||   $0.00
11      D  4/2/87  Brother-in-Law Repay $25 loan   $25.00       ||   $0.00
12   1002  4/2/87  Bookstore      "Iacocca"        ($8.95)      ||   $0.00
13   1003  4/3/87  Local S&L      Mortgage        ($600.00)     ||   $0.00
14     CW  4/3/87  Cash           Cash Machine    ($200.00)     ||   $0.00
15   1004  4/4/87  GMAC           Car Payment     ($205.00)     ||   $0.00
16   1005  4/4/87  First Bank     MasterCard Bill ($127.35)     ||   $0.00
17   1006  4/4/87  ELSI           Student Loan    ($115.00)     ||   $0.00
18   1007  4/4/87  Power Company  Electric Bill   ($135.00)     ||   $0.00
19   1008  4/4/87  Water Company  Water Bill       ($35.00)     ||   $0.00
F9                         CALC                               POSTING.WKS
Press ALT to choose commands.
```

Figure 4-7.

Now, give every transaction an account code. Most checks and other transactions will probably fit into one of the accounts you've defined. If you can't figure out where to post a transaction, post it to the account labeled Other. The only time you won't give a transaction a code is when you need to post that transaction to two or more accounts. You'll learn how to do that later in this chapter.

You'll probably have difficulty remembering all your account numbers. To find the number of an account, press the Window key ([F6]) to move the cursor into the right-hand window, and then press the Right Arrow key to scroll through the Account Posting area until you find it. As you move the cursor to the right, one account after another appears in the right-hand window. When you find the account you are looking for, press [F6] again to move the cursor back to the left-hand window and enter the account number for that account in the appropriate cell. If you scroll too far to the right, simply press the Left Arrow key to move the cursor to the left. (If you have a mouse, you can use the horizontal scroll bar in the right-hand window to scroll the accounts to the left or right.)

Manual Posting

Although you can post most of your checks and deposits to a single account, you might need to post a few to two or more accounts. For example, you might write a check at the grocery store for groceries, cleaning materials, and makeup; and then want to code this check to three accounts: Food, Household Supplies, and Personal Supplies. Or you might set up your accounts system so that the interest and principal portions of each loan payment are recorded separately.

Although the Simple General Ledger can't automatically post a transaction to two or more accounts, you can easily do so manually. Instead of giving this kind of transaction an account code, you simply enter the appropriate amounts manually in two or three accounts.

For example, suppose that you want to post check 1014 in Figure 4-5 on page 108 to two accounts. You want to enter $70.00 of the total amount in the Food account and the remaining $5.56 in the Household Supplies account. First, move the cursor to row 26 and press the Window key ([F6]) to move the cursor into the right-hand window. Then, press the Right Arrow key to move the cursor through the accounts until you reach column L, which contains the Food account. Now, enter the number –70. Next, move the cursor to the right again until it is in column O, which contains the Household Supplies account, and enter the value –5.56.

If you post a check manually to two or more accounts, be sure that the sum of the values you post equals the amount of the check. If the amounts you post don't add up, the account totals in row 110 will be incorrect. In a few pages, you'll learn a way to modify the template so that it detects this kind of error.

Recalculating

After you code all the transactions in the Check Register, you're ready to recalculate the spreadsheet. Press the Calc key ([F9]) or choose Calculate Now from the Options menu. When you do so, Works evaluates each formula in the range G9:X109. These formulas compare the account codes you entered in column F to the account numbers in row 8. In those cases where the account code in column F matches the account number in row 8, the formula posts the value from column E to that account. All the other formulas return the value 0.

For example, suppose you coded each transaction you imported into the template, as shown in Figure 4-8 beginning on page 112. When you press [F9] or choose Calculate Now from the Options menu, Works posts each transaction to an account in the Account Posting area. Figure 4-9 shows the result. Notice that the first check, which you coded for account 15, has been posted to account 15. Similarly, the second check, which has the account code 12, has been posted to account 12, and so on.

When you press the Calc key ([F9]), the formulas in row 110 compute the total of the items in each account and the total of the transactions you've entered. For example, the formula in cell E110 in Figure 4-8 returns the value –$619.09, indicating that checks and deposits equaling –$619.09 have been entered in the Check Register. The

Figure 4-8.

SIMPLE GENERAL LEDGER — SIMPLE GENERAL LEDGER
CHECK REGISTER — ACCOUNT POSTING — For Period Ending — 4/30/87

						INCOME		EXPENSES		Furniture/	
Check						Taxable	Tax Free	Housing	Utilities	Imprvmnts	Food
Number	Date	Payee/Payor	Notation	Amount	Accnt	1	2	10	11	12	13
1000	4/1/87	Cleaners	Shirt Laundry	($7.50)	15	$0.00	$0.00	$0.00	$0.00	$0.00	$0.00
1001	4/1/87	Hardware Store	Paint Brushes	($12.35)	12	$0.00	$0.00	$0.00	$0.00	$0.00	$0.00
D	4/2/87	Brother-in-Law	Repay $25 loan	$25.00	2	$0.00	$0.00	$0.00	$0.00	$0.00	$0.00
1002	4/2/87	Bookstore	"Iacocca"	($8.95)	18	$0.00	$0.00	$0.00	$0.00	$0.00	$0.00
1003	4/3/87	Local S&L	Mortgage	($600.00)	10	$0.00	$0.00	$0.00	$0.00	$0.00	$0.00
CW	4/3/87	Cash	Cash Machine	($200.00)	25	$0.00	$0.00	$0.00	$0.00	$0.00	$0.00
1004	4/4/87	GMAC	Car Payment	($205.00)	20	$0.00	$0.00	$0.00	$0.00	$0.00	$0.00
1005	4/4/87	First Bank	MasterCard Bill	($127.35)	22	$0.00	$0.00	$0.00	$0.00	$0.00	$0.00
1006	4/4/87	ELSI	Student Loan	($115.00)	23	$0.00	$0.00	$0.00	$0.00	$0.00	$0.00
1007	4/4/87	Power Company	Electric Bill	($135.00)	11	$0.00	$0.00	$0.00	$0.00	$0.00	$0.00
1008	4/4/87	Water Company	Water Bill	($35.00)	11	$0.00	$0.00	$0.00	$0.00	$0.00	$0.00
1009	4/4/87	SCB	Telephone Bill	($56.00)	11	$0.00	$0.00	$0.00	$0.00	$0.00	$0.00
D	4/4/87	ABC Corp.	Pay 3/15-3/31	$1,500.00	1	$0.00	$0.00	$0.00	$0.00	$0.00	$0.00
1010	4/5/87	Carpet World	Carpet Cleaning	($36.00)	10	$0.00	$0.00	$0.00	$0.00	$0.00	$0.00
1011	4/7/87	Storer	Cable TV	($35.15)	25	$0.00	$0.00	$0.00	$0.00	$0.00	$0.00
1012	4/8/87	LS Ayres	Cosmetics	($25.73)	17	$0.00	$0.00	$0.00	$0.00	$0.00	$0.00
1013	4/11/87	Heleringers	Sofa	($551.45)	12	$0.00	$0.00	$0.00	$0.00	$0.00	$0.00
1014	4/13/87	Kroger	Groceries	($75.56)		$0.00	$0.00	$0.00	$0.00	$0.00	($70.00)
1015	4/14/87	IRS	Taxes	($879.00)	24	$0.00	$0.00	$0.00	$0.00	$0.00	$0.00
1016	4/19/87	Dr. Chen	Office Visit	($30.00)	19	$0.00	$0.00	$0.00	$0.00	$0.00	$0.00
1017	4/19/87	Johnson Drugs	Prescription	($12.50)	19	$0.00	$0.00	$0.00	$0.00		
D	4/21/87	ABC Corp.	Pay 4/1-4/15	$1,500.00	1	$0.00	$0.00				
1018	4/23/87	Maxie's	Clothing	($245.00)	14	$0.00					
								$0.00	$0.00	$0.00	$0.00
107								$0.00	$0.00	$0.00	$0.00
108								$0.00	$0.00	$0.00	$0.00
109				--------				--------	--------	--------	--------
110				$0.00				$0.00	$0.00	$0.00	$0.00
111				========				========	========	========	========

Figure 4-9.

SIMPLE GENERAL LEDGER — SIMPLE GENERAL LEDGER
CHECK REGISTER — ACCOUNT POSTING — For Period Ending — 4/30/87

						INCOME		EXPENSES		Furniture/	
Check						Taxable	Tax Free	Housing	Utilities	Imprvmnts	Food
Number	Date	Payee/Payor	Notation	Amount	Accnt	1	2	10	11	12	13
1000	4/1/87	Cleaners	Shirt Laundry	($7.50)	15	$0.00	$0.00	$0.00	$0.00	$0.00	$0.00
1001	4/1/87	Hardware Store	Paint Brushes	($12.35)	12	$0.00	$0.00	$0.00	$0.00	($12.35)	$0.00
D	4/2/87	Brother-in-Law	Repay $25 loan	$25.00	2	$0.00	$25.00	$0.00	$0.00	$0.00	$0.00
1002	4/2/87	Bookstore	"Iacocca"	($8.95)	18	$0.00	$0.00	$0.00	$0.00	$0.00	$0.00
1003	4/3/87	Local S&L	Mortgage	($600.00)	10	$0.00	$0.00	($600.00)	$0.00	$0.00	$0.00
CW	4/3/87	Cash	Cash Machine	($200.00)	25	$0.00	$0.00	$0.00	$0.00	$0.00	$0.00
1004	4/4/87	GMAC	Car Payment	($205.00)	20	$0.00	$0.00	$0.00	$0.00	$0.00	$0.00
1005	4/4/87	First Bank	MasterCard Bill	($127.35)	22	$0.00	$0.00	$0.00	$0.00	$0.00	$0.00
1006	4/4/87	ELSI	Student Loan	($115.00)	23	$0.00	$0.00	$0.00	$0.00	$0.00	$0.00
1007	4/4/87	Power Company	Electric Bill	($135.00)	11	$0.00	$0.00	$0.00	($135.00)	$0.00	$0.00
1008	4/4/87	Water Company	Water Bill	($35.00)	11	$0.00	$0.00	$0.00	($35.00)	$0.00	$0.00
1009	4/4/87	SCB	Telephone Bill	($56.00)	11	$0.00	$0.00	$0.00	($56.00)	$0.00	$0.00
D	4/4/87	ABC Corp.	Pay 3/15-3/31	$1,500.00	1	$1,500.00	$0.00	$0.00	$0.00	$0.00	$0.00
1010	4/5/87	Carpet World	Carpet Cleaning	($36.00)	10	$0.00	$0.00	($36.00)	$0.00	$0.00	$0.00
1011	4/7/87	Storer	Cable TV	($35.15)	25	$0.00	$0.00	$0.00	$0.00		
1012	4/8/87	LS Ayres	Cosmetics	($25.73)	17	$0.00	$0.00	$0.00			
1013	4/11/87	Heleringers	Sofa	($551.45)	12	$0.00	$0.00				
1014	4/13/87	Kroger	Groceries	($75.56)		$0.00					
								$0.00	$0.00	$0.00	$0.00
106								$0.00	$0.00	$0.00	$0.00
107								$0.00	$0.00	$0.00	$0.00
108								$0.00	$0.00	$0.00	$0.00
109				--------				--------	--------	--------	--------
110				($873.79)		$3,000.00	$25.00	($636.00)	($226.00)	($878.80)	($207.50)
111				========		========	========	========	========	========	========

M	N	O	P	Q	R	S	T	U	V	W	X
	Cleaning/	Household	Personal					Credit			
Clothing	Laundry	Supplies	Expenses	Entrtnmnt	Medical	Autos		Cards	Debt	Taxes	Other
14	15	16	17	18	19	20	21	22	23	24	25
$0.00	$0.00	$0.00	$0.00	$0.00	$0.00	$0.00	$0.00	$0.00	$0.00	$0.00	$0.00
$0.00	$0.00	$0.00	$0.00	$0.00	$0.00	$0.00	$0.00	$0.00	$0.00	$0.00	$0.00
$0.00	$0.00	$0.00	$0.00	$0.00	$0.00	$0.00	$0.00	$0.00	$0.00	$0.00	$0.00
$0.00	$0.00	$0.00	$0.00	$0.00	$0.00	$0.00	$0.00	$0.00	$0.00	$0.00	$0.00
$0.00	$0.00	$0.00	$0.00	$0.00	$0.00	$0.00	$0.00	$0.00	$0.00	$0.00	$0.00
$0.00	$0.00	$0.00	$0.00	$0.00	$0.00	$0.00	$0.00	$0.00	$0.00	$0.00	$0.00
$0.00	$0.00	$0.00	$0.00	$0.00	$0.00	$0.00	$0.00	$0.00	$0.00	$0.00	$0.00
$0.00	$0.00	$0.00	$0.00	$0.00	$0.00	$0.00	$0.00	$0.00	$0.00	$0.00	$0.00
$0.00	$0.00	$0.00	$0.00	$0.00	$0.00	$0.00	$0.00	$0.00	$0.00	$0.00	$0.00
$0.00	$0.00	$0.00	$0.00	$0.00	$0.00	$0.00	$0.00	$0.00	$0.00	$0.00	$0.00
$0.00	$0.00	$0.00	$0.00	$0.00	$0.00	$0.00	$0.00	$0.00	$0.00	$0.00	$0.00
$0.00	$0.00	$0.00	$0.00	$0.00	$0.00	$0.00	$0.00	$0.00	$0.00	$0.00	$0.00
$0.00	$0.00	$0.00	$0.00	$0.00	$0.00	$0.00	$0.00	$0.00	$0.00	$0.00	$0.00
$0.00	$0.00	$0.00	$0.00	$0.00	$0.00	$0.00	$0.00	$0.00	$0.00	$0.00	$0.00
$0.00	$0.00	($5.56)	$0.00	$0.00	$0.00	$0.00	$0.00	$0.00	$0.00	$0.00	$0.00
$0.00	$0.00	$0.00	$0.00	$0.00	$0.00	$0.00	$0.00	$0.00	$0.00	$0.00	$0.00
$0.00	$0.00	$0.00	$0.00	$0.00	$0.00	$0.00	$0.00	$0.00	$0.00	$0.00	$0.00
$0.00	$0.00	$0.00	$0.00	$0.00	$0.00	$0.00				$0.00	$0.00
$0.00	$0.00	$0.00	$0.00								$0.00
$0.00	$0.00	$0.00				$0.00	$0.00	$0.00	$0.00	$0.00	
			$0.00	$0.00	$0.00	$0.00	$0.00	$0.00	$0.00	$0.00	$0.00
$0.00	$0.00	$0.00	$0.00	$0.00	$0.00	$0.00	$0.00	$0.00	$0.00	$0.00	$0.00
--------	--------	--------	--------	--------	--------	--------	--------	--------	--------	--------	--------
$0.00	$0.00	$0.00	$0.00	$0.00	$0.00	$0.00	$0.00	$0.00	$0.00	$0.00	$0.00
========	========	========	========	========	========	========	========	========	========	========	========

M	N	O	P	Q	R	S	T	U	V	W	X
	Cleaning/	Household	Personal					Credit			
Clothing	Laundry	Supplies	Expenses	Entrtnmnt	Medical	Autos		Cards	Debt	Taxes	Other
14	15	16	17	18	19	20	21	22	23	24	25
$0.00	($7.50)	$0.00	$0.00	$0.00	$0.00	$0.00	$0.00	$0.00	$0.00	$0.00	$0.00
$0.00	$0.00	$0.00	$0.00	$0.00	$0.00	$0.00	$0.00	$0.00	$0.00	$0.00	$0.00
$0.00	$0.00	$0.00	$0.00	$0.00	$0.00	$0.00	$0.00	$0.00	$0.00	$0.00	$0.00
$0.00	$0.00	$0.00	$0.00	($8.95)	$0.00	$0.00	$0.00	$0.00	$0.00	$0.00	$0.00
$0.00	$0.00	$0.00	$0.00	$0.00	$0.00	$0.00	$0.00	$0.00	$0.00	$0.00	$0.00
$0.00	$0.00	$0.00	$0.00	$0.00	$0.00	$0.00	$0.00	$0.00	$0.00	$0.00	($200.00)
$0.00	$0.00	$0.00	$0.00	$0.00	$0.00	($205.00)	$0.00	$0.00	$0.00	$0.00	$0.00
$0.00	$0.00	$0.00	$0.00	$0.00	$0.00	$0.00	$0.00	($127.35)	$0.00	$0.00	$0.00
$0.00	$0.00	$0.00	$0.00	$0.00	$0.00	$0.00	$0.00	$0.00	($115.00)	$0.00	$0.00
$0.00	$0.00	$0.00	$0.00	$0.00	$0.00	$0.00	$0.00	$0.00	$0.00	$0.00	$0.00
$0.00	$0.00	$0.00	$0.00	$0.00	$0.00	$0.00	$0.00	$0.00	$0.00	$0.00	$0.00
$0.00	$0.00	$0.00	$0.00	$0.00	$0.00	$0.00	$0.00	$0.00	$0.00	$0.00	$0.00
$0.00	$0.00	$0.00	$0.00	$0.00	$0.00	$0.00	$0.00	$0.00	$0.00	$0.00	($35.15)
$0.00	$0.00	$0.00	($25.73)	$0.00	$0.00	$0.00	$0.00	$0.00	$0.00	$0.00	$0.00
$0.00	$0.00	$0.00	$0.00	$0.00							
$0.00	$0.00	($5.56)	$0.00				$0.00	$0.00	$0.00		
$0.00	$0.00				$0.00	$0.00	$0.00	$0.00	$0.00	$0.00	$0.00
				$0.00	$0.00	$0.00	$0.00	$0.00	$0.00	$0.00	$0.00
			$0.00	$0.00	$0.00	$0.00	$0.00	$0.00	$0.00	$0.00	$0.00
$0.00	$0.00	$0.00	$0.00	$0.00	$0.00	$0.00	$0.00	$0.00	$0.00	$0.00	$0.00
$0.00	$0.00	$0.00	$0.00	$0.00	$0.00	$0.00	$0.00	$0.00	$0.00	$0.00	$0.00
--------	--------	--------	--------	--------	--------	--------	--------	--------	--------	--------	--------
($245.00)	($7.50)	($42.31)	($25.73)	($25.95)	($42.50)	($205.00)	$0.00	($127.35)	($115.00)	($879.00)	($235.15)
========	========	========	========	========	========	========	========	========	========	========	========

formula in cell G110 in Figure 4-9 returns the value $3,000.00, indicating that you posted a total of $3,000.00 of income to the Taxable Income account. Similarly, the value in cell I110, $636.00, indicates that you posted that amount in withdrawals to the Housing account.

You can use the totals in cells G110 through X110 in a variety of ways. Some of the totals (such as Housing Expenses, Medical Expenses, and so on) might help you prepare your tax return. By comparing these totals to your monthly (or annual) budget, you can determine whether you are overspending or underspending your budget.

Printing and Saving

After you enter and code your transactions and recalculate the spreadsheet, you'll probably want to save your spreadsheet in a new file. To do so, select Save As from the File menu and, if necessary, change the current directory. Next, type a new name for the spreadsheet and press Enter or choose OK to save the file. Choose a filename that clearly identifies the contents of the spreadsheet. For example, you might save the sample spreadsheet under the name SGLAPR87.WKS (for Simple General Ledger April, 1987). After you save the spreadsheet under a new name, you can retrieve it by selecting Open from the File menu, typing the new name, and pressing Enter or choosing OK.

Always be sure to save your filled-in Simple General Ledger spreadsheets under a name other than that of the original, empty template. If you save a filled-in spreadsheet under the same name as the original template, the filled-in version replaces the original version.

You'll probably also want to print the Simple General Ledger after you enter and post a set of transactions. You can print either the entire spreadsheet or any specific portion of it that you need. To print the entire spreadsheet, first choose Layout from the Print menu and make any necessary changes to the print settings. If you have a wide-carriage printer and plan to print this worksheet on 11-inch-by-14-inch paper, you can change the Page Width setting from *8.5"* to *14"*. You can also change the Top, Bottom, Left, and Right margins, and define a header and a footer.

Next, you can use the Font command to select the font you want Works to use to print the report. If you want to squeeze the entire report onto one page, choose a relatively compressed font (such as Elite) and a small point size (such as 6 or 8).

After you adjust the settings, select Print from the Print menu. When you see the Print dialog box, adjust any of the settings in that dialog box and then choose Print to print the worksheet. Because this spreadsheet is too large to fit on one sheet of paper, Works splits the printed spreadsheet into logical sections and prints each section on a separate sheet.

To print only a portion of the spreadsheet, begin by using the Set Print Area command on the Print menu to define the cells to print. For example, if you want to print only the Check Register, highlight the range A9:F38 and select Set Print Area from the Print menu to define the cells you want to print. Then, use the Layout and Font commands to make any needed adjustments to the print settings. Finally, select Print from the Print menu and press Enter or choose Print to print the selected range. If the Freeze Titles command is active, Works prints the entries in the frozen rows in columns A through F and then the defined print area.

MODIFICATIONS

You might want (or need) to modify your spreadsheet. First, you might want to change the formula in cell E110 so that it checks the sums of the values in column E against the total of the sums in cells G110 through X110. Second, you might need to add a few rows to the spreadsheet so that you can post more than the standard 100 transactions.

A Checksum Formula

The basic spreadsheet we've created in this chapter has one weakness: It does not offer a good way to verify that every transaction was posted to an account. If you want to verify that every transaction was posted, you need to compute the sum of the account totals in cells G110 through X110 and compare that result to the value in cell E110. If the two totals agree, then every transaction was posted. Otherwise, you have a problem.

Computing these sums manually can be tedious. As you might expect, however, you can have Works do all the work for you. Simply replace the formula in cell E110 with the formula

```
IF(ROUND(SUM(E9:E109),2)=ROUND(SUM(G110:X110),2),SUM(E9:E109),0)
```

This formula simply compares the sums of the values in column E with the total of the sums in cells G110 through X110. If the two sums are equal, then the formula returns the result of the formula SUM(E9:E109). Otherwise, the formula returns 0.

This formula lets you see at a glance whether every transaction was posted to an account. If the value in cell E110 is 0, something is amiss. If the result is anything other than 0, then you can assume that every transaction has been posted.

Notice that we used the ROUND function in this formula to round the result of the formulas SUM(E9:E109) and SUM(G110:X110) to 2 decimal places. These ROUND functions are made necessary by a quirk of the floating-point calculator in your personal computer. Sometimes the floating-point calculator introduces very, very small errors into calculations. By "very, very small," we mean errors in the fifteenth digit to the right of the decimal. These errors are completely meaningless until you try to compare the result of a SUM to another SUM or to a fixed value. Then, these very small errors may cause Works to think that two numbers which really are equal are not equal. The ROUND functions remove the chance for this kind of problem by rounding these small errors out of the values you want to compare. You'll want to keep this quirk in mind as you use the IF and SUM functions in your own spreadsheets.

Adding Rows

The Simple General Ledger has room for exactly 100 transactions. If the number of transactions does not greatly exceed 100, you can use the Insert command on the Edit menu to add a few rows to the spreadsheet. After you add the new row or rows, copy the formulas for columns G through X into those rows.

Let's look at an example. Suppose you need to add five additional rows to the spreadsheet. To begin, highlight rows 109, 110, 111, 112, and 113. Then, select Insert from the Edit menu to insert five empty rows in the spreadsheet. In addition, the Insert command moves the labels in rows 109 and 111 to rows 114 and 116 and the formulas in row 110 to row 115. It also adjusts the formulas in row 116 so that they refer to the five new rows. For example, after you insert the new rows, cell G115 contains the formula *=SUM(G9:G114)*.

Now, copy the formulas for columns G through X into the new rows. To do so, select the range G108:X113, which includes the last row of formulas and the cells in columns G through X of the new rows. Now, select Fill Down from the Edit menu to copy the formulas from row 108 into rows 109, 110, 111, 112, and 113. You can now enter and code as many as five additional transactions.

If you add too many additional rows, you might exceed the available computer memory. Because the IF formulas in each row consume a significant amount of memory, expanding the spreadsheet can rapidly lead to a shortage.

CONCLUSION

The Simple General Ledger you built in this chapter is a simple accounting system that lets you track your income and expenses at home or at work. While it does not offer some features of stand-alone general ledger systems, it is adequate for most households and many small businesses.

Even if you don't use this template, you learned some generally useful techniques: the use of mixed references to create a formula that can be copied into a rectangular range and the use of the IF function to post values. You'll find these techniques handy when you build your own spreadsheets.

Loan Amortization Calculator

Although most of us would wish it weren't so, nearly all of us have to borrow money. We borrow to buy houses and cars, to finance major purchases, to pay for vacations, to cover the cost of college, and for a hundred other reasons. The purpose of a loan generally determines its characteristics. For instance, mortgage loans normally have long terms and high principal balances, while student loans have unusually low interest rates. All loans, however, have one dogged characteristic in common: They have to be repaid.

The process of repaying a loan is called amortizing the loan. When you borrow money, the bank (or other lender) usually gives you a schedule of payments called an amortization schedule, or amortization table. It lists the date and amount of each payment, and the amount of the principal that remains after each payment is made. The table might also tell what portion of each payment is interest and what portion is principal.

You might find the bank's payment schedule useful, but you'll discover some excellent reasons to create your own schedule using Microsoft Works. First, the schedule from the bank probably can't show you the effect of paying a little extra principal each month. Second, it probably can't show you how much your payment will change if the interest rate changes. And it almost certainly doesn't tell you (for fear of scaring you off) the total amount you'll pay to amortize the loan. To analyze your loans carefully and thoroughly, you'll want to create your own amortization table, one that tells you what the schedule from the bank does not.

The Loan Amortization Calculator enables you to do just that. With this spreadsheet, you can create an amortization table for any monthly-payment loan. The Loan Amortization Calculator can handle any combination of principal balance, term (as many as 360 months, or 30 years), and interest rate, and can handle special situations that frequently arise, such as additional monthly principal payments and variable interest rates. The spreadsheet can also help you analyze a loan. For example, it computes the total amount you will pay to amortize a loan and the portion of that total that constitutes interest. You can also use it to analyze the status of a loan at any point in its term of repayment.

This template demonstrates several interesting features of Works. It uses the PMT, CHOOSE, YEAR, MONTH, SUM, MOD, and VLOOKUP functions to perform calculations. It also shows a technique for passing changes through a series of values, and it uses several clever formulas to head off potential problems.

ABOUT THE TEMPLATE

Figure 5-1 shows the entire Loan Amortization Calculator template as it will appear after you create it. Figure 5-2 on page 120 shows the Loan Amortization Calculator in use. The template has three distinct areas: the Assumptions area, the Amortization table, and the Analysis area. The Assumptions area occupies the top half of the first screen (cells A4:D9 shown in Figure 5-3 on page 121). In this area, you enter the basic information required to create the Amortization table—the date of the first payment, the beginning principal, the annual rate, the term (in months), and the additional principal you want to pay each month (cells D4:D8). Cell D9 contains a PMT function that can then compute the monthly payment required to amortize the loan.

The Amortization table occupies the range A20:H383. Figure 5-4 on page 121 shows the first screen of this area. The table uses the information in the Assumptions area to create a full payment schedule for the loan. For each monthly payment, the table includes the payment number, date, rate, total payment amount, interest amount, principal amount, and ending principal balance. The formulas that compute these figures are designed to handle a variety of special circumstances, including additional monthly principal payments and variable interest rates.

The Analysis area occupies the lower half of the screen shown in Figure 5-3 (the range A11:G19). The formulas in this area compute the total amount you'll pay to amortize a loan and the interest portion of that total. This area also lets you compute the status of the loan at any point in its term: the principal paid to date, the interest paid to date, the remaining principal, the remaining interest, and the total of the remaining payments.

	A	B	C	D	E	F	G	H
1	==
2	LOAN AMORTIZATION CALCULATOR
3	==
4	Date of First Payment			1/1/88				
5	Beginning Principal			$0.00				
6	Annual Rate			0.00%				
7	Term (in months)			0 Months				
8	Additional Principal			$0.00				
9	Monthly Payment			$0.00				
10								
11	Total Payments			$0.00 Total Interest			$0.00	
12								
13	Current Payment			0				
14	Principal Portion			$0.00 Interest Portion			$0.00	
15								
16	Principal Paid to Date			$0.00 Interest Paid to Date			$0.00	
17	Remaining Principal			$0.00 Remaining Interest			$0.00	
18	Total Remaining			$0.00				
19								
20				Total			Ending	
21				Monthly	Interest	Principal	Principal	Total
22	Payment	Date	Rate	Payment	Payment	Payment	Balance	Interest
23	-------	------	------	----------	----------	----------	----------	----------
24	1	1/1/88	0.00%	$0.00	$0.00	$0.00	$0.00	$0.00
25	2	2/1/88	0.00%	$0.00	$0.00	$0.00	$0.00	$0.00
26	3	3/1/88	0.00%	$0.00	$0.00	$0.00	$0.00	$0.00
27	4	4/1/88	0.00%	$0.00	$0.00	$0.00	$0.00	$0.00
28	5	5/1/88	0.00%	$0.00	$0.00	$0.00	$0.00	$0.00
29	6	6/1/88	0.00%	$0.00	$0.00	$0.00	$0.00	$0.00
30	7	7/1/88	0.00%	$0.00	$0.00	$0.00	$0.00	$0.00
31	8	8/1/88	0.00%	$0.00	$0.00	$0.00	$0.00	$0.00
32	9	9/1/88	0.00%	$0.00	$0.00	$0.00	$0.00	$0.00
33	10	10/1/88	0.00%	$0.00	$0.00	$0.00	$0.00	$0.00
34	11	11/1/88	0.00%	$0.00	$0.00	$0.00	$0.00	$0.00
35	12	12/1/88	0.00%	$0.00	$0.00	$0.00	$0.00	$0.00
36	13	1/1/89	0.00%	$0.00	$0.00	$0.00	$0.00	$0.00
37	14	2/1/89	0.00%	$0.00	$0.00	$0.00	$0.00	$0.00
38	15	3/1/89	0.00%	$0.00	$0.00	$0.00	$0.00	$0.00
39	16	4/1/89	0.00%	$0.00	$0.00	$0.00	$0.00	$0.00
40				$0.00	$0.00	$0.00	$0.00	
		1/1/18	0.00%		$0.00	$0.00	$0.00	
370	347	11/1/16	0.00%	$0.00				$0.00
371	348	12/1/16	0.00%	$0.00				$0.00
372	349	1/1/17	0.00%	$0.00	$0.00	$0.00	$0.00	$0.00
373	350	2/1/17	0.00%	$0.00	$0.00	$0.00	$0.00	$0.00
374	351	3/1/17	0.00%	$0.00	$0.00	$0.00	$0.00	$0.00
375	352	4/1/17	0.00%	$0.00	$0.00	$0.00	$0.00	$0.00
376	353	5/1/17	0.00%	$0.00	$0.00	$0.00	$0.00	$0.00
377	354	6/1/17	0.00%	$0.00	$0.00	$0.00	$0.00	$0.00
378	355	7/1/17	0.00%	$0.00	$0.00	$0.00	$0.00	$0.00
379	356	8/1/17	0.00%	$0.00	$0.00	$0.00	$0.00	$0.00
380	357	9/1/17	0.00%	$0.00	$0.00	$0.00	$0.00	$0.00
381	358	10/1/17	0.00%	$0.00	$0.00	$0.00	$0.00	$0.00
382	359	11/1/17	0.00%	$0.00	$0.00	$0.00	$0.00	$0.00
383	360	12/1/17	0.00%	$0.00	$0.00	$0.00	$0.00	$0.00

Figure 5-1.

	A	B	C	D	E	F	G	H
1	==						
2	LOAN AMORTIZATION CALCULATOR						
3	==						
4	Date of First Payment			2/1/88				
5	Beginning Principal			$95,000.00				
6	Annual Rate			9.25%				
7	Term (in months)			360 Months				
8	Additional Principal			$25.00				
9	Monthly Payment			$806.54				
10								
11	Total Payments			$261,535.88	Total Interest		$166,535.88	
12								
13	Current Payment			12				
14	Principal Portion			$197.38	Interest Portion		$709.17	
15								
16	Principal Paid to Date			$3,197.44	Interest Paid to Date		$8,681.06	
17	Remaining Principal			$91,802.56	Remaining Interest		$157,854.82	
18	Total Remaining			$249,657.38				
19								

	Payment	Date	Rate	Total Monthly Payment	Interest Payment	Principal Payment	Ending Principal Balance	Total Interest
24	1	2/1/88	9.25%	$906.54	$732.29	$174.25	$94,825.75	$732.29
25	2	3/1/88	9.25%	$906.54	$730.95	$175.59	$94,650.16	$1,463.24
26	3	4/1/88	9.25%	$906.54	$729.59	$176.95	$94,473.21	$2,192.84
27	4	5/1/88	9.25%	$906.54	$728.23	$178.31	$94,294.90	$2,921.07
28	5	6/1/88	9.25%	$906.54	$726.86	$179.69	$94,115.21	$3,647.92
29	6	7/1/88	9.25%	$906.54	$725.47	$181.07	$93,934.14	$4,373.39
30	7	8/1/88	9.25%	$906.54	$724.08	$182.47	$93,751.68	$5,097.47
31	8	9/1/88	9.25%	$906.54	$722.67	$183.87	$93,567.81	$5,820.14
32	9	10/1/88	9.25%	$906.54	$721.25	$185.29	$93,382.52	$6,541.39
33	10	11/1/88	9.25%	$1,906.54	$719.82	$1,186.72	$92,195.80	$7,261.21
34	11	12/1/88	9.25%	$906.54	$710.68	$195.87	$91,999.93	$7,971.89
35	12	1/1/89	9.25%	$906.54	$709.17	$197.38	$91,802.56	$8,681.06
36	13	2/1/89	9.25%	$806.54	$707.64	$98.90	$91,703.66	$9,388.70
37	14	3/1/89	9.25%	$806.54	$706.88	$99.66	$91,604.00	$10,095.58
38	15	4/1/89	9.25%	$806.54	$706.11	$100.43	$91,503.57	$10,801.70
39	16	5/1/89	9.25%	$806.54	$705.34	$101.20	$91,402.37	$11,507.04
40				$806.54	$704.56	$101.98	$91,300.39	$12,211.60
	304	5/1/13	10.00%	$830.06	$703.77	$102.77	$91,197.62	$12,915.77
328	305	6/1/13	10.00%	$830.06	$60.??	$???	$?,???.??	$???.98
329	306	7/1/13	10.00%	$830.06	$54.03	$776.02	$5,707.90	$166,341.01
330	307	8/1/13	10.00%	$830.06	$47.57	$782.49	$4,925.41	$166,388.57
331	308	9/1/13	10.00%	$830.06	$41.05	$789.01	$4,136.39	$166,429.62
332	309	10/1/13	10.00%	$830.06	$34.47	$795.59	$3,340.81	$166,464.09
333	310	11/1/13	10.00%	$830.06	$27.84	$802.22	$2,538.59	$166,491.93
334	311	12/1/13	10.00%	$830.06	$21.15	$808.90	$1,729.69	$166,513.08
335	312	1/1/14	10.00%	$830.06	$14.41	$815.64	$914.05	$166,527.50
336	313	2/1/14	10.00%	$830.06	$7.62	$822.44	$91.61	$166,535.12
337	314	3/1/14	10.00%	$92.37	$0.76	$91.61	$0.00	$166,535.88
338	315	4/1/14	10.00%	$0.00	$0.00	$0.00	$0.00	$166,535.88
339	316	5/1/14	10.00%	$0.00	$0.00	$0.00	$0.00	$166,535.88
340	317	6/1/14	10.00%	$0.00	$0.00	$0.00	$0.00	$166,535.88

Figure 5-2.

```
 File  Edit  Print  Select  Format  Options  Chart  Window
"========
      A       B        C        D          E        F          G
1   ========================================================================
2   LOAN AMORTIZATION CALCULATOR
3   ========================================================================
4   Date of First Payment        2/1/88
5   Beginning Principal      $95,000.00
6   Annual Rate                   9.25%
7   Term (in months)           360 Months
8   Additional Principal        $25.00
9   Monthly Payment            $806.54
10
11  Total Payments          $261,535.88 Total Interest       $166,535.88
12
13  Current Payment                 12
14  Principal Portion          $197.38 Interest Portion        $709.17
15
16  Principal Paid to Date   $3,197.44 Interest Paid to Date  $8,681.06
17  Remaining Principal     $91,802.56 Remaining Interest   $157,854.82
18  Total Remaining        $249,657.38
19
A1                                                          LOAN.WKS
Press ALT to choose commands.
```

Figure 5-3.

```
 File  Edit  Print  Select  Format  Options  Chart  Window

      A       B        C        D          E          F          G
20                             Total                            Ending
21                           Monthly    Interest   Principal  Principal
22  Payment  Date    Rate    Payment    Payment    Payment    Balance
23  -------  ------  ------  ---------  ---------  ---------  ---------
24       1   2/1/88  9.25%    $906.54    $732.29    $174.25   $94,825.75
25       2   3/1/88  9.25%    $906.54    $730.95    $175.59   $94,650.16
26       3   4/1/88  9.25%    $906.54    $729.59    $176.95   $94,473.21
27       4   5/1/88  9.25%    $906.54    $728.23    $178.31   $94,294.90
28       5   6/1/88  9.25%    $906.54    $726.86    $179.69   $94,115.21
29       6   7/1/88  9.25%    $906.54    $725.47    $181.07   $93,934.14
30       7   8/1/88  9.25%    $906.54    $724.08    $182.47   $93,751.68
31       8   9/1/88  9.25%    $906.54    $722.67    $183.87   $93,567.81
32       9  10/1/88  9.25%    $906.54    $721.25    $185.29   $93,382.52
33      10  11/1/88  9.25%  $1,906.54    $719.82  $1,186.72   $92,195.80
34      11  12/1/88  9.25%    $906.54    $710.68    $195.87   $91,999.93
35      12   1/1/89  9.25%    $906.54    $709.17    $197.38   $91,802.56
36      13   2/1/89  9.25%    $806.54    $707.64     $98.90   $91,703.66
37      14   3/1/89  9.25%    $806.54    $706.88     $99.66   $91,604.00
38      15   4/1/89  9.25%    $806.54    $706.11    $100.43   $91,503.57
A20                                                         LOAN.WKS
Press ALT to choose commands.
```

Figure 5-4.

CREATING THE TEMPLATE

To create the Loan Amortization Calculator, first select New from the File menu, choose Spreadsheet, and choose the New button to create a new spreadsheet. Then, select Manual Calculation from the Options menu. This command puts Works in the manual recalculation mode—a necessity in a large spreadsheet like this one.

Next, you need to change the widths of some columns in the spreadsheet. To change the width of a column, position the cursor in that column, select Width from the Format menu, type the new column width, and press Enter or choose OK. The table in Figure 5-5 shows the new widths for each column in the template.

Column	Width
A	8
B	8
C	8
D	12
E	11
F	12
G	12
H	12

Figure 5-5.   Column widths for the Loan Amortization Calculator.

The Assumptions Area

Now you're ready to start making entries. To begin, enter the header labels for the spreadsheet in rows 1, 2, and 3. The double lines in rows 1 and 3 span columns A through H. To create these double-line labels, enter a label made up of a series of equal signs (=) in each cell in row 1, and then copy that series of labels from row 1 into row 3. To enter each label in row 1, type a quotation mark (") followed by the proper number of equal signs. For example, to enter the label in cell A1, you would move the cursor to cell A1, type a quotation mark, and then type a string of eight equal signs ("========). If you forget the quotation mark, Works will try to interpret the entry as a formula.

After you enter a label in each cell in row 1, you can use the Copy command to copy the labels from row 1 into row 3. To do this, highlight the range A1:G1, select Copy from the Edit menu, point to cell A3, and press Enter. Next, move the cursor to cell A2 and enter the label *LOAN AMORTIZATION CALCULATOR*.

Then, enter the labels *Date of First Payment, Beginning Principal, Annual Rate, Term (in months), Additional Principal,* and *Monthly Payment* in cells A4 through A9 and the label *Months* in cell E7.

Next, you need to enter values for Date of First Payment, Beginning Principal, Annual Rate, and Term (in months) in cells D4, D5, D6, and D7. At this point, you can enter fictitious numbers in these cells. (You might want to use the numbers that appear in the example in Figure 5-3 on page 121.) These entries will help you to understand how the template works as you create it. In cell D4, enter a date in the form MM/DD/YY. In cells D5, D6, and D7, enter numbers. (For the Annual Rate in cell D6, enter a decimal number, such as *.12* or *.08*.)

As you enter the "dummy" values for these cells, assign each cell the proper format. Assign Dollar format with two decimal places to cells D5 and D8, and assign Percent format with two decimals to cell D6. Default formatting is satisfactory for cell D7. To format cell D5, highlight the cell, select Dollar from the Format menu, and press Enter or choose OK. (Because the default number of decimal places is 2, you need not change that setting.) Next, move the cursor to cell D6, select Percent from the Format menu, and press Enter or choose OK. (Once again, you need not change the number of decimal places.) Format cell D8 exactly as you formatted D5.

Next, move to cell D9 and enter the formula

`=IF(D5=0,0,PMT(D5,D6/12,D7)+D8)`

This function first tests the value in cell D5. If D5 contains the value 0, this function returns the value 0. Otherwise, the function computes the monthly payment required to amortize the loan described by your entries in cells D5, D6, and D7. The total monthly payment is the sum of that amount and any additional monthly payment toward the principal that you enter in cell D8. After you enter the formula, select Dollar from the Format menu and press Enter or choose OK.

The Amortization Table

Now you are ready to build the Amortization table. To begin, move the cursor to cell A20. (Press Ctrl-Home followed by PgDn.) Next, enter the labels that appear in cells A20 through H23 in Figure 5-1 on page 119 at the corresponding locations in your spreadsheet. To center the labels, highlight the range A20:H22. Then, select Style from the Format menu, choose the Center option, and press Enter or choose OK.

The Payment Number column

After you enter the table headers, enter the payment numbers in column A. Beginning in cell A24, enter the number *1*. Then move the cursor to cell A25 and enter the formula *=A24+1*. This formula sets the value of cell A25 to be one greater than the value in cell A24. Now, highlight the range A25:A383 and choose Fill Down from the Edit menu. This command copies the formula in cell A25 to the range A26:A383. To check your progress, press the Calc key ([F9]) to recalculate the spreadsheet, and then move the cursor to cell A383. The formula in that cell should return the value 360.

The Payment Date column

Now you're ready to fill in column B of the Amortization table. This column contains formulas that compute the date of each payment. First, assign Month, Day, Year format to the range B24:B383. To do so, highlight the range B24:B383 and then choose Time/Date from the Format menu. In the resulting dialog box, choose Month, Day, Year (with Short date form), and press Enter or choose OK.

Next, move the cursor to cell B24 and enter the formula *=D4* to link cell B24 to cell D4 in the Assumptions area, the cell in which you entered the first payment date. Now, move the cursor to cell B25 and enter the formula

```
=B24+CHOOSE(MONTH(B24)-1,31,IF(MOD(YEAR(B24),4)=0,29,28),
31,30,31,30,31,31,30,31,30,31)
```

This complex formula allows the spreadsheet to compute the next payment date for the loan. The next payment date is the sum of the preceding date and the appropriate number of additional days. Because different months have different numbers of days, the formula evaluates the month in which the previous date falls, and then uses the CHOOSE function to select the proper number of days from a list. CHOOSE enables Works to select a value from a list based on the position of that value in the list. The form of the CHOOSE function is

CHOOSE(*offset,item1,item2,item3,...,itemn*)

where *item1*, *item2*, and so on are the components of the list, and *offset* specifies the position of the value you want the function to return. If the offset is 0, then the CHOOSE function returns *item1*. If the offset is 1, the function returns *item2*. If the offset is n–1, the function will return *itemn*.

The first expression of the CHOOSE function in cell B25, *MONTH(B24)–1*, computes the month number of the previous payment date and then subtracts one from that number. For example, if the previous payment occurred in May (month 5), then this expression returns the value 4.

We subtract one from the result of the MONTH function because of the way CHOOSE selects the items from its list. Remember that CHOOSE selects the first item from the list if the offset is 0, the second item from the list if the offset is 1, and so on. We want our CHOOSE function to return the first item from the list when the MONTH function returns the value 1, the second item when the MONTH function returns the value 2, and so on. To make this work, we have to subtract 1 from the result of the MONTH function.

The CHOOSE function uses this first expression to select one of its remaining 12 expressions. In our formula, these expressions are simply the number of days in each month of the year: 31 (January), 28 or 29 (February), 31 (March), and so on. Since February can have either 28 or (in leap years) 29 days, the third expression of the CHOOSE function is a little more complex than the others. This argument,

IF(MOD(YEAR(B24),4)=0,29,28), can be translated into English like this: If the remainder after dividing the year value of the date in cell B24 by 4 is 0, then return 29; otherwise, return 28. In other words, if the year portion of the date in cell B24 is evenly divisible by 4 (meaning that it is a leap year), then return 29, the number of days in February in a leap year; otherwise, return 28.

The result of the CHOOSE function is the number of days in the month in which the previous payment was made. Adding this value to the date of the previous payment (in cell B24) returns the date of the next payment. For example, if the date in cell B24 is 4/1/87, then the formula in cell B25 returns the date 5/1/87. This result is the sum of 30 (days in April) and the value for the preceding date, April 1, 1987.

After you enter the formula in cell B25, copy it to the range B26:B383. To do this, highlight the range B25:B383 and select Fill Down from the Edit menu. Now, press the Calc key ([F9]) to recalculate the spreadsheet. Column B now contains a series of dates, each of which falls exactly one month after the previous date.

The Rate column

Now you are ready to fill in column C. The entries in this column are the monthly interest rates for each payment. Including these rates in the table makes it possible to produce an Amortization table for a variable-rate loan.

To begin, give the cells in column C Percent format with two decimal places. To do this, highlight the range C24:C383, select Percent from the Format menu, and press Enter or choose OK. Next, move the cursor to cell C24 and enter the formula *=D6*. This formula links cell C24 to cell D6, which contains the interest rate you specified. Now, move the cursor down one cell to cell C25 and enter the formula *=C24* to equate the value in cell C25 to the value in cell C24.

Finally, copy the formula in cell C25 to the range C26:C383. To do so, highlight the range C25:C383 and select Fill Down from the Edit menu. To recalculate the spreadsheet, press the Calc key ([F9]). Column C now contains a series of percentages, all identical to the value in cell D6.

The Total Monthly Payment column

The entries you make in column D compute the correct monthly payments for the loan. To begin, give the cells in this column Dollar format with two decimal places. To do so, highlight the range D24:D383, select Dollar from the Format menu, and press Enter or choose OK. Next, move the cursor to cell D24 and enter the formula *=D9*. This formula links cell D24 to cell D9, the cell that contains the formula that computes your monthly payment.

Now move the cursor to cell D25 and enter the formula

```
=IF(C25=C24,IF(G24<D24-(G24*(C25/12)),G24*(1+C25/12),D24),
PMT(G24,C25/12,$D$7-A25-1)+$D$8)
```

This complex formula computes the monthly payment for the second month in the amortization. The formula is so lengthy because it must handle two special cases.

First, the formula lets you change the interest rate at any point in the amortization of the loan. Whenever you change the rate, the formula adjusts the monthly payment. Second, the formula handles the case where the final payment is smaller than the normal monthly payment. This situation arises when you pay additional principal with all or some monthly payments.

Here's how the formula works. The first IF function compares the interest rate for the current period (cell C25) with the interest rate for the previous period (cell C24). If these values are equal—meaning that the interest rate has not changed—the second IF function compares the value in cell G24 (the principal balance remaining after the previous payment) to the value in cell D24 (the previous month's payment) minus the result of multiplying the value in cell G24 (remaining principal) times the value in cell C25 (the current interest rate) divided by 12.

If the value in G24 is less than the value of the second expression—meaning that the total remaining principal is less than the principal portion of a regular monthly payment—then the formula computes a special final payment. This calculation is made by multiplying the remaining principal (cell G24) by 1 plus the result of dividing the current interest rate (cell C25) by 12.

On the other hand, if the remaining principal (cell G24) is not less than the result of the expression D24–(G24*(C25/12)), then the formula returns the value from D24 (the previous monthly payment). In other words, the current payment is the same as the previous payment.

If the value in cell C25 does not equal the value in cell C24—meaning that the interest rate has changed between the previous payment and the current payment— then the function PMT(G24,C25/12,$D$7–A25–1)+$D$8 computes a new payment. The first expression in this function, G24, is the remaining principal. The second expression, C25/12, computes the current monthly interest rate. The third expression, $D$7–A25–1, computes the remaining term of the loan by subtracting the number of the current payment in cell A25 from the total term in cell D7 and then subtracting 1 from that result. The last term of the argument, +$D$8, adds the additional monthly payment from cell D8 to the computed monthly payment.

After you enter the formula in cell D25, copy it to the range D26:D383. To do so, highlight the range D25:D383 and select Fill Down from the Edit menu. Don't recalculate the spreadsheet at this time—the values in column D will not be correct until you make entries in column G.

The Interest Payment column

Now, move to column E—the Interest Payment column. The formulas you enter in this column compute the interest portion of each monthly payment. To begin, give the cells in this column Dollar format with two decimal places: Highlight the range E24:E383, select Dollar from the Format menu, and press Enter or choose OK.

The interest portion of any monthly payment is equal to the monthly interest rate times the principal that remains after the previous payment. To compute the interest portion of the first payment, move the cursor to cell E24 and enter the formula

=(C24/12)*D5. This formula multiplies the beginning principal in cell D5 by the monthly interest rate, the current rate (cell C24) divided by 12.

Now, move the cursor to cell E25 and enter the formula *=(C25/12)*G24*. This formula is very similar to the formula in cell E24, except that this one refers to the value in cell G24, the principal remaining after the first payment.

Now, copy the formula in cell G25 to the range E26:E383. To do this, highlight the range E25:E383 and select Fill Down from the Edit menu. As before, you need not recalculate the spreadsheet—the values in this column will not be correct until you make entries in column G.

The Principal Payment column

You have only three more columns to complete in the Amortization table. The formulas you enter in column F compute the principal portion of each monthly payment by subtracting the interest portion in column E from the total monthly payment in column D.

To fill in this column, first highlight the range F24:F383, select Dollar from the Format menu, and press Enter or choose OK. This command assigns Dollar format with two decimal places to the cells in column F. Now, move the cursor to cell F24 and enter the formula *=D24−E24*. This formula computes the principal portion of the first monthly payment.

Next, move the cursor to cell F25 and enter the formula

```
=IF(D25=0,0,D25-E25)
```

This formula compares the current monthly payment (cell D25) with 0; if the value in cell D25 equals 0, the function returns 0; otherwise, it returns the difference between the value in cell D25 and the value in cell E25. In other words, if the monthly payment is 0, then the principal portion is also 0; if the monthly payment is not 0, then the principal payment is the difference between the amount of the total payment and the interest payment. The conditional test prevents the table from continuing to amortize the loan after it is fully repaid.

Now, copy the formula in cell F25 to the range F26:F383. To do so, highlight the range F25:F383 and select Fill Down from the Edit menu.

The Ending Principal Balance column

The formulas you enter in the Ending Principal Balance column compute the principal balance after each monthly payment. They simply subtract the principal portion of each monthly payment from the preceding principal balance.

To fill in column G, first highlight the range G24:G383, select Dollar from the Format menu, and press Enter or choose OK. Now, move the cursor to cell G24 and enter the formula *=D5−F24*. To compute the principal balance after the first monthly payment, this formula subtracts the principal portion of the first payment from the initial principal balance for the loan.

Next, move the cursor to cell G25 and enter the formula =G24−F25. To compute the principal balance after the second payment, this formula subtracts the principal portion of the second payment from the principal balance after the first payment.

Finally, highlight the range G25:G383 and select Fill Down from the Edit menu to copy the formula from cell G25 into the range G26:G383. To recalculate the spreadsheet, press the Calc key ([F9]). Column G now contains a series of dollar amounts, the gradually decreasing principal balance.

The Total Interest column

The last column in the Amortization table, Total Interest (column H), is optional. Use it only if you want the spreadsheet to let you compute the interest paid to date and the total unpaid interest on your loan at any point. The formulas in this column simply compute a running balance of the total interest paid.

To fill in this column, first highlight the range H24:H383, select Dollar from the Format menu, and press Enter or choose OK. Next, move the cursor to cell H24 and enter the formula =E24. This formula computes the total interest paid after the first payment simply by referring to the interest portion of the first payment.

Now, move the cursor to cell H25 and enter the formula =H24+E25. This formula computes the total interest paid after the second monthly payment by adding the interest portion of the second payment (cell E25) to the total interest paid after the first payment (cell H24). Next, highlight the range H25:H383 and select Fill Down from the Edit menu to copy the formula from cell H25 into the range H26:H383. To recalculate the spreadsheet, press the Calc key ([F9]) once. Column H now contains an increasing series of dollar amounts—and the Amortization table is complete!

The Analysis Area

Now you're ready to enter the labels and formulas that make up the Analysis area. To begin, move the cursor to cell A11. (Use the arrow keys, the Go To key, or Ctrl-Home or PgUp with the arrow keys.) Now, enter the labels from cells A11, A13, A14, A16, A17, A18, E11, E14, E16, and E17 in Figure 5-1 on page 119 in the same cells in your spreadsheet.

The Total Payments and Total Interest

When the labels are in place, move the cursor to cell D11 and enter the function

```
=SUM(D24:D383)
```

This function computes the total of all your payments to amortize the loan. To format cell D11, select Dollar from the Format menu and press Enter or choose OK.

The result of the formula in cell D11 is considerably larger than the initial principal balance in cell D5. The difference represents the interest you pay on the loan. To compute this number exactly, move the cursor to cell G11 and enter the formula =*D11–D5*. This formula computes the total interest you'll pay by subtracting the initial principal balance (in cell D5) from the total of all payments (in cell D11). To assign Dollar format to cell D11, select Dollar from the Format menu and then press Enter or choose OK.

The Current Status Area

The remaining formulas allow you to analyze the status of a loan at any point in its life. All these formulas depend, either directly or indirectly, on the value in cell D13. For now, enter any whole number from 0 to the number of months in the term of the loan (the value in cell D7) in cell D13. (You might enter the number used in Figure 5-3 on page 121.) This value prevents the formulas you enter in this area from returning the error message *ERR*.

Now, move the cursor to cell D14 and enter the formula

=IF(D13=0,0,VLOOKUP(D13,A24:G383,5))

This formula uses the VLOOKUP function to "look up" the principal portion of the specified payment from column F of the Amortization table. The form of the VLOOKUP function is

=VLOOKUP(*key,table_range,offset*)

where *table range* defines the lookup table you want to use, *key* is the value you want to look up in the first column of the table, and *offset* is the column of the table from which to retrieve the function's result. VLOOKUP moves down the first column of the lookup table and finds the largest value that is not greater than the key value. Then, it looks across the row that contains that value to the column specified by the offset. VLOOKUP considers the first column of the table an offset of 0, the second column an offset of 1, and so on.

The formula in cell D14 says: If the value in cell D13 is 0, then return 0; otherwise, look up the value from cell D13 in the lookup table A24:G383 (the Amortization table) and return the value from the sixth column in that table (five columns to the right of the current column). Consider an example: If D13 contains the value 4, the formula returns the value from cell F27. VLOOKUP locates this value by looking down column A (the first column in the lookup table) beginning with cell A24. The function searches for the greatest value that is not greater than the key value, 4. Because the value in cell A27, 4, is the greatest value in column A that is not greater than the key, VLOOKUP retrieves its result from row 27. The function counts across to the column with an offset of 5, beginning with column A, which has an offset of 0. The result of the function is thus the value from cell F27: $50.40.

After you enter the formula in cell D14, assign Dollar format with two decimal places to that cell. To do so, select Dollar from the Format menu and then press Enter or choose OK.

Next, move the cursor to cell G14 and enter the formula

```
=IF(D13=0,0,VLOOKUP(D13,A24:G383,4))
```

This formula, which is very similar to the one in cell D14, computes the interest portion of the specified payment by looking up the appropriate value from column E in the Amortization table. The only difference between this formula and the one in cell D14 is that this one uses an offset of 4 rather than an offset of 5 to specify the column that contains the value to be returned.

To assign Dollar format with two decimal places to cell G14, select Dollar from the Format menu and press Enter or choose OK.

Next, move the cursor to cell D16 and enter the formula *=D5–D17*. This formula computes the principal paid to date, including the principal portion of the payment indicated by the entry in cell D13. This formula references cell D5, which contains the initial principal balance for the loan, and cell D17, which will contain a formula to compute the remaining principal. Because cell D17 is currently blank, the formula in cell D16 simply returns the value from D5.

Now, move the cursor to cell D17 and enter the formula

```
=IF(D13=0,D5,VLOOKUP(D13,A24:G383,6))
```

This formula computes the unpaid principal after the payment indicated by the value in cell D13. It says: If the entry in cell D13 is 0, then the remaining principal balance equals the initial principal balance from cell D5. Otherwise, look up the principal remaining after the indicated payment from column G of the Amortization table, using the value in cell D13 as the key value.

Next, move the cursor to cell D18 and enter the formula *=D17+G17*. This formula computes the total amount unpaid by adding the remaining principal in cell D17 to the value in cell G17. Cell G17 will contain a formula that computes the total unpaid interest. Because cell G17 is currently blank, however, the formula in cell D18 simply returns the value from cell D17.

After you've entered the formulas in cells D16, D17, and D18, assign Dollar format with two decimal places to those cells. To do so, highlight the range D16:D18, select Dollar from the Format menu, and press Enter or choose OK.

Just two more formulas to go! The first computes the interest paid to date, including the interest portion of the payment specified in cell D13. Move the cursor to cell G16 and enter the formula

```
=IF(D13=0,0,VLOOKUP(D13,A24:H383,7))
```

This formula says: If the current payment entry in cell D13 is 0, then no interest has been paid to date. Otherwise, look up the interest paid to date from column H of the Amortization table, using the value in cell D13 as the key value. Remember that column H already contains a series of formulas that calculate a running total of interest paid throughout the life of the loan.

Finally, move the cursor to cell G17 and enter the formula *=G11–G16*. This formula computes the total unpaid interest by subtracting the amount of interest paid to date (cell G16) from the total interest payable across the term of the loan (cell G11).

After you've entered the formulas in cells G16 and G17, assign Dollar format with two decimal places to those cells. To do this, highlight the range G16:G17, select Dollar from the Format menu, and press Enter or choose OK.

Saving the Template

That's it! You're finished. At this point, press the Calc key ([F9]) to recalculate the spreadsheet and update all the formulas. Because the spreadsheet is so large and contains so many formulas, Works may need several minutes to complete the recalculation. Once the spreadsheet has been recalculated, check it over to be sure that all of the results look reasonable and that the values in the Analysis area agree with the values in that area in Figure 5-1 on page 119. If you find any disparities, you may need to edit and correct one or more formulas.

When you are confident that the template has been built correctly, "zero it out" to prepare it for your real assumptions. Simply replace the date in cell D4 with a base date (such as 1/1/80), and replace the dummy assumptions in cells D5, D6, D7, D8, and D13 with zeros. To make these changes, move the cursor to cell D4 and type *1/1/80*. Then, move the cursor down one cell and type *0*. Continue to move the cursor down column D, entering zeros in cells D6, D7, D8, and D13. After you zero out all the assumptions, press [F9] again to recalculate the spreadsheet. Recalculating the spreadsheet resets the value of every formula to 0.

Now, save the spreadsheet. To do this, select Save As from the File menu. Then, if you want to save the file in a directory other than the current directory, choose that directory from the Other Drives & Directories box and choose OK. Next, type a name (such as *LOAN.WKS*) and press Enter to save the file. If you want to save the file in the current directory, simply type a name and press Enter or choose OK.

USING THE TEMPLATE

Now, you're ready to put the Loan Amortization Calculator to work. To begin, open the spreadsheet. (If you just created it, skip this step.) First, choose Open from the File menu. Then, if the file you want to open is in the current directory, type the filename under which you saved the spreadsheet, including the extension (for example, *LOAN.WKS*) or highlight the name of the spreadsheet in the list. Then, press Enter or choose OK to open the file. If the file you want to open is not in the current directory, select the directory that contains the file from the Other Drives & Directories list box and choose OK. Then either type the filename or choose it from the list of filenames and press Enter or choose OK.

Entering the Assumptions

When the Loan Amortization Calculator appears on the screen, enter the assumptions that define the loan you want to analyze in cells D4, D5, D6, and D7. Suppose, for example, you want to analyze a loan with a beginning principal balance of $100,000.00, an annual interest rate of 9.25%, and a term of 360 months. Assume that the first payment is to occur on February 1, 1988.

To begin, move the cursor to cell D4 and enter the first payment date, *2/1/88*. Then, move to cell D5 and enter the beginning principal balance, *100000*. Next, move to cell D6 and enter the annual interest rate, *.0925*. Finally, move to cell D7 and enter the term, *360*.

Now, press the Calc key ([F9]) to recalculate the spreadsheet and create the Amortization table. After a few seconds, the formula in cell D9 returns the monthly payment for the loan: $822.68. A few seconds later, the formulas in cells D11, G11, D17, G17, and D18 also return results, as shown in Figure 5-6.

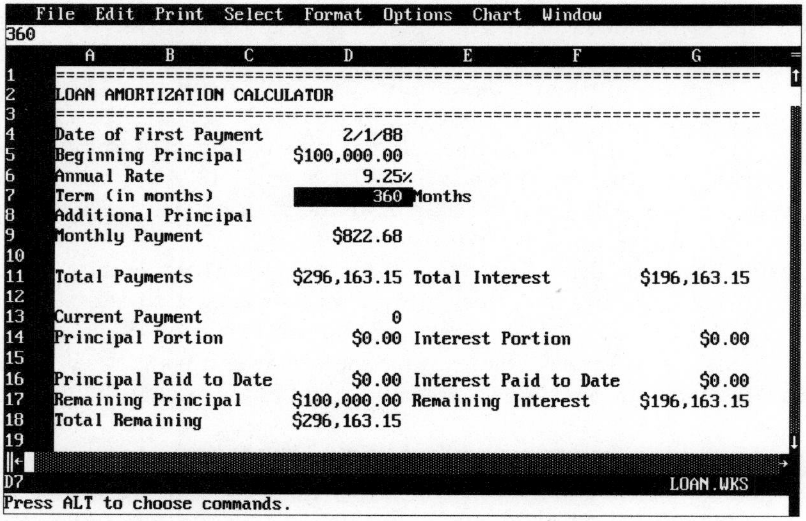

```
 File  Edit  Print  Select  Format  Options  Chart  Window
360
        A        B       C        D          E        F        G          =
1   =============================================================================
2   LOAN AMORTIZATION CALCULATOR
3   =============================================================================
4   Date of First Payment         2/1/88
5   Beginning Principal        $100,000.00
6   Annual Rate                    9.25%
7   Term (in months)                  360 Months
8   Additional Principal
9   Monthly Payment                $822.68
10
11  Total Payments             $296,163.15 Total Interest     $196,163.15
12
13  Current Payment                     0
14  Principal Portion               $0.00 Interest Portion          $0.00
15
16  Principal Paid to Date          $0.00 Interest Paid to Date     $0.00
17  Remaining Principal        $100,000.00 Remaining Interest  $196,163.15
18  Total Remaining            $296,163.15
19
D7                                                                  LOAN.WKS
Press ALT to choose commands.
```

Figure 5-6.

Looking at the Amortization Table

After the spreadsheet calculates the monthly payment and other values, press PgDn to look at the Amortization table for the loan. Figure 5-7 shows the first part of the table. As you can see, the table contains the payment, date, rate, total amount, interest amount, principal amount, and ending principal balance for each payment. Although you can't see it on the current screen, column H contains a running total of the interest paid.

```
 File  Edit  Print  Select  Format  Options  Chart  Window
=IF(C26=C25,IF(G25<D25-(G25*(C26/12)),G25*(1+C26/12),D25),PMT(G25,C26/12,$D$7-A2
      A       B       C       D         E          F          G
20                          Total                           Ending
21                          Monthly    Interest   Principal  Principal
22   Payment  Date    Rate   Payment    Payment    Payment   Balance
23
24       1   2/1/88  9.25%   $822.68    $770.83    $51.84    $99,948.16
25       2   3/1/88  9.25%   $822.68    $770.43    $52.24    $99,895.92
26       3   4/1/88  9.25%   $822.68    $770.03    $52.64    $99,843.27
27       4   5/1/88  9.25%   $822.68    $769.63    $53.05    $99,790.22
28       5   6/1/88  9.25%   $822.68    $769.22    $53.46    $99,736.76
29       6   7/1/88  9.25%   $822.68    $768.80    $53.87    $99,682.89
30       7   8/1/88  9.25%   $822.68    $768.39    $54.29    $99,628.60
31       8   9/1/88  9.25%   $822.68    $767.97    $54.70    $99,573.90
32       9  10/1/88  9.25%   $822.68    $767.55    $55.13    $99,518.77
33      10  11/1/88  9.25%   $822.68    $767.12    $55.55    $99,463.22
34      11  12/1/88  9.25%   $822.68    $766.70    $55.98    $99,407.24
35      12   1/1/89  9.25%   $822.68    $766.26    $56.41    $99,350.83
36      13   2/1/89  9.25%   $822.68    $765.83    $56.85    $99,293.98
37      14   3/1/89  9.25%   $822.68    $765.39    $57.28    $99,236.70
38      15   4/1/89  9.25%   $822.68    $764.95    $57.73    $99,178.97
D26                                                         LOAN.WKS
Press ALT to choose commands.
```

Figure 5-7.

To look at a different part of the Amortization table, use your mouse or the cursor movement keys to move to the cell you want to see. For example, to view the next screenful of payments, press PgDn. To move directly to the bottom of the table, press Ctrl-Down Arrow. To return to the top, press Ctrl-Up Arrow. To move to a figure in column H, press Ctrl-Right Arrow. To see column A, press Ctrl-Left Arrow.

To move to a specific row, press the Go To key ([F5]), type *A* followed by the row number, and press Enter or choose OK. For example, to move to row 200, press [F5], type *A200*, and press Enter or choose OK. Now, press Ctrl-Home to move the cursor to cell A1 and display the Assumptions and Analysis areas.

Analyzing the Loan

The Analysis area occupies the lower half of the first screen in the template. The formulas in this area compute several important statistics about your loan. For example, the formula in cell D11 calculates the total amount you'll have to pay to repay the loan: $296,163.15 in the example. Cell G11 computes the total amount of interest you'll pay: $196,163.15.

The formulas in rows 13, 14, 16, 17, and 18 allow you to analyze the status of the loan at any time. All these formulas depend on the payment number you enter in cell D13. To use this part of the spreadsheet, enter a number in cell D13 and recalculate the spreadsheet. To analyze the status of the loan after payment number 12, for example, you would enter the value *12* in cell D13 and press [F9] to recalculate the spreadsheet. Do not enter a value in cell D13 that is less than 0 or greater than the number of payments in the term of the loan.

Because cell D13 in the example contains the value 0, the values in this area represent the status of the loan before any payments have been made. Cell D17 shows the remaining principal, $100,000.00, which matches the beginning principal balance. Cell G17 computes the total unpaid interest, $196,163.15, which matches the total amount of interest to be paid across the life of the loan (calculated in cell G17). Cell C18 returns the total amount unpaid, $296,163.15, which matches the total amount payable to amortize the loan (calculated in cell D11). The other formulas, which compute the principal and interest portion of the current payment and the total amounts of principal and interest paid to date, return the value 0.

If you enter a number other than 0 in cell D13, these formulas return the status of the loan at a specific point. To see how these formulas work, check the status of the loan after 12 payments. Enter the value *12* in cell D13 and press the Calc key ([F9]). After a moment, your screen looks like Figure 5-8.

The numbers in rows 14, 16, 17, and 18 now represent the status of the loan after payment number 12. The value in cell D14, $56.41, is the principal portion of the twelfth payment; the value in cell G14, $766.26, is the interest portion. The value in cell D16, $649.17, is the total amount of principal repaid. Similarly, the value in cell G16, $9,222.94, is the total amount of interest paid to date. The value in cell D17, $99,350.83, is the unpaid principal after the twelfth payment, and the value in cell G17, $9,222.94, is the unpaid interest, assuming that the loan is not paid off early. Finally, the value in cell D18, $296,291.05, is the total amount remaining to be paid.

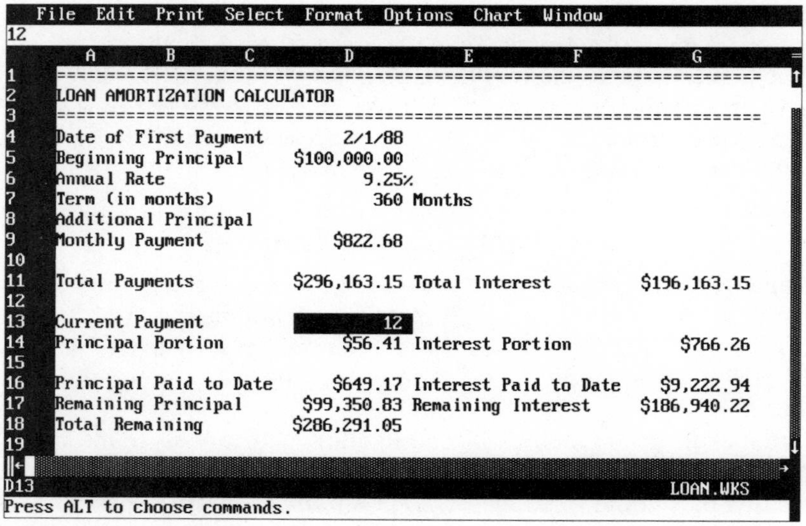

Figure 5-8.

Changing Assumptions

You can change any of your assumptions—date of first payment, beginning principal balance, annual rate, or term assumptions—at any time. You might change an assumption to correct an error or to test its effect. To change an assumption, simply move the cursor to the appropriate cell, type the new value, and then recalculate the spreadsheet.

For example, suppose you want to see the effect of changing the amount you borrow from $100,000.00 to $95,000.00. Move the cursor to cell D5, type *95000*, and press [F9] to recalculate the spreadsheet. Changing the principal from $100,000.00 to $95,000.00 reduces the monthly payment by nearly $40.00. In addition, all the numbers in the Analysis area change to reflect the new terms of the loan.

Here's a little trick to let you gauge the effect of a changed assumption on the monthly payment without taking the time to recalculate the entire spreadsheet. Works lets you recalculate any cell merely by editing the cell. Simply move the cursor to that cell, press the Edit key ([F2]), and then press Enter. For example, suppose you want to see how much your monthly payment will change if the annual interest rate falls to 9.00%. First, move the cursor to cell D6 and enter the number *.09*. Then move to cell D9, press [F2], and press Enter. Works recomputes the monthly payment without recalculating the rest of the spreadsheet. Figure 5-9 shows the result.

If you use this technique, be sure to "clean up after yourself." In other words, either restore the assumptions to their original condition or recalculate the entire spreadsheet so that the Amortization table and the Analysis area reflect the new

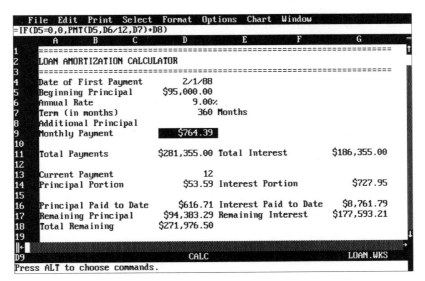

Figure 5-9.

assumptions. In the preceding example, you can clean up by moving the cursor back to cell D6 and typing the value .0925. (Then, you can recalculate cell D9 to restore its previous value.)

Special Features

So far, we've looked at only the basic capabilities of the Loan Amortization Calculator. This spreadsheet has a few additional features to handle special situations. First, the template allows you to make additional principal payments—monthly or only for selected months. Second, it lets you change the interest rate at any point in the term of the loan.

Paying additional principal

One of the best ways to speed up the repayment of a loan is to pay extra principal each month in addition to your normal monthly payment. Paying even a little extra principal each month can have a tremendous impact on the amount of time required to repay the loan and on the total amount of interest you pay. The Loan Amortization Calculator allows you to pay extra principal in two ways. You can elect to pay a fixed amount of additional principal each month, or you can choose to pay additional principal only in selected months.

If you plan to pay extra principal each month, enter the additional monthly amount in cell D8 and then recalculate the spreadsheet. The spreadsheet recomputes your monthly payment and updates the values in the Amortization table to reflect the change.

Suppose, for example, you plan to pay an additional $25.00 toward the principal each month. First, move the cursor to cell D8, type *25*, and press Enter. Then, press the Calc key ([F9]) to recalculate the spreadsheet. Figure 5-10 shows the result. Notice that the total amount you have to repay decreased from $281,355.00 to just $250,543.03. Also notice that the total interest you pay decreased to $155,543.03. Now, use the Go To key ([F5]) to move the cursor to cell A334; notice that paying $25.00 of additional principal each month also decreased the effective term of the loan from 360 months to only 311 months.

To make special additional principal payments whenever you choose, edit the entry in the Total Monthly Payment column of the Amortization table (column D) for the payment you want to change. Add the additional amount to the formula in that cell. The spreadsheet then carries the additional payment forward through the table until you explicitly reedit the formula. To do that, move down the table to the row for the payment you want to reduce, edit the formula in column D, and subtract the additional amount from that formula.

For example, suppose that you want to pay $100.00 of additional principal each month for the first 12 months of the loan. Begin by editing the formula in cell D24 (the entry in the Total Monthly Payment column for the first payment) to include

```
  File  Edit  Print  Select  Format  Options  Chart  Window
25
        A       B       C        D         E        F          G
1  ============================================================
2  LOAN AMORTIZATION CALCULATOR
3  ============================================================
4  Date of First Payment        2/1/88
5  Beginning Principal     $95,000.00
6  Annual Rate                  9.25%
7  Term (in months)          360 Months
8  Additional Principal        $25.00
9  Monthly Payment            $806.54
10
11 Total Payments         $250,543.03 Total Interest       $155,543.03
12
13 Current Payment             12
14 Principal Portion          $80.79 Interest Portion       $725.75
15
16 Principal Paid to Date    $929.76 Interest Paid to Date   $8,748.74
17 Remaining Principal    $94,070.24 Remaining Interest   $146,794.29
18 Total Remaining       $240,864.53
19
D8                                                   LOAN.WKS
Press ALT to choose commands.
```

Figure 5-10.

your $100.00 special payment. To do so, move the cursor to cell D24, press the Edit key ([F2]), type *+100*, and press Enter. Next, move down to cell D36 (the cell in the Total Monthly Payment column for the month in which you want to stop paying extra principal), press [F2], type *–100*, and press Enter.

Now, press the Calc key ([F9]) to recalculate the entire spreadsheet. Figure 5-11 on the following page shows the first screen of the Amortization table after the addition of the special payment. Notice that the total amount for payments 1 through 12 is now $906.54, but that the total amount of payment 13 is only $806.54. The spreadsheet passed your change through the table from row 24 to row 35. Figure 5-12 shows the home screen (the screen displayed when you press Ctrl-Home) after this change is made. Notice that all the numbers in the Analysis area changed slightly as a result of the additional payments.

To take another example, suppose that you get a special gift of $1000.00 shortly before you're due to make the tenth payment on your loan. You decide to use this gift to repay a portion of your principal. To enter this payment, edit the formula in cell D33 (the entry in the Total Monthly Payment column for the tenth payment) to include your $1000.00 special payment. To do this, move the cursor to cell D33, press the Edit key ([F2]), type *+1000*, and press Enter. Then, move the cursor down one cell, press [F2], type *–1000*, and press Enter. Finally, press the Calc key ([F9]) to recalculate the entire spreadsheet. Figure 5-13 on page 139 shows the first screen of the Amortization table after the addition of the special payment. Notice that payment number 10 is now $1906.54, while all the other payments are still $906.54 or $806.54.

```
  File   Edit   Print   Select   Format   Options   Chart   Window
=IF(C36=C35,IF(G35<D35-(G35*(C36/12)),G35*(1+C36/12),D35),PMT(G35,C36/12,$D$7-A3
         A        B       C         D          E          F          G
18  Total Remaining              $229,096.01                                      ↑
19
20                            Total                                  Ending
21                           Monthly     Interest    Principal     Principal
22  Payment    Date    Rate  Payment     Payment      Payment       Balance
23  ───────  ──────  ─────  ────────   ──────────   ──────────   ──────────
24     1     2/1/88   9.25%  $906.54     $732.29      $174.25     $94,825.75
25     2     3/1/88   9.25%  $906.54     $730.95      $175.59     $94,650.16
26     3     4/1/88   9.25%  $906.54     $729.59      $176.95     $94,473.21
27     4     5/1/88   9.25%  $906.54     $728.23      $178.31     $94,294.90
28     5     6/1/88   9.25%  $906.54     $726.86      $179.69     $94,115.21
29     6     7/1/88   9.25%  $906.54     $725.47      $181.07     $93,934.14
30     7     8/1/88   9.25%  $906.54     $724.08      $182.47     $93,751.68
31     8     9/1/88   9.25%  $906.54     $722.67      $183.87     $93,567.81
32     9    10/1/88   9.25%  $906.54     $721.25      $185.29     $93,382.52
33    10    11/1/88   9.25%  $906.54     $719.82      $186.72     $93,195.80
34    11    12/1/88   9.25%  $906.54     $718.38      $188.16     $93,007.64
35    12     1/1/89   9.25%  $906.54     $716.93      $189.61     $92,818.03
36    13     2/1/89   9.25%  $806.54     $715.47       $91.07     $92,726.96      ↓
‖←▓▓                                                                    →
D36                                                              LOAN.WKS
Press ALT to choose commands.
```

Figure 5-11.

```
  File   Edit   Print   Select   Format   Options   Chart   Window
"========
         A        B       C         D          E          F          G
1   ========================================================================
2   LOAN AMORTIZATION CALCULATOR                                              ↑
3   ========================================================================
4   Date of First Payment         2/1/88
5   Beginning Principal        $95,000.00
6   Annual Rate                     9.25%
7   Term (in months)              360 Months
8   Additional Principal          $25.00
9   Monthly Payment              $806.54
10
11  Total Payments            $239,974.51 Total Interest          $144,974.51
12
13  Current Payment                   12
14  Principal Portion            $189.61 Interest Portion            $716.93
15
16  Principal Paid to Date     $2,181.97 Interest Paid to Date     $8,696.53
17  Remaining Principal       $92,818.03 Remaining Interest      $136,277.98
18  Total Remaining          $229,096.01                                      ↓
19
‖←▓▓                                                                    →
A1                                                              LOAN.WKS
Press ALT to choose commands.
```

Figure 5-12.

```
 File   Edit   Print   Select   Format   Options   Chart   Window
=IF(C34=C33,IF(G33<D33-(G33*(C34/12)),G33*(1+C34/12),D33),PMT(G33,C34/12,$D$7-A3
       A        B         C          D           E          F            G
20                                 Total                                Ending
21                                 Monthly     Interest   Principal   Principal
22  Payment     Date     Rate      Payment     Payment    Payment     Balance
23  -------   -------   ------    ---------   ---------   ---------   ---------
24        1   2/1/88    9.25%      $906.54     $732.29     $174.25   $94,825.75
25        2   3/1/88    9.25%      $906.54     $730.95     $175.59   $94,650.16
26        3   4/1/88    9.25%      $906.54     $729.59     $176.95   $94,473.21
27        4   5/1/88    9.25%      $906.54     $728.23     $178.31   $94,294.90
28        5   6/1/88    9.25%      $906.54     $726.86     $179.69   $94,115.21
29        6   7/1/88    9.25%      $906.54     $725.47     $181.07   $93,934.14
30        7   8/1/88    9.25%      $906.54     $724.08     $182.47   $93,751.68
31        8   9/1/88    9.25%      $906.54     $722.67     $183.87   $93,567.81
32        9  10/1/88    9.25%      $906.54     $721.25     $185.29   $93,382.52
33       10  11/1/88    9.25%    $1,906.54     $719.82   $1,186.72   $92,195.80
34       11  12/1/88    9.25%      $906.54     $710.68     $195.87   $91,999.93
35       12   1/1/89    9.25%      $906.54     $709.17     $197.38   $91,802.56
36       13   2/1/89    9.25%      $806.54     $707.64      $98.90   $91,703.66
37       14   3/1/89    9.25%      $806.54     $706.88      $99.66   $91,604.00
38       15   4/1/89    9.25%      $806.54     $706.11     $100.43   $91,503.57
D34                                                           LOAN.WKS
Press ALT to choose commands.
```

Figure 5-13.

Variable interest rates

These days, many mortgages offer variable interest rates. While the specifics of these variable-rate loans differ greatly, they all have more or less the same structure: After a certain period of time, the bank can raise or lower the annual rate on your loan. Typically, an increase in the annual rate means an increase in your monthly payment, and a decrease in the rate means a decrease in the payment.

If you are considering a variable rate mortgage (or if you already have one), then you'll be glad to know that the Loan Amortization Calculator can handle it. To enter a new interest rate, change the entry in the Rate column of the Amortization table (column C) for the payment in which the new rate takes effect. The spreadsheet passes this change through the Amortization table.

For example, suppose that the rate rises from 9.25% to 10.00% at the end of the second year of the mortgage. To update the Amortization table, move the cursor to cell C48 (the cell in the Rate column for payment 25, the first payment at the new rate), type .1, and press Enter. Now, press the Calc key ([F9]) to recalculate the spreadsheet. As shown in Figure 5-14 on the following page, the rate for each payment after payment 25 has changed to 10.00%, and the total amount of each payment has changed to reflect the new rate.

You can change the interest rate as often as you wish. You can even use a different interest rate for every payment. To make each change, move the cursor to the appropriate cell in column C and enter the new rate. Each new rate you enter remains in effect until you enter another new rate or until the loan is fully amortized.

```
     File  Edit  Print  Select  Format  Options  Chart  Window
0.1
        A       B        C         D          E          F         G
46      23  12/1/89    9.25%    $806.54    $699.75    $106.79   $90,671.78
47      24   1/1/90    9.25%    $806.54    $698.93    $107.61   $90,564.16
48      25   2/1/90   10.00%    $830.06    $754.70     $75.36   $90,488.81
49      26   3/1/90   10.00%    $830.06    $754.07     $75.98   $90,412.82
50      27   4/1/90   10.00%    $830.06    $753.44     $76.62   $90,336.21
51      28   5/1/90   10.00%    $830.06    $752.80     $77.26   $90,258.95
52      29   6/1/90   10.00%    $830.06    $752.16     $77.90   $90,181.05
53      30   7/1/90   10.00%    $830.06    $751.51     $78.55   $90,102.50
54      31   8/1/90   10.00%    $830.06    $750.85     $79.20   $90,023.30
55      32   9/1/90   10.00%    $830.06    $750.19     $79.86   $89,943.44
56      33  10/1/90   10.00%    $830.06    $749.53     $80.53   $89,862.91
57      34  11/1/90   10.00%    $830.06    $748.86     $81.20   $89,781.71
58      35  12/1/90   10.00%    $830.06    $748.18     $81.88   $89,699.83
59      36   1/1/91   10.00%    $830.06    $747.50     $82.56   $89,617.28
60      37   2/1/91   10.00%    $830.06    $746.81     $83.25   $89,534.03
61      38   3/1/91   10.00%    $830.06    $746.12     $83.94   $89,450.09
62      39   4/1/91   10.00%    $830.06    $745.42     $84.64   $89,365.45
63      40   5/1/91   10.00%    $830.06    $744.71     $85.35   $89,280.10
64      41   6/1/91   10.00%    $830.06    $744.00     $86.06   $89,194.05
C48                                                              LOAN.WKS
Press ALT to choose commands.
```

Figure 5-14.

Printing and Saving

After you set up an Amortization table for a new loan, save that spreadsheet to a new file. To do this, select Save As from the File menu. Then, if you want to save the file in a directory other than the current directory, choose that directory from the Other Drives & Directories box and choose OK. Next, type a new name for the spreadsheet, and press Enter to save the file. If you want to save the file in the current directory, simply type a name and press Enter or choose OK. Choose a name for the file that clearly identifies its contents.

Be sure to save your filled-in amortization spreadsheets under a name other than the name you used for the original, empty Loan Amortization Calculator. If you save a filled-in spreadsheet under the same name as the template, the original version is replaced with the filled-in version.

To print the entire Loan Amortization Calculator, first choose Layout from the Print menu and change any print settings you want to change. You might want to change the margins and define a header and footer. Because this template is narrow enough to be printed on standard 8 1/2-inch-wide paper, you probably don't need to change the Page Width setting. Next, use the Font command to select the font you want Works to use to print the report. If you want to squeeze the entire report onto one page, choose a relatively compressed font (such as Elite) and a small point size (such as 6 or 8).

After you adjust the settings, choose Print from the Print menu to display the Print dialog box. Then, adjust any settings and choose Print to print the report.

To print only a portion of the Loan Amortization Calculator, you need to define the print area before you begin printing. For example, if you want to print only the Assumptions and Analysis areas—the first screen of the spreadsheet—first highlight the range A1:G19 and select the Set Print Area command from the Print menu. Then, use the Layout and Font commands to make any needed adjustments to the Works print settings. Finally, select Print from the Print menu and choose the Print button to print the selected range.

CONCLUSION

The Loan Amortization Calculator is one of the most useful and interesting spreadsheets in this book. You're likely to find a reason to use it sometime soon. Even if you don't use the spreadsheet, however, you can employ some of the tricks and techniques you learned in building it. Feel free to borrow from or modify the template in any way you wish. Your only limit is your imagination!

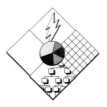

Breakeven Analysis

Have you ever started a business? Or are you responsible for managing new products at the company for which you work? If so, then you've probably used breakeven analysis at some time or another. It is a critical part of the evaluation of any new business venture or product. Breakeven analysis allows you to determine the breakeven point—the number of units of a product or service you have to sell before total costs exactly match total revenues. If you sell more than the breakeven number of units, you make a profit; if you sell less than the breakeven volume, you lose money.

This template calculates the breakeven point for a product, given its price, per unit variable costs, and total fixed costs. It also includes a breakeven chart that plots the relationship between your costs and sales and identifies the precise breakeven point. The spreadsheet also demonstrates a clever technique that lets you create a chart dynamically, based on the result of a formula.

ABOUT THE TEMPLATE

Figure 6-1 on the following page shows the template for Breakeven Analysis as it looks when you first create it. Figure 6-2, also on the following page, shows the spreadsheet with some sample information entered in it. As you can see, the template has only one section. You enter your assumptions about unit price, unit variable costs, and total fixed costs in cells C5 through C7. Cell C9 contains a formula that computes the actual breakeven point.

Cells B14 through F14 contain formulas that compute the dollar sales, variable costs, fixed costs, total costs, and net income (profit) at each of five levels of sales. Cells A14 through A18 contain formulas that compute these five levels of sales by referring to the breakeven result in cell C9. These formulas create a range of sales volumes that brackets the breakeven point. The value in cell A14 is always 0, and the value in cell A18 is always approximately twice the breakeven volume.

The results in cells A14 through F18 are the basis for a chart that depicts the relationships between unit sales and dollar sales, variable costs, fixed costs, total costs, and net income.

```
 File  Edit  Print  Select  Format  Options  Chart  Window
"============
       A          B          C          D          E          F        =
1   =========================================================================↑
2   BREAKEVEN ANALYSIS
3   =========================================================================
4
5   Sale Price/Unit:
6   Variable Cost/Unit:
7   Fixed Costs:
8
9   Breakeven Volume:              ERR
10
11     Unit      Dollar     Variable     Fixed      Total        Net
12     Sales      Sales       Costs       Costs      Costs      Income
13   --------   --------   --------    --------   --------   --------
14        0        $0         $0          $0         $0         $0
15      ERR        $0         $0          $0         $0         $0
16      ERR        $0         $0          $0         $0         $0
17      ERR        $0         $0          $0         $0         $0
18      ERR        $0         $0          $0         $0         $0
19                                                                       ↓
‖←█                                                                     →
A1                            CALC                    CL    SHEET1.WKS
Press ALT to choose commands.
```

Figure 6-1.

```
 File  Edit  Print  Select  Format  Options  Chart  Window
"============
       A          B          C          D          E          F        =
1   =========================================================================↑
2   BREAKEVEN ANALYSIS
3   =========================================================================
4
5   Sale Price/Unit:           $25.00
6   Variable Cost/Unit:        $16.00
7   Fixed Costs:              $120,000
8
9   Breakeven Volume:          13,333
10
11     Unit      Dollar     Variable     Fixed      Total        Net
12     Sales      Sales       Costs       Costs      Costs      Income
13   --------   --------   --------    --------   --------   --------
14        0        $0         $0      $120,000   $120,000   ($120,000)
15     7500    $187,500   $120,000    $120,000   $240,000    ($52,500)
16    15000    $375,000   $240,000    $120,000   $360,000     $15,000
17    22500    $562,500   $360,000    $120,000   $480,000     $82,500
18    30000    $750,000   $480,000    $120,000   $600,000    $150,000
19                                                                       ↓
‖←█                                                                     →
A1                                                    CL    PROD1BE.WKS
Press ALT to choose commands.
```

Figure 6-2.

CREATING THE TEMPLATE

Breakeven Analysis is one of the easiest templates in this book to create. To begin, select New on the File menu if the New dialog box is not already on your screen. Next, choose Spreadsheet and select New to open a new spreadsheet. Now, select Manual Calculation from the Options menu. Putting Works in the manual recalculation mode eliminates delays as you build the spreadsheet because it prevents the program from recalculating the entire spreadsheet after each entry.

Next, you need to change the widths of columns B through F from 10 characters to 12. To do this, highlight at least one cell in each of these columns, select Width from the Format menu, type *12*, and press Enter or choose OK.

Next, change the default format for the spreadsheet from General to Dollar with zero decimal places. To do so, you need to highlight the entire spreadsheet and then choose the appropriate command from the Format menu. First, hold down the Shift and Ctrl keys and press [F8]. When the entire spreadsheet is highlighted, select Dollar from the Format menu. When the Dollar dialog box appears, type *0* and then press Enter or choose OK.

Making Entries

Now, you are ready to make entries in the spreadsheet, beginning with the header labels in rows 1, 2, and 3. First, enter a label consisting of a quotation mark followed by 12 equal signs (*"============*) in cell A1. Then, highlight the range A1:G1 and select Fill Right from the Edit menu to copy this label to cells B1 through G1. Then, highlight the range A1:G1 (if it's not still highlighted), select Copy from the Edit menu, highlight cell A3, and press Enter. This command copies the labels from the range A1:G1 to the range A3:G3.

Next, move the cell pointer to cell A2 and enter the label *BREAKEVEN ANALYSIS*. Then, enter the labels *Sale Price/Unit:, Variable Cost/Unit:,* and *Fixed Costs:* in cells A5, A6, and A7. When these labels are in place, assign Dollar format with two decimal places to cells C5 and C6. To do this, highlight the range C5:C6, select Dollar from the Format menu, type *2*, and press Enter or choose OK.

Now, enter the label *Breakeven Volume:* in cell A9. Then, move to cell C9 and enter the formula

=C7/(C5-C6)

This formula uses the values in cells C5, C6, and C7 to calculate the breakeven volume. The formula simply divides the total fixed costs by the difference between the unit sales price and the unit variable costs. (This difference is sometimes called the contribution margin.) Because cells C5, C6, and C7 are currently empty (and thus have the value 0), this formula will return the message *ERR*. (Works always returns *ERR* when it tries to divide by 0.) These ERR results will go away when you enter your assumptions in cells C5, C6, and C7. After you enter this breakeven formula, assign Comma (0) format to cell C9. To do this, select Comma from the Format menu, type *0*, and press Enter or choose OK.

The rest of the template calculates the values that Works graphs in the breakeven chart. To create this portion of the spreadsheet, begin by entering the labels *Unit, Dollar, Variable, Fixed, Total*, and *Net* in cells A11, B11, C11, D11, E11, and F11. Then, enter *Sales, Sales, Costs, Costs, Costs*, and *Income* in cells A12, B12, C12, D12, E12, and F12.

Next, enter a label consisting of a quotation mark followed by eight hyphens ("--------) in cell A13. Then, highlight the range A13:F13 and select Fill Right from the Edit menu to copy this label to cells B13 through F13.

Now, change the alignment of the labels in cells A11 through F13 to right-aligned. To do this, highlight the range A11:F13, select Style from the Format menu, choose Right, and press Enter or choose OK.

Next, enter the formulas in cells A14 through F18 that compute the values Works uses to create the breakeven chart. To begin, enter the value *0* in cell A14. Then, move to cell A18 and enter the complex formula

```
=ROUND(C9*2,
IF(C9>10000000,-7,
IF(C9>1000000,-6,
IF(C9>100000,-5,
IF(C9>10000,-4,
IF(C9>1000,-3,
IF(C9>100,-2,
IF(C9>10,-1,
C9))))))))
```

(Of course, you'll actually enter the formula on one line; it appears here on several lines to make it easier to understand.) Works uses the value returned by this formula as the top limit for the x axis in the chart. The formula simply doubles the breakeven volume in cell C9, and then rounds the result to one significant digit. If the breakeven point is 11, for example, the formula returns the value 20; if the breakeven point is 251, the formula returns the value 500; if the breakeven point is 3289, the function returns the value 7000; and so forth.

This formula uses the ROUND function to round the result of the formula C9*2. The ROUND function has the form

=ROUND(*value,number of places*)

where *value* is the number you want to round, and *number of places* is the number of places you want after the decimal point in the rounded result. For example, the function =ROUND(123.45678,2) returns the value 123.46. If you reduce the number of places, the function =ROUND(123.45678,0) returns the value 123.

Although the number of places is usually expressed as a positive number or as 0, it can also be negative. A negative expression for *number of places* in a ROUND function tells it to round to the left of the decimal point. For example, the function =ROUND(123.45678,–1) returns the value 120. The function =ROUND(123.45678,–2) returns the value 100.

The series of IF functions tests the value in cell C9 and supplies the appropriate expression for *number of places* in the ROUND function based on the size of the value in that cell. For example, if cell C9 contains a value greater than 100, then *number of places* is –2. If cell C8 contains a value greater than 100,000, then *number of places* is –5.

After you enter this formula in cell A18, move to cell A15 and enter the formula

=A14+ (A$18/4)

This formula divides the value in cell A18 by 4 and adds the result to the value in cell A14. In fact, because cell A14 contains the value 0, the result of this formula is always one-fourth of the value in cell A18. Highlight the range A15:A17 and select Fill Down from the Edit menu to copy the formula from cell A15 to cells A16 and A17. Because the reference to cell A14 in the original formula is relative, it changes as you copy the formula to the new cells. The mixed reference to cell A18, however, does not change (as you copy it vertically). For instance, the formula copied in cell A16 is *=A15+(A$18/4)*. The result of the formula in cell A16 is exactly one-half of the value in cell A18. The value in cell A17 is three-quarters of the value in cell A18. The results of these formulas split the range between 0 and the value in cell A18 into four equal increments.

Because the formulas in cells A15, A16, A17, and A18 refer to cell C9—which currently returns *ERR*—these formulas also return *ERR*. These ERR results will go away when you enter your assumptions in cells C5, C6, and C7.

Before you go on, change the format of cells A14 through A18 from Dollar with zero decimals to Fixed with zero decimals. To do this, highlight the range A14:A18, choose Fixed from the Format menu, type *0*, and press Enter or choose OK.

Next, enter the formula *=C$5*A14* in cell B14. This formula computes the dollar sales for the first level of unit sales (0). Then, move to cell C14 and enter the formula *=C$6*A14*, which computes the total variable costs at the first level of sales. Now, move to cell D14 and enter the formula *=C$7* to reference the total fixed costs assumption in cell C7. Next, enter the formula *=C14+D14* in cell E14. This formula computes total costs at the first level of sales by adding the total variable costs (cell C14) to the total fixed costs (cell D14). Finally, enter the formula *=B14–E14* in cell F14. This formula computes the net income at the first level of sales by subtracting the total costs at that level of sales (cell E14) from the total dollar sales (cell B14).

After you enter these formulas, copy them to cells B15:F18. To do this, highlight the range B14:F18 and select Fill Down from the Edit menu. The relative references in these formulas change as Works copies the formulas down the spreadsheet. However, the mixed references to cells C5, C6, and C7 in the formulas remain unchanged. For example, cell B15 contains the formula *=C$5*A15*, cell C16 contains the formula *=C$6*A16*, cell D17 contains the formula *=C$7*, and so forth. These formulas calculate the dollar sales, variable costs, fixed costs, total costs, and net income at each of the levels of unit sales specified by the formulas in cells A14 through A18.

Figure 6-3 shows your spreadsheet as it now appears. As you can see, many formulas in the spreadsheet return the message *ERR*. This occurs because cells C5, C6, and C7 are currently empty and thus have a value of 0. These ERR results go away when you enter your assumptions in cells C5, C6, and C7.

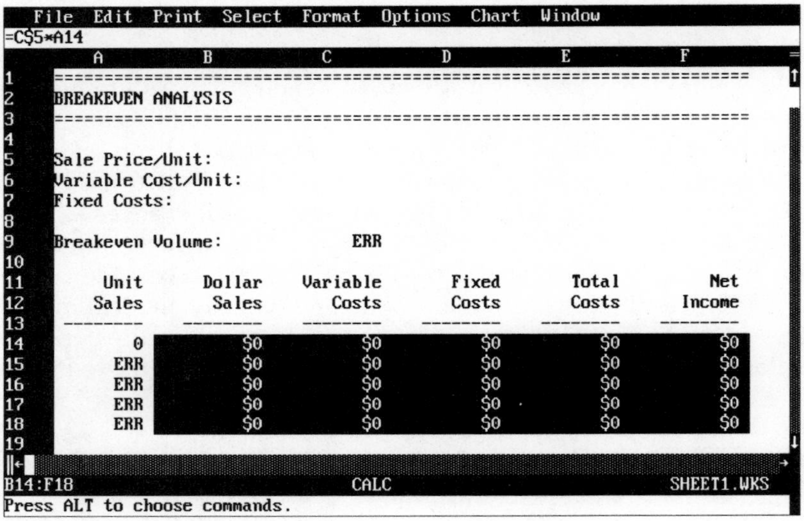

```
 File  Edit  Print  Select  Format  Options  Chart  Window
=C$5*A14
         A           B           C           D           E           F
==============================================================================
1
2  BREAKEVEN ANALYSIS
3  ==============================================================================
4
5  Sale Price/Unit:
6  Variable Cost/Unit:
7  Fixed Costs:
8
9  Breakeven Volume:             ERR
10
11     Unit       Dollar     Variable      Fixed       Total        Net
12     Sales      Sales       Costs        Costs       Costs       Income
13    --------   --------   ---------    --------    --------    --------
14        0         $0         $0          $0          $0          $0
15       ERR        $0         $0          $0          $0          $0
16       ERR        $0         $0          $0          $0          $0
17       ERR        $0         $0          $0 .        $0          $0
18       ERR        $0         $0          $0          $0          $0
19
B14:F18                         CALC                        SHEET1.WKS
Press ALT to choose commands.
```

Figure 6-3.

Creating the Chart

Now you're ready to set up a chart to show the relationships between unit sales and the other values in the table. To begin, select Define from the Chart menu. When you do this, Works creates a new chart and drops you to the chart sublevel. At this point, you can begin to define the chart. First, pull down the Format menu and choose Line to create a Line chart.

Next, you need to specify the series of y values for the chart. This chart actually has five y series. The first y series includes the range B14:B18 (Dollar Sales), the second y series the range C14:C18 (Variable Costs), the third series the range D14:D18 (Fixed Costs), the fourth the range E14:E18 (Total Costs), and the fifth the range F14:F18 (Net Income).

To specify the range B14:B18 as the first y series, highlight the range B14:B18 and select 1st Y-Series from the Data menu. Then, highlight the range C14:C18 and select 2nd Y-Series to define the range C14:C18 as the second y series. Highlight the range D14:D18 and select 3rd Y-Series. To define the fourth y series, highlight the range E14:E18 and select 4th Y-Series. Finally, highlight the range F14:F18 and select 5th Y-Series from the Data menu.

After you define the five y ranges, specify the range A14:A18 as the x range. To do this, highlight the range A14:A18 and select X-Series from the Data menu.

Next, you need to add some titles to the chart. Pull down the Data menu and choose Titles to display the Titles dialog box. Then, type the name of your company or the name of the product you are analyzing in the Chart Title entry box (we'll type *ANY COMPANY, INC.*). Next, move to the Subtitle entry box and type *Breakeven Analysis*. Then, enter the title *Unit Sales* in the X-Axis entry box. Finally, enter the title *Dollars* in the Y-Axis entry box. After you type these titles, press Enter or choose OK.

In addition to the titles, add some legends—one to identify each of the five y ranges in the chart. Because you can assign a legend to only a single y series each time you access the Legends dialog box, you have to select Legends five times to define legends for all five y series.

To specify the legend for the first y series, pull down the Data menu, select Legends, highlight 1st Y in the Series box, move the cursor to the Legend entry box, type *Dollar Sales*, and press Enter or choose OK. To specify the legend for the second y series, pull down the Data menu again, select Legends again, highlight 2nd Y in the Series box, type *Variable Costs* in the Legend entry box, and press Enter or choose OK. Now, repeat these steps to assign the legends *Fixed Costs*, *Total Costs*, and *Net Income* to the third, fourth, and fifth y series, respectively.

The breakeven chart is now completely defined. However, if you select View from the Chart menu at this point, your screen will look like Figure 6-4. Because you haven't entered any values in cells C5, C6, and C7 of the spreadsheet, the chart doesn't look like much yet. When you enter those values, the chart will begin to display results. (Press the Esc key or click with your mouse to exit the View mode.)

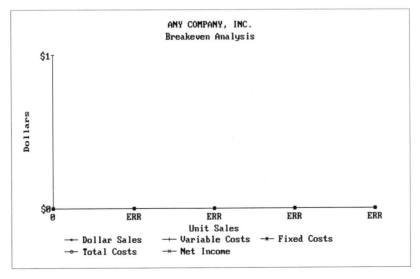

Figure 6-4.

Naming the Chart

Works assigns a default name to each chart you create. When you created the chart shown in Figure 6-4, for example, Works gave it the name CHART1. Although these default names are perfectly adequate, you may want to give your charts names that describe their purposes. For example, you might give the chart shown in Figure 6-4 the name BREAKEVEN. To do so, press Enter or click with your mouse to return to the chart creation sublevel. Next, pull down the Chart menu, choose Charts, and highlight the name CHART1 (the current name of the chart) in the Charts list box. Then, type *BREAKEVEN* in the Name box and choose Rename.

Saving the Spreadsheet

After you create this spreadsheet, save it for future use. The first time you save the template, select Save As from the File menu. Then, if you want to save the file in a directory other than the current one, choose that directory from the Other Drives & Directories list box and choose OK. Next, type a name (such as *BRKEVEN.WKS*), and press Enter or choose OK to save the file. If you want to save the file in the current directory, simply type a filename and press Enter or choose OK. Because the chart is an integral part of the spreadsheet, Works saves it along with the spreadsheet. If you've already saved the spreadsheet, you can save it again by choosing Save from the File menu.

USING THE SPREADSHEET

To use the spreadsheet you created for Breakeven Analysis, begin by opening the template. (If you just created the template, skip this step.) First, choose Open from the File menu. Then, if the file you want to open is in the current directory, either type the filename under which you saved the template, including the extension (for example, *BRKEVEN.WKS*) or choose the name of the template in the list; then, press Enter or choose OK to open the file. If the file you want to open is not in the current directory, select the directory that contains the file from the Other Drives & Directories list box and press Enter or choose OK. Then, either type the filename or choose it from the list of filenames and press Enter or choose OK.

To analyze the breakeven point for a product, you enter three values in the spreadsheet, recalculate it, and select View from the Chart menu. First, enter the unit sales price (the amount for which you plan to sell each unit of your product) in cell C5. Next, enter the variable cost per unit sold in cell C6. Variable costs are the incremental costs involved in producing each extra unit of the product. Variable costs usually include such things as raw material and labor that vary directly with the number of units you produce and sell. Third, enter your total fixed costs in cell C7. Fixed costs are the costs you incur as a going concern, whether you sell 1 unit or 100 million units—rent, management payroll, interest on bank debt, and the like.

After you make these entries, press the Calc key ([F9]) or select Calculate Now from the Options menu to recalculate the spreadsheet. When you do this, Works recalculates the formula in cell C9, which returns the breakeven volume for the spreadsheet. Then, it recalculates the formulas in the breakeven table (cells A14 through F18), creating a series of unit sales values that span a range from 0 to roughly twice the breakeven volume. The table also contains the dollar sales, variable costs, fixed costs, total costs, and net income values that correspond to each unit sales value.

After you note the result of the breakeven formula, you can display the spreadsheet results in chart form. To do this, simply pull down the Chart menu, check to see that BREAKEVEN is the current chart, and then choose the View command.

An Example

Let's look at an example. Suppose you want to go into the business of manufacturing widgets. You estimate that it will cost $16 in parts and labor to produce each widget and that you will be able to sell the widgets for $25 apiece. You estimate that overhead expenses (lease of factory space, administrative expenses, and so forth) will be $120,000. Given these estimates, you want to know how many widgets you must sell to break even.

To analyze this situation with Breakeven Analysis, begin by entering the value *25* in cell C5, the value *16* in cell C6, and the value *120000* in cell C7. Now, recalculate either by pressing [F9] or by selecting Calculate Now from the Options menu.

Figure 6-5 on the following page shows the spreadsheet after you enter the assumptions and recalculate. As you can see, the formula in cell C9 returns the value *13,333*—the breakeven volume. If you sell fewer than 13,333 widgets, you lose money (that is, costs exceed revenues). If you sell more than 13,333 widgets, you make money (that is, revenues exceed costs).

As you can also see, the formula in cell A18 returns the value *30000*, which is approximately twice the breakeven volume. The formulas in cells A15, A16, and A17 use this value to calculate the other unit sales values: *7500, 15000,* and *22500.* Notice that these values are exactly one-fourth, one-half, and three-fourths of the value in cell A18. The formulas in cells B14:F18 calculate the dollar sales, variable costs, fixed costs, total costs, and net income values at each volume point.

After you note the breakeven value, pull down the Chart menu, check to see that BREAKEVEN is highlighted, and then select the View command. When you do, Works draws the chart shown in Figure 6-6 on the following page. The chart shows five lines—one for each of the five y ranges. The topmost line at the y axis plots the total cost information for the five volume points displayed on the x axis. The horizontal line at $120,000 plots fixed costs. The third line (the one at the top on the right edge of the chart) plots dollar sales. The fourth line (which rises from $0.00 to $480,000) plots variable costs. The fifth line (the bottom line at the y axis) plots net income.

```
   File  Edit  Print  Select  Format  Options  Chart  Window
120000
          A          B          C          D          E          F          =
1  ================================================================
2  BREAKEVEN ANALYSIS
3  ================================================================
4
5  Sale Price/Unit:        $25.00
6  Variable Cost/Unit:     $16.00
7  Fixed Costs:            $120,000
8
9  Breakeven Volume:       13,333
10
11    Unit       Dollar    Variable    Fixed       Total       Net
12    Sales      Sales      Costs       Costs      Costs      Income
13  ---------  ---------  ---------  ---------  ---------  ---------
14        0         $0         $0    $120,000    $120,000   ($120,000)
15     7500    $187,500   $120,000   $120,000    $240,000    ($52,500)
16    15000    $375,000   $240,000   $120,000    $360,000      $15,000
17    22500    $562,500   $360,000   $120,000    $480,000      $82,500
18    30000    $750,000   $480,000   $120,000    $600,000     $150,000
19
C7                                                     CL   BRKEVEN.WKS
Press ALT to choose commands.
```

Figure 6-5.

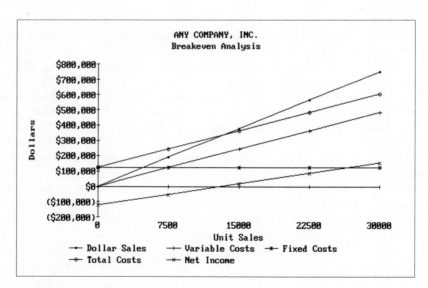

Figure 6-6.

As you can see, the dollar sales and total cost lines cross about midway between the tick mark for the value 7500 and the tick mark for the value 15000 on the x axis. The point of intersection is the breakeven point. At volumes lower than the breakeven volume, the total cost line is above the revenue line (that is, costs exceed revenues). At volumes higher than the breakeven volume, the revenue line is above the total cost line (that is, revenues exceed costs). Because the net income line plots the difference between revenues and total costs, it crosses the x axis at the breakeven point. Of course, the resolution of this chart does not show you the breakeven volume as precisely as the spreadsheet. However, you can see the relationships between revenues and the various costs more clearly than you can in the spreadsheet.

Printing and Saving

After you set up your analysis, save the spreadsheet in a new file. To do this, select Save As from the File menu. Then, if you want to save the file in a directory other than the current directory, choose that directory from the Other Drives & Directories box and choose OK. Next, type a new name for the spreadsheet and press Enter or choose OK to save the file. If you want to save the file in the current directory, simply type a name and press Enter or choose OK. Choose a name for the file that clearly identifies its contents—for example, PROD1BE for product 1 breakeven analysis.

Always be sure to save your filled-in Breakeven Analysis under a name other than the name you used for the original, empty template. If you save a filled-in spreadsheet under the same name as the original template, the filled-in version replaces the original version.

To print the spreadsheet, first choose the Layout command from the Print menu and change any print settings you want to change. You might want to change the margins and define a header and a footer. Because this template is narrow enough to be printed on standard 8 1/2-inch-wide paper, you probably don't need to change the Page Width setting. Next, use the Font command to select the font you want Works to use to print the report. If you want to squeeze the entire report onto one page, choose a relatively compressed font (such as Elite) and a small point size (such as 6 or 8).

After you adjust the settings, select Print from the Print menu to display the Print dialog box. Then, adjust the settings in that dialog box and choose the Print button to print the report.

You can also print the chart that illustrates the breakeven relationships. To do so, first select the chart you want to print from the list of charts on the Chart menu. (If you created only one chart, Works highlights that chart.) Next, select Print Chart from the Print menu. When the Print Chart dialog box appears, press Enter or choose the Print button to print the current chart.

CONCLUSION

Breakeven analysis is a useful tool for analyzing the potential success of a new product or company. It allows you to figure out your "breakeven volume"—the number of units of a product you have to sell before you begin to make money. Sell more than the breakeven volume, and you make a profit; sell less than that volume, and you lose money. The template you created in this chapter is a handy tool for performing breakeven analysis. You simply enter the unit price, unit variable costs, and total fixed costs, and the spreadsheet does the rest. It even creates a chart that illustrates the relationships between your revenues and your various costs.

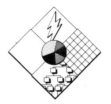

Ratio Analysis

Ratio analysis is one of the tools financial analysts and investors use to measure the financial condition of a company. Financial ratios are to financial analysis what blood pressure and temperature are to medicine: standardized measures of critical (corporate) health factors. Ratios measure such important factors as a company's ability to repay debt or to collect its accounts receivable. Using ratios, you can easily determine how well a company is doing and how its performance stacks up against forecasts or against the performances of other, similar companies.

This template allows you to enter the financial information for a company into a generic income statement and a generic balance sheet. Then, it uses that information to compute several of the most common financial ratios and statistics for the company. With the resulting figures, you can analyze the financial condition of the company. The spreadsheet is easy to set up and to use. If you need to perform financial analysis, consider using this template.

ABOUT THE TEMPLATE

Figure 7-1, beginning on the next page, shows the Ratio Analysis template as it looks when you first create it. As you can see, the template has three areas, labeled INCOME STATEMENT, BALANCE SHEET, and RATIOS AND ANALYSIS. The Income Statement occupies columns A through G and rows 4 through 21. The top part of the Income Statement, with sample data entered in it, is shown in Figure 7-2 on page 157. In this area, you enter the income information for the company you want to analyze: sales, cost of goods sold, operating expenses, and so on. Some of the cells in column F contain formulas that compute sums of the amounts you enter. The formulas in column G compute the percentage of sales represented by each number in column F.

```
             A        B        C        D        E        F        G
1     =================================================================
2     RATIO ANALYSIS
3     =================================================================
4     INCOME STATEMENT                                    Dollars  Percent
5     ===========================================         =======  =======
6
7     Sales                                                        ERR
8     Cost of Goods Sold                                           ERR
9                                                         -------  -------
10    Gross Margin                                           $0    ERR
11    Selling, General, and Administrative Expenses                ERR
12    Depreciation                                                 ERR
13                                                         -------  -------
14    Profit Before Interest and Taxes                      $0    ERR
15    Interest Expense                                             ERR
16                                                         -------  -------
17    Profit Before Taxes                                   $0    ERR
18    Income Taxes                                                 ERR
19                                                         -------  -------
20    Net Income                                            $0    ERR
21                                                         =======  =======
22    =================================================================
23    BALANCE SHEET                                       Dollars  Percent
24    ===========================================         =======  =======
25
26    Assets
27     Cash and Marketable Securities                              ERR
28     Accounts Receivable (Net of Allowance for Bad Debts)        ERR
29     Inventory                                                   ERR
30     Other Current Assets                                        ERR
31                                                         -------  -------
32      Total Current Assets                                 $0    ERR
33
34     Total Plant, Property, and Equipment                        ERR
35     Accumulated Depreciation                                    ERR
36     Other Non-Current Assets                                    ERR
37                                                         -------  -------
38      Net Non-Current Assets                               $0    ERR
39                                                         -------  -------
40    Total Assets                                          $0    ERR
41                                                         =======  =======
42    Liabilities
43     Accounts Payable                                            ERR
44     Short-Term Debt                                             ERR
45     Other Current Liabilities                                   ERR
46                                                         -------  -------
47      Total Current Liabilities                            $0    ERR
48
49     Long-Term Debt                                              ERR
50     Other Non-Current Liabilities                               ERR
51                                                         -------  -------
52      Total Non-Current Liabilities                        $0    ERR
53                                                         -------  -------
54    Total Liabilities                                     $0    ERR
55
56     Paid-in Capital                                             ERR
57     Retained Earnings                                           ERR
58                                                         -------  -------
59     Total Stockholders Equity                             $0    ERR
60                                                         -------  -------
61    Total Liabilities and Equity                          $0    ERR
62                                                         =======  =======
```

Figure 7-1.   (continued)

Figure 7-1. Continued.

```
63  =================================================================
64  RATIOS AND ANALYSIS                              Dollars   Percent
65  =============================================    =======   =======
66  Debt/Equity Ratio                                  ERR
67  Times Interest Earned                              ERR Times
68
69  Net Working Capital                                 $0
70  Current Ratio                                      ERR
71  Quick Ratio                                        ERR
72  Cash Ratio                                         ERR
73
74  Days Sales in Accounts Receivable                  ERR Days
75  Days Cost of Goods Sold in Accounts Payable        ERR Days
76  Days Cost of Goods Sold in Inventory               ERR Days
77  Inventory Turnover                                 ERR Turns/Year
78
79  Return on Sales                                    ERR
80  Return on Assets                                   ERR
81  Return on Equity                                   ERR
```

```
 File  Edit  Print  Select  Format  Options  Chart  Window
       A        B       C       D       E       F        G
3   ===============================================================
4   INCOME STATEMENT                               Dollars   Percent
5   ===========================================    =======   =======
6
7   Sales                                          $975,000   100.00%
8   Cost of Goods Sold                             $417,000    42.77%
9                                                  --------   -------
10  Gross Margin                                   $558,000    57.23%
11  Selling, General, and Administrative Expenses  $350,000    35.90%
12  Depreciation                                    $56,000     5.74%
13                                                 --------   -------
14  Profit Before Interest and Taxes              $152,000    15.59%
15  Interest Expense                                $35,000     3.59%
16                                                 --------   -------
17  Profit Before Taxes                            $117,000    12.00%
18  Income Taxes                                    $27,000     2.77%
19                                                 --------   -------
20  Net Income                                      $90,000     9.23%
21                                                 =======   =======
A21                                                          RATIO.WKS
Press ALT to choose commands.
```

Figure 7-2.

The Balance Sheet area occupies the range A22:G62. Figure 7-3 on the following page shows the top portion of the Balance Sheet as it appears on the screen. In this area, you enter the balance sheet data for the company you want to analyze—cash; accounts receivable; plant, property, and equipment; and so on. As in the Income

```
  File  Edit  Print  Select  Format  Options  Chart  Window
"==============
                A      B      C       D       E        F          G       =
==============================================================================
22
23  BALANCE SHEET                                          Dollars   Percent
24  =========================================================  =======   =======
25
26  Assets
27   Cash and Marketable Securities                         $92,000   17.08%
28   Accounts Receivable (Net of Allowance for Bad Debts) $103,250   19.16%
29   Inventory                                             $100,500   18.65%
30   Other Current Assets                                     $500    0.09%
31                                                         -------   -------
32    Total Current Assets                                $296,250   54.99%
33
34   Total Plant, Property, and Equipment                 $275,000   51.04%
35   Accumulated Depreciation                            ($35,000)   -6.50%
36   Other Non-Current Assets                               $2,500    0.46%
37                                                         -------   -------
38   Net Non-Current Assets                               $242,500   45.01%
39                                                         -------   -------
40  Total Assets                                          $538,750  100.00%
||+
A22                                                                  RATIO.WKS
Press ALT to choose commands.
```

Figure 7-3.

Statement, some cells in column F contain formulas that total the amounts you enter. The formulas in column G compute the percentage of total assets (or total liabilities and equity) represented by each number in column F.

The last area, Ratios and Analysis, begins in row 63. This area contains formulas that compute commonly used financial measures, such as the current ratio, debt equity ratio, and days sales in receivables. Figure 7-4 shows the top of this section on the screen, and Figure 7-5 beginning on page 160 shows the entire sample spreadsheet.

CREATING THE TEMPLATE

The template for Ratio Analysis is easy to create. To begin, use the New command on the File menu to open a new spreadsheet. Next, change the width of column A from 10 characters (the default) to 13 characters. To do this, move the cursor to any cell in column A, select Width from the Format menu, type *13*, and press Enter or choose OK.

Now, assign Dollar format with zero decimal places to the cells in column F, and assign Percent format with two decimal places to the cells in column G. To begin, move to cell F7, highlight the range F7:F61, and select Dollar from the Format menu. When the Decimals dialog box appears, type *0* and then press Enter or choose OK. Next, highlight the range G7:G61, select Percent from the Format menu, and press Enter or choose OK to accept the default number of decimal places (2).

```
 File  Edit  Print  Select  Format  Options  Chart  Window
"============
          A         B         C         D         E         F         G
63  ============|===================================================================
64  RATIOS AND ANALYSIS                                         Dollars   Percent
65  =================================================================  =======   =======
66  Debt/Equity Ratio                                            0.84
67  Times Interest Earned                                        3.57 Times
68
69  Net Working Capital                                       $209,500
70  Current Ratio                                                3.41
71  Quick Ratio                                                  2.25
72  Cash Ratio                                                   1.06
73
74  Days Sales in Accounts Receivable                           38.12 Days
75  Days Cost of Goods Sold in Accounts Payable                 26.55 Days
76  Days Cost of Goods Sold in Inventory                        86.76 Days
77  Inventory Turnover                                           4.15 Turns/Year
78
79  Return on Sales                                              9.23%
80  Return on Assets                                            16.71%
81  Return on Equity                                            30.66%

A63                                                                    RATIO.WKS
Press ALT to choose commands.
```

Figure 7-4.

Entering Column Headers

Now you're ready to begin making entries. First, enter the header labels for the template in rows 1, 2, and 3. The double lines in rows 1 and 3 span columns A through F. To create these double lines, enter a label made up of equal signs (=) in each cell in row 1, and then copy that series of labels from row 1 to rows 3 and 5. To enter each label, type a quotation mark (") followed by the proper number of equal signs (corresponding to the column width). For example, to enter the label in cell A1, move the cursor to cell A1, type a quotation mark, and then type a string of 13 equal signs ("=============). If you forget the quotation mark, Works tries to interpret the entry as a formula and displays the message *Error: Missing Operand*. After you enter a label in each cell in row 1, highlight the range A1:G1, select Copy from the Edit menu, point to cell A3, and press Enter.

The entry in cell A2 is a simple label. To enter it, move the cursor to cell A2 and type *RATIO ANALYSIS*.

Now you're ready to create the labels for the Income Statement area. To create the double-line labels in row 5, begin by copying the labels in row 3. First select the range A3:E3, select Copy from the Edit menu, point to cell A5, and press Enter. Next, move to cell F5, type two spaces followed by a series of seven equal signs, and press Enter. Then, highlight the range F5:G5 and select Fill Right from the Edit Menu.

The entries in cells A4, F4, and G4 are column labels. To make these entries, move the cursor to cell A4 and type *INCOME STATEMENT*. Then, type two spaces followed by the label *Dollars* in cell F4 and two spaces followed by the label *Percent* in cell G4. These labels identify the columns that make up the Income Statement.

```
         A        B        C        D        E        F        G
1  ===================================================================
2  RATIO ANALYSIS
3  ===================================================================
4  INCOME STATEMENT                               Dollars  Percent
5  ===========================================  =======  =======
6
7  Sales                                        $975,000  100.00%
8  Cost of Goods Sold                           $417,000   42.77%
9                                               -------   -------
10 Gross Margin                                 $558,000   57.23%
11 Selling, General, and Administrative Expenses $350,000   35.90%
12 Depreciation                                  $56,000    5.74%
13                                               -------   -------
14 Profit Before Interest and Taxes            $152,000   15.59%
15 Interest Expense                             $35,000    3.59%
16                                               -------   -------
17 Profit Before Taxes                         $117,000   12.00%
18 Income Taxes                                 $27,000    2.77%
19                                               -------   -------
20 Net Income                                   $90,000    9.23%
21                                               =======   =======
22 ===================================================================
23 BALANCE SHEET                                  Dollars  Percent
24 ===========================================  =======  =======
25
26 Assets
27  Cash and Marketable Securities              $92,000   17.08%
28  Accounts Receivable (Net of Allowance for Bad Debts) $103,250  19.16%
29  Inventory                                  $100,500   18.65%
30  Other Current Assets                          $500    0.09%
31                                              -------   -------
32   Total Current Assets                      $296,250   54.99%
33
34 Total Plant, Property, and Equipment        $275,000   51.04%
35 Accumulated Depreciation                   ($35,000)   -6.50%
36 Other Non-Current Assets                      $2,500    0.46%
37                                              -------   -------
38   Net Non-Current Assets                    $242,500   45.01%
39                                              -------   -------
40 Total Assets                                $538,750  100.00%
41                                              =======   =======
42 Liabilities
43  Accounts Payable                            $30,750    5.71%
44  Short-Term Debt                             $55,000   10.21%
45  Other Current Liabilities                    $1,000    0.19%
46                                              -------   -------
47   Total Current Liabilities                  $86,750   16.10%
48
49 Long-Term Debt                              $155,000   28.77%
50 Other Non-Current Liabilities                 $3,500    0.65%
51                                              -------   -------
52   Total Non-Current Liabilities             $158,500   29.42%
53                                              -------   -------
54 Total Liabilities                           $245,250   45.52%
55
56 Paid-in Capital                             $150,000   27.84%
57 Retained Earnings                           $143,500   26.64%
58                                              -------   -------
59   Total Stockholders Equity                 $293,500   54.48%
60                                              -------   -------
61 Total Liabilities and Equity                $538,750  100.00%
62                                              =======   =======
```

Figure 7-5.

(continued)

Figure 7-5. *Continued.*

```
63  =============================================================
64  RATIOS AND ANALYSIS                               Dollars   Percent
65  ===========================================       =======   =======
66  Debt/Equity Ratio                                   0.84
67  Times Interest Earned                               3.57 Times
68
69  Net Working Capital                             $209,500
70  Current Ratio                                       3.41
71  Quick Ratio                                         2.25
72  Cash Ratio                                          1.06
73
74  Days Sales in Accounts Receivable                  38.12 Days
75  Days Cost of Goods Sold in Accounts Payable        26.55 Days
76  Days Cost of Goods Sold in Inventory               86.76 Days
77  Inventory Turnover                                  4.15 Turns/Year
78
79  Return on Sales                                     9.23%
80  Return on Assets                                   16.71%
81  Return on Equity                                   30.66%
```

Now you can use the header for the Income Statement to create the headers for the Balance Sheet and for the Ratios and Analysis area. To do this, simply copy the contents of rows 3, 4, and 5 to the appropriate locations in the spreadsheet and then change the label INCOME STATEMENT to either BALANCE SHEET or RATIOS AND ANALYSIS. (Of course, you could create these headers from scratch, but why waste the effort?)

To begin, highlight the range A3:G5 and select Copy from the Edit menu. When you issue this command, the legend COPY appears in the lower right region of the screen. Now, move the cursor to cell A22 (the upper left cell in the Balance Sheet) and press Enter. Next, use the newly copied header in cells A22:G24 to create the header for the Ratios and Analysis area. To do so, select Copy from the Edit menu, highlight cell A63, and press Enter. (Because the copied header in the range A22:G24 is already highlighted, you don't have to highlight it before you reselect the Copy command.)

Now, replace the label *INCOME STATEMENT* in each of the copied section headers with the appropriate label. To begin, move the cursor to cell A23 and enter the label *BALANCE SHEET*. Then, move to cell A64 and enter the label *RATIOS AND ANALYSIS*. (Press [F5] and enter the cell coordinates to move quickly to the specified cell. If you have a mouse, you can also use the scroll bar to move the cursor.)

Entering Row Headers

Now you're ready to begin entering the row headers in column A. To begin, move the cursor to cell A7 and enter the label *Sales*. Then, move to cell A8 and enter the label *Cost of Goods Sold*. Next, move to cell A10 and enter the label *Gross Margin*. Continue in this fashion—moving down column A and entering labels—until all the row headers shown in column A in Figure 7-1 beginning on page 156 are in place.

Notice that some labels in column A are indented one space and others two spaces from the left edge of the column. These indentions help to make the spreadsheet easier to read and understand. To indent a label, type the appropriate number of spaces before you begin typing the label itself.

The Income Statement

Now you're ready to create the Income Statement. Most of the cells in column F in this area are input cells: When you use the spreadsheet, you enter the income information for the company you are analyzing in these cells. Other cells in this column, however, contain formulas that compute simple sums. Enter those formulas now from the list in Figure 7-6. To enter each formula, move the cursor to the appropriate cell, type the formula, and press Enter. For example, to enter the formula in cell F10, move the cursor to cell F10, type *=F7–F8*, and press Enter.

The cells in column G in the Income Statement contain formulas that compute the percentage of sales represented by each number in column F. To create these formulas, move the cursor to cell G7 and enter the formula *=F7/F$7*. Because cell F7 is empty, this formula returns the message *ERR*. Don't worry—when you recalculate with a value entered in cell F7, the *ERR* disappears. (To avoid getting the *ERR* result, enter *1* in cell F7.)

After you enter the formula for cell G7, copy that formula to the range G8:G20. To do this, highlight the range G7:G20 and select Fill Down from the Edit menu. Selecting this command duplicates the formula in cell G7 into the other cells in the highlighted range. Because the first reference to cell F7 in the original formula is a relative reference, it changes as you copy the formula. However, because the second reference to cell F7 in the original formula is mixed (F$7), it does not change. For example, the formula copied in cell G8 is *=F8/F$7*, the formula in cell G10 is *=F10/F$7*, and so on. Because cell F7 is empty, all these formulas return the message *ERR*.

Next, you need to enter dashed-line labels in some of the cells in columns F and G. To begin, move the cursor to cell F9, press the Spacebar twice, and type seven hyphens (-------). Then, highlight the range F9:G9 and select Fill Right to copy the

Cell	Formula
F10	=F7–F8
F14	=F10–F11–F12
F17	=F14–F15
F20	=F17–F18

Figure 7-6. Formulas for column F of the Income Statement.

label to cell G9. When the labels are in place in cells F9 and G9, use the Copy command to copy them to cells F13 and G13, F16 and G16, and F19 and G19. To do so, select the range F9:G9, select Copy from the Edit menu, highlight cell F13, and press Enter. Then, select the Copy command again, highlight cell F16, and press Enter. Finally, select Copy once more, highlight cell F19, and press Enter.

Now, move the cursor to cell F21 and enter a double-line label made up of two spaces followed by seven equal signs (=). Then, highlight the range F21:G21 and select Fill Right from the Edit menu to copy the double-line label from F21 to G21.

The Balance Sheet

Now you're ready to create the Balance Sheet. As in the Income Statement, most of the cells in column F in this area are input cells. When you use the spreadsheet, you enter the balance sheet information for the company you are analyzing in these cells. However, other cells in this column contain formulas, which are listed in the table in Figure 7-7. To enter each formula, move the cursor to the appropriate cell, type the formula, and press Enter. For example, to enter the formula for cell F32, move the cursor to cell F32, type *=SUM(F27:F31)*, and press Enter.

Column G in the Balance Sheet contains formulas that compute the percentage of total assets represented by each number in column F. To create these formulas, move the cursor to cell G27 and enter the formula *=F27/F$40*. Because the formula in cell F40 currently returns the value 0, this formula returns the message *ERR*. The formula returns a number result when you enter a value in cell F40.

After you enter the formula for cell G27, copy that formula to the range G28:G61. To do this, highlight the range G27:G61 and select Fill Down from the Edit menu. Because the reference to cell F27 in the original formula is a relative reference, it changes as you copy the formula. However, because the reference to cell F40 in the

Cell	Formula
F32	=SUM(F27:F31)
F38	=SUM(F34:F37)
F40	=F32+F38
F47	=SUM(F43:F46)
F52	=SUM(F49:F51)
F54	=F47+F52
F59	=SUM(F56:F58)
F61	=F54+F59

Figure 7-7. Formulas for column F of the Balance Sheet.

original formula is mixed (F$40), it remains fixed when you copy it vertically. For example, the formula in cell G28 is *=F28/F$40*, the formula in cell G32 is *=F32/F$40*, and so on. Because cell F40 currently has the value 0, all these formulas return the message *ERR* for now.

Next, enter dashed-line labels in some of the cells in columns F and G. You can use the Copy command to create them. To begin, highlight the range F19:G19 in the Income Statement and select Copy from the Edit menu. Then, highlight cell F31 and press Enter to copy the labels from cells F19 and G19 to cells F31 and G31. Now, select the Copy command again, highlight cell F37, and press Enter to copy the labels again. Repeat these steps to duplicate the labels into cells F39 and G39, F46 and G46, F51 and G51, F53 and G53, F58 and G58, and F60 and G60.

Now, enter double-line labels in cells F41 and G41 and cells F62 and G62. To do this quickly, copy the labels in cells F21 and G21. First, move the cursor to cell F21 and highlight the range F21:G21. Then, select Copy from the Edit menu, highlight cell F41, and press Enter. Next, select the Copy command again, highlight cell F62, and press Enter to copy the labels a second time.

Finally, you need to erase a few cells in column G. Move the cursor to cell G33 and select Clear from the Edit menu. Next, move to cell G42 and use the Clear command to erase that cell. Repeat these steps to erase cells G48 and G55.

The Ratios and Analysis Area

Now you're ready to create the Ratios and Analysis area. The formulas in this area compute common financial measures—such as the ratio of debt to equity and the number of days sales in accounts receivable—from the data in the Income Statement and in the Balance Sheet. To begin creating this area, assign Fixed format with two decimal places to the cells in the range F66:F77. To do this, highlight the range F66:F77, select Fixed from the Format menu, and press Enter to accept the default number of decimal places (2).

To start entering formulas, move the cursor to cell F66 and enter the formula *=F54/F59*. This formula computes the Debt/Equity Ratio for the company being analyzed. It divides the company's total liabilities (computed in cell F54) by its total equity (cell F59).

Now, move to cell F67 and enter the formula *=(F20+F15)/F15*. This formula computes the ratio of the company's earnings (before paying interest expense) to its interest expense. This ratio is commonly called Times Interest Earned. The formula divides the sum of the company's net income (cell F20) and its interest expense (cell F15) by its interest expense (cell F15). After you enter the formula in cell F67, move the cursor to cell G67 and enter the label *Times*.

Next, move to cell F69 and enter the formula *=F32–F47*. This formula computes the company's Net Working Capital by subtracting its total current liabilities (cell

F47) from its total current assets (cell F32). After you enter the formula, select Dollar from the Format menu, type *0*, and press Enter or choose OK to give cell F69 the currency format with zero decimal places.

Now, move the cursor to cell F70 and enter the formula *=F32/F47*. This formula computes the company's Current Ratio by dividing its total current assets (cell F32) by its total current liabilities (cell F47).

Next, move to cell F71 and enter the formula *=(F32–F29–F30)/F47*. This formula computes the ratio of the company's current assets, not including inventory or "other" current assets, to its current liabilities. This ratio is commonly called the Quick Ratio. The formula first subtracts the company's inventory (cell F29) and its other current assets (cell F30) from its total current assets (cell F32) and then divides the difference by the total current liabilities (cell F47).

Next, move the cursor to cell F72 and enter the formula *=F27/F47.* to compute the ratio between the company's cash (cell F27) and its total current liabilities (cell F47). This ratio is commonly called the Cash Ratio.

Now, move the cursor to cell F74 and enter the formula *=F28/(F7/360)*. This formula computes the ratio between the company's accounts receivable and its daily sales, commonly called the Days Sales in Accounts Receivable. The formula first divides the company's total sales (cell F7) by 360 (days) to compute its daily sales. Then, it divides the company's accounts receivable (cell F28) by its daily sales. After you enter the formula in cell F74, move the cursor to cell G74 and enter the label *Days*.

Now, move the cursor to cell F75 and enter the formula *=F43/(F8/360)*. This formula computes the ratio between the company's accounts payable and its daily cost of goods sold, commonly called the Days Cost of Goods Sold in Accounts Payable. The formula first divides the company's total cost of goods sold (cell F8) by 360 (days) to compute daily cost of goods sold. Then it divides the company's accounts payable (cell F43) by its daily cost of goods sold. Next, move the cursor to cell G75 and enter the label *Days*.

Next, move to cell 76 and enter the formula *=F29/(F8/360)*. This formula divides the company's inventory (cell F29) by its daily cost of goods sold (computed by dividing the total cost of goods sold in cell F8 by 360). The result of this calculation is commonly called the Days Cost of Goods Sold in Inventory. Next, move the cursor to cell G76 and enter the label *Days*.

Now, move the cursor to cell F77 and enter the formula *=F8/F29*. This formula computes the ratio between the company's cost of goods sold (cell F8) and its inventory (cell F29). This ratio is commonly called Inventory Turnover. After you enter the formula in cell F77, move the cursor to cell G77 and enter the label *Turns/Year*.

The last three formulas return percentages. To format the appropriate cells, highlight the range F79:F81, select Percent from the Format menu, and press Enter or choose OK to assign these cells the Percent format with two decimals. Then, move to cell F79 and enter the formula *=F20/F7*. This formula computes the ratio between the company's net income (cell F20) and its total sales (cell F7). The result is called the Return on Sales. Next, move to cell F80 and enter the formula *=F20/F40*. This formula computes the company's Return on Assets by dividing its net income (cell F20) by its total assets (cell F40). Finally, move to cell F81 and enter the formula *=F20/F59*. This formula computes the ratio between the company's net income (cell F20) and its total equity (cell F59), commonly called Return on Equity.

Saving the Template

That's all there is to it—the template is built. Before you do anything else, save the finished template. To do this, select Save As from the File menu. Then, if you want to save the file in a directory other than the current directory, choose that directory from the Other Drives & Directories box and choose OK. Next, type a name (such as *RATIO.WKS*) and press Enter or choose OK to save the file. If you want to save the file in the current directory, simply type a name and press Enter or choose OK.

USING THE TEMPLATE

After you create the template for Ratio Analysis, you're ready to put it to work. First, open the spreadsheet. (If you just created the template, skip this step.) To begin, choose Open from the File menu. Then, if the file you want to open is in the current directory, simply type the filename under which you saved the template, including the extension (for example, RATIO.WKS), or highlight the name of the template in the list, and then press Enter or choose OK to open the file. If the file you want to open is not in the current directory, select the directory that contains the file from the Other Drives & Directories list box and choose OK. Then, either type the filename or choose it from the list and press Enter or choose OK to open the file.

Moving the Cursor

As shown in Figure 7-3 on page 158, the Income Statement appears on the home screen when you load the spreadsheet. To look at a different part of the template, use your mouse or the cursor movement keys to move the cursor to the appropriate cell. For example, to see the Balance Sheet, you need only press PgDn. To see the Ratios and Analysis area, press PgDn twice more. To move back up through the template, press PgUp. If you have a mouse, use the vertical scroll bar to move from area to area in the template.

To move to a specific row, just press the Go To key ([F5]), type *A*, followed by the number of the row, and press Enter or choose OK. For example, to move to row 63 (the first row in the Ratios and Analysis area), press [F5], type *A63*, and press Enter or choose OK.

Entering Company Data

After you load the template, simply enter the necessary information for the company you want to analyze in the Income Statement and the Balance Sheet. The table in Figure 7-8 lists the cells in which you enter company information. Because the spreadsheet is set up for automatic recalculation, Works updates the formulas in columns F and G as soon as you begin making entries.

Cell	Contents
F7	Sales (including other revenue, if any, but net of returns and credits, if any)
F8	Cost of Goods Sold
F11	Selling, General, and Administrative Expenses
F12	Depreciation
F15	Interest Expense
F18	Income Taxes
F27	Cash and Marketable Securities
F28	Accounts Receivable (Net of Allowance for Bad Debts)
F29	Inventory
F30	Other Current Assets (if any)
F34	Total Plant, Property, and Equipment
F35	Accumulated Depreciation (enter as a negative value)
F36	Other Non-Current Assets (if any)
F43	Accounts Payable (including accrued expenses, if any)
F44	Short-Term Debt (including current portion of long-term debt)
F45	Other Current Liabilities (if any)
F49	Long-Term Debt
F50	Other Non-Current Liabilities (if any)
F56	Paid-In Capital (includes common stock and preferred stock, if any)
F57	Retained Earnings

Figure 7-8. Ratio Analysis input cells.

The Income Statement and Balance Sheet we created in the template are generic. For this reason, the income statement and balance sheet for the company you want to analyze are not likely to match those in the template exactly. You have to use your judgment to decide exactly how to enter the information for the company you want to analyze. Usually, you can overcome any problems simply by combining less important or unusual items from the company's financial statements into the accounts offered on the spreadsheet. However, you might be compelled, at times, to modify the structure of the Income Statement or the Balance Sheet in the spreadsheet to accommodate the financial statements of a particular company. You'll learn how to do that later in this chapter.

One word of warning: It is easy to make a mistake as you're entering values in the spreadsheet and to create an unbalanced balance sheet in the process. Be certain that the Balance Sheet in the spreadsheet balances; that is, be sure that the total assets in cell F40 equals the total liabilities and equity in cell F61. You can check the Balance Sheet by looking at the result of the formula in cell G61. If the Balance Sheet is in balance, this result is 100%. If cell G61 contains any value other than 100%, the Balance Sheet is not balanced. You should find and fix the problem before you begin your analysis.

Printing and Saving

After you enter the information in the Balance Sheet and Income Statement for the company you want to evaluate, save that spreadsheet into a new file. To do this, select Save As from the File menu. Then, if you want to save the file in a directory other than the current directory, choose that directory from the Other Drives & Directories box and choose OK. Next, type a new name for the spreadsheet and press Enter or choose OK to save the file. If you want to save the file in the current directory, simply type a name and press Enter or choose OK. Choose a name for the file that clearly identifies its contents. To retrieve a file, select Open from the File menu, type or highlight the name, and press Enter or choose OK.

Be sure to save your filled-in Ratio Analysis spreadsheets under a name other than the name you used for the original, empty template. If you save a filled-in spreadsheet under the same name as the original template, the filled-in version replaces the original version.

To print the entire spreadsheet, first choose the Layout command from the Print menu and change any print settings you want to change. You might want to adjust the margins and define a header and a footer. Because this template is narrow enough to be printed on standard 8.5-inch-wide paper, you probably don't need to change the Page Width setting. Next, use the Font command to select the font you want Works to use to print the report. If you want to squeeze the entire report onto one page, choose a relatively compressed font (such as Elite) and a small point size (such as 6 or 8).

After you adjust the settings, select Print from the Print menu to display the Print dialog box. Then, adjust the settings in that dialog box and choose the Print button to print the report.

To print only a portion of the Ratio Analysis spreadsheet, you'll need to define the print area before you begin to print. For example, if you want to print only the Ratios and Analysis area, first highlight the range A63:G81. Then, select Set Print Area from the Print menu. Now, use the Layout and Font commands to make any needed adjustments to the Works print settings. Finally, select Print from the Print menu and choose the Print button to print the selected range.

Interpreting the Results

The real key to using Ratio Analysis is understanding how to interpret the numbers it produces. The percentages and ratios the spreadsheet computes are tools that let you measure the performance of the company. While the figures can have meaning in and of themselves (for example, a negative return on equity always indicates a loss and may indicate a company in serious trouble), they are most useful when compared to forecasts, to figures for comparable companies, or to industry averages. Comparing the ratios for the company you are analyzing to forecasts helps you to figure out whether the company is doing as well as expected. Comparing the ratios to those of other companies or to industry averages lets you see how the company is doing in relation to other companies in the same industry.

This is a point worth repeating: Ratios are more useful as comparative tools than as absolute measures of performance. Although you can apply accepted rules of thumb to many ratios in the spreadsheet, those rules may not be valid for the company or industry you are analyzing. Before you can use ratio analysis effectively, you must have a good understanding of the industry and the company you are analyzing.

Having recognized this point, let's walk through a sample ratio analysis, looking at the ratios for a fictional company. The table in Figure 7-9 lists the income statement

Cell	Item	Enter
F7	Sales	975000
F8	Cost of Goods Sold	417000
F11	Selling, General, and Administrative Expenses	350000
F12	Depreciation	56000
F15	Interest Expense	35000
F18	Income Taxes	27000
F27	Cash	92000
F28	Accounts Receivable	103250
F29	Inventory	100500
F30	Other Current Assets	500
F34	Total Plant, Property, and Equipment	275000
F35	Accumulated Depreciation	−35000
F36	Other Non-Current Assets	2500
F43	Accounts Payable	30750
F44	Short-Term Debt	55000
F45	Other Current Liabilities	1000
F49	Long-Term Debt	155000
F50	Other Non-Current Liabilities	3500
F56	Paid-In Capital	150000
F57	Retained Earnings	143500

Figure 7-9.

and balance sheet data for this company. Figure 7-5 on page 160 shows this data in the spreadsheet. Figure 7-4 on page 159 shows the Ratios and Analysis area of the filled-in spreadsheet on the screen.

Financial Statement Percentages

The percentages in column G help you to understand the relationships between the numbers in the financial statement. For example, the percentage in cell G8, 42.77%, shows you at a glance that our sample company spends about 42 cents of every dollar of sales on cost of goods sold. Likewise, the percentage in cell G20, 9.23%, tells you that the company earns 9 cents of profit on each dollar of sales. And the percentage in cell G34, 51.04%, shows you that more than half of this company's assets are fixed assets—plant, property, and equipment.

You can also use these percentages to compare one company's performance to that of others in the same industry. For example, our company has a profit of 9.23 percent of sales (cell F79). If its competitors are earning 10.25 percent of sales, our company may be doing something wrong.

By the way, you can easily add percentages such as those in column G to any Works spreadsheet that includes a balance sheet or an income statement.

Debt/Equity Ratio

A company's Debt/Equity Ratio describes the mix of debt and equity (stock) used to finance the company. For example, the Debt/Equity Ratio of our sample company, 0.84, indicates that the company has 84 cents of debt for every dollar of equity. We used the conservative definition of debt in our calculation: We assumed that all liabilities, including accounts payable, notes payable, bank debt, and so on, are "debt." Equity is composed of paid-in capital and retained earnings.

What is an acceptable Debt/Equity Ratio? The answer depends both on the company being analyzed and on the industry in which that company operates. A rule of thumb is that Debt/Equity Ratios over 1 to 1 are risky, but in many industries, ratios of 2 to 1 or 3 to 1 are common. In addition, high Debt/Equity Ratios have become more acceptable in recent times than they were in the past.

Times Interest Earned

The Times Interest Earned statistic lets you measure the sufficiency of the resources available to a company to pay interest on its debt. This ratio compares a company's net income (before paying interest expense) to its interest expense. Generally, this number is greater than 1, meaning that the company can still earn a profit after it pays its interest. It is often much greater than 1. For instance, the Times Interest Earned statistic for our sample company is 3.57. This means that our company earns 3.57 times what it needs to pay the interest on its debt.

Net Working Capital

A company's Net Working Capital is simply the difference between its current assets (the cash and other near-cash assets such as accounts receivable and inventory) and its current liabilities (obligations such as accounts payable and notes payable that come due in the current year). Net Working Capital is the "cushion" between the company's cash (and near-cash assets) and its immediate obligations. Because the current assets of a company are the resources it must use to pay its current liabilities, financial health generally requires that Net Working Capital be positive—that is, that current assets exceed current liabilities. If Net Working Capital is negative for very long, the company will have a difficult time paying its bills.

The Net Working Capital of our sample company is $209,500. While this seems to be a large positive amount, it really means little by itself. For instance, $209,500 of Net Working Capital might be a healthy cushion for a company with only $86,000 in current liabilities, but it would be frighteningly slim for a company with $10,000,000 in current liabilities. However, you can use the next three ratios—the Current Ratio, the Quick Ratio, and the Cash Ratio—to measure Net Working Capital as a percentage of liabilities.

The Current Ratio

The Current Ratio is computed by dividing a company's current assets by its current liabilities. The Current Ratio measures the liquidity of a company. In general, the Current Ratio for a healthy company is at least 1 to 1, indicating that the company's current assets equal or exceed its current liabilities. In some cases, it can be much higher. The Current Ratio for the sample company, 3.41, indicates that it has plenty of cushion between its resources and its immediate obligations.

The Quick Ratio

The Quick Ratio is very similar to the Current Ratio. Both help you determine the short-term health of a company by comparing its current resources to its immediate obligations. The Quick Ratio is slightly more conservative than the Current Ratio, however, because it excludes inventory, the least liquid (convertible to cash) current asset, from the total current assets. As a result, the Quick Ratios of most companies are smaller than their Current Ratios. The ratio in the example, 2.25, tells us that the example company has a healthy cushion. Whether a ratio greater than 1 is desirable depends on how conservative you are.

The Cash Ratio

The Cash Ratio also compares a company's short-term resources to its immediate obligations. However, it is even more conservative than the Quick Ratio, because it excludes all current assets but cash—including accounts receivable—from the calculation. A Cash Ratio greater than 1 to 1 indicates that the company has more cash than it has immediate liabilities. The ratio for our sample company, 1.06, tells us that the company has enough cash to repay all of its current liabilities without converting any accounts receivable or inventory to cash. As with the Quick Ratio, the desirability of a ratio greater than 1 depends on how conservative you are.

Days Sales in Accounts Receivable

Days Sales in Accounts Receivable is a statistic that measures the efficiency with which a company manages its accounts receivable. Most companies that extend credit to their customers state the terms of that credit in days: net 10 days, net 30 days, net 90 days, and so on. Of course, the actual collection period is usually longer than the company's stated terms. For example, a company that offers terms of net 30 days might collect its accounts in an average of 35 or 45 days.

Days Sales in Accounts Receivable measures the actual collection period of accounts receivable. This statistic is computed by dividing the accounts receivable balance by average daily sales (total sales divided by 360). The result in the example, 38.12 days, indicates that the accounts receivable balance represents about 38 days of sales or that the average collection period for receivables is 38 days. If this company offers terms of net 30 days, then a 38-day average collection cycle is probably pretty good. If the company offers terms of net 10 days, on the other hand, it might have a problem with collections or a problem with receivables management.

Days Cost of Goods Sold in Accounts Payable

Days Cost of Goods Sold in Accounts Payable measures the size of the company's accounts payable in relation to its cost of goods sold. This statistic is computed by dividing the accounts payable balance by the average daily cost of goods sold (total cost of goods sold divided by 360). In general, a large number of Days Cost of Goods Sold in Accounts Payable indicates that the company is taking full advantage of credit terms offered by its suppliers. The result in the example, 26.55 days, indicates that the company's current accounts payable balance represents about 26 days of cost of goods sold.

Days Cost of Goods Sold in Inventory

Days Cost of Goods Sold in Inventory measures the size of the company's investment in inventory relative to its cost of goods sold. This statistic is computed by dividing the inventory balance by average daily cost of goods sold (total cost of goods sold divided by 360). In general, a large number of Days Cost of Goods Sold in Inventory indicates large inventories in relation to sales. A company with a low number of Days Cost of Goods Sold in Inventory is keeping its inventory levels low in relation to sales. The result in the example, 86.76 days, indicates that the company's current inventory balance represents nearly 90 days, or three months, of cost of goods sold.

Inventory Turnover

Inventory Turnover is a simple tool for measuring the efficiency with which a company's inventory is managed. Generally speaking, a company with a high number of inventory turns per year is keeping its inventory levels low in relation to sales, which frees up cash for other uses. A low number of turns indicates large inventories in relation to sales, which could imply poor inventory management. (Of course, there are costs associated with ordering or producing inventory in a hurry and with being out of stock, so a high number of turns does not always imply perfect inventory management.)

The Inventory Turnover statistic in the example, 4.15, indicates that this company is turning over its inventory about four times per year, or that inventory at any given time is equal to about 25 percent of a year's sales.

Return on Sales

Return on Sales is simply the percentage of sales represented by net income. In other words, Return on Sales tells you how many cents of every dollar of sales turn into profit. The figure given in the example, 9.23 percent, indicates that our sample company is earning nearly 10 cents for every dollar of sales. Although this seems like a good return, you get a better picture by comparing this result to that of similar companies. Like the other ratios, Return on Sales is a comparative, not an absolute, tool.

Return on Assets

Return on Assets is computed by dividing the company's net income by the total value of its assets. It measures the productivity of the assets that have been put to work in the business. If this ratio, usually expressed as a percentage, is lower than those of similar companies in the same industry, or lower than the ratio that could be generated by redeploying the assets in another way, then the company may be in trouble. The figure given in the example, 16.71 percent, indicates that the assets employed in this business are earning a return of about 17 percent, which is probably not too bad.

Return on Equity

Return on Equity compares a company's net income to its equity—the amount invested in the company. Equity includes not only paid-in capital but also past earnings retained in the business. Think of Return on Equity as the "rate of interest" that the stockholders of the business earn on their investment. The Return on Equity figure in the example, 30.66 percent, indicates that the owners of this business are earning a rate of return on their investment of over 30 percent. In some industries, a Return on Equity of 30 percent is extraordinarily good; in others, it is only average.

MODIFICATIONS

As mentioned earlier, the income statement and balance sheet for the company you want to analyze are unlikely to match exactly the generic set of accounts in the template. You can usually avoid problems by combining less important or unusual items from the company's financial statements into the accounts offered by the Ratio Analysis template.

If necessary, however, you can modify the structure of the Income Statement or the Balance Sheet in the template to accommodate the financial statements of a particular company. To do that, simply insert a row at the appropriate spot in the spreadsheet and then enter the label for the new account in column A, the amount for the account in column F, and a formula in column G to compute the appropriate percentage for the new account. Finally, adjust any formulas in column F that should be affected by the new account. Be careful! If you add an account and then forget to change the formulas it affects, you will get inaccurate results—which can lead to bad decisions.

You might also modify the spreadsheet by adding one or more ratios. To do this, simply insert a row in the Ratios and Analysis area, enter the description of the ratio in column A, and enter the formula that computes the ratio in column F.

CONCLUSION

The template for Ratio Analysis you built in this chapter is a simple tool for performing financial analysis. If you need to analyze a business—your own business, a client's, or a potential investment—you can put this template to work for you.

The Mailing-List Manager

One of the most popular uses for integrated programs such as Microsoft Works is mailing-list management. You can use the Works Database environment to store the names and addresses of the people to whom you want to write: friends, business associates, sales prospects, association members, charitable contributors, and so on. Then, you can create mail-merge documents in the Works Word Processor that draw information from the fields of the database into printed documents—mailing labels, form letters, bills, statements, or any other kind of correspondence or report. You can print the document for every record in a database, or you can use a query to select a subset of the records and then print the document for that subset. You can also use the Sort command to sort the database before you print.

The Mailing-List Manager provides the basic tools you need to manage your mailing list in Works. It is at the same time one of the most useful templates in the book and one of the easiest to create. You can use it at home to store the names and addresses of your friends and acquaintances or at work to hold the names of your employees, customers, prospects, and so on. As you build the template, you learn how to create, query, and sort databases, and you learn how to create merge documents in Works.

ABOUT THE TEMPLATE

The Mailing-List Manager has three parts: a database, a mailing-label document, and a form-letter document. The database stores the names, addresses, and other information about the people to whom you want to write: friends, prospects, business associates, and so on. The mailing-label document is a mail-merge document that, when printed, draws information from the fields of the database and then prints that information in the form of a mailing label. The form-letter document is also a mail-merge document. When you print the form letter, it merges information from the database with literal text to produce a form letter.

Figure 8-1 shows the form we'll use to work with this database. As you can see, this database contains all the fields you need to produce mailing labels and letters: First Name, Last Name, City, State, Zip, and so forth. It also contains five fields that you might not expect: Field 12, Field 13, Field 14, Field 15, and Field 16. You can use these fields to store additional information about each name in the list, information that is specific to your use of the database. For example, if you use this database to store the names of sales prospects, you might use these fields to record information such as the source of the prospect, the salesperson who is assigned to follow up, and so on. You can change the names of these fields, or you can add or omit one or more fields.

Figure 8-2 shows the upper left corner of the List screen. The sample records simply appear in the order in which they were entered. Works gives you the option of sorting the database before you print, or of selecting a subset of your records for printing. Sorting the database controls the order in which Works prints your labels or form letters. The program's ability to select records that match a criterion you define lets you print labels or form letters for only those selected records.

The mailing-label merge document is shown in Figure 8-3. The merge fields in this document draw information from the fields of the database. As you can see, these fields are arranged in the form of a standard mailing label.

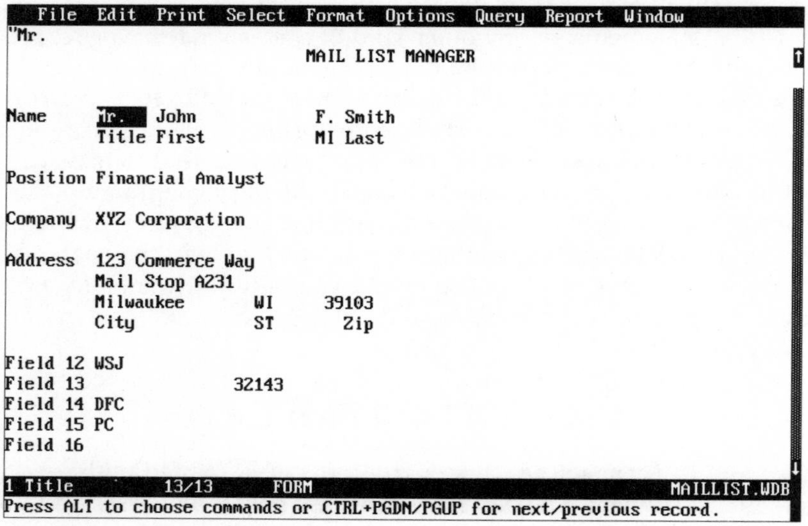

Figure 8-1.

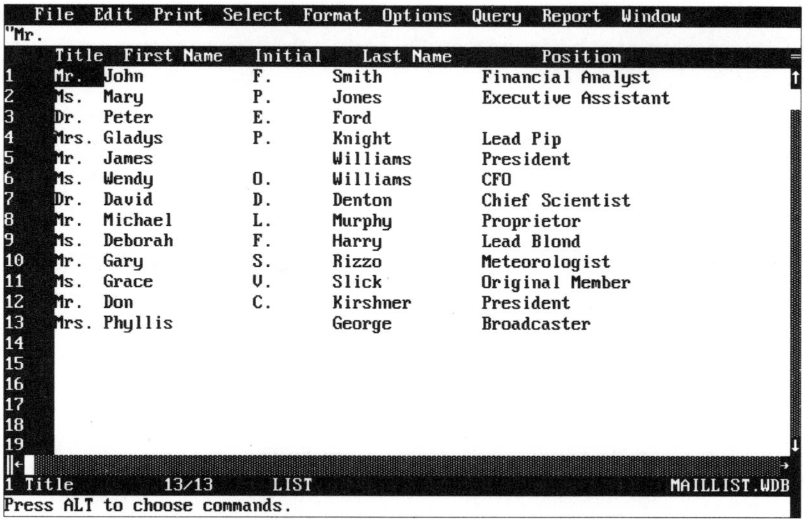

```
 File  Edit  Print  Select  Format  Options  Query  Report  Window
"Mr.
     Title  First Name  Initial   Last Name        Position
1   Mr.  John       F.    Smith      Financial Analyst        ↑
2   Ms.  Mary       P.    Jones      Executive Assistant
3   Dr.  Peter      E.    Ford
4   Mrs. Gladys     P.    Knight     Lead Pip
5   Mr.  James            Williams   President
6   Ms.  Wendy      O.    Williams   CFO
7   Dr.  David      D.    Denton     Chief Scientist
8   Mr.  Michael    L.    Murphy     Proprietor
9   Ms.  Deborah    F.    Harry      Lead Blond
10  Mr.  Gary       S.    Rizzo      Meteorologist
11  Ms.  Grace      V.    Slick      Original Member
12  Mr.  Don        C.    Kirshner   President
13  Mrs. Phyllis          George     Broadcaster
14
15
16
17
18
19
‖←
1 Title          13/13        LIST                   MAILLIST.WDB
Press ALT to choose commands.
```

Figure 8-2.

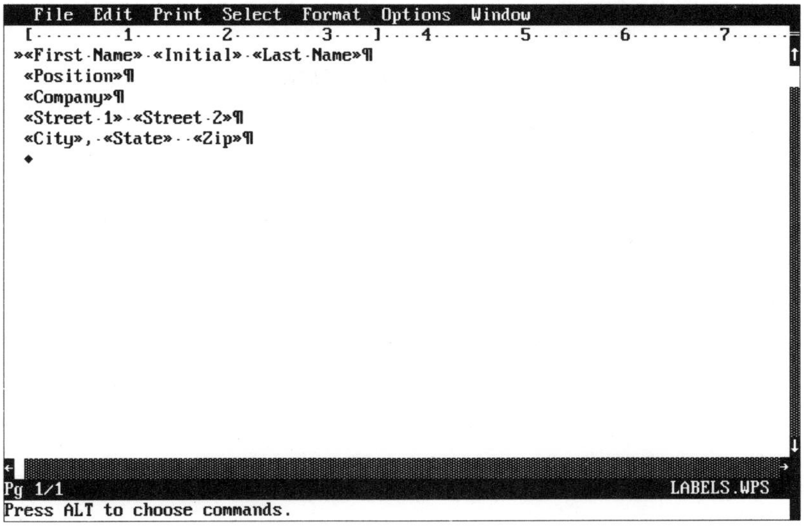

```
 File  Edit  Print  Select  Format  Options  Window
[········1·········2·········3···]····4·········5·········6·········7·····
»«First·Name»·«Initial»·«Last·Name»¶                                     ↑
 «Position»¶
 «Company»¶
 «Street·1»·«Street·2»¶
 «City»,·«State»···«Zip»¶
 ◆

←
Pg 1/1                                              LABELS.WPS
Press ALT to choose commands.
```

Figure 8-3.

Figure 8-4 shows the form-letter merge document. The address and salutation portions of this document draw information from the fields of the database. (In fact, the address portion of the document is very similar to the mailing-label document.) As you can see, the body of this letter is simply the statement *Replace this sentence with the body of your letter.* When you use the document, you replace this line with your own letter. You can use the same address and salutation whenever you employ this template, however.

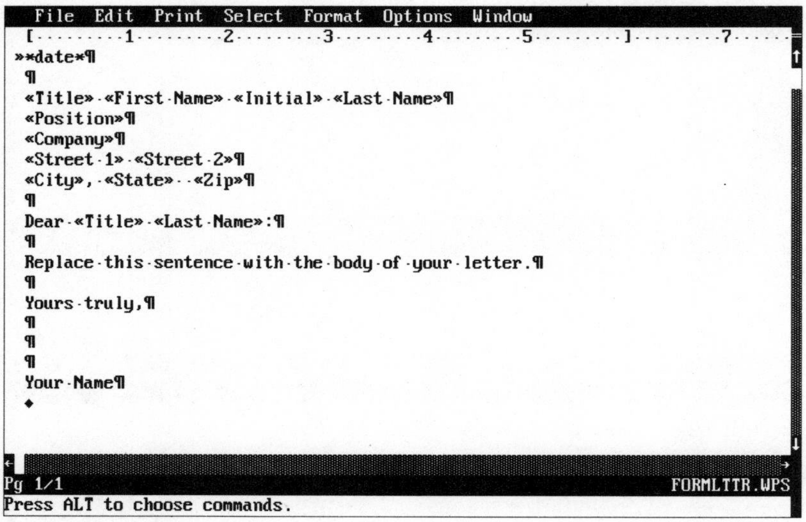

```
 File  Edit  Print  Select  Format  Options  Window
[·········1·········2·········3·········4·········5·········]·········7·····
»*date*¶
¶
«Title»·«First·Name»·«Initial»·«Last·Name»¶
«Position»¶
«Company»¶
«Street·1»·«Street·2»¶
«City»,·«State»···«Zip»¶
¶
Dear·«Title»·«Last·Name»:¶
¶
Replace·this·sentence·with·the·body·of·your·letter.¶
¶
Yours·truly,¶
¶
¶
Your·Name¶
◆

Pg 1/1                                                    FORMLTTR.WPS
Press ALT to choose commands.
```

Figure 8-4.

CREATING THE TEMPLATE

A database is the heart of any mail-merge template, because it stores the information from which Works prints your mailing labels and form letters. Before you can print labels and letters, then, you must create a database to hold the name and address information.

Creating the Database

The first step in creating the mail-merge template is creating the database that holds the information you want to print in mailing labels and form letters. To create the database shown in Figure 8-1 on page 176, first select New from the File menu if the New dialog box is not already on your screen. Then, choose Database and choose New. Works displays a blank form design screen like the one shown in Figure 8-5.

In Works, you can create a database simply by building a form for the database. Now that you have reached the form design screen, you can take advantage of that shortcut to create your mailing-list database. Figure 8-6 shows the form you must build to create the database. The subsequent table, Figure 8-7 on the following page, lists the width of each field in the form and the database.

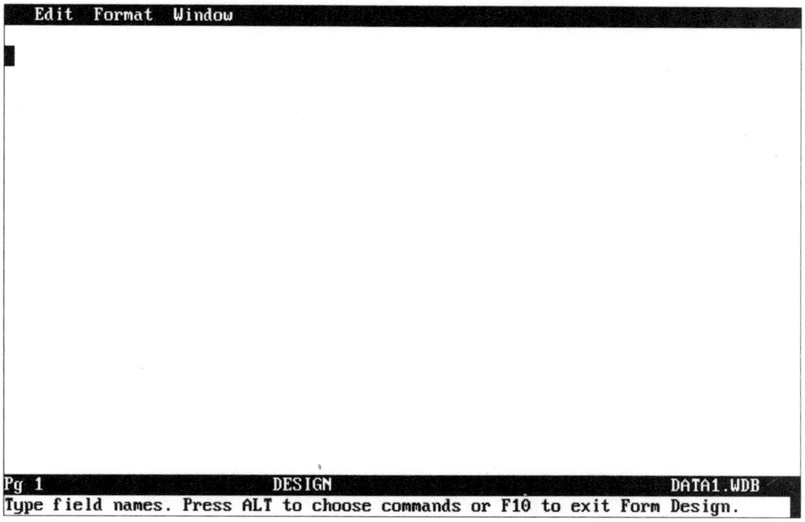

```
 Edit  Format  Window

▌



















Pg 1                          DESIGN                          DATA1.WDB
Type field names. Press ALT to choose commands or F10 to exit Form Design.
```

Figure 8-5.

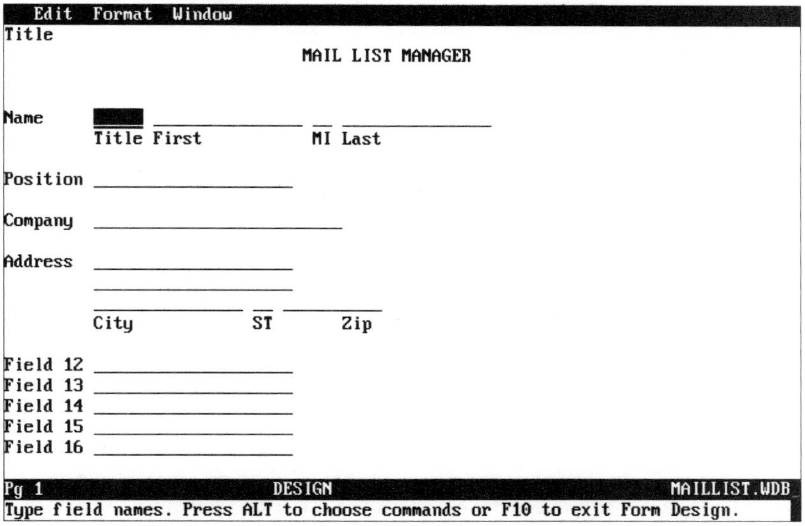

```
 Edit  Format  Window
Title
                         MAIL LIST MANAGER


Name     ████▌ _____ __ _____
         Title First        MI Last

Position _____

Company  _____

Address  _____
         _____
         _____ __ _____
         City       ST   Zip

Field 12 _____
Field 13 _____
Field 14 _____
Field 15 _____
Field 16 _____

Pg 1                          DESIGN                       MAILLIST.WDB
Type field names. Press ALT to choose commands or F10 to exit Form Design.
```

Figure 8-6.

Field	Width
Title	5
First Name	15
Initial	2
Last Name	15
Position	20
Company	25
Street 1	20
Street 2	20
City	15
State	2
Zip	10
Field 12	15
Field 13	15
Field 14	15
Field 15	15
Field 16	15

Figure 8-7. Names and widths of all fields in the mailing-list database.

When you design a form, begin at the top. To enter a title on the first line of the form, press the Right Arrow key 30 times, type *MAIL LIST MANAGER*, and press Enter.

Next, enter four fields on the fourth line of the form: Title, First Name, Initial, and Last Name. To begin, press the Down Arrow key three times to move the cursor to line 4, press Home to move the cursor to the beginning of the line, type the text *Name*, and press Enter. To place the Title field, type the name of the field, followed by a colon, at the appropriate position. In this case, press the Right Arrow key six times, type *Title:*, and press Enter. To remove the field name from the display, select Show Field Name from the Format menu. (You will relabel the field later, on line 5.) Then, to reduce the width of the field to five characters, select Width from the Format menu, type *5*, and press Enter or choose OK.

To place the First Name field, press the Right Arrow key twice, type *First Name:*, and press Enter. To remove the field name from the display, select Show Field Name from the Format menu. To set the width of the field to 15 characters, select Width from the Format menu, type *15*, and press Enter or choose OK.

Next, press the Right Arrow key two times, type *Initial:*, and press Enter. Then, choose Show Field Name, choose Width, type *2*, and press Enter or choose OK. To place the Last Name field to the right of the Initial field, press Right Arrow two more times, type *Last Name:*, and press Enter. Then, choose Show Field Name, choose Width, type *15*, and press Enter or choose OK.

After you create these fields on line 4 of the form, enter text that describes them on line 5. To do so, first press the Down Arrow key and Home to move the cursor to the beginning of the fifth line. Then, press the Right Arrow key nine times, type *Title*, press the Right Arrow key two more times, type *First*, press the Right Arrow key 12 more times, type *MI*, press the Right Arrow key twice, type *Last*, and press Enter.

As shown in Figure 8-8, the form currently contains four fields: Title, First Name, Initial, and Last Name. The names of these fields are hidden; the text on line 5 and at the beginning of line 4 describes these fields.

Notice that this form uses text instead of the built-in field names to identify the field blanks. To achieve this effect, you need to turn off the Show Field Name option for each field and then type descriptions for the fields in the form. This approach makes it possible to align both the field blanks and the field names in the form, instead of only one or the other. It also allows you to reduce the width of the fields without obscuring the field names.

Next, press the Home key and press the Down Arrow key twice to position the cursor on line 7 of the form. To label the Position field, type *Position* and then press the Right Arrow key twice to move the cursor to the tenth column. To place the field itself, type *Position:* and press Enter. Then, choose Show Field Name from the Format menu to hide the field name, and choose Width from the Format menu, type *20*, and press Enter to change the field width.

Now, use the same techniques you used to place the fields on lines 4 and 7 to place the remainder of the fields listed in Figure 8-7. Most of the fields are aligned below the Position field and opposite their labels. The Street 1 field is on line 11, opposite the label *Address*, with the Street 2 field directly below it. The City, State, and

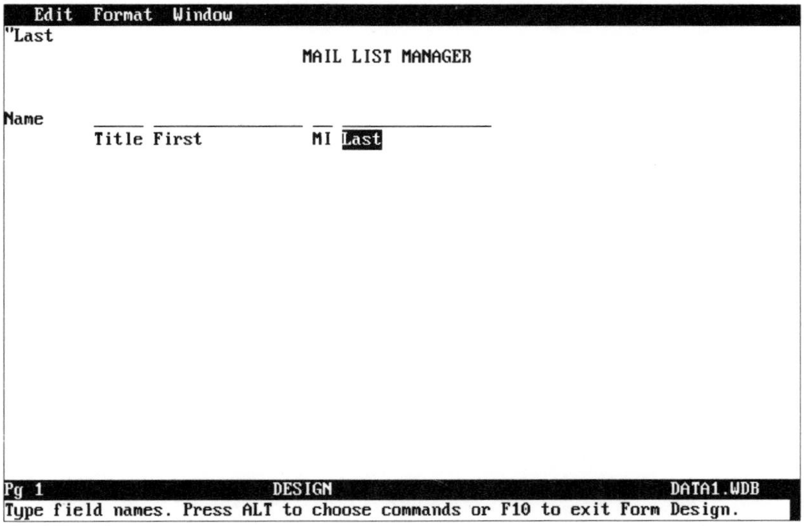

Figure 8-8.

Zip fields, like the Name fields on line 4, are arranged consecutively, with the field labels on the next line.

When your form looks like Figure 8-6 on page 179, exit the form design screen. To do this, select the Exit Design command from the Edit menu or simply press [F10]. In either case, Works exits the form design screen and creates a database according to the specifications in the form.

After you create the database, save it. To save the database for the first time, select Save As from the File menu, type a name (such as MAILLIST.WDB), and press Enter or choose Save.

Creating the mailing-label merge document

To print information from the MAILLIST database in the form of mailing labels, set up a merge document like the one shown in Figure 8-2 on page 177. This document contains placeholders for most of the fields in the MAILLIST database. When you print a report from this document, Works draws information from the fields specified by the placeholders and prints it in the report.

To create this document, first select New from the File menu, choose Word Processor as the document type, and then choose New to create a new document like the one shown in Figure 8-9.

Now, insert placeholders in the new document that refer to the fields in the database. Arrange the placeholders like a mailing label—as you intend to print them. In brief, the procedure for inserting a placeholder requires that you open the database

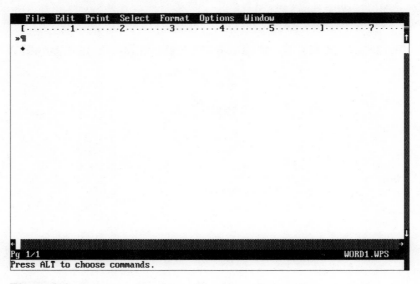

Figure 8-9.

that contains the field from which you want to retrieve information. Then, you need to position the cursor in your document where you want that field to appear and use the Insert Field command on the Edit menu to specify the database and field you want to reference.

To create the merge document shown in Figure 8-3 on page 177, you need to retrieve information from 10 fields in the MAILLIST database shown in Figure 8-1 on page 176: First Name, Initial, Last Name, Position, Company, Street 1, Street 2, City, State, and Zip. To begin placing fields, select Open from the File menu and open the MAILLIST database. (If the MAILLIST database is already open, skip this step.) Then, choose WORD1 from the Windows menu to make it the active document again. Now, move the cursor to the upper left corner of the screen (if it is not there already), select Insert Field from the Edit menu, choose MAILLIST.WDB from the Databases box, choose First Name from the Fields box, and then press Enter or choose OK. As you see in Figure 8-10, Works inserts the placeholder <<*First Name*>> at the upper left corner of the document.

To complete the first line of the document, place the Initial and Last Name fields. To retrieve entries from the Initial field, first press the Spacebar once to insert a blank space after the placeholder for the First Name field. Then, select Insert Field from the Edit menu, choose Initial from the Fields list box (MAILLIST.WDB is still the selected database), and then press Enter or choose OK. To place the Last Name field, press the Spacebar once more, select Insert Field, select Last Name from the Fields box, and then press Enter or choose OK.

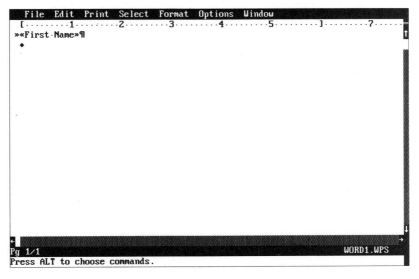

Figure 8-10.

After you place the fields on the first line, repeat the same steps to retrieve information from the remaining fields (Position, Company, Street 1, Street 2, City, State, and Zip). Place the Position field at the left edge of the second line, the Company field at the left edge of the third line, the Street 1 field at the left edge of the fourth line, and the City field at the left edge of the fifth line. Then, go back and put the placeholder for the Street 2 field to the right of the Street 1 field on the fourth line. The placeholder for the State field belongs on the fifth line, separated from the City placeholder by a comma and a space. Finally, put the placeholder for the Zip field to the right of the State placeholder, separated from it by two spaces. Figure 8-3 on page 177 shows the completed merge document.

After you create this document, save it. To do so, select Save As from the File menu, type a name (such as *LABELS.WPS*), and press Enter or choose OK.

Creating the generic form-letter merge document

To print information from the mailing-list database within form letters, set up a Word Processor merge document like the one shown in Figure 8-4 on page 178. Like the merge document you created to print mailing labels, this document contains placeholders to retrieve information from most of the fields in the MAILLIST database. In addition to these placeholders, however, it also contains text that serves as the body of the letter. When you print a report from this document, Works prints a customized letter for each selected record in the database.

To create this document, first select New from the File menu, choose Word Processor as the document type, and then choose New to create a new Word Processor document. Now you're ready to begin placing fields.

The first line of the sample letter in Figure 8-4 on page 178 contains a special date field which instructs Works to print the current date at the top of each letter. To place this field, position the cursor at the upper left corner of the document (if it is not there already). Then, select Insert Special from the Edit menu to display the Insert Special dialog box. The choices in this dialog box allow you to place various special fields in your documents. When the box appears, choose Print Date and then choose OK. Works places the marker *date* at the upper left corner of the document.

The third through seventh lines of the document contain placeholders for the fields from the MAILLIST database. As you can see, the arrangement of these fields is almost exactly the same as the arrangement of the fields in the mailing label shown in Figure 8-3 on page 177. The only difference is that in the form letter, a placeholder for the Title field appears to the left of the First Name, Initial, and Last Name fields on the third line. You can create these field placeholders in exactly the same way you created the placeholders in the mailing-label document. First, use the Open command on the File menu to open the MAILLIST database. Then place each field as you did in the other document: Position the cursor where you want the field to appear, select Insert Field from the Edit menu, select MAILLIST.WDB as the database, and choose the field from which you want to retrieve information from the Fields selection box. Finally, press Enter or choose OK.

The ninth line of the document contains the salutation, a combination of text and placeholders for the Title and Last Name fields. To create this line, first move the cursor to the beginning of the ninth line and type *Dear* followed by a single space. Next, insert a placemarker for the Title field by selecting Insert Field from the Edit menu, choosing Title from the Fields box, and then pressing Enter or choosing OK. Now, press the Spacebar to insert one blank space and use the Insert Field command to insert a placemarker for the Last Name field. Finally, type a colon (:).

Although the layout of the date, address, and salutation is the same for almost any form letter, the body of the letter varies greatly. What you include in the body of the form letter depends on the message you want to send; your letter might announce a meeting, convey a birthday greeting, respond to a request for information, or do any of a hundred other things. At this point, move to the eleventh line of the document and type a filler statement: *Replace this sentence with the body of your letter.* Before you print any form letters, replace this line with the message you want to send.

Like the body of a letter, the closing varies with the purpose of the letter. The standard form letter contains a fairly standard closing. To include this closing in the document, move the cursor to the beginning of the thirteenth line; then, type *Yours truly,* and press Enter four times. Type *Your Name* on line 17.

Now, save the completed form-letter document. To do so, pull down the File menu and select Save As. Then, if you want to save the file in a directory other than the current one, choose that directory from the Other Drives and Directories list box and choose OK. Next, type a name (such as *FORMLTTR.WPS*), and then press Enter or choose OK to save the file. If you want to save the file in the current directory, simply type a filename and press Enter or choose OK. Then, choose Close from the File menu to close the FORMLTTR document.

USING THE TEMPLATE

After you create the MAILLIST database, the mailing-label document, and the form-letter document, you can use them to print mailing labels and form letters. First, though, you have to enter the names, addresses, and other information for the people to whom you intend to write. After you enter this information in the database, you might want to sort the database or specify some selection criteria. Then, you can use either mail-merge document to print the information.

Filling in the Database

For the most part, the names of the fields in the MAILLIST database explain the type of information you need to enter in each field. The Title field holds a title of address, such as Mr., Ms., or Dr.; the First Name field holds a first name; the Last Name field holds a last name; and so forth.

The type of information you enter in the last five fields depends on your purpose in creating the database. If you are creating a personal database, you might want to store birthdays in one field, telephone numbers in another field, spouses' names in a third field, and so forth. If you are using the database for business purposes, you might use these fields to store social security numbers, salaries, dates of employment, and so forth. In any case, you can use as many of these extra fields as you need. These fields simply allow you to record more information about each individual in the database and to use that new information to select the records you want to print.

To begin filling in the database, open the MAILLIST database and make it the active document. (If MAILLIST.WDB is already open, make it the active document by pulling down the Window menu and selecting its name.) To open the database, choose Open from the File menu. Then, either type the filename under which you saved the database, including the extension (for example, *MAILLIST.WDB*), or highlight the name of the database in the list, and choose OK or press Enter. Works displays the Form screen for the empty database and positions the cursor in the first field (Title), as shown in Figure 8-6 on page 179.

To enter information, simply position the cursor on the field in which you want to make an entry, type that entry, and press Enter or one of the arrow keys. If you press the Enter key, Works stores the entry and keeps the cursor block on that entry. If you press one of the arrow keys, Works stores the entry and moves the cursor to a different field.

As you enter records, you will probably make a few mistakes. To modify an entry, move the cursor to it, press the Edit key ([F2]), make the change, and press Enter. To overwrite an entry, simply move the cursor to it, type the new entry, and then press Enter. To delete an entire record, use the Ctrl-PgUp or Ctrl-PgDn combinations to display it, pull down the Edit menu, and select Delete. To insert a blank record into the database above the current one, pull down the Edit menu and select Insert.

An example

To see how this template works, enter the information about sales leads (prospects) shown in Figure 8-11 in the MAILLIST database. Use Field 12 to store the source of each lead, Field 13 to store the date of each lead, Field 14 to store the initials

	Title	First Name	Initial	Last Name	Position	Company	Street 1
1	Mr.	John	F.	Smith	Financial Analyst	XYZ Corporation	123 Commerce Way
2	Ms.	Mary	P.	Jones	Executive Asst.	Reagan, Nixon & Ford	234 W. 52nd Street
3	Dr.	Peter	E.	Ford			3125 Meadow Road
4	Mrs.	Gladys	P.	Knight	Lead Pip	Gladys Knight & The Pips	8532 Peachtree Pl.
5	Mr.	James		Williams	President	James Williams, Inc.	2415 Main Street
6	Ms.	Wendy	O.	Williams	CFO	Alameda Corp.	2415 3rd Street
7	Dr.	David	D.	Denton	Chief Scientist	Modern Sleepwear	5617 Any Street
8	Mr.	Michael	L.	Murphy	Proprietor	Murphy's Bar & Grill	855 Broadway
9	Ms.	Deborah	F.	Harry	Lead Blond	Blondie	243 E. 11th Street
10	Mr.	Gary	S.	Rizzo	Meteorologist	WHAS TV	145 S. 6th Street
11	Ms.	Grace	V.	Slick	Original Member	Spaceship, Inc.	287 Fulton Street
12	Mr.	Don	C.	Kirshner	President	DCK, Inc.	3096 Fifth Avenue
13	Mrs.	Phyllis		George	Broadcaster	United Conservatives	328 Market Street

Figure 8-11.

of the salesperson who will follow up on each lead, and Field 15 to store the type of product that interests each prospective customer.

To enter these records, begin by making MAILLIST.WDB the active document. Then, type *Mr.*, press the Right Arrow key, type *John*, press Right Arrow, type *F.*, press Right Arrow, type *Smith*, press Right Arrow, and so forth. After you enter the label *PC* in Field 15 of the first record, press the Right Arrow key to move the cursor to Field 16, which is unused. Then, press the Right Arrow key again to move the cursor to the Title field of the next record and enter the information for the second sales lead. Enter the remaining 12 records in the same fashion.

Saving the database

After you enter these records in the database, save it again. To do this, select Save As from the File menu, type a new name, and press Enter or choose OK. Choose a name for the file that clearly identifies its contents—for example, *PROSPECT.WDB* for your prospect mailing list. Be sure to save your filled-in mailing-list database under a name other than the name you used for the original, empty template. If you save a filled-in database under the same name as the original template, the filled-in version replaces the original version.

As you continue to use the database, you will edit and delete existing records and add new records to it. Always resave the database after you make changes. As your databases get bigger, be sure to save a backup copy of them on a floppy disk for safety.

Multiple databases

To get the most from this template, create several different databases of names and addresses. At work you might have one database that stores the names of your prospects, one for the names of your customers, and one for the names of your employees. To create the second and subsequent databases, open the empty MAILLIST database, enter the appropriate information in it, and then use the Save As command to save it under a new name. For example, to create a database to hold the names of your customers, you would use the Open command to open the MAILLIST

Street 2	City	State	Zip	Field 12	Field 13	Field 14	Field 15	Field 16
Mail Stop A231	Milwaukee	WI	39103	WSJ	32143	DFC	PC	
Suite 123	New York	NY	10023	Phone	32174	JTC	PC	
	Evansville	IN	38901	Phone	32178	JLM	MF	
Suite 3256	Atlanta	GA	21675	PCW	32183	JLM	MINI	
	Denver	CO	87143	Info	32194	DFC	MF	
	Alameda	CA	45618	WSJ	32207	SSC	MF	
Suite 581	Palo Alto	CA	45819	Phone	32218	DFC	MF	
	Louisville	KY	40200	Local	32226	DFC	PC	
Apt 4C	New York	NY	10001	RS	32235	JTC	PC	
	Louisville	KY	40201	Local	32270	JLM	PC	
	San Francisco	CA	43970	RS	32272	JTC	PC	
Suite 199	New York	NY	10030	WSJ	32274	JTC	MINI	
	Birmingham	AL	32981	Phone	32285	SSC	PC	

database, enter your customer names into it, and then use the Save As command to save it under the name CUST.WDB. Because all versions of the MAILLIST database have the same structure (that is, the same fields), you can use any of them with the mailing-label and form-letter documents you will create.

Selecting Records

When Works prints a database report, it extracts information from only the records that are selected at the time. If all the records are selected, Works prints one mailing label or form letter for each record in the database. If only certain records are selected, Works prints a document for only those certain records.

To select a subset of the records in a database, use the Define command on the Query menu to create a query form. Then, enter one or more selection conditions (criteria) in the query form and apply those criteria to the database. When you do this, Works displays only the matching records. If you then print the database, Works prints only the displayed records.

For example, suppose you want to select only those prospects with the entry *Phone* in the Source field (Field 12). To do so, select Define from the Query menu to display the query form for the database. The query form, shown in Figure 8-12, looks exactly like the entry form.

Because you want Works to select only those records that have the entry *Phone* in the Source field, enter that word in the corresponding field in the query form. To do this, press the Right Arrow key 11 times to position the cursor on that field (field 12),

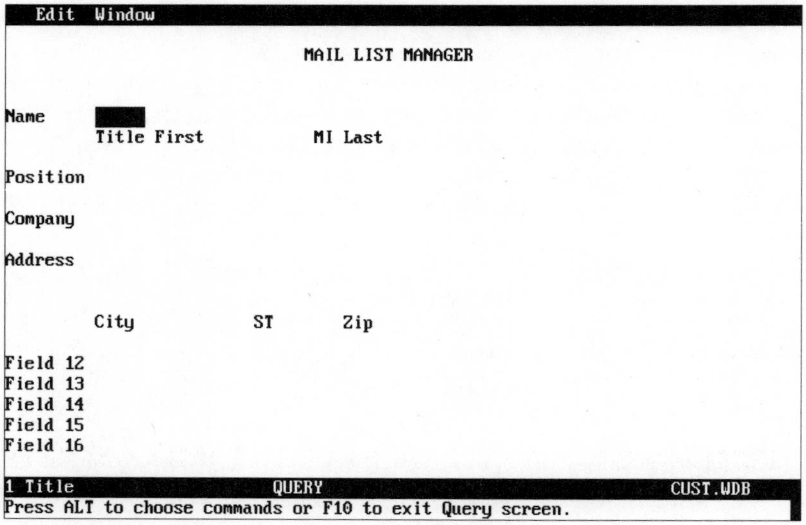

Figure 8-12.

type *Phone*, and press Enter. Now, to execute this selection, press [F10] or select Exit Query from the Edit menu. Works then exits the define query mode and returns to the database. Instead of showing you all the records in that database, however, Works displays only those records that meet the condition you set. If you chose View Form from the Options menu, you see the first matching record in the database, as shown in Figure 8-13. You also see the message *4/13* at the bottom of the screen, which tells you that only 4 of the 13 records in the database were selected. If you chose View List from the Options menu, the screen displays only the selected records, as shown in Figure 8-14 on the following page.

To view all the records in a database again, choose Show All Records from the Query menu. When you issue this command, Works lets you display all the records in the database, and you see the message *13/13* in the Status line. To reapply the criterion, select Apply Query again from the Query menu.

To define a different query, select Define from the Query menu to enter the query form again. To change the criteria completely, select Delete from the Edit menu to delete any existing criteria, and then enter your new criteria. If you want to modify the current query, you can edit the existing criteria or add additional criteria to the form. When the query is ready, simply press [F10] or select Exit Query from the Edit menu to activate it.

Of course, this example barely scratches the surface of the various criteria you can use to select records from a Works database. For more on the use of criteria, see pages 406–416 in the *Microsoft Works Reference*.

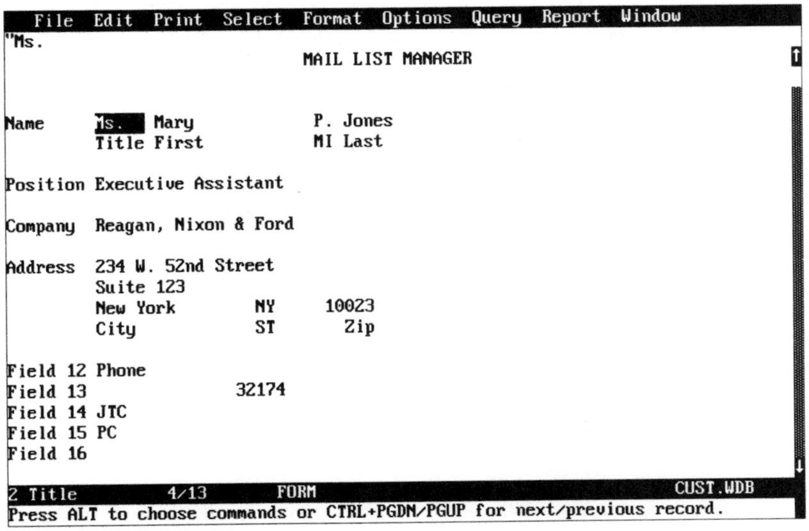

Figure 8-13.

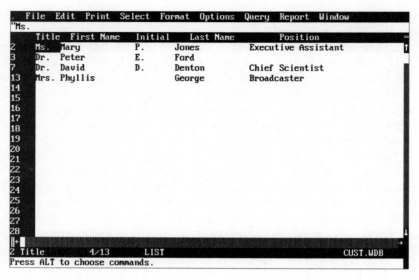

Figure 8-14.

Sorting Records

When you print a database report, Works orders the records as they appear in the database. In most cases, that is the order in which you entered them in the database. Sorting the database enables you to change the order of the records in the database— and therefore in the printed report.

Sorting a Works database is a relatively simple process. To begin, pull down the Query menu and select the Sort command. Works then presents a Sort dialog box, like the one shown in Figure 8-15, that allows you to define as many as three sort fields. Then, move the cursor to the entry box for the first sort field, type the name of the field on which you want to sort the database, and select a sort order (either Ascend or Descend) for that field. When you choose OK, Works closes the Sort dialog box and sorts the database into the order you specified.

For example, suppose you want to sort the PROSPECT database into ascending order on the basis of the entries in the Last Name field. To do this, pull down the Query menu, select Sort, type *Last Name* in the 1st Field entry box, and select Ascend (if it is not selected already). Then choose OK to sort the database. As shown in Figure 8-16, Works arranges the records in the database in ascending alphabetical order on the basis of the entries in the Last Name field.

Once again, this simple example doesn't begin to exploit the full potential for sorting a database using Works. For more information on sorting, see pages 422–425 in the *Microsoft Works Reference*.

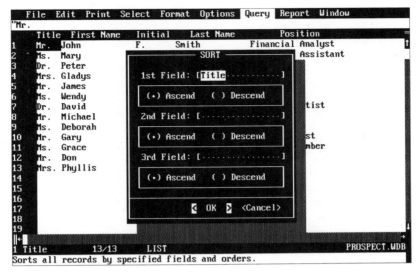

Figure 8-15.

```
 File   Edit   Print   Select   Format   Options   Query   Report   Window
"Dr.
    Title  First Name   Initial    Last Name        Position              ≡
1   Dr.  David          D.      Denton         Chief Scientist               ↑
2   Dr.  Peter          E.      Ford
3   Mrs. Phyllis                George         Broadcaster
4   Ms.  Deborah        F.      Harry          Lead Blond
5   Ms.  Mary           P.      Jones          Executive Assistant
6   Mr.  Don            C.      Kirshner       President
7   Mrs. Gladys         P.      Knight         Lead Pip
8   Mr.  Michael        L.      Murphy         Proprietor
9   Mr.  Gary           S.      Rizzo          Meteorologist
10  Ms.  Grace          V.      Slick          Original Member
11  Mr.  John           F.      Smith          Financial Analyst
12  Mr.  James                  Williams       President
13  Ms.  Wendy          O.      Williams       CFO
14
15
16
17
18
19
‖←
1 Title        13/13      LIST                            PROSPECT.WDB
Press ALT to choose commands.
```

Figure 8-16.

Printing Mailing Labels

Next, you need to adjust the page layout settings for printing labels. To do this, first make LABELS.WPS the active document (by opening it or choosing it from the Window menu). Next, select Layout from the Print menu to display the Layout dialog box shown in Figure 8-17. When this dialog box appears, set all margins to 0 (including the Header Margin and the Footer Margin) and set the page dimensions to match the size of the label stock you are using. Also, be sure to clear the Header and Footer text boxes.

Next, select Print Labels from the Print menu to display the Print Labels dialog box shown in Figure 8-18. The options in this dialog box allow you to select the database from which you want Works to retrieve information and to set the dimensions and the arrangement of the labels you want to print. The Databases selection box contains a list of the database files that are currently open. Choose the name of the database from which you want to print. Because the Databases box lists only databases that are currently open, you won't be able to print from a database unless it appears in the list.

Your choices for the other options depend on the sheets of labels on which you are going to print. The Label Spacing settings need to match the dimensions of your labels. Enter the Vertical and Horizontal settings to match the height and width of your labels. The Number of Labels Across Page setting tells Works how many labels you want to print across each page. For example, to print single-column labels on

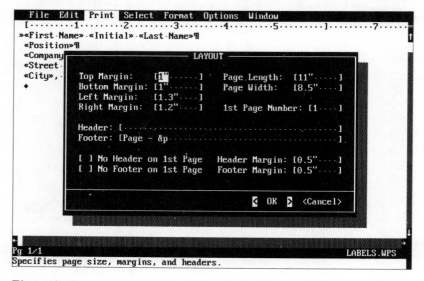

Figure 8-17.

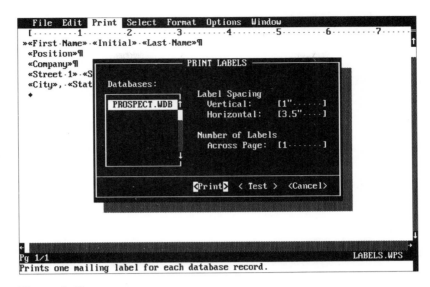

Figure 8-18.

stock that is ¹⁵/₁₆ inch by 3¹/₂ inches, specify *1* for the vertical spacing, *3.5* for the
horizontal spacing, and *1* label across each page. (Works supplies the default unit of
measure, inches.)

Now, choose Print or Test from the bottom of the dialog box to display the Print
dialog box shown in Figure 8-19 on the following page. The first setting in this dialog
box lets you specify the number of copies of each label you want to print. In most
cases, you want to print only one copy (the default setting). The second setting, Print
Specific Pages, is not meaningful when you are printing mailing labels. The third setting, Print to File, allows you to print the labels to a text file instead of to your printer. To do so, select this option and specify the name of the text file. The final setting,
Draft Quality, lets you cancel out any special print attributes (styles, fonts, and so
forth) that you have assigned to the placeholders or text in the merge document.

After you adjust any settings you want to change in the Print dialog box, you can
print the labels. Before you start the process, however, align the labels in your printer
so that the print head is on the first line of the first row of labels. Then, simply
choose Print from the bottom of the Print dialog box.

If you chose Test from the Print Labels dialog box, Works prints only the first
row of labels and then displays the dialog box shown in Figure 8-20 on the following
page. If the sample mailing labels are aligned correctly on the sheet, choose Print to
print the remaining labels. If the labels are not properly positioned, adjust the alignment and choose Test to print the first label or row of labels again. If the alignment is
correct, choose Print. Otherwise, adjust the alignment of the labels again and repeat
the Test command.

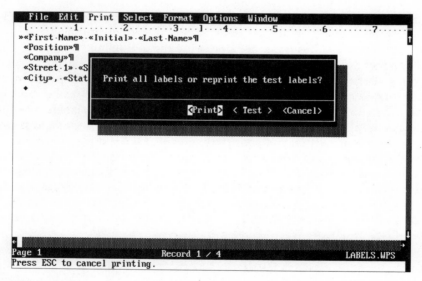

Figure 8-19.

Figure 8-20.

If you choose Print from the Print Labels dialog box, Works does not print a test row. Instead, it simply prints the labels—one label for each selected record, in the order that those records appear in the database. If you want to cancel the printing process before Works prints every label, simply press the Esc key. When you do, Works will display a dialog box that offers two options, labeled OK and Cancel. If you choose OK from this box, Works terminates the printing process. If you choose Cancel, Works cancels the interruption and continues to print labels.

An example

To demonstrate the process, let's print a label for each record in the PROSPECT database that has the entry *PC* in Field 15. We'll arrange the records in ascending order based on the entries in the Zip field, and print them on two-across mailing labels, $^{15}/_{16}$ inch deep and $3^{1}/_{2}$ inches wide.

To begin, check to see that PROSPECT.WDB and LABELS.WPS are open, with PROSPECT.WDB the active window. Then, select Sort from the Query menu, specify Zip as the first sort field, choose ascending order, and then choose OK. Works sorts the PROSPECT database in ascending order based on the entries in the Zip field. Next, select Define from the Query menu, type *PC* in the Field 15 blank of the query form, press Enter, and then press [F10] to display only those records that have the entry *PC* in Field 15.

After sorting and selecting the records, begin printing the labels. To do this, first activate the LABELS merge document by selecting its name from the Window menu. From within this document, choose Layout from the Print menu to activate the Layout dialog box. Now, adjust the Page Length and Page Width settings to match the label stock you are using, set all the margin settings to 0, and press Enter or choose OK. Next, select Print Labels from the Print menu to display the Print Labels dialog box. Choose PROSPECT.WDB as the source database and specify *1* for the vertical spacing, *3.5* for the horizontal spacing, and *2* labels across each page. Then choose Print to store these settings and to display the Print dialog box. Be sure that the Number of Copies option is set to 1 and that the other three options are off.

Finally, choose Print at the bottom of the Print dialog box to begin printing labels. As shown in Figure 8-21 on the following page, these labels are arranged in ascending order based on the entries in the Zip field, and only those records with the Field 15 entry *PC* are printed.

Printing Form Letters

The merge document shown in Figure 8-4 on page 178 lets you print the information from the PROSPECT database in form letters. Like printing mailing labels, printing form letters is a multiple-step process. First, make the merge document active and then customize the form letter so that it conveys the message you want to send. When the form letter is ready to print, perform a series of steps similar to those for printing mailing labels.

```
Deborah F. Harry                    Mary P. Jones
Lead Blond                          Executive Asst.
Blondie                             Reagan, Nixon & Ford
243 E. 11th Street Apt 4C           234 W. 52nd Street Suite 123
New York, NY  10001                 New York, NY  10023


Phyllis  George                     John F. Smith
Broadcaster                         Financial Analyst
United Conservatives                XYZ Corporation
328 Market Street                   123 Commerce Way Mail Stop A231
Birmingham, AL  32981               Milwaukee, WI  39103


Michael L. Murphy                   Gary S. Rizzo
Proprietor                          Meteorologist
Murphy's Bar & Grill                WHAS TV
855 Broadway                        145 S. 6th Street
Louisville, KY  40200               Louisville, KY  40201


Grace V. Slick
Original Member
Spaceship, Inc.
287 Fulton Street
San Francisco, CA  43970
```

Figure 8-21.

Customizing the form letter

Because the body and typed signature of our form letter are generic, replace them with the text you actually want to send before you print each batch of form letters. To replace the generic text statement with your custom message, simply expand the cursor to cover that statement and type the new body copy. To replace the phrase *Your Name* in the closing with your actual name, expand the cursor to cover that phrase and type your name.

In addition to text, the body of your form letter can contain merge fields. To insert a placeholder for a merge field in the body of the letter, repeat the steps you used to place a field in the address or salutation portions of the letter: Position the cursor where you want that field to appear, select Insert Field from the Edit menu, choose a database, select a field, and then choose OK.

Because we stored information on sales leads in PROSPECT, let's customize the form letter to serve as cover letter for product information that we want to send to each prospect. Then, type the following paragraphs and placeholders in place of the statement *Replace this sentence with the body of your letter.*

Thank you for your recent inquiry about XYZ Corporation's products. The information you requested is enclosed.

<<Title>> <<Last Name>>, many thousands of people just like you have found XYZ's products to be perfect for their business and personal computing needs. We think you will agree that the XYZ Corporation makes the finest computer supplies available anywhere.

Once again, thank you for your inquiry.

Now, replace the generic phrase *Your Name* in the closing with the text

**Smiley G. Handshaker
V.P. Sales and Marketing**

Figure 8-22 shows the customized letter.

To alter the layout of the form letter—its margins, page length, page width, headers, footers, and so forth—select Layout from the Print menu. For most reports, the default settings shown in the Page Layout dialog box are satisfactory. If you want to change any settings, however, make your changes and then choose OK.

You also can assign special print attributes to the merge fields and text within a merge document. To do this, expand the cursor to mark the text or placeholder of the field you want to adjust, pull down the Format menu, and select the attribute(s) you want to assign to that text or field. You can use the commands in the middle section of the Format menu to alter the line spacing of the letter.

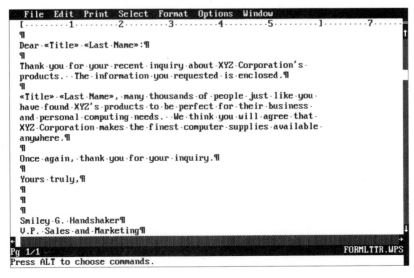

Figure 8-22.

Printing the form letter

Now, prepare to print the form letter. As you might expect, the process of printing form letters is somewhat like that of printing mailing labels. To begin, be sure that the source database (in this case, PROSPECT.WDB) and the form-letter merge document (in this case, FORMLTTR.WPS) are open, and that the merge document is the active document. Next, select Print Merge from the Print menu. When you issue this command, Works displays the Print Merge dialog box shown in Figure 8-23. Now, choose the name of the database from which the form letter extracts information (in this case, PROSPECT.WDB) and then choose OK.

When you choose OK, Works displays the Print dialog box shown in Figure 8-24. The options in this box allow you to specify the number of copies of the letter you want to print for each record, the pages you want to print, and the destination— whether it be your printer or a file. You can also indicate whether you want the printer to ignore special print attributes (boldfacing, underlining, special type faces, and so forth) in the document by choosing the Draft Quality check box. In most cases, you can simply use the default settings shown in Figure 8-24.

Now, choose Print to print the form letters, one for each selected record, in the order that they appear in the database. To cancel the printing process before Works prints every letter, simply press the Esc key and then choose Cancel.

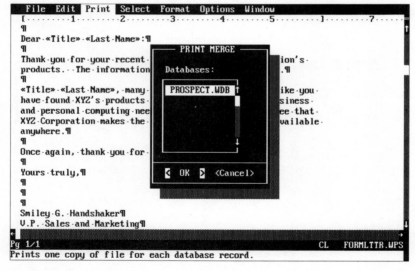

Figure 8-23.

```
  File  Edit  Print  Select  Format  Options  Window
[·········1·········2·········3·········4·········5·········]·········7·····
¶
Dear·«Title»··«Last·Name»:¶
¶                          ┌──────── PRINT ────────┐
Thank·you·for·y            │                        │
products.··The             │ Number of Copies: [1····] │
¶                          │                        │
«Title»··«Last·N           │ [ ] Print Specific Pages │
have·found·XYZ'            │                 Pages: [··········] │
and·personal·co            │                        │
XYZ·Corporation            │ [ ] Print to File      │
anywhere.¶                 │           File Name: [···········] │
¶                          │                        │
Once·again,··tha           │ [ ] Draft Quality      │
¶                          │                        │
Yours·truly,¶              │                        │
¶                          │         ◀Print▶  <Cancel> │
¶                          │                        │
¶                          └────────────────────────┘
Smiley·G.·Handshaker¶
V.P.·Sales·and·Marketing¶
                                                        FORMLTTR.WPS
Prints one copy of file for each database record.
```

Figure 8-24.

A simple example

As a simple example of printing form letters, print the letter shown in Figure 8-22 on page 197 once for each of the seven individuals selected from the PROSPECT database by the previous query. To do this, begin by checking to see that both the mailing-list database (PROSPECT.WDB) and the form-letter merge document (FORMLTTR.WPS) are open. If they are not, use the Open command on the File menu to open them. Next, be sure that PROSPECT is the active window and that only the seven records that meet the condition are selected. If not, choose Define from the Query menu, type *PC*, press Enter, and press [F10] or choose Exit Query from the Edit menu.

To print the form letters, activate the FORMLTTR merge document by selecting its name from the Window menu. Next, select Print Merge from the Print menu to display the Print Merge dialog box, and choose PROSPECT.WDB as the source database. Then, choose Print to display the Print dialog box. Be sure that the Number of Copies option is set to 1 and that the other three options are off. Finally, align the paper in your printer, turn the printer on, and choose Print. When you do this, Works prints one form letter for each record in the database. Figure 8-25 on the following page shows one of the letters.

Adding complexity

As you can see, defining a query lets you select only those records that match the criteria that you define; Works then prints the form letter for only a subset of the records in the database. Sorting a database before you print enables you to print the form letters in the new, sorted order.

1/4/88

Ms. Deborah F. Harry
Lead Blond
Blondie
243 E. 11th Street Apt 4C
New York, NY 10001

Dear Ms. Harry:

Thank you for your recent inquiry about XYZ Corporation's
products. The information you requested is enclosed.

Ms. Harry, many thousands of people just like you have found
XYZ's products to be perfect for their business and personal
computing needs. We think you will agree that XYZ
Corporation makes the finest computer supplies available
anywhere.

Once again, thank you for your inquiry.

Yours truly,

Smiley G. Handshaker
V.P. Sales and Marketing

Figure 8-25.

MODIFICATIONS

You might want to make a couple of important modifications to the mailing-label
and form-letter documents you've created. First, you might modify the documents by
removing the Company and Position field placeholders. Second, you might assign
special formats to some of the field placeholders in the form-letter or label
documents.

Eliminating the Company and Position Fields

Although most records in the PROSPECT database have entries in the Position
and Company fields, some do not. Because the placeholders for these fields are the
only entries on two of the lines in the LABELS merge document, Works leaves a
blank line in the label if the record lacks an entry in either field, and it leaves two

blank lines in the label if the record lacks an entry in both fields. Blank lines also appear when you print form letters for these records.

The only way to eliminate these blank lines is to remove the Position and Company fields from the merge document. Unfortunately, this keeps Works from printing Position and Company information from those records that have entries in those fields. If you are using the MAILLIST database for personal rather than business purposes, you might prefer to remove the Position and Company fields from the LABELS merge document. Figure 8-26 shows the resulting document. This change eliminates the two unwanted blank lines from mailing labels. By modifying your form-letter document in exactly the same way, you can avoid similar problems with blank Position and Company fields.

Formatting the Document

Works lets you assign special print attributes (boldfacing, underlining, alternative fonts and sizes, and so forth) to the field placeholders in your mailing-label or form-letter documents. To use this feature, simply highlight at least the first letter of the placeholder of the field you want to adjust, pull down the Format menu, and select the attribute(s) you want to assign to that field. When you print the mailing label or form letter, Works prints each entry from that field in the style you assigned to its placeholder.

Figure 8-26.

CONCLUSION

Mailing-list management is one of the most popular uses for Microsoft Works. In this chapter, you created a system you can use to manage almost any mailing list. Along the way, you learned how to create, query, and sort databases, and you learned how to create merge documents in Works. If you want to use Works for mailing-list management, you'll probably be able to use this template as is. Even if you don't use the template, you can probably apply the techniques you learned to your own Works files.

The Time Tracker

As the American economy becomes more and more a service economy, people and companies increasingly use time as their fundamental measure of output. Accountants, lawyers, graphic artists, consultants, copywriters, and many other professionals sell their services in units of time. For example, a lawyer preparing a bill typically charges each client for a certain number of hours spent on a certain project at a certain rate. These professionals use time as a convenient measure of the services they provide.

Companies and individuals who bill by the hour obviously have a great need to keep track of their time. Fortunately, Microsoft Works is a terrific tool for tracking time. You can use the Works database to record the time you and your staff spend on each task, project, and client. Then, use queries to select specific information from the database, such as the information for a certain client, project, or employee. You can also create reports that present the information in the database in a variety of forms.

The Time Tracker provides the basic tools you need to begin tracking time in Works. Easy to create and use, the template can nevertheless be extremely useful. And as you build the template, you'll learn how to create, query, and sort databases, and how to create and use database reports in Works.

ABOUT THE TEMPLATE

The Time Tracker is based on a simple Works database named TIMECARD. Figure 9-1 on the following page shows the form we'll use to work with this database. Figure 9-2, also on the following page, shows the database with some sample records entered in it. Figure 9-3 on page 205 shows the upper left corner of the List screen.

```
 File  Edit  Print  Select  Format  Options  Query  Report  Window
"Smith
                                                                            ↑


                              TIME TRACKER
                            Personal Time Card


        Last Name      Smith
        First Name     Mary

        Client         ABC Corp.
        Project        Annual Report
        Task           Manage

        Date              9/1/87
        Time               4.0      (hours and tenths)
        Hourly Rate       $60
        Charge         $240.00




 1 Last Name    19/19      FORM                            TIMECARD.WDB
 Press ALT to choose commands or CTRL+PGDN/PGUP for next/previous record.
```

Figure 9-1.

	Last Name	First Name	Client	Project	Task	Date	Time	Rate	Charge
1	Smith	Mary	ABC Corp.	Annual Report	Manage	9/1/87	4.0	$60	$240.00
2	Williams	Beth	XYZ Inc.	Brochure	Design	9/1/87	10.0	$45	$450.00
3	Jones	John	JLM Limited	Fall Catalog	Design	9/1/87	6.0	$50	$300.00
4	Jones	John	JLM Limited	Fall Catalog	Mockup	9/1/87	3.0	$40	$120.00
5	Smith	Mary	ABC Corp.	Sales Piece	Manage	9/1/87	4.0	$60	$240.00
6	Jones	John	ABC Corp.	Annual Report	Copy	9/2/87	3.0	$40	$120.00
7	Smith	Mary	XYZ Inc.	Brochure	Copy	9/2/87	6.5	$75	$487.50
8	Williams	Beth	XYZ Inc.	Brochure	Mockup	9/2/87	4.0	$40	$160.00
9	Jones	John	ABC Corp.	Sales Piece	Copy	9/2/87	6.0	$40	$240.00
10	Smith	Mary	XYZ Inc.	Slide Show	Manage	9/2/87	1.5	$60	$90.00
11	Williams	Beth	XYZ Inc.	Slide Show	Photo	9/2/87	3.0	$50	$150.00
12	Williams	Beth	DEF Co.	Xmas Mailer	Copy	9/2/87	2.0	$40	$80.00
13	Jones	John	DEF Co.	Annual Report	Design	9/3/87	4.0	$50	$200.00
14	Smith	Mary	DEF Co.	Annual Report	Manage	9/3/87	6.0	$60	$360.00
15	Williams	Beth	TCG Inc.	Annual Report	Photo	9/3/87	6.0	$50	$300.00
16	Williams	Beth	P&Q Manufacturing	Brochure	Design	9/3/87	4.0	$45	$180.00
17	Smith	Mary	AAA Enterprises	New Client Call		9/3/87	2.0	$0	$0.00
18	Jones	John	DEF Co.	Xmas Mailer	Copy	9/3/87	4.0	$40	$160.00
19	Smith	Mary	DEF Co.	Xmas Mailer	Manage	9/3/87	2.0	$60	$120.00

Figure 9-2.

As you can see in the figures above, this database has nine fields, labeled Last
Name, First Name, Client, Project, Task, Date, Time, Rate, and Charge. Each record
stores the time spent by one person on one task within one project for one client. The
Last Name and First Name fields store the name of the person who performed the
work, and the Client field stores the name of the client for whom the work was done.

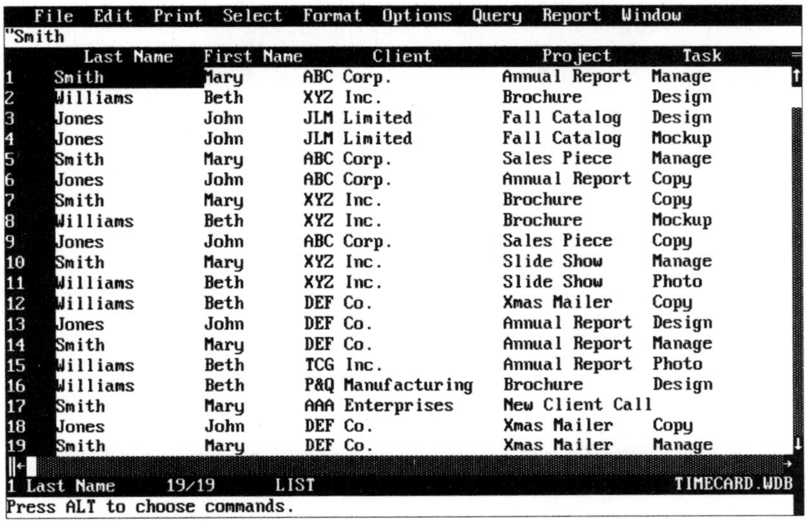

```
  File  Edit  Print  Select  Format  Options  Query  Report  Window
"Smith
          Last Name    First Name        Client            Project        Task        =
1    Smith           Mary       ABC Corp.         Annual Report  Manage         ↑
2    Williams        Beth       XYZ Inc.          Brochure       Design
3    Jones           John       JLM Limited       Fall Catalog   Design
4    Jones           John       JLM Limited       Fall Catalog   Mockup
5    Smith           Mary       ABC Corp.         Sales Piece    Manage
6    Jones           John       ABC Corp.         Annual Report  Copy
7    Smith           Mary       XYZ Inc.          Brochure       Copy
8    Williams        Beth       XYZ Inc.          Brochure       Mockup
9    Jones           John       ABC Corp.         Sales Piece    Copy
10   Smith           Mary       XYZ Inc.          Slide Show     Manage
11   Williams        Beth       XYZ Inc.          Slide Show     Photo
12   Williams        Beth       DEF Co.           Xmas Mailer    Copy
13   Jones           John       DEF Co.           Annual Report  Design
14   Smith           Mary       DEF Co.           Annual Report  Manage
15   Williams        Beth       TCG Inc.          Annual Report  Photo
16   Williams        Beth       P&Q Manufacturing Brochure       Design
17   Smith           Mary       AAA Enterprises   New Client Call
18   Jones           John       DEF Co.           Xmas Mailer    Copy
19   Smith           Mary       DEF Co.           Xmas Mailer    Manage         ↓
|←■                                                                             →
1 Last Name      19/19        LIST                              TIMECARD.WDB
Press ALT to choose commands.
```

Figure 9-3.

The Project and Task fields identify the job that was performed. The Date field records the date on which work was done, the Time field records the amount of time spent on the task, and the Rate field records the hourly rate to be charged for that work. The Charge field contains a formula that computes the total charge for the work by multiplying the value in the Time field by the value in the Rate field.

To supplement this database, we create four reports. The first report, BASIC, is a simple listing of the TIMECARD database. The second report, BILLING SUMMARY, summarizes the total charges for each project and each client. BILLING SUMMARY includes only the Client, Project, and Charge fields. The third report you create, BILLING DETAIL, shows exactly how much work has been done on each project for each client and how much that work has cost. The information in both the second and third reports is grouped by client and by project. This report includes the Client, Last Name, Project, Task, Time, Rate, and Charge fields. Finally, the STAFFING report shows what each person has done. This report is grouped by project, client, and the last name of the staff member. It includes the fields Last Name, First Name, Client, Project, Task, Time, Rate, and Charge.

In this chapter, you also learn to use queries to select information from the TIMECARD database. For example, you can use queries to select only the records for a particular person, or for a particular client, or for a particular project done for a particular client. We also use the Sort command on the Query menu to sort the records in the database.

CREATING THE TEMPLATE

The heart of the Time Tracker is the database that stores the information about what work has been performed by whom for which client. As you might expect, then, the first step in creating the template is creating the TIMECARD database shown in Figure 9-1 on page 204. To begin, select New from the File menu, choose Database, and then choose New. When you do this, Works displays a blank form design screen like the one shown in Figure 9-4.

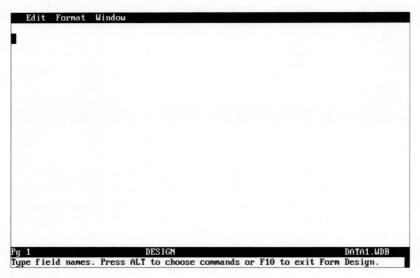

Figure 9-4.

Designing the Form

In Works, you can create a database merely by creating a form for the database. You can take advantage of that shortcut to create the TIMECARD database. Having reached the Design sublevel, you can create the database by building the form shown in Figure 9-5. The table in Figure 9-6 lists the field names and widths for each field you will place in the form and the database.

When you design a form, the best place to begin is the top. First, enter the label TIME TRACKER on the third line of the form. To do this, press the Down Arrow key twice to move the cursor to the third line; then, press the Right Arrow key 33 times to move the cursor toward the middle of the form, type *TIME TRACKER*, and press Enter. Next, press the Down Arrow key once to move the cursor to the fourth line, press the Left Arrow key three times to move the cursor to the left, type *Personal Time Card*, and press Enter.

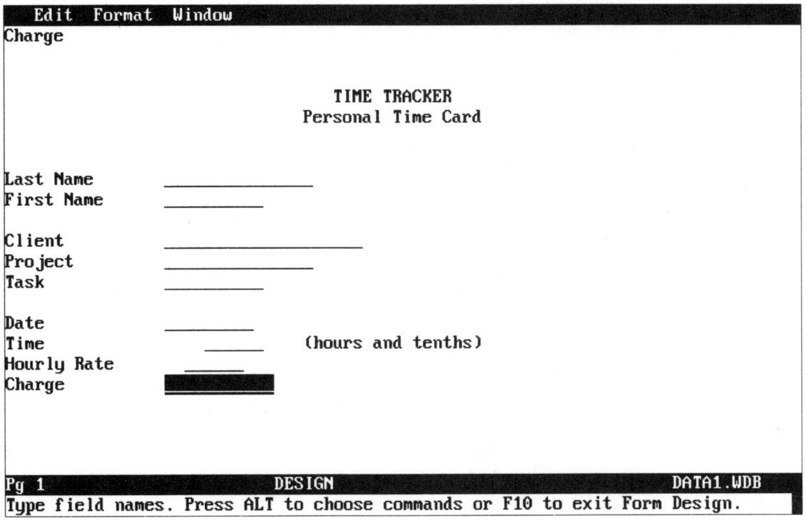

Figure 9-5.

Field	Width
Last Name	15
First Name	10
Client	20
Project	15
Task	10
Date	9
Time	6
Rate	6
Charge	11

Figure 9-6. *Fields and widths for the TIMECARD database.*

Entering the field labels

If you look at Figure 9-2 on page 204, you'll see that we've used text instead of the built-in field names to identify the field blanks in this form. To achieve this effect, we turn off the Show Field Name option for each field and then type descriptions for the fields into the form. This approach makes it possible to align both the field blanks and the field names in the form, and it lets you reduce the width of the fields without obscuring the field names. It also allows you to abbreviate the actual field names (to conserve space in the List screen) without having to use those abbreviated field names as labels in the Form screen.

Now, enter the labels that identify the contents of each field in the form (before you enter the fields themselves). To begin, press the Home key to move the cursor to the left edge of the form, and press the Down Arrow key three times to move the cursor down to the seventh line in the form. Then, type *Last Name* and press Enter. Next, press the Down Arrow key again to move the cursor down one more line, type *First Name*, and press Enter. Then press the Down Arrow key twice to move the cursor to the tenth line, type *Client*, and press Enter.

Continue in this way until you've entered all the labels along the left edge of the form (Figure 9-1). Figure 9-7 shows how your screen looks with all these labels.

Creating the fields

Now you're ready to enter the fields themselves. To begin, press the Up Arrow key to move the cursor to the seventh line of the form, containing the label *Last Name*. Then, press the Right Arrow key eight times, type *Last Name:*, and press Enter. To remove the field name from the display, select Show Field Name from the Format menu. Then, to change the width of the field to 15 characters, select Width from the Format menu, type *15*, and press Enter.

To place the First Name field, press the Down Arrow key once, type *First Name:*, and press Enter. To remove the field name from the display, select Show Field Name from the Format menu. Next, change the width of the field to 10 characters: Select Width from the Format menu, type *10*, and press Enter.

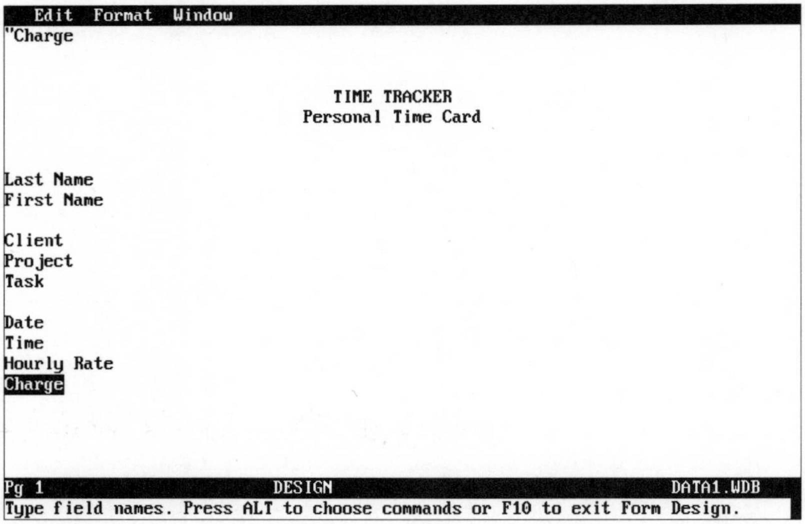

Figure 9-7.

To place the Client field, press the Down Arrow key twice, type *Client:*, and press Enter. Then, select the Show Field Name command to hide the field name, and select Width, type *20*, and press Enter to set the width of the field. To place the Project field, press the Down Arrow key again, type *Project:*, and press Enter. Select the Show Field Name command to hide the field name; select Width, type *15*, and press Enter. To place the Task field, press the Down Arrow key, type *Task:*, and press Enter. Then, select Show Field Name to hide the field name; select Width, type *10*, and press Enter.

To place the Date field, press the Down Arrow key twice, type *Date:*, and press Enter. Then, select Show Field Name to hide the field name; select Width, type *9*, and press Enter. To assign MM/DD/YY format to the Date field, select Time/Date from the Format menu, choose the Month, Day, Year option (with Short date format), and press Enter or choose OK.

To place the Time field, press the Down Arrow key to move the cursor down one line, and press the Right Arrow key four times. Then, type *Time:* and press Enter. Next, select Show Field Name to hide the field name, and select Width, type *6*, and press Enter to set the width of the field. Next, select Fixed from the Format menu, type *1* to set the number of decimal places, and press Enter or choose OK. This command assigns Fixed format with one decimal to the Time field. Next, press the Right Arrow key five times and type the prompt *(hours and tenths)*.

To place the Rate field, press the Down Arrow key again to move the cursor down one line, and then press the Left Arrow key 12 times. Then, type *Rate:* and press Enter. Next, select the Show Field Name command to hide the field name; select Width, type *6*, and press Enter. Next, select Dollar from the Format menu, type *0*, and press Enter or choose OK. This command assigns Dollar format with zero decimals to the Rate field.

Finally, to place the Charge field, press the Down Arrow key again and press the Left Arrow key twice to move the cursor to the left. Then, type *Charge:* and press Enter. Next, select the Show Field Name command to hide the field name; select Width, type *11*, and press Enter to set the width of the field. To assign Dollar format with two decimal places, select Dollar from the Format menu, and press Enter or choose OK to accept the default number of decimal places.

That's it. Your form should now look like the one shown in Figure 9-5 on page 207. Now, exit the Design screen: Select Exit Design from the Edit menu or simply press [F10]. In either case, Works exits the Design screen and creates a database according to the specifications in the form. Before you go on, press Ctrl-Home to move the cursor to the Last Name field. Figure 9-8 on the following page shows the current appearance of your screen.

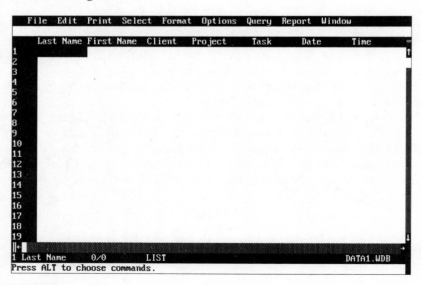

```
 File  Edit  Print  Select  Format  Options  Query  Report  Window
                                                                        ↑
                              TIME TRACKER
                            Personal Time Card

Last Name        ███████████████
First Name

Client
Project
Task

Date
Time                      (hours and tenths)
Hourly Rate
Charge


                                                                        ↓
1 Last Name      0/0        FORM                          DATA1.WDB
Press ALT to choose commands or CTRL+PGDN/PGUP for next/previous record.
```

Figure 9-8.

The List Screen

Now you need to use the List screen of the database to make a few more changes to its structure. To begin, choose View List from the Options menu to display the List screen, as shown in Figure 9-9.

```
 File  Edit  Print  Select  Format  Options  Query  Report  Window
                                                                        =
     Last Name  First Name  Client    Project      Task     Date     Time
1                                                                       ↑
2
3
4
5
6
7
8
9
10
11
12
13
14
15
16
17
18
19                                                                      ↓
‖←                                                                      →
1 Last Name     0/0         LIST                          DATA1.WDB
Press ALT to choose commands.
```

Figure 9-9.

Now, change the widths of the fields in the List screen to match the widths of those fields in the form. These widths are listed in Figure 9-6 on page 207. To change the width of a field on the List screen, move the cursor to that field, select Width from the Format menu, type the new width, and press Enter or choose OK. For example, to change the width of the Last Name field from 10 characters to 15 characters, simply move the cursor to the Last Name field (if it is not there already), select Width from the Format menu, type *15*, and press Enter or choose OK.

After you change the widths of the fields, enter a formula in the Charge field that defines its contents. To do this, move the cursor to the first cell in the Charge field, type *=Time∗Rate*, and press Enter. Because you have not yet entered data in these fields, nothing will happen right away. However, as soon as you enter information in the first record, this formula will return a value based on the contents of the Time and Rate fields for that record. As you enter data in subsequent records, Works uses this formula to compute the correct charge for each record.

Saving the Database

After you create the database, save it. To do so for the first time, select Save As from the File menu. Then, if you want to save the file in a directory other than the current one, choose that directory from the Other Drives & Directories list box and choose OK. Next, type a name (such as *TIMECARD.WDB*), and press Enter or choose Save to save the file. If you want to save the file in the current directory, simply type a filename and press Enter or choose OK.

Creating the Reports

Now you need to create the four reports for the TIMECARD database. To create a new report form, you'll first use the Sort dialog box to define as many as three fields on which you want to sort or group the records in the report. Works uses these fields to determine the printing order of the records and the types of summary group rows you can insert in the new report. If you do not want your new report to group or sort the records it prints, clear all key fields from the dialog box.

After you complete this step, select New from the Report menu to create a new report, like the one shown in Figure 9-10 on the following page. As you can see, this definition includes several types of rows: two Intr Page rows, a Record row, and a Summ Report row. These rows are used to hold field labels and field formulas that specify the information you want to include in the report, as well as where and how you want it to appear.

Works also inserts one summary group row in the default report definition for each field specified in the Sort dialog box.

Within the default report rows, Works inserts the appropriate labels and formulas for each database field that contains entries. In this case, we've entered information only in the Charge field, so only that field contains these labels and formulas.

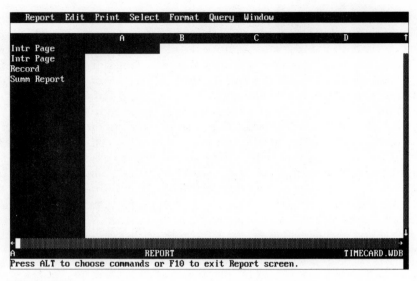

Figure 9-10.

You can either build your report from this default definition prepared by Works, or you can use the Delete command on the Edit menu to clear the report definition so that you can start from scratch. You'll usually begin by clearing the default definition to build your own report. To do this, highlight all the rows in the definition and choose Delete from the Edit menu. After you delete the default rows, use the Insert command on the Edit menu to insert bands of various types into the report design screen. Next, enter labels and formulas in the design screen that define what you want Works to print and where. Next, use the commands on the Format menu to format and change the widths of the columns in the report. Finally, use the Layout command to set the margins for the report and to define a header or a footer (or both).

The BASIC report

Let's begin by creating the BASIC report. As mentioned previously, this report simply lists the records in the TIMECARD database and computes two sums: the total of the entries in the Time field and the total of the entries in the Charge field for the entire report.

To create the BASIC report, first choose Sort from the Query menu. Because this report should neither group nor sort the records it prints, you'll want to delete the field names identified in the Sort dialog box. To do this, simply press the Del key and then press Enter or choose OK. Now, choose New from the Report menu to create a new default report definition, as shown in Figure 9-10.

Now you're ready to define the report. To begin, you need to enter labels and formulas in the existing rows that specify the information you want Works to print and where it should appear in the report. First, you need to enter field names in the first row of the definition. To begin, enter the label *Last Name* in column A of the first Intr Page row. (You can also enter this label by selecting Field Name from the Edit menu, choosing Last Name from the Field Name dialog box, and then choosing OK.) Then, press the Right Arrow key to move the cursor to column B and enter the label *First Name*. To provide a space between this label and the label for column C, increase the width of column B: With the cursor in column B, choose Width from the Format menu, type *11*, and press Enter or choose OK. Now, enter the labels *Client* in column C, *Project* in column D, *Task* in column E, *Date* in column F, *Time* in column G, and *Rate* in column H. Column I already contains the label *Charge*. This row will now place field header labels across the top of each page of the report. By leaving the second Intr Page row blank, you tell Works to insert a blank line below these labels.

Next, you need to enter a series of field formulas in the Record row. To begin, press the Home key and then press the Down Arrow twice to move the cursor to column A of the Record row. Then, enter the formula *=Last Name*. (You can also enter this formula by first selecting Field Value from the Edit menu, choosing Last Name from the Field Value box, and then choosing OK.) Now, enter the formulas *=Client* in column C, *=Project* in column D, *=Task* in column E, *=Date* in column F, *=Time* in column G, and *=Rate* in column H. Column I already contains the formula *=Charge*. These formulas will cause Works to print the entries from the Last Name, Client, Project, Task, Date, Time, Rate, and Charge fields in each record in the report.

Finally, you need to create formulas that will compute totals for the Time and Charges fields. To do this, move to the Summ Report row and enter the formula *=SUM(Time)* in column G and the formula *=SUM(Charge)* in column I. (Another way to enter these formulas is to select the Field Summary command from the Edit menu, choose the field to summarize and SUM as type of calculation, and then choose OK.) These SUM functions compute the sum of the entries in the Time and Charge fields for the entire report. Works prints these values once at the end of the report. Figure 9-11 on the following page shows columns D through I of the completed report definition.

Next, use the Layout command to set the margins for the report and to define a header and a footer for the report. To do this, select Layout from the Print menu to display the Layout dialog box. Move to the Left Margin text box and type *0.5*. This new setting replaces the original setting, *1.3"*, and sets the left margin of the printed report to one-half inch. Next, move to the Right Margin text box and type *0.5*. This change sets the right margin of the printed report to one-half inch. Then, if you have a wide-carriage printer, move the cursor to the Page Width entry box and replace the default width, *8.5"*, with a new setting of *14*.

Figure 9-11.

Now, move to the Header entry box and enter the header definition

&lDate: &d &cBASIC LISTING &rPage: &p

This definition tells Works to print a header with three parts. On each page of the
report, Works prints the label *Date:*, followed by the current date, at the left edge of
the header line; the label *BASIC LISTING* in the center of the header line; and the
label *Page:*, followed by the current page number, at the right edge of the header line.

After you enter the header definition, delete the existing footer definition. To do
this, press the Tab key to advance to the Footer text box, highlighting the existing
definition. Now, simply press the Del key to clear the text box. Figure 9-12 shows the
completed Layout dialog box. When you're finished, press Enter or choose OK to
store the changes you made.

That's all there is to it! The report is now defined. Before you do anything else,
select the Reports command from the Report menu. Selecting this command displays
the dialog box. When you see this, move to the Name entry box and type the name
BASIC as shown in Figure 9-13. Then, press Enter or choose Rename to change the
name of the report you just defined from Report1 to BASIC. Next, select Exit Report
from the Report menu to return to the TIMECARD database and select Save from the
File menu to save the database and the completed report.

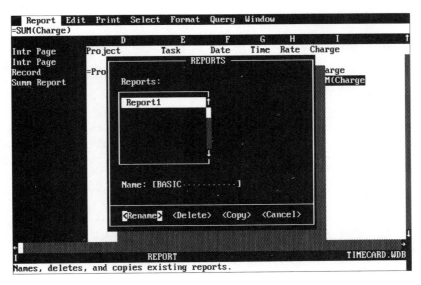

```
 Report  Edit  Print  Select  Format  Query  Window
"Last Name
                      A              B              C                    ↑
Intr Page     Last Name        First Name Client
Intr Page  ┌──────────────────── LAYOUT ────────────────────────┐
Record     │                                                     │
Summ Repor │  Top Margin:    [1"·····]   Page Length:  [11"·····] │
           │  Bottom Margin: [1"······]  Page Width:   [8.5"····] │
           │  Left Margin:   [0.5"····]                           │
           │  Right Margin:  [0.5"····]  1st Page Number: [1····] │
           │                                                     │
           │  Header: [&lDate: &d &cBASIC LISTING &rPage: &p·····] │
           │  Footer: [·········································]   │
           │                                                     │
           │  [ ] No Header on 1st Page   Header Margin: [0.5"····] │
           │  [ ] No Footer on 1st Page   Footer Margin: [0.5"····] │
           │                                                     │
           │                              <  OK  >  <Cancel>     │
           └─────────────────────────────────────────────────────┘
                                                                  ↓
A                     REPORT                         TIMECARD.WDB
Specifies page size, margins, and headers.
```

Figure 9-12.

```
 Report  Edit  Print  Select  Format  Query  Window
=SUM(Charge)
                   D         E        F      G    H      I              ↑
Intr Page     Project      Task     Date   Time Rate  Charge
Intr Page  ┌───────────── REPORTS ─────────────┐
Record     =Pro│                               │arge
Summ Report│  Reports:                         │M(Charge
           │  ┌────────────────────┐↑          │
           │  │ Report1            ││           │
           │  │                    ││           │
           │  │                    ││           │
           │  │                    ││           │
           │  │                    │↓          │
           │  └────────────────────┘           │
           │                                    │
           │  Name: [BASIC···········]          │
           │                                    │
           │  <Rename>  <Delete>  <Copy>  <Cancel> │
           └────────────────────────────────────┘
                                                                  ↓
I                     REPORT                         TIMECARD.WDB
Names, deletes, and copies existing reports.
```

Figure 9-13.

The BILLING SUMMARY

Now let's create another report, the BILLING SUMMARY. As mentioned earlier, this report simply summarizes the total charges for each project and each client. The BILLING SUMMARY includes only the Client, Project, and Charge fields and groups records by the entries in the Client and Project fields.

To create the BILLING SUMMARY report, first select the Sort command from the Query menu to display the Sort dialog box, as shown in Figure 9-14. The Sort dialog box lets you define the fields on which you want to group the report. To do this, enter the field name Client in the 1st Field text box and the field name Project in the 2nd Field text box. Then, press Enter or choose OK to leave the dialog box.

Now, select New from the Report menu to create a new default report definition. Works will now create a report definition similar to the one in Figure 9-10 on page 212. However, in this new report, Works will insert a Summ Client group row followed by a Summ Project group row just above the Summ Report row.

Because this default definition is not similar to the report definition you are creating, begin by deleting it. Simply highlight all six rows in the new definition and select Delete from the Edit menu to empty the report definition.

Now you're ready to begin defining the report. First, you will use the Insert command on the Edit menu to insert a band into the report design screen. Then, you'll enter labels and formulas in that band to define what information you want Works to print and where it should appear in the printed report.

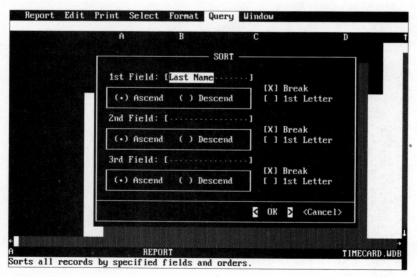

Figure 9-14.

   To begin, highlight the first row in the design screen. To do this, move the cursor
to any cell in that row and select Row from the Select menu. If you have a mouse,
you can select the row by clicking in the area just to the left of row 1. Next, select
Insert from the Edit menu to display the Insert dialog box, as shown in Figure 9-15.
This box lists the different kinds of bands you can use in this report: Intr Report, Intr
Page, Intr Client, and so on. Choose Intr Page and then press Enter or choose OK to
insert an Intr Page band into the report design screen.

   Now you're ready to define the contents of the new band. To begin, type the label
Client in column A of the new band. Then, press the Right Arrow key to move the
cursor to column B, and enter the label *Project*. Finally, move the cursor to column C,
type the label *Charge*, and press Enter. After you enter this last label, select Style
from the Format menu, choose the Right option, and press Enter or choose OK. This
command right-aligns the label in column C.

   Next, highlight row 2 and select Insert from the Edit menu to display the Insert
dialog box. Then, choose Summ Project and press Enter or choose OK to insert a
Summ Project band into the report design screen. Next, type the formula *=Client* in
column A of the new band, press the Right Arrow key to move to column B, and enter the formula *=Project*. Finally, move the cursor to column C and type the formula
=SUM(Charge). Because these formulas are in a Summ Project band, Works computes
and prints their results only once for each different project in the report. The formulas in columns A and B simply display the name of the project and the client for
whom that project is being performed. The formula *=SUM(Charge)* computes the sum
of the entries in the Charge field for that project.

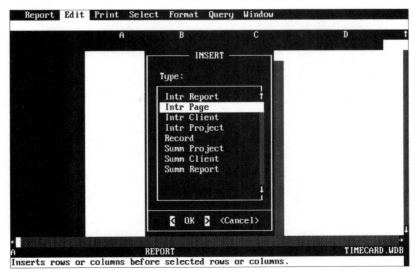

Figure 9-15.

Next, highlight row 3 and select Insert from the Edit menu yet again. When the Insert dialog box appears, choose Summ Client and press Enter or choose OK. Selecting this command inserts a Summ Client band into the report design screen. Next, press the Right Arrow key to move the cursor to column B, and enter the label *Client Total:*. Then, move the cursor to column C and type the formula *=SUM(Charge)*. Because this formula is in a Summ Client band, Works computes and prints its result only once for each different client in the report. The formula computes the sum of the entries in the Charge field for each client.

Next, highlight row 4 and select Insert from the Edit menu. Choose Summ Client from the Insert dialog box and press Enter or choose OK. Selecting this command inserts a Summ Client band into the report design screen. Because this band is used only for spacing, we won't enter any information into it. When you print the report, Works uses this band to place a blank line between each client group in the report.

Finally, highlight row 5 and select the Insert command again. When the Insert dialog box appears, choose Summ Report and press Enter or choose OK to insert a Summ Report band into the report design screen. Next, press the Right Arrow key to move the cursor to column B, and enter the label *Report Total:*. Then, move the cursor to column C and type the formula *=SUM(Charge)*. Because this formula is in a Summ Report band, Works computes and prints its results only once, at the end of the report. The formula computes the sum of the entries in the Charge field for the entire report.

Now, change the widths of columns A, B, and C. Do so in the same way that you change the width of a column in a spreadsheet or a database: Move the cursor to that column, select Width from the Format menu, type the new width, and press Enter or choose OK. The table in Figure 9-16 lists the widths of the columns in the BILLING SUMMARY.

Next, change the format of column C, which contains the Charge field, to Dollar with two decimal places. To begin, highlight column C. Do this either by moving the cursor to any cell in column C and selecting Column from the Select menu or, if you have a mouse, by clicking on the letter C at the top of the column. Next, select Dollar from the Format menu and press Enter or choose OK. Figure 9-17 shows the report definition at this point.

Column	Width
A	20
B	15
C	11

Figure 9-16. Column widths for the BILLING SUMMARY.

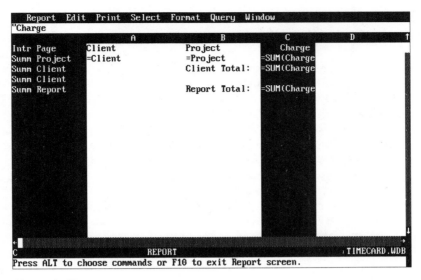

Figure 9-17.

Finally, use the Layout command to set the margins and to define a header and a footer for the report. To do this, select Layout from the Print menu to display the Layout dialog box. Now, move to the Left Margin text box and type *0.5* to replace the original setting, *1.3"*, and to set the left margin of the printed report to one-half inch. Next, move to the Right Margin text box and type *0.5* to set the right margin to one-half inch.

Now move to the Header text box and enter the header definition

&lDate: &d &cBILLING SUMMARY &rPage: &p

This definition tells Works to print a header with three parts. On each page of the report, Works prints the label *Date:*, followed by the current date, at the left edge of the header line; the label *BILLING SUMMARY* in the center; and the label *Page:*, followed by the current page number, at the right edge of the header line.

After you enter the header definition, delete the existing footer definition. To do this, press the Tab key to advance to the Footer text box and highlight the existing definition. Now, simply press the Del key to clear the text box. When you're finished, press Enter or choose OK to save your changes.

The report is finished. Before you do anything else, select Reports from the Report menu to display the Reports dialog box. Move to the Name entry box, type the name *BILLING SUMMARY*, and choose the Rename option. Choosing this option changes the name of the report you defined from Report1 to BILLING SUMMARY. Next, select Exit Report from the Report menu to return to the TIMECARD database. Then, select Save from the File menu to save the database and the completed report.

The BILLING DETAIL report

The BILLING DETAIL report shows exactly how much work has been done on each project for each client and the charge to the client for that work. The information in this report—from the Client, Last Name, Project, Task, Time, Rate, and Charge fields—is grouped by client and by project.

To create the BILLING DETAIL report, first choose Sort from the Query menu to display the Sort dialog box. Because the Sort dialog box retains its most recent field entries, the field names Client and Project are still identified as the 1st Field and 2nd Field entries. If they are not present, enter them in the appropriate text boxes. Then, press Enter or choose OK to leave the dialog box.

Now, select New from the Report menu to create a new default report definition. Works creates a report definition similar to the one in Figure 9-10 on page 212, but with a Summ Client row and a Summ Project row above the Summ Report row.

Because the default definition is not similar to the report definition you are creating, begin by deleting the contents of this new definition. Highlight all six rows in the new definition and select Delete from the Edit menu to empty the report definition.

Now you're ready to define the report itself. To begin, highlight the first row in the design screen and select Insert from the Edit menu to display the Insert dialog box. Choose Intr Client and press Enter or choose OK to insert an Intr Client band into the report design screen. Next, type the label *Client:* in column A of the new band. Then, press the Right Arrow key to move the cursor to column B, and enter the formula *=Client*. Because these entries are in an Intr Client band, Works prints them only once for each client in the report. The formula in column B simply displays the name of each client immediately before the information reported for that client.

Next, highlight row 2 and select Insert from the Edit menu. Choose Intr Client from the Insert dialog box and press Enter or choose OK to insert an Intr Client band into the report design screen. Because this band is used only for spacing, you don't enter any information in it. When you print the report, Works uses this band to place a blank line immediately before the information reported for each client.

Now, highlight row 3 and select Insert from the Edit menu. To insert another Intr Client band into the report design screen, choose Intr Client from the Insert dialog box and press Enter or choose OK. Next, type the label *Name* in column A of the new band. Press the Right Arrow key to move the cursor to column B and enter the label *Project*. Next, enter the labels *Task* in column C, *Date* in column D, *Time* in column E, *Rate* in column F, and *Charges* in column G. Highlight columns D, E, F, and G in the new band, select Style from the Format menu, choose Right, and press Enter or choose OK. This command right-aligns the labels in columns D, E, F, and G.

Next, highlight row 4 and select Insert from the Edit menu. When the Insert dialog box appears, choose Record and press Enter or choose OK to insert a Record band into the report definition. Next, enter the formula *=Last Name* in column A of the new band, the formula *=Project* in column B, the formula *=Task* in column C, the formula *=Date* in column D, the formula *=Time* in column E, the formula *=Rate* in column F, and the formula *=Charge* in column G. Because these formulas are in a Record band, Works prints them once for each record in the report. These formulas simply display the contents of the Last Name, Project, Task, Date, Time, Rate, and Charge fields for each record in TIMECARD.

Next, highlight row 5 and select Insert from the Edit menu to display the Insert dialog box. To insert a Summ Project band into the report design screen, choose Summ Project and press Enter or choose OK. Next, enter the label *Project Total:* in column D of the new band and the formula *=SUM(Charge)* in column G. Because these entries are in a Summ Project band, Works prints the specified information only once for each project in the report. The formula in column G computes the sum of the Charge fields for each project.

Now, highlight row 6 and select Insert from the Edit menu. To insert another Summ Project band into the report design screen, choose Summ Project again and press Enter or choose OK. Because you are inserting this band only for spacing, you need not enter any information in it. When you print the report, Works uses this band to place a blank line after each project group.

Next, highlight row 7 and select Insert from the Edit menu. Choose Summ Client and press Enter or choose OK to insert a Summ Client band into the report design screen. Next, enter the label *Client Total:* in column D of the new band and the formula *=SUM(Charge)* in column G. Because these entries are in a Summ Client band, Works prints the information only once for each client. The formula in column G computes the sum of the entries in the Charge field for each client.

Now, highlight row 8 and select Insert from the Edit menu. To insert another Summ Client band into the report design screen, choose Summ Client again, and press Enter or choose OK. Because you insert this band only for spacing, you need not enter any information in it. When you print the report, Works uses this band to place a blank line after each client group.

Finally, highlight row 9 and select the Insert command again. When the Insert dialog box appears, choose Summ Report and press Enter or choose OK to insert a Summ Report band into the report definition. Next, move the cursor to column D and enter the label *Report Total:*. Then, move the cursor to column G and type the formula *=SUM(Charge)*. Because these entries are in a Summ Report band, Works prints the specified information only once, at the end of the report. The formula in column G computes the sum of the entries in the Charge field for the entire report.

Now you need to change the widths of the columns in the report definition. Figure 9-18 on the following page lists the appropriate column widths.

Next, change the format of columns D, E, F, and G. To begin, highlight column D either by moving the cursor to any cell in column D and selecting Column from the Select menu or, if you have a mouse, by clicking on the letter D at the top of the column. When the column is highlighted, select Time/Date from the Format menu, choose the Month, Day, Year option, and press Enter or choose OK. This command assigns MM/DD/YY format to column D.

Column	Width
A	15
B	15
C	10
D	8
E	6
F	6
G	11

Figure 9-18. Column widths for the BILLING DETAIL report.

Next, highlight column E, select Fixed from the Format menu, type *1*, and press Enter or choose OK. This command assigns Fixed format with one decimal place to column E. Then, highlight column F, select Dollar from the Format menu, type *0*, and press Enter or choose OK to assign Dollar format with zero decimal places to column F. Finally, highlight column G, select Dollar from the Format menu, and press Enter or choose OK to assign Dollar format with two decimal places to that column. Figure 9-19 shows columns B through G of the report definition at this point.

Last, use the Layout command to set the margins for the report and to define a header and a footer for the report. To do so, select Layout from the Print menu to display the LAYOUT dialog box. Then, move to the Left Margin entry box and type *0.5*. Next, move to the Right Margin text box and type *0.5*. These changes set the left and right margins of the printed report at one-half inch.

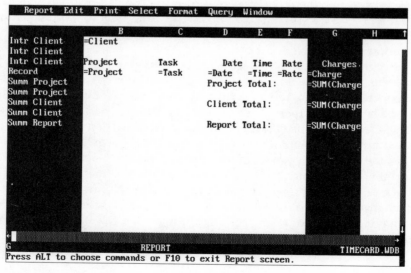

Figure 9-19.

Now, move to the Header entry box and enter the header definition

```
&lDate: &d &cBILLING DETAIL &rPage: &p
```

This definition tells Works to print a header with three parts: the label *Date:*, followed by the current date, at the left edge of the header line; the label *BILLING DETAIL* in the center of the header line; and the label *Page:*, followed by the current page number, at the right edge of the header line. Works prints the header on each page of the report.

After you enter the header definition, delete the existing footer definition. To do this, press the Tab key to advance to the Footer text box and highlight the existing definition. Now, simply press the Del key to clear the text box. When you're finished, press Enter or choose OK to save your changes.

Now you're ready to save the completed report definition. First, select Reports from the Report menu. When you see the Report dialog box, move to the Name entry box and type the name *BILLING DETAIL*. Then, choose the Rename option to change the name of the report you defined from Report1 to BILLING DETAIL. Next, select Exit Report from the Report menu to return to the TIMECARD database. Then, select Save from the File menu to save the database and the completed report.

The STAFFING report

The fourth report, STAFFING, lists the work each person has done. This report is grouped by last name of the staff member, client, and project and includes the Last Name, First Name, Client, Project, Task, Time, Rate, and Charge fields.

To create the STAFFING report, first choose Sort from the Query menu to activate the main Sort dialog box. Next, replace the existing sort field entries: Enter *Last Name* in the 1st Field text box and *Client* in the 2nd Field text box. Then, press Enter or choose OK to leave the dialog box.

Now, select New from the Report menu to create a new default report definition.

Because this default definition is not similar to the report definition you are creating, delete the contents of this new definition. To do this, simply highlight all seven rows in the new definition and select Delete from the Edit menu.

Now you're ready to define the report. To begin, highlight the first row in the design screen and select Insert from the Edit menu. When you see the Insert dialog box, choose Intr Last Name and press Enter or choose OK to insert an Intr Last Name band into the report design screen. Next, type the label *Last Name:* in column A of the new band. Then, press the Right Arrow key to move the cursor to column B, and enter the formula *=Last Name*. Because these entries are in an Intr Last Name band, they appear only once for each different client in the printed report. The formula in column B simply displays the last name of each staff member before the group for that staff member.

Next, highlight row 2 and select Insert from the Edit menu. To insert another Intr Last Name band, choose Intr Last Name from the Insert dialog box and press Enter or choose OK. Because you insert this band only for spacing, you need not enter anything in it. When you print the report, Works uses this band to place a blank line before each Last Name group.

Now, highlight row 3 and select the Insert command from the Edit menu. To insert an Intr Client band into the report definition, choose Intr Client from the Insert dialog box and press Enter or choose OK. Next, type the label *Client* in column A of the new band. Then, enter the labels *Project* in column B, *Task* in column C, *Date* in column D, *Time* in column E, *Rate* in column F, and *Charges* in column G. After you enter this last label, highlight columns D, E, F, and G in the new band, select Style from the Format menu, choose Right, and press Enter or choose OK. This command right-aligns the labels in columns D, E, F, and G.

Next, highlight row 4 and select Insert from the Edit menu. When the Insert dialog box appears, choose the Record option and press Enter or choose OK to insert a Record band into the report definition. Next, enter the formula *=Client* in column A of the new band, the formula *=Project* in column B, the formula *=Task* in column C, the formula *=Date* in column D, the formula *=Time* in column E, the formula *=Rate* in column F, and the formula *=Charge* in column G. Because these formulas are in a Record band, their results appear only once for each record in the printed report. These formulas simply display the contents of the Client, Project, Task, Date, Time, Rate, and Charge fields for each record in TIMECARD.

Next, highlight row 5 and select Insert from the Edit menu. When the Insert dialog box appears, choose Summ Project and press Enter or choose OK to insert a Summ Project band into the report design screen. Next, enter the label *Project Total:* in column C of the new band, the formula *=SUM(Time)* in column E, and the formula *=SUM(Charge)* in column G. Because these entries are in a Summ Project band, they appear only once for each project in the printed report. The formulas in columns E and G compute the sum of the entries in the Time and Charge fields for each project.

Now, highlight row 6 and select Insert from the Edit menu. Choose Summ Project again and press Enter or choose OK to insert another Summ Project band. Because you insert this band only for spacing, you need not enter any information in it. When you print the report, Works uses this band to place a blank line after each project group.

Next, highlight row 7 and select Insert from the Edit menu. Choose Summ Client from the Insert dialog box and press Enter or choose OK to insert a Summ Client band into the report design screen. Next, enter the label *Client Total:* in column C of the new band, the formula *=SUM(Time)* in column E, and the formula *=SUM(Charge)* in column G. Because these entries are in a Summ Client band, they appear once for each client in the printed report. The formulas in columns E and G compute the sum of the entries in the Time and Charge fields for each client group.

Now, highlight row 8 and select Insert from the Edit menu. Choose Summ Client again and press Enter or choose OK to insert another Summ Client band. Because you insert this extra band only for spacing, you need not enter any information in it. When you print the report, Works uses this band to place a blank line after each group of records associated with a particular client.

Next, highlight row 9 and select Insert from the Edit menu. When the Insert dialog box appears, choose Summ Last Name and press Enter or choose OK to insert a Summ Last Name band into the report design screen. Next, enter the label *Person Total:* in column C of the new band, the formula *=SUM(Time)* in column E, and the formula *=SUM(Charge)* in column G. Because these entries are in a Summ Last Name band, they appear only once for each staff member in the report. The formulas in columns E and G compute the sum of the entries in the Time and Charge fields for each group of records associated with a particular last name.

Now, highlight row 10, select Insert from the Edit menu, choose Summ Last Name again, and press Enter or choose OK. Once again, you insert this band only for spacing, so you need not enter any information in it. When you print the report, Works places a blank line after each group of records associated with a particular last name.

Finally, highlight row 11 and select the Insert command again. When the Insert dialog box appears, choose Summ Report and press Enter or choose OK to insert a Summ Report band into the report definition. Move the cursor to column C in the new band and enter the label *Report Total:*. Then, move the cursor to column E and enter the formula *=SUM(Time)*. Next, move the cursor to column G and type the formula *=SUM(Charge)*. Because these entries are in a Summ Report band, they appear only once, at the end of the printed report. The formulas compute the sum of the entries in the Time and Charge fields for the entire report.

Now you need to change the widths of the columns in the report definition. The table in Figure 9-20 lists the appropriate column widths.

Next, change the format of columns D, E, F, and G. To begin, highlight column D by moving the cursor to any cell in column D and selecting Column from the Select menu or, if you have a mouse, by clicking on the letter D at the top of the column.

Column	Width
A	20
B	15
C	10
D	8
E	6
F	6
G	11

Figure 9-20. Column widths for the STAFFING report.

Next, select Time/Date from the Format menu, choose Month, Day, Year, and press Enter or choose OK to assign MM/DD/YY format to column D.

Next, highlight column E, select Fixed from the Format menu, type 1, and press Enter or choose OK. This command assigns Fixed format with one decimal place to column E. Then, highlight column F, select Dollar from the Format menu, type 0, and press Enter or choose OK to assign Dollar format with zero decimal places to column F. Finally, highlight column G, select Dollar from the Format menu, and press Enter or choose OK to assign Dollar format with two decimal places to that column. Figure 9-21 shows the screen at this point.

Last, use the Layout command to set the margins for the report and to define a header and a footer for the report. To do so, select Layout from the Print menu to display the Layout dialog box. Then, move to the Left Margin entry box and type 0.5 to set the left margin of the printed report to one-half inch. Next, move to the Right Margin entry box and type 0.5 to set the right margin to one-half inch.

Now, move to the Header entry box and enter the header definition

&lDate: &d &cSTAFFING REPORT &rPage: &p

This definition tells Works to print a header with three parts: the label *Date:*, followed by the current date, at the left edge of the header line; the label *STAFFING REPORT* in the center of the header line; and the label *Page:*, followed by the current page number, at the right edge of the header line. Works prints the header information on each page of the report.

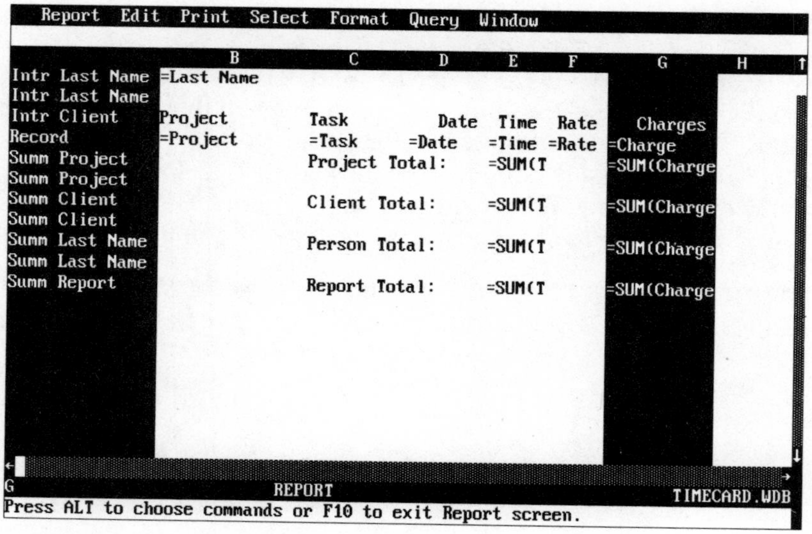

Figure 9-21.

After you enter the header definition, delete the existing footer definition. To do this, press the Tab key to advance to the Footer text box and highlight the existing definition. Now, simply press the Del key to clear the text box and press Enter or choose OK to save your changes.

Now you're ready to save the completed report definition. First, select Reports from the Report menu to display the Report dialog box, move to the Name entry box, and type the name *STAFFING REPORT*. Then, choose the Rename option to change the name of the report you defined from Report1 to STAFFING. Next, select Exit Report from the Report menu to return to the TIMECARD database. Then, select Save from the File menu to save the database and the completed report.

USING THE TEMPLATE

Once you have created the TIMECARD database and the three reports that accompany it, you can begin to use the template: Simply record the activities of your staff in the TIMECARD database. Then, from time to time, you can query, sort, and print reports from the database.

Entering Data

The first step in using this template is to record your activity and the activity of your staff in the TIMECARD database. You can enter this information at any interval that is comfortable for you—every day, once a week, once a month. You can either enter the data yourself, have a clerk make the entries, or have staff members enter the information about their own projects directly.

For the most part, the names of the fields in the TIMECARD database explain the type of information you enter in each field. Each record shows the time spent by one person on one task within one project for one client. The Last Name and First Name fields store the name of the person who performed the work being recorded. The Client field stores the name of the client for whom the work was done. The Project and Task fields identify the job that was performed. The Project field holds the name of the overall job—for instance, 1987 Annual Report—and the Task field the name of a task within that job—Write Copy, for example, or Design, or Mockup. The Date field records the date on which the work was done and the Time field records the amount of time spent on the task. The Rate field records the hourly rate you plan to charge for the work. You won't make entries in the Charge field because that field contains a formula that computes the total charge for the work by multiplying the value in the Time field by the value in the Rate field.

Although the three fields that describe the job are called Client, Project, and Task, you can use these fields in any way you want to describe the tasks your people perform. For example, your company might not perform projects for specific clients. In that event, you might use the Client field to record the division of your company for which the work was performed. Or you might use the Client field to record the name of a project—*Microsoft Works Book*—the Project field to record the name of the task—*Chapter 9*—and the Task field to record the Subtask—*Write*. And as you'll see later, you can even change the names of the fields.

To make entries, open the TIMECARD database. (If you just created the template, skip this step.) To begin, choose Open from the File menu. Then, either type the filename under which you saved the template, including the extension (for example, *TIMECARD.WDB*), or highlight the name of the database in the list, and press Enter or choose OK. If TIMECARD.WDB is already open but is not the active document, make it the active document by pulling down the Window menu and selecting it. In either case, Works displays the List screen for the empty database.

After you open the database, choose View Form from the Options menu to move to the Form screen. (If you already see the form on the screen, skip this step.) Figure 9-8 on page 210 shows the form on the screen. To enter information through a form, position the cursor on the field in which you want to make an entry, type that entry, and press Enter or one of the arrow keys to lock it in. If you press Enter, Works locks in the entry and keeps the cell pointer on that entry. If you press one of the arrow keys, Works locks in the entry and moves the cursor to a new field.

As you enter records in the database, you will probably make a few mistakes. To modify an entry, move the cursor to it, press the Edit key ([F2]), make the change, and press Enter. To overwrite an entry, simply move the cursor to it, type the new entry, and then press Enter. To delete an entire record, press Ctrl-PgUp or Ctrl-PgDn to display it, pull down the Edit menu, and select Delete. To insert a blank record into the database above the current one, pull down the Edit menu and select Insert.

An example

To learn how this template works, enter the information shown in Figure 9-2 on page 204 in the TIMECARD database. Begin by making TIMECARD.WDB the active document. To begin entering data, first be sure the cursor is positioned on the Last Name field of the first record. If it is not, press Ctrl-Home to reposition it. Then, type the last name *Smith* and press the Right Arrow key, type *Mary* and press the Right Arrow key, type *ABC Corp.* and press the Right Arrow key, type *Annual Report* and press the Right Arrow key, type *Manage* and press the Right Arrow key, type *9/1/87* and press the Right Arrow key, type *4.0* and press the Right Arrow key, type *60*, and then press Enter. When you enter the value *60* in the Rate field, Works computes the value for the Charge field and displays that value, *$240*. Figure 9-22 shows the form at this point.

After you type the value *60* in the Rate field of the first record and press Enter, press the Right Arrow key twice to move the cursor to the Last Name field of the second record. At that point, enter the second record, and then continue in the same fashion until you have entered all 19 records in the sample database in Figure 9-2.

```
┌─────────────────────────────────────────────────────────────────────┐
│  File  Edit  Print  Select  Format  Options  Query  Report  Window    │
│60                                                                   ↑ │
│                                    ·                                  │
│                              TIME TRACKER                             │
│                            Personal Time Card                         │
│                                                                       │
│                                                                       │
│  Last Name      Smith                                                 │
│  First Name     Mary                                                  │
│                                                                       │
│  Client         ABC Corp.                                             │
│  Project        Annual Report                                         │
│  Task           Manage                                                │
│                                                                       │
│  Date           9/1/87                                                │
│  Time               4.0        (hours and tenths)                     │
│  Hourly Rate    ▓$60▓                                                 │
│  Charge         $240.00                                               │
│                                                                       │
│                                                                     ↓ │
│ 1 Rate            1/1        FORM                       TIMECARD.WDB   │
│ Press ALT to choose commands or CTRL+PGDN/PGUP for next/previous record.│
└─────────────────────────────────────────────────────────────────────┘
```

Figure 9-22.

Saving the Database

After you enter all the records, save the database. The first time you save the
Time Tracker after you enter records, save it under a new name. To do this, select
Save As from the File menu, type a new name, and press Enter or choose OK. Choose
a name for the file that clearly identifies its contents, such as *TCSEPT87.WDB* for your
September 1987 records. Be sure to choose a name other than TIMECARD.WDB when
you save a filled-in database. If you save a filled-in database under the same name as
the original template, the filled-in version replaces the template.

Always resave the database after you make any changes. After you save the database for the first time, you don't have to give it a new name. Instead, simply use the
Save command to save the database under the name you gave it previously.

To avoid memory capacity problems, open a fresh database every so often. For
example, you might want to start over at the beginning of each month. That way,
each database includes the records for only a single month. If you are entering a
large number of transactions into the database, you may need to start over every
week. If you are entering only a few records each month, you might want to start
over once every quarter or even once a year.

To "start over," use the Open command to open the original, empty TIMECARD
database and make any entries that apply to the new period. Then, use the Save As
command to save the database under a new name, one that clearly identifies the contents of the file. For instance, you might save the file that contains the records for October 1987 under the name TCOCT87.WDB.

Querying the Database

Queries are tools that let you select specific records from a database. To specify a subset of the records in a database, use the Define command on the Query menu to create a query form for your database. Then, enter selection conditions (criteria) in the query form that tell Works which records you want to select. When you apply those criteria to the database, Works hides the records that do not match the stated criteria, displaying only the matching records. If you then print the database, the report contains only the selected records.

To view all the records in a database again, select Show All Records from the Query menu. Works then selects all the records in the database. To reapply the criteria, select Apply Query from the Query menu.

To define a second query for a database, select Define from the Query menu to enter the query form again. Then, if you want to change the criteria completely, select Delete from the Edit menu to delete any existing criteria, and then enter your new criteria. To modify the existing query, you can edit the current criteria or add additional criteria to the form. When the query is ready, simply press [F10] or pull down the Edit menu and select Exit Query to activate it.

An example

You can query the TIMECARD database in many interesting ways. For example, suppose you want to select only those records for the client ABC Corp. To do this, select Define from the Query menu to display the query form, which looks exactly like the entry form.

Because you want Works to select only those records that have the entry *ABC Corp.*, enter that criterion in the Client field on the query form. To do this, position the cursor on the Client field, type *ABC Corp.*, and press Enter. Figure 9-23 shows the completed query.

To activate this selection condition, simply press [F10] or select Exit Query from the Edit menu. Works exits the define query mode and returns to the database. Instead of showing you all the records, however, Works lets you view only those records that have the entry *ABC Corp.* in the Client field.

If you are looking at the Form screen for the database, the screen looks like Figure 9-24. You'll see the first matching record in the database in the form, with the message *4/19* at the bottom of the screen. This message tells you that only 4 of the 19 records in the database were selected. As you move from one record to the next, Works displays only the matching records. If you are viewing the database in the List screen, the list contains only the selected records, as shown in Figure 9-25 on page 232.

When you want to view the entire database again, select Show All Records from the Query menu. Works selects all the records in the database. If you are viewing the database in the Form screen, the message *19/19* appears at the bottom of the screen. If you are viewing the List screen, Works displays all the records in the database.

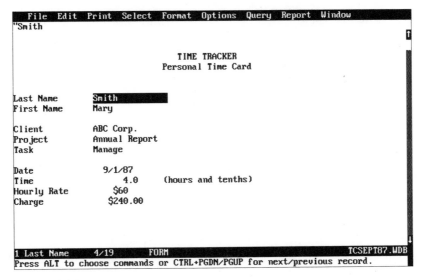

Figure 9-23.

Figure 9-24.

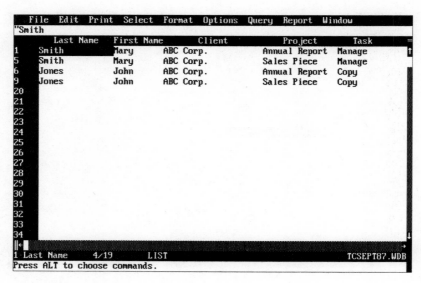

Figure 9-25.

Another example

Let's consider another example. Suppose you want to select only those records for work performed by the staff member John Jones. To begin, select Define from the Query menu to enter the query form again. Then, select Delete from the Edit menu to delete any existing criteria. Now, enter the label *Jones* in the Last Name field and press Enter. To activate this selection condition, simply press [F10] or select Exit Query from the Edit menu. Works exits the define query mode and returns to the database, where it displays only those records that have the entry *Jones* in the Last Name field. If you are viewing the List screen, it will look like Figure 9-26. As you can see, only the selected records are visible.

To view the entire database again, select Show All Records from the Query menu. When you issue this command, Works displays all the records in the database.

A more complex example

Let's look at one more example. Suppose you want to select the records for the client XYZ Inc. that relate to work done on the Slide Show project. To begin, select Define from the Query menu and then select Delete from the Edit menu to delete any existing criteria. Now, move the cursor to the Client field and enter the label *XYZ Inc.* Then, move to the Project field and enter the label *Slide Show*. To activate these criteria, simply press [F10] or select Exit Query from the Edit menu. Works returns to the database and displays only those records that have the entry *XYZ Inc.* in the Client field and the entry *Slide Show* in the Project field. If you are viewing the List screen, you see the screen shown in Figure 9-27. As you can see, only the selected records are visible.

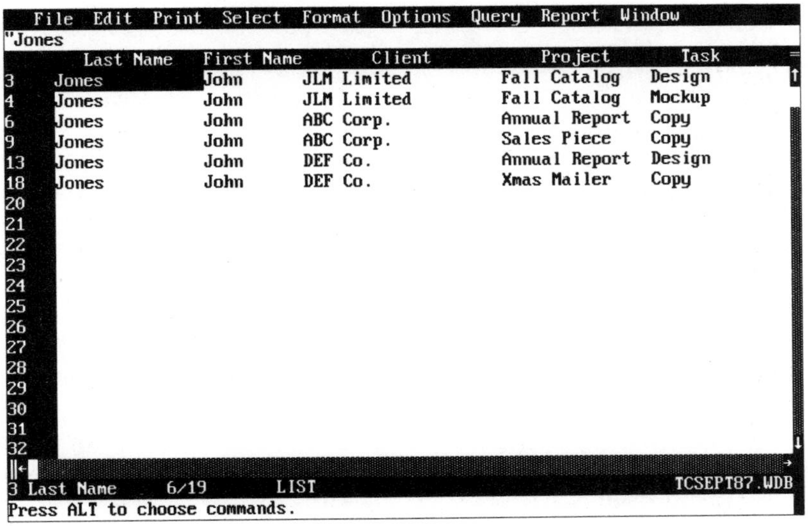

```
 File  Edit  Print  Select  Format  Options  Query  Report  Window
"Jones
         Last Name    First Name        Client           Project        Task
3    Jones           John        JLM Limited        Fall Catalog    Design      ↑
4    Jones           John        JLM Limited        Fall Catalog    Mockup
6    Jones           John        ABC Corp.          Annual Report   Copy
9    Jones           John        ABC Corp.          Sales Piece     Copy
13   Jones           John        DEF Co.            Annual Report   Design
18   Jones           John        DEF Co.            Xmas Mailer     Copy
20
21
22
23
24
25
26
27
28
29
30
31
32                                                                               ↓
‖←■                                                                              →
3 Last Name      6/19         LIST                              TCSEPT87.WDB
Press ALT to choose commands.
```

Figure 9-26.

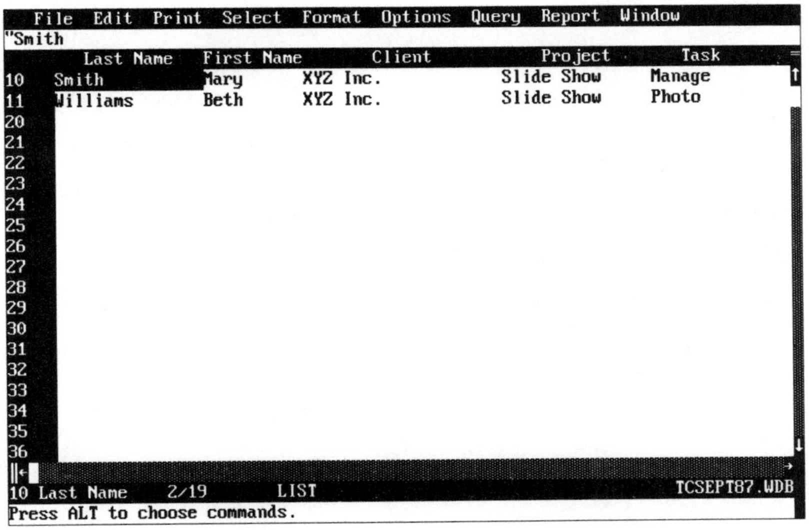

```
 File  Edit  Print  Select  Format  Options  Query  Report  Window
"Smith
         Last Name    First Name        Client           Project        Task
10   Smith           Mary        XYZ Inc.           Slide Show      Manage      ↑
11   Williams        Beth        XYZ Inc.           Slide Show      Photo
20
21
22
23
24
25
26
27
28
29
30
31
32
33
34
35
36                                                                               ↓
‖←■                                                                              →
10 Last Name     2/19         LIST                              TCSEPT87.WDB
Press ALT to choose commands.
```

Figure 9-27.

To view the entire database again, select Show All Records from the Query menu. When you issue this command, Works selects all the records in the database.

Sorting Records

The Sort command on the Query menu allows you to sort a Works database. It arranges the database so that the entries in one, two, or three fields are presented in ascending or descending order. Sorting arranges the database so that specific records are easier to locate.

Sorting a Works database is a relatively simple process, normally performed on the List screen. To begin, pull down the Query menu and select the Sort command to display a Sort dialog box like the one shown in Figure 9-28. This box allows you to define as many as three sort fields. To define the first sort field for a database, move the cursor to the 1st Field text box, type the name of the field on which you want to sort the database, and select a sort order (either Ascend or Descend) for that field. When you choose OK, Works closes the Sort dialog box and sorts the database into the order you specified.

Works remembers the settings you enter in the Sort dialog box. After you specify a group of sort settings, they appear in the dialog box the next time you select the Sort command. If you want to use those settings, simply press Enter or choose OK to sort the database. If you want to use different settings, replace some or all of those settings with new ones and delete any unneeded settings from the dialog box before you sort. To delete an unwanted entry, move to the box that contains that entry and press the Backspace key.

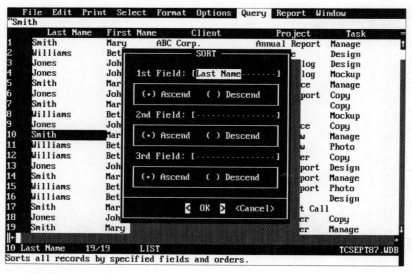

Figure 9-28.

For example, suppose you want to sort the TCSEPT87 database into ascending order based on the entries in the Client field. To do this, pull down the Query menu, select Sort, type *Client* in the 1st Field entry box, and select Ascend (if it is not selected already). Then, if the 2nd Field and 3rd Field entry boxes are not blank, delete those entries. Finally, press Enter or choose OK to sort the database. Figure 9-29 shows the result. As you can see, Works arranges the records in ascending order based on the entries in the Client field. In effect, the records in the database are now grouped by client.

Now suppose you want to sort the TIMECARD database again so that the records in each client group are arranged in ascending order based on the entries in the Project field. To do this, pull down the Query menu and select Sort. When the Sort dialog box appears, the 1st Field entry box still contains the entry *Client*. Because you want to use this setting, you don't need to change or delete that entry. Instead, move the cursor to the 2nd Field entry box, type *Project*, and then select Ascend (if it is not selected already). Finally, press Enter or choose OK to sort the database. Figure 9-30 on the following page shows the result. As in the preceding example, Works arranges the records in the database in ascending order based on the entries in the Client field. This time, however, it also sorts the records (grouped by Client) in ascending order based on the entries in the Project field.

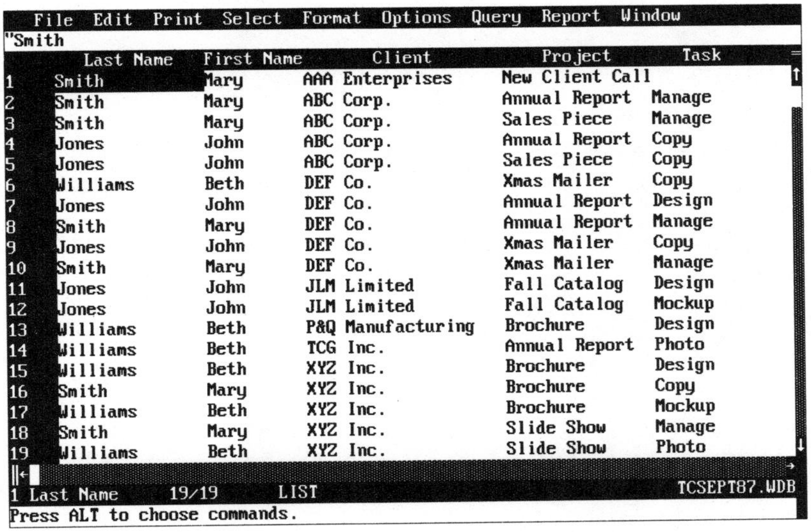

Figure 9-29.

```
 File  Edit  Print  Select  Format  Options  Query  Report  Window
"Smith
         Last Name    First Name        Client          Project        Task      =
1   Smith         Mary     AAA Enterprises   New Client Call                       ↑
2   Smith         Mary     ABC Corp.         Annual Report   Manage
3   Jones         John     ABC Corp.         Annual Report   Copy
4   Smith         Mary     ABC Corp.         Sales Piece     Manage
5   Jones         John     ABC Corp.         Sales Piece     Copy
6   Jones         John     DEF Co.           Annual Report   Design
7   Smith         Mary     DEF Co.           Annual Report   Manage
8   Williams      Beth     DEF Co.           Xmas Mailer     Copy
9   Jones         John     DEF Co.           Xmas Mailer     Copy
10  Smith         Mary     DEF Co.           Xmas Mailer     Manage
11  Jones         John     JLM Limited       Fall Catalog    Design
12  Jones         John     JLM Limited       Fall Catalog    Mockup
13  Williams      Beth     P&Q Manufacturing Brochure        Design
14  Williams      Beth     TCG Inc.          Annual Report   Photo
15  Williams      Beth     XYZ Inc.          Brochure        Design
16  Smith         Mary     XYZ Inc.          Brochure        Copy
17  Williams      Beth     XYZ Inc.          Brochure        Mockup
18  Smith         Mary     XYZ Inc.          Slide Show      Manage
19  Williams      Beth     XYZ Inc.          Slide Show      Photo      ↓
←
1 Last Name      19/19      LIST                              TCSEPT87.WDB
Press ALT to choose commands.
```

Figure 9-30.

Printing the Reports

You can use the four reports you have already created to print the information from the TCSEPT87 database in a variety of ways. Printing database reports is a simple process. If you want to print only a selected group of records, begin by using a query to select those records. Then, pull down the Report menu and select the report you want to print. Next, select Print Report from the Print menu and choose Print or press Enter.

To interrupt the printing process before Works prints every record, simply press the Esc key. When you do, Works displays a dialog box that offers two options, labeled OK and Cancel. If you choose OK, Works exits the printing process. If you choose Cancel, Works continues to print labels.

A simple example

Suppose you want to print a copy of the BASIC report for the entire TCSEPT87 database. To begin, select Show All Records from the Query menu to be sure that all records are selected. Then, pull down the Report menu. As you can see in Figure 9-31, this menu includes the names of each of the four reports you defined. To select the BASIC report, highlight its name in the list and press Enter.

Before you continue further, you need to set up Works for the specific text printer and paper type you plan to use. To do this, first select Define from the Report menu. Now, choose Select Text Printer from the Print menu, and then choose the appropriate printer, paper feed method, and printer connection from the resulting dialog box.

```
 File  Edit  Print  Select  Format  Options  Query | Report  Window
"Smith
        Last Name    First Name      Client         | Define
1    Smith         Mary      AAA Enterprises   Ne| iew
2    Smith         Mary      ABC Corp.         An| View
3    Jones         John      ABC Corp.         An|
4    Smith         Mary      ABC Corp.         Sa| Save As...
5    Jones         John      ABC Corp.         Sa|
6    Jones         John      DEF Co.           An| Reports...
7    Smith         Mary      DEF Co.           An|
8    Williams      Beth      DEF Co.           Xm| 1 BASIC
9    Jones         John      DEF Co.           Xm| 2 BILLING SUMMARY
10   Smith         Mary      DEF Co.           Xm| 3 BILLING DETAIL
11   Jones         John      JLM Limited       Fa| 4 STAFFING
12   Jones         John      JLM Limited       Fa|
13   Williams      Beth      P&Q Manufacturing  Broc
14   Williams      Beth      TCG Inc.          Annual Report    Photo
15   Williams      Beth      XYZ Inc.          Brochure         Design
16   Smith         Mary      XYZ Inc.          Brochure         Copy
17   Williams      Beth      XYZ Inc.          Brochure         Mockup
18   Smith         Mary      XYZ Inc.          Slide Show       Manage
19   Williams      Beth      XYZ Inc.          Slide Show       Photo
1 Last Name              LIST                              TCSEPT87.WDB
Enters Report screen.
```

Figure 9-31.

Then, select Font from the Print menu and choose the text font and size from the resulting Font dialog box. If you are trying to squeeze the report onto one sheet, you'll probably want to choose a small font and size.

Next, select Print from the Print menu to display the Print dialog box shown in Figure 9-32 on the following page. The first setting in this dialog box allows you to specify the number of copies of the report you want Works to print. In most cases, you will want to print only one copy (the default number). The second setting, Print Specific Pages, enables you to select the pages you want to print. For instance, you could use this option to tell Works to print only the first page of the report, or pages 1 through 5, or pages 3 and 4, or pages 1, 3, and 5. You will usually skip this option when you are printing a database report. The third setting, Print to File, allows you to print the labels to a text file instead of to your printer. To do this, select this option and specify the name of the file to which you want Works to print the labels. The final setting, Print All But Record Rows, allows you to print only the Intr and Summ rows from the report definition. Once again, you will usually skip this option.

After you adjust any settings you want to change in the Print dialog box, you can print the report. Before you do, however, place the proper kind of paper (8.5-inch-wide paper for this report) in your printer and align the paper so that the print head is on the first line of a new sheet. Also, be sure that your printer is properly connected to your computer and that it is turned on and on-line. After you do these things, simply choose Print from the bottom of the Print dialog box to produce the printed report, shown in Figure 9-33 on the following page.

Figure 9-32.

Date: 9/4/87			BASIC LISTING						Page: 1
Last Name	First Name	Client	Project	Task	Date	Time	Rate	Charge	
Smith	Mary	ABC Corp.	Annual Report	Manage	9/1/87	4.0	$60	$240.00	
Williams	Beth	XYZ Inc.	Brochure	Design	9/1/87	10.0	$45	$450.00	
Jones	John	JLM Limited	Fall Catalog	Design	9/1/87	6.0	$50	$300.00	
Jones	John	JLM Limited	Fall Catalog	Mockup	9/1/87	3.0	$40	$120.00	
Smith	Mary	ABC Corp.	Sales Piece	Manage	9/1/87	4.0	$60	$240.00	
Jones	John	ABC Corp.	Annual Report	Copy	9/2/87	3.0	$40	$120.00	
Smith	Mary	XYZ Inc.	Brochure	Copy	9/2/87	6.5	$75	$487.50	
Williams	Beth	XYZ Inc.	Brochure	Mockup	9/2/87	4.0	$40	$160.00	
Jones	John	ABC Corp.	Sales Piece	Copy	9/2/87	6.0	$40	$240.00	
Smith	Mary	XYZ Inc.	Slide Show	Manage	9/2/87	1.5	$60	$90.00	
Williams	Beth	XYZ Inc.	Slide Show	Photo	9/2/87	3.0	$50	$150.00	
Williams	Beth	DEF Co.	Xmas Mailer	Copy	9/2/87	2.0	$40	$80.00	
Jones	John	DEF Co.	Annual Report	Design	9/3/87	4.0	$50	$200.00	
Smith	Mary	DEF Co.	Annual Report	Manage	9/3/87	6.0	$60	$360.00	
Williams	Beth	TCG Inc.	Annual Report	Photo	9/3/87	6.0	$50	$300.00	
Williams	Beth	P&Q Manufacturing	Brochure	Design	9/3/87	4.0	$45	$180.00	
Smith	Mary	AAA Enterprises	New Client Call		9/3/87	2.0	$0	$0.00	
Jones	John	DEF Co.	Xmas Mailer	Copy	9/3/87	4.0	$40	$160.00	
Smith	Mary	DEF Co.	Xmas Mailer	Manage	9/3/87	2.0	$60	$120.00	
						81.0		$3,997.50	

Figure 9-33.

Printing selected records

When Works prints a database report, it extracts information from only the records that are selected at the time; that is, those that meet current query criteria. If all records are selected, then the report includes every record in the database. If only certain records are selected, Works prints the selected records only.

To illustrate, suppose you want to print a copy of the BASIC report for only those records in the TCSEPT87 database that have the Date field entry *9/3/87*. To begin, select Exit Report from the Report menu to return to the database. Then, if the List screen is not displayed, select View List from the Options menu. Now, select Define from the Query menu to enter the query form. Then, select Delete from the Edit menu to delete any existing criteria, enter the date *9/3/87* in the Date field, and press Enter. To activate this selection condition, simply press [F10] or pull down the Edit menu and select Exit Query. Works then exits the define query mode, returns to the database, and displays only those records that have the entry *9/3/87* in the Date field.

Next, pull down the Report menu and confirm that the BASIC report is selected. Because you already defined the printer and page layout settings, you're ready to print. To proceed, select Print Report from the Print menu, double-check your paper and your printer, and choose Print from the bottom of the Print dialog box. Figure 9-34 shows the printed report. Notice that this report contains only the selected records from the database.

Printing a grouped report

Now suppose that you want to print a BILLING DETAIL report that contains all the records in the database. To begin, select Show All Records from the Query menu to be sure that all records are selected. Then, pull down the Report menu and select the BILLING DETAIL report. Next, select Print Report from the Print menu to display the Print dialog box. Before you begin printing, place the proper kind of paper (8.5-inch-wide paper for this report) in your printer and align the paper so that the print head is on the first line of a new sheet. Make sure that your printer is properly connected to your computer and that it is turned on and on-line. Finally, choose Print to print the report.

Figure 9-35 beginning on page 240 shows the printed report. As you can see, this report is grouped by client. The name of each client is printed on a line before the group of records for that client, and the records within each client group are further

Date: 9/4/87			BASIC LISTING						Page: 1
Last Name	First Name	Client	Project	Task	Date	Time	Rate	Charge	
Jones	John	DEF Co.	Annual Report	Design	9/3/87	4.0	$50	$200.00	
Smith	Mary	DEF Co.	Annual Report	Manage	9/3/87	6.0	$60	$360.00	
Williams	Beth	TCG Inc.	Annual Report	Photo	9/3/87	6.0	$50	$300.00	
Williams	Beth	P&Q Manufacturing	Brochure	Design	9/3/87	4.0	$45	$180.00	
Smith	Mary	AAA Enterprises	New Client Call		9/3/87	2.0	$0	$0.00	
Jones	John	DEF Co.	Xmas Mailer	Copy	9/3/87	4.0	$40	$160.00	
Smith	Mary	DEF Co.	Xmas Mailer	Manage	9/3/87	2.0	$60	$120.00	
						28.0		$1,320.00	

Figure 9-34.

```
Date: 9/4/87                  BILLING DETAIL                  Page: 1


    Client:        AAA Enterprises

    Name           Project         Task       Date  Time  Rate   Charges
    Smith          New Client Call            9/3/87  2.0   $0    $0.00
                                          Project Total:            $0.00

                                          Client Total:             $0.00


    Client:        ABC Corp.

    Name           Project         Task       Date  Time  Rate   Charges
    Smith          Annual Report   Manage   9/1/87  4.0   $60    $240.00
    Jones          Annual Report   Copy     9/2/87  3.0   $40    $120.00
                                          Project Total:          $360.00

    Smith          Sales Piece     Manage   9/1/87  4.0   $60    $240.00
    Jones          Sales Piece     Copy     9/2/87  6.0   $40    $240.00
                                          Project Total:          $480.00

                                          Client Total:           $840.00


    Client:        DEF Co.

    Name           Project         Task       Date  Time  Rate   Charges
    Jones          Annual Report   Design   9/3/87  4.0   $50    $200.00
    Smith          Annual Report   Manage   9/3/87  6.0   $60    $360.00
                                          Project Total:          $560.00

    Williams       Xmas Mailer     Copy     9/2/87  2.0   $40    $80.00
    Jones          Xmas Mailer     Copy     9/3/87  4.0   $40    $160.00
    Smith          Xmas Mailer     Manage   9/3/87  2.0   $60    $120.00
                                          Project Total:          $360.00

                                          Client Total:           $920.00


    Client:        JLM Limited

    Name           Project         Task       Date  Time  Rate   Charges
    Jones          Fall Catalog    Design   9/1/87  6.0   $50    $300.00
    Jones          Fall Catalog    Mockup   9/1/87  3.0   $40    $120.00
                                          Project Total:          $420.00

                                          Client Total:           $420.00
```

Figure 9-35.   (continued)

Figure 9-35. Continued.

```
Date: 9/4/87                    BILLING DETAIL                      Page: 2


   Client:        P&Q Manufacturing

   Name           Project        Task        Date  Time  Rate    Charges
   Williams       Brochure       Design     9/3/87  4.0   $45    $180.00
                                            Project Total:        $180.00

                                            Client Total:         $180.00

   Client:        TCG Inc.

   Name           Project        Task        Date  Time  Rate    Charges
   Williams       Annual Report  Photo      9/3/87  6.0   $50    $300.00
                                            Project Total:        $300.00

                                            Client Total:         $300.00

   Client:        XYZ Inc.

   Name           Project        Task        Date  Time  Rate    Charges
   Williams       Brochure       Design     9/1/87 10.0   $45    $450.00
   Smith          Brochure       Copy       9/2/87  6.5   $75    $487.50
   Williams       Brochure       Mockup     9/2/87  4.0   $40    $160.00
                                            Project Total:      $1,097.50


   Smith          Slide Show     Manage     9/2/87  1.5   $60     $90.00
   Williams       Slide Show     Photo      9/2/87  3.0   $50    $150.00
                                            Project Total:        $240.00

                                            Client Total:       $1,337.50

                                            Report Total:       $3,997.50
```

grouped by project. For example, notice that the records in the ABC Corp. group are divided into two groups, one for the Annual Report project and one for the Sales Piece project. In addition, Works computed and printed a total for the Charge field for each project group, for each client group, and for the report as a whole.

Printing a grouped report for selected records only

Let's look at one more example. Suppose you want to print a copy of the STAFF-ING report for only those records in the sample TIMECARD database that have the Client field entry *DEF Co.* To begin, select Define from the Query menu to display the query form. Then, select the Delete command from the Edit menu to delete any existing criteria. Now, enter the label *DEF Co.* in the Client field and press Enter. To activate this selection condition, simply press [F10] or pull down the Edit menu and select Exit Query. Works exits the define query mode and returns to the database, where it displays only those records that have the entry *DEF Co.* in the Client field. Figure 9-36 shows a List screen with these selected records.

Next, pull down the Report menu and select the STAFFING report. Because this is an especially wide report, you need to select Define from the Report menu to modify the printing instructions. Now, choose Font from the Print menu, and select a compact text font and font size. Then, press Enter or choose OK to execute this change. Finally, select Print from the Print menu, double-check your paper and your printer, and choose Print from the bottom of the Print dialog box to print the report. Figure 9-37 shows the printed report. Notice that this report contains only the selected records. Also, notice that this report is grouped by the entries in the Last Name field and that the name of each staff member is printed on a line before the group of records for that person. Within each group, the records are further grouped by client and by project. (Because the report contains only the records for a single client, however, the client groups are not evident.) Works computed and printed a total for the Charge field for each project group, for each client group, and for the report as a whole.

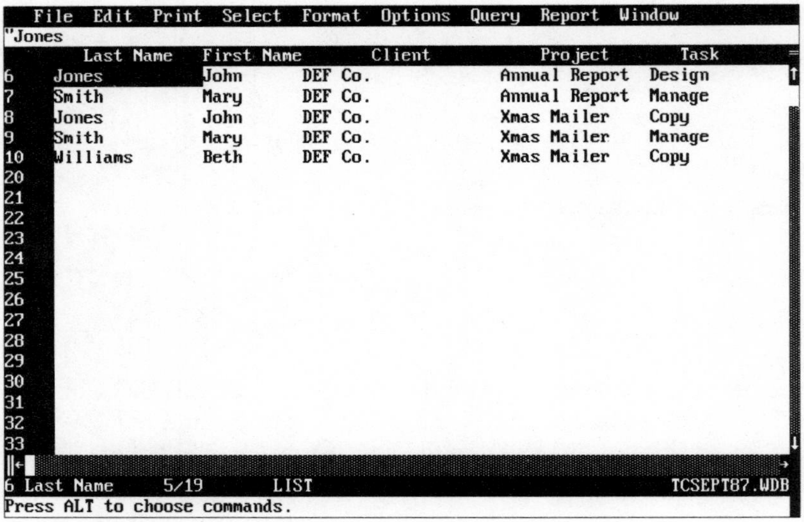

```
 File   Edit   Print   Select   Format   Options   Query   Report   Window
"Jones
         Last Name    First Name      Client          Project       Task
6     Jones          John       DEF Co.          Annual Report  Design
7     Smith          Mary       DEF Co.          Annual Report  Manage
8     Jones          John       DEF Co.          Xmas Mailer    Copy
9     Smith          Mary       DEF Co.          Xmas Mailer    Manage
10    Williams       Beth       DEF Co.          Xmas Mailer    Copy
20
21
22
23
24
25
26
27
28
29
30
31
32
33
6 Last Name      5/19        LIST                        TCSEPT87.WDB
Press ALT to choose commands.
```

Figure 9-36.

```
Date: 9/4/87                    STAFFING REPORT                    Page: 1


Last Name:        Jones

Client            Project       Task        Date   Time   Rate   Charges
DEF Co.           Annual Report Design    9/3/87    4.0    $50    $200.00
                                Project Total:      4.0           $200.00

DEF Co.           Xmas Mailer   Copy      9/3/87    4.0    $40    $160.00
                                Project Total:      4.0           $160.00

                                Client Total:       8.0           $360.00

                                Person Total:       8.0           $360.00

Last Name:        Smith

Client            Project       Task        Date   Time   Rate   Charges
DEF Co.           Annual Report Manage    9/3/87    6.0    $60    $360.00
                                Project Total:      6.0           $360.00

DEF Co.           Xmas Mailer   Manage    9/3/87    2.0    $60    $120.00
                                Project Total:      2.0           $120.00

                                Client Total:       8.0           $480.00

                                Person Total:       8.0           $480.00

Last Name:        Williams

Client            Project       Task        Date   Time   Rate   Charges
DEF Co.           Xmas Mailer   Copy      9/2/87    2.0    $40    $80.00
                                Project Total:      2.0           $80.00

                                Client Total:       2.0           $80.00

                                Person Total:       2.0           $80.00

                                Report Total:      18.0           $920.00
```

Figure 9-37.

MODIFICATIONS

You can make several interesting modifications to the Time Tracker. For one thing, you might create more reports for the database. Creating these additional reports is no more difficult than creating the four reports explained in this chapter. Simply select New from the Report menu, delete the default definition, insert bands, and make entries in the bands. You could, of course, create any number of different reports from this database. However, Works allows you to create a maximum of eight reports for a single database, so be careful when deciding which reports to add and which to leave out.

You might also choose to modify one or more of the reports you created for the template. You might want to add or delete fields, add additional statistics, or add or delete spacing bands. You can also use the Style command on the Format menu to boldface, underline, or italicize parts of your reports.

Third, you might want to change the names of one or more fields in the TIMECARD database. For example, you might change the name of the Client field to Job so that you can use the database to record time information for projects that are not client-specific. Unfortunately, it is not especially easy to change the name of a field. If you edit the form to change the name of a field, you lose all the data stored in that field. Instead, you have to add a new field with the preferred name, move the data from the old field to the new field, delete the old field, and then move the new field to the position of the old field in both the List screen and the Form screen. Then, you have to redesign any reports that included the old field. In fact, the process is sufficiently difficult that you might be better off to leave the field names as they are or to start over from scratch.

CONCLUSION

If you bill for your services on the basis of time, you need a system that helps you keep track of your time. In this chapter, you created a system you can use to track your time. And along the way, you learned how to create, query, and sort databases, and how to create and use database reports.

The Accounts
Receivable Tracker

If you sell your goods or services on credit, you need a good way to track the money that your customers or clients owe you—your accounts receivable. Managing accounts receivable is one of the most difficult—and important—jobs for the manager of a small business. Failing to manage accounts receivable can lead to cash flow problems that can kill a small business. Managing receivables carefully can help you to maintain good cash flow and improve customer relationships.

In this chapter, we'll create the Accounts Receivable Tracker, a tracking system that provides the basic tools you'll need to manage accounts receivable in Works. This template is fairly easy to create and use; at the same time, it can be extremely useful. And as you build the Accounts Receivable Tracker, you'll learn how to create, query, and sort databases, and how to create and use database reports in Works.

ABOUT THE TEMPLATE

The Accounts Receivable Tracker is based on the Works database shown in Figure 10-1 on the following page. Figure 10-2 shows the form we'll use to work with this database. Figure 10-3 shows the upper left portion of the List screen.

As you can see in Figure 10-1, the accounts receivable database has 22 fields, identified by the labels shown along the top of the List screen. The Inv # field stores the number of the invoice. The Inv Date field holds the date on which the invoice was written, and the Net Amount field stores the original amount of the invoice. The Date Due field contains a formula that computes the date on which payment is due.

The Pmt1 Date, Pmt1 Amnt, Pmt2 Date, and Pmt2 Amnt fields record the date and amount of any payments made against the invoice. The Balance field contains a formula that computes the current balance by subtracting the values in the Pmt1 Amnt and Pmnt2 Amnt fields from the values in the Net Amount field.

	Inv #	Inv Date	Net Amount	Date Due	Pmt1 Date	Pmt1 Amnt	Pmt2 Date	Pmt2 Amnt	Balance	0-30 Days	31-60 Days	61-90 Days	Over 90 Days
1	10001	1/2/87	$1,234.56	2/1/87					$1,234.56	$0.00	$0.00	$0.00	$1,234.56
2	10002	1/5/87	$416.00	2/4/87	2/3/87	$416.00			$0.00	$0.00	$0.00	$0.00	$0.00
3	10003	1/9/87	$333.67	2/8/87	2/5/87	$333.00	4/12/87	$0.67	$0.00	$0.00	$0.00	$0.00	$0.00
4	10004	1/15/87	$415.76	2/14/87	2/15/87	$215.00	3/7/87	$200.00	$0.76	$0.00	$0.00	$0.00	$0.76
5	10005	1/22/87	$1,278.09	2/21/87	2/14/87	$1,278.09			$0.00	$0.00	$0.00	$0.00	$0.00
6	10006	1/26/87	$367.32	2/25/87	3/5/87	$367.32			$0.00	$0.00	$0.00	$0.00	$0.00
7	10007	1/30/87	$872.55	3/1/87					$872.55	$0.00	$0.00	$0.00	$872.55
8	10008	2/1/87	$55.00	3/3/87	3/2/87	$55.00			$0.00	$0.00	$0.00	$0.00	$0.00
9	10009	2/4/87	$81.90	3/6/87	2/28/87	$80.00	5/1/87	$1.90	$0.00	$0.00	$0.00	$0.00	$0.00
10	10010	2/8/87	$109.52	3/10/87					$109.52	$0.00	$0.00	$0.00	$109.52
11	10011	2/11/87	$261.00	3/13/87	3/15/87	$261.00			$0.00	$0.00	$0.00	$0.00	$0.00
12	10012	2/17/87	$630.00	3/19/87	3/19/87	$630.00			$0.00	$0.00	$0.00	$0.00	$0.00
13	10013	2/24/87	$1,234.56	3/26/87					$1,234.56	$0.00	$0.00	$0.00	$1,234.56
14	10014	3/2/87	$721.33	4/1/87	4/5/87	$721.33			$0.00	$0.00	$0.00	$0.00	$0.00
15	10015	3/7/87	$911.50	4/6/87	4/6/87	$911.50			$0.00	$0.00	$0.00	$0.00	$0.00
16	10016	3/8/87	$700.43	4/7/87					$700.43	$0.00	$0.00	$0.00	$700.43
17	10017	3/15/87	$848.00	4/14/87	4/12/87	$848.00			$0.00	$0.00	$0.00	$0.00	$0.00
18	10018	3/20/87	$916.00	4/19/87	4/17/87	$900.00			$16.00	$0.00	$0.00	$0.00	$16.00
19	10019	3/22/87	$494.34	4/21/87					$494.34	$0.00	$0.00	$0.00	$494.34
20	10020	4/2/87	$900.00	5/2/87	5/2/87	$900.00			$0.00	$0.00	$0.00	$0.00	$0.00
21	10021	4/7/87	$377.80	5/7/87					$377.80	$0.00	$0.00	$0.00	$377.80
22	10022	4/16/87	$165.75	5/16/87					$165.75	$0.00	$0.00	$0.00	$165.75
23	10023	4/22/87	$2,100.00	5/22/87					$2,100.00	$0.00	$0.00	$0.00	$2,100.00
24	10024	4/25/87	$1,467.33	5/25/87					$1,467.33	$0.00	$0.00	$0.00	$1,467.33
25	10025	4/30/87	$210.55	5/30/87					$210.55	$0.00	$0.00	$0.00	$210.55
26	10026	5/2/87	$167.88	6/1/87					$167.88	$0.00	$0.00	$0.00	$167.88
27	10027	5/7/87	$944.44	6/6/87					$944.44	$0.00	$0.00	$0.00	$944.44
28	10028	5/10/87	$744.00	6/9/87					$744.00	$0.00	$0.00	$0.00	$744.00

Figure 10-1.

```
   File   Edit   Print   Select   Format   Options   Query   Report   Window

                        ACCOUNTS RECEIVABLE TRACKER                              ↑

   INVOICE DATA        ▇▇▇▇▇▇▇
                       Invoice Number    Invoice Date   Net Amount    Date Due

                       Comments

   PAYMENT HISTORY              Date          Amount        Balance Due
                       Payment 1
                       Payment 2

   ACCOUNT AGING
                       0-30 Days     31-60 Days    61-90 Days    Over 90 Days   Days

   CUSTOMER INFO
                       Name                              Customer PO

                       Address

                       City            ST  Zip           Phone

1 Inv #             0/0        FORM                            AR.WDB
Press ALT to choose commands or CTRL+PGDN/PGUP for next/previous record.
```

Figure 10-2.

The 0-30 Days, 31-60 Days, 61-90 Days, and Over 90 Days fields contain formulas that "age" the invoice into one of four categories: less than 31 days old, more than 30 days old but less than 61 days old, more than 60 days old but less than 91 days old, and over 90 days old. The Days Past Due field contains a formula that computes the actual number of days that have elapsed since the invoice was due.

Days Past Due	Cust PO #	Cust Name	Cust Address	Cust City	Cust State	Cust Zip	Cust Phone	Comments
311	32005	XYZ, Inc.	55 W. Market St.	Louisville	KY	40223	(502) 896-3344	
0	123	ABC Corp.	123 Commerce Dr.	Louisville	KY	40202	(502) 452-1188	
0		Consolidated Company	225 River Road	Clarksville	IN	47130	(812) 288-8899	
298	5991	L&M Manufacturing	30001 Highway 60	Shelbyville	KY	40065	(502) 456-6655	
0	6672	AAA Enterprises	213 E. Jackson St.	Chicago	IL	60619	(312) 555-6519	
0	1234	ZZZ Limited	901 Main Street	Louisville	KY	40018	(502) 377-8766	
283	92	R&R Partners	875 N. Meridian St.	Indianapolis	IN	46250	(317) 842-7162	Ch 11; referred to legal
0		Bigville Warehousing	441 Warehouse Place	Louisville	KY	40011	(502) 566-1234	
0		Bill Smith Sales Co.	123 Rupp Road	Lexington	KY	40511	(606) 776-1556	
274	445	Williams, Jobs, & Lutz	266 Clark Road	Springfield	IL	62763	(217) 690-8333	
0	712	Associated Companies	7332 Lakeshore Dr.	Chicago	IL	60601	(312) 521-0087	
0	A3442	SmallTown Processing	777 Spring St.	New Albany	IN	47150	(812) 288-6611	
258	145	XYZ, Inc.	55 W. Market St.	Louisville	KY	40223	(502) 896-3344	
0	8011	Rivertown Food Supply	123 Oak Street	Louisville	KY	40202	(502) 452-1848	
0	7012	Heckle & Jeckle, Inc.	3366 Wright Blvd.	Dayton	OH	45435	(513) 431-6992	
246		Consolidated Company	225 River Road	Clarksville	IN	47130	(812) 288-8899	
0	1001	Davis and Sons	23 Riverfront Place	Cincinatti	OH	45244	(513) 722-3988	
234	5176	QMF Rock & Gravel	3417 E. 82nd St.	Indianapolis	IN	46321	(317) 844-7733	
232	7794	Bigville Warehousing	411 Warehouse Place	Louisville	KY	40011	(502) 566-1234	
0	904	John Doe & Assoc.	222 Lake Road	South Bend	IN	46615	(219) 382-8722	
216	XY123	Bigtown Manufacturing	931 Busch Rd.	St. Louis	MO	63121	(314) 555-7809	
207		Anytown Artists	321 University Ave.	Columbus	OH	43210	(614) 333-1256	
201	A3510	SmallTown Processing	777 Spring St.	New Albany	IN	47150	(812) 288-6611	
198	6044	L&M Manufacturing	30001 Highway 60	Shelbyville	KY	40065	(502) 456-6655	
193	1677	ZZZ Limited	901 Main Street	Louisville	KY	40018	(502) 377-8766	
191	3295	ABC Corp.	123 Commerce Dr.	Louisville	KY	40202	(502) 452-1188	
186	179	XYZ, Inc.	55 W. Market St.	Louisville	KY	40220	(502) 896-3344	CREDIT HOLD!
183	3312	BWI, Inc.	12345 Liberty St.	Louisville	KY	40207	(502) 590-6930	

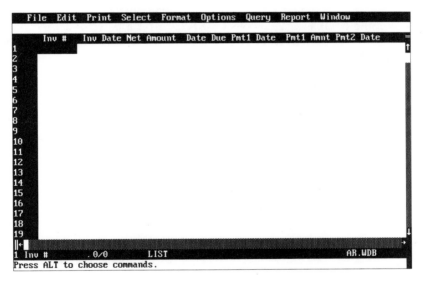

Figure 10-3.

The Cust PO # field identifies the customer's purchase order number. The Cust Name, Cust Address, Cust City, Cust State, Cust Zip, and Cust Phone fields contain the name, address, and phone number of the customer from whom payment is due. The last field, Comments, holds any comments you want to make about a customer or an invoice.

We'll create six reports to accompany this database. The first, INVOICELIST, is a simple listing of the invoices in the database. This report includes the fields Inv #, Inv Date, Net Amount, Date Due, Cust Name, and Cust PO #. The second report, AGING, includes the fields Inv #, Inv Date, Cust Name, Balance, 0-30 Days, 31-60 Days, 61-90 Days, and Over 90 Days. This report simply lists each invoice and classifies its balance by age. The OVERDUE report lists only overdue invoices. It includes the fields Cust Name, Inv #, Net Amount, Balance, and Days Past Due and groups records on the Days Past Due and the Balance fields. The fourth report, CUSTLIST, is a listing of the Customers with invoices in the database. This report groups records by Cust Name and includes the fields Cust Name, Cust Address, Cust City, Cust State, Cust Zip, Cust Phone, and Balance. The OPENBYCUST report lists the open invoices in the database by customer. The records in this report are grouped by Cust Name and Inv #. It includes the fields Cust Name, Inv #, Inv Date, Net Amount, Date Due, Balance, and Days Past Due. The last report, STATEMENT, is a billing statement. It includes the fields Cust Name, Cust Address, Cust City, Cust State, Cust Zip, Inv Date, Inv #, Cust PO #, Pmt1 Amnt, Pmt2 Amnt, and Balance. This rather unusual report groups records on the Cust Name field.

We'll also use queries in a variety of ways to select information from the accounts receivable database. We'll select the record for a particular invoice, the records for a particular company, or the records for all invoices that are a certain age. We'll also use the Sort command on the Query menu to sort the database.

CREATING THE TEMPLATE

The heart of the Accounts Receivable Tracker is the database that stores the information about each invoice. For this reason, the first step in creating the template is to create the database. To begin, select New from the File menu if the New dialog box is not already on your screen. Then, choose Database, and choose the New button. A blank form definition then appears on which you can design your form.

In Works, you can create a database merely by creating a form for the database. We'll take advantage of that shortcut to create the AR database. Figure 10-4 shows the form we'll build, and the table in Figure 10-5 on page 250 lists the field names and widths for each field.

To create this form, begin by entering the label that appears on the top line. To do this, press the Right Arrow key 27 times to move the cursor toward the middle of the form, type *ACCOUNTS RECEIVABLE TRACKER*, and press Enter.

Next, enter the labels that appear along the left edge of the form. First, press the Home key to return the cursor to the left end of the current line and press the Down Arrow key twice to move it to the third line. Then, press the Right Arrow key once, type *INVOICE DATA*, and press Enter. Next, press the Down Arrow key five times and enter the label *PAYMENT HISTORY*. Then, press the Down Arrow key four times and enter the label *ACCOUNT AGING*. Finally, press the Down Arrow key three more times, type *CUSTOMER INFO*, and press Enter.

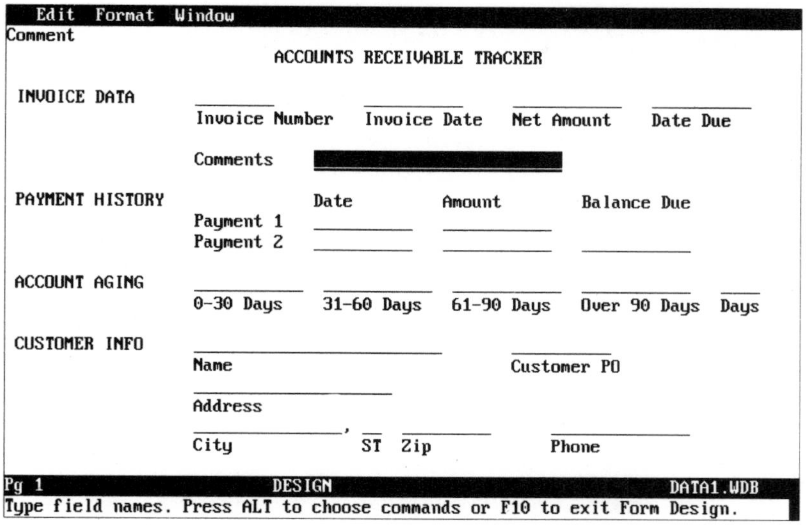

Figure 10-4.

Entering the Field Labels

Now you're ready to begin creating fields. First, notice in Figure 10-4 that the form uses text instead of the built-in field names to identify the field blanks. To do this, we turn off the Show Field Name option for each field and then type a description for each field into the form. This approach makes it possible to align both the field blanks and the field names in the form. It also allows you to reduce the width of the fields without obscuring the field names. Finally, it allows you to abbreviate the actual field names (to conserve space on the List screen) without restricting you to those abbreviated field names as labels in the form.

Let's begin by entering the labels that identify the contents of each field. First, press the Home key to move the cursor to the left edge of the form, and then press the Up Arrow key 11 times to move the cursor to line 4. Then, press the Right Arrow key 19 times, enter *Invoice Number*, press the Right Arrow key four more times, and enter *Invoice Date*. Next, press the Right Arrow key four more times and enter *Net Amount*. Finally, press the Right Arrow key five times, type *Date Due*, and press Enter.

Now, press the Down Arrow key twice to move the cursor down two lines and then to the left until it is directly under the letter *I* in the label *Invoice Number*. When the cursor is in place, enter the label *Comments*.

Next, press the Down Arrow key twice, press the Right Arrow key 12 times, and enter *Date*. Next, press the Right Arrow key 10 times, enter the label *Amount*, press the Right Arrow key nine more times, and enter *Balance Due*.

Field	Width	Format, Decimal Places
Inv #	8	
Inv Date	10	Short Month, Day, Year (MM/DD/YY)
Net Amount	11	Dollar, 2
Date Due	10	Short Month, Day, Year (MM/DD/YY)
Pmt1 Date	10	Short Month, Day, Year (MM/DD/YY)
Pmt1 Amnt	11	Dollar, 2
Pmt2 Date	10	Short Month, Day, Year (MM/DD/YY)
Pmt2 Amnt	11	Dollar, 2
Balance	11	Dollar, 2
0-30 Days	11	Dollar, 2
31-60 Days	11	Dollar, 2
61-90 Days	11	Dollar, 2
Over 90 Days	11	Dollar, 2
Days Past Due	4	Fixed, 0
Cust PO #	10	
Cust Name	25	
Cust Address	20	
Cust City	15	
Cust State	2	
Cust Zip	9	
Cust Phone	14	
Comments	25	

Figure 10-5. *Fields and widths for the AR database.*

Now, press the Down Arrow key once, press the Home key, press the Right Arrow key 19 times, and enter *Payment 1*. Then, press the Down Arrow key again and enter *Payment 2*. Next, press the Down Arrow key three times, type *0-30 Days*, and press Enter. Then, press the Right Arrow key five times, enter *31-60 Days*, press the Right Arrow key four times, enter *61-90 Days*, press the Right Arrow key four more times, and enter *Over 90 Days*. Finally, press the Right Arrow key three times, type *Days*, and press Enter.

Now, press the Down Arrow key three times, press the Home key, press the Right Arrow key 19 times, and enter *Name*. Then, press the Right Arrow key 29 times and enter *Customer PO*. Next, press the Down Arrow key twice, press the Left Arrow key 32 times, and enter *Address*. Then, press the Down Arrow key twice, enter *City*, press the Right Arrow key 12 more times, press the Up Arrow key once, and type a comma (,). Then, press the Down Arrow key once, press the Right Arrow key twice, and enter *ST*. Next, press the Right Arrow key three times, enter *Zip*, press the Right Arrow key 13 times, and enter *Phone*.

Figure 10-6 shows the form design screen at this point with the labels in place.

```
 Edit  Format  Window
"Phone
                    ACCOUNTS RECEIVABLE TRACKER

INVOICE DATA
               Invoice Number   Invoice Date   Net Amount    Date Due

               Comments

PAYMENT HISTORY          Date         Amount        Balance Due
               Payment 1
               Payment 2

ACCOUNT AGING
               0-30 Days    31-60 Days   61-90 Days   Over 90 Days  Days

CUSTOMER INFO
               Name                            Customer PO

               Address

               City          '  ST  Zip        Phone
Pg 1                      DESIGN                          DATA1.WDB
Type field names. Press ALT to choose commands or F10 to exit Form Design.
```

Figure 10-6.

Creating the Fields

Now you're ready to enter the fields. Before you start, remember that the order in which you place the fields in a form determines the order of the fields on the List screen. Because that order is important in this template, be careful to enter the fields in the order shown in Figure 10-6. This requires that you skip around the form a bit as you place fields.

To begin placing fields, press Ctrl-Home to move the cursor to the upper right corner of the screen. Then, press the Down Arrow key twice, press the Right Arrow key eight times, type *Inv #:*, and press Enter. This step inserts the Inv # field into the form. To remove the field name from the display, select Show Field Name from the Format menu. Then, to increase the width of the field to eight characters, select Width from the Format menu, type *8*, and press Enter.

To place the Inv Date field, press the Right Arrow key 10 times and enter *Inv Date:*. To remove the field name from the display, select Show Field Name from the Format menu. To set the width of the field to 10 characters, select Width from the Format menu, type *10*, and press Enter. Then, select Time/Date from the Format menu, choose the Month, Day, Year option (with Short date form), and press Enter or choose OK. This command assigns the MM/DD/YY date format to the Inv Date field.

To place the Net Amount field, press the Right Arrow key six times and enter *Net Amount:*. Then, select the Show Field Name command to hide the field name and select the Width command, type *11*, and press Enter to set the field width. Next, select Dollar from the Format menu and press Enter or choose OK to assign the Dollar format with two decimal places to the Net Amount field.

To place the Date Due field, press the Right Arrow key four more times and enter *Date Due:*. Then, select the Show Field Name command to hide the field name and select the Width command, type *10*, and press Enter to set the field width. Then, select Time/Date from the Format menu, choose the Month, Day, Year option (Short date form), and press Enter or choose OK.

To create the proper field order, place the Pmt1 Date field next. To do so, press the Down Arrow key six times, press the Left Arrow key 27 times, and enter *Pmt1 Date:*. Then, select the Show Field Name command to hide the field name and select the Width command, type *10*, and press Enter to set the field width. To assign this field MM/DD/YY date format, select Time/Date from the Format menu, choose the Month, Day, Year option (Short date form), and press Enter or choose OK.

To place the Pmt1 Amnt field, press the Right Arrow key four times, type *Pmt1 Amnt:*, and press Enter. Then, select the Show Field Name command, select the Width command, type *11*, and press Enter. To assign this field Dollar format with two decimal places, select Dollar from the Format menu and press Enter or choose OK.

To place the Pmt2 Date field, press the Down Arrow key once, press the Left Arrow key 13 times, type *Pmt2 Date:*, and press Enter. Then, select the Show Field Name command, select the Width command, type *10*, and press Enter. To assign this field MM/DD/YY date format, select Time/Date from the Format menu, choose the Month, Day, Year option (with Short date form), and press Enter or choose OK.

To place the Pmt2 Amnt field, press the Right Arrow key four times, type *Pmt2 Amnt:*, and press Enter. Then, select the Show Field Name command, select the Width command, type *11*, and press Enter. To assign this field Dollar format with two decimal places, select Dollar from the Format menu and press Enter or choose OK.

To place the Balance field, press the Right Arrow key four times, type *Balance:*, and press Enter. Then, select the Show Field Name command, select the Width command, type *11*, and press Enter. To assign the proper format to the field, select Dollar from the Format menu and press Enter or choose OK.

Now press the Down Arrow key twice and press the Home key to move the cursor to the beginning of line 12 of the form. Then, to place the 0-30 Days field, press the Right Arrow key seven times, type *0-30 Days:*, and press Enter. Select the Show Field Name command, select the Width command, type *11*, and press Enter. To assign the proper format, select Dollar from the Format menu and press Enter or choose OK.

To place the 31-60 Days field, press the Right Arrow key three times, type *31-60 Days:*, and press Enter. Then, select the Show Field Name command, select the Width command, type *11*, and press Enter. Select Dollar from the Format menu and press Enter or choose OK.

To place the 61-90 Days field, press the Right Arrow key three times, type *61-90 Days:*, and press Enter. Then, select the Show Field Name command, select the Width command, type *11*, and press Enter. Select Dollar from the Format menu and press Enter or choose OK.

Next, to place the Over 90 Days field, press the Right Arrow key three times, type *Over 90 Days:*, and press Enter. Then, select the Show Field Name command, select the Width command, type *11*, and press Enter. Select Dollar from the Format menu and press Enter or choose OK.

Now, press the Right Arrow key four times, type *Days Past Due:*, and press Enter. Select the Show Field Name command, select the Width command, type *4*, and press Enter. To assign Fixed format with zero decimal places, select Fixed from the Format menu, type *0*, and press Enter or choose OK.

To place the Cust PO # field, press the Down Arrow key three times and then press the Left Arrow key 21 times to align the cursor with the *D* in *61–90 Days*. Then, type *Cust PO #:* and press Enter. Next, select the Show Field Name command, select the Width command, type *10*, and press Enter.

To place the Cust Name field, press the Left Arrow key 32 times, type *Cust Name:*, and press Enter. Next, select the Show Field Name command, select the Width command, type *25*, and press Enter. Then, press the Down Arrow key twice, type *Cust Address:*, and press Enter to place the Cust Address field. Select the Show Field Name command, select the Width command, type *20*, and press Enter.

To place the Cust City field, press the Down Arrow key twice, type *Cust City:*, and press Enter. Then, select the Show Field Name command, select the Width command, type *15*, and press Enter. Then, press the Right Arrow key three times, type *Cust State:*, and press Enter to place the Cust State field. Next, select the Show Field Name command, select the Width command, type *2*, and press Enter. Then, press the Right Arrow key three times, type *Cust Zip:*, and press Enter to place the Cust Zip field. Next, select the Show Field Name command, select the Width command, type *9*, and press Enter.

Next, to place the Cust Phone field, press the Right Arrow key seven times, type *Cust Phone:*, and press Enter. Then, select the Show Field Name command, select the Width command, type *14*, and press Enter.

Finally, you need to go back and place the Comments field. To do this, press Ctrl-Home to move the cursor to the upper left corner of the screen. Next, press the Down Arrow key five times and press the Right Arrow key 24 times. Then, type *Comment:* and press Enter. Then, select the Show Field Name command, select the Width command, type *25*, and press Enter.

That's it. Your form should now look like Figure 10-4. At this point, select Exit Design from the Edit menu or simply press [F10]. In either case, Works exits the form definition screen and creates the database specified by the form. You can modify the design of the form by choosing Define Form from the Options menu. Notice, however, that the Define Form command appears on the Options menu of the Form screen, as shown in Figure 10-7, but not on the Options menu of the List screen.

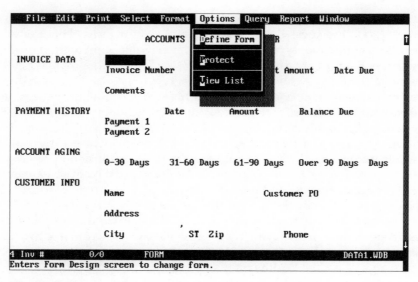

Figure 10-7.

The List Screen

Now you need to use the List screen to change the structure of the database. To begin, choose View List from the Options menu and then press Ctrl-Home. These actions take you to the upper left corner of the List screen, as shown in Figure 10-8.

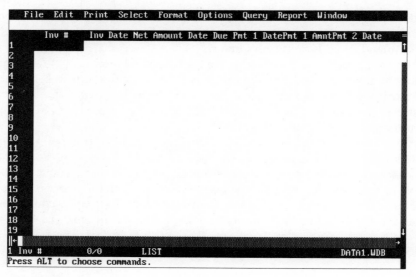

Figure 10-8.

Because the cursor was in the Comment field when you pressed [F10], it also appeared in the Comment field when you switched to the List screen. Pressing the Ctrl-Home key sequence returns the cursor to the home screen, which comprises the upper left corner of the List screen or the first record if you are looking at the Form screen.

Now you're ready to begin making changes. First, you need to change the field widths on the List screen to match those listed in the table in Figure 10-9. (With a few exceptions, the final widths of the fields on the List screen match those on the Form screen.) To change the width of a field on the List screen, move the cursor to that field, select Width from the Format menu, type the new width, and press Enter or choose OK. For example, to change the width of the Inv # field from 10 characters to 8 characters, move the cursor to that field (it may already be there), select Width from the Format menu, type *8*, and press Enter or choose OK.

Next, you need to change the format of the Cust PO # field. To right-align data in this field, move to the Cust PO # field, select Style from the Format menu, choose Right from the Alignment options box, and then press Enter or choose OK.

Field	Width
Inv #	8
Inv Date	10
Net Amount	11
Date Due	10
Pmt1 Date	10
Pmt1 Amnt	11
Pmt2 Date	10
Pmnt2 Amnt	11
Balance	11
0-30 Days	11
31-60 Days	11
61-90 Days	11
Over 90 Days	13
Days Past Due	14
Cust PO #	10
Cust Name	25
Cust Address	20
Cust City	15
Cust State	10
Cust Zip	10
Cust Phone	15
Comments	25

Figure 10-9. *Fields and widths for the AR database (List screen).*

After you change the field widths, you need to enter formulas that define the contents of the Date Due, Balance, 0-30 Days, 31-60 Days, 61-90 Days, Over 90 Days, and Days Past Due fields. To begin, move the cursor to the first cell in the Date Due field, type *=Inv Date+30*, and press Enter. When you do this, Works enters this formula in the first record of the Date Due field. This formula sets the value of the entries in the Date Due field to be equal to the value in the Inv Date of the same record plus 30 days. Until you enter records in the database, this formula remains hidden in each cell of this field. As you enter information in the fields of the database, Works uses this formula to compute the correct due date for each invoice.

Next, move the cursor to the first cell in the Balance field and enter the formula

=Net Amount-Pmt1 Amnt-Pmt2 Amnt

This formula sets the value of the entries in the Balance field equal to the value in the Net Amount field of the same record minus the values in the Pmt1 Amnt and Pmt2 Amnt fields for that record. In other words, the current balance is equal to the original balance minus any payments made to date.

Now move the cursor to the 0-30 Days field and enter the formula

=IF(NOW()-30<=Date Due,Balance,0)

This formula says: If the result of subtracting 30 from the current date (as computed by the NOW function) is less than or equal to the date in the Date Due field, then return the value from the Balance field. Otherwise, return 0. In other words, if the date in the Date Due field is 30 days or less before today, then the invoice is no more than 30 days old, and the value from the Balance field should be posted to the 0-30 Days field.

Next, move to the 31-60 Days field and enter the formula

=IF(NOW()-30>Date Due,IF(NOW()-60<=Date Due,Balance,0),0)

This formula says: If the result of subtracting 30 from the current date is greater than the date in the Date Due field, then if the result of subtracting 60 from the current date is less than or equal to the date in the Date Due field, return the value from the Balance field. Otherwise, return 0. If the result of subtracting 30 from the current date is less than or equal to the date in the Date Due field, then return 0. In other words, this formula posts the value from the Balance field to the 31-60 Days field if the date in the Date Due field is from 60 days to 31 days before the current date.

Now, move the cursor to the 61-90 Days field and enter the formula

=IF(NOW()-60>Date Due,IF(NOW()-90<=Date Due,Balance,0),0)

This formula says: If the result of subtracting 60 from the current date is greater than the date in the Date Due field, then if the result of subtracting 90 from the current date is less than or equal to the date in the Date Due field, return the value from the

Balance field. Otherwise, return 0. If the result of subtracting 60 from the current date is less than or equal to the date in the Date Due field, then return 0. In other words, this formula posts the value from the Balance field to the 61-90 Days field if the date in the Date Due field is from 90 days to 61 days before the current date.

Now, move the cursor to the Over 90 Days field and enter the formula

```
=IF(NOW()-90>Date Due,Balance,0)
```

This formula says: If the result of subtracting 90 from the current date is greater than the date in the Date Due field, then return the value from the Balance field. Otherwise, return 0. In other words, this formula posts the value from the Balance field to the Over 90 Days field if the date in the Date Due field is more than 90 days before the current date.

Next, move the cursor to the Days Past Due field and enter the formula

```
=IF(NOW()>Date Due&Balance>0.01,INT(NOW()-Date Due),0)
```

This formula says: If the current date is greater than the Date Due on the invoice, and if the current balance is greater than $0.01, then return the integer of the difference between the Date Due and the current date. In other words, if the invoice is overdue (that is, if its due date has passed) and if it has not yet been paid off (that is, if its balance is greater than 1 cent), then return the number of days it is past due (that is, the number of days that have elapsed between its due date and the current date).

Saving the Database

After you create the database, save it. To do so for the first time, select Save As from the File menu, type a name (such as *AR.WDB*), and press Enter or choose Save.

Creating the Reports

Now you need to create the reports for the AR database. The basic process for creating reports is always the same: You first use the Sort command on the Query menu to define the fields (if any) on which you want to group the report. If you don't want the report to be grouped by the entries in a particular field, you delete the default entry in the 1st Field text box in the Sort dialog box. (When you select the Sort command for the first time, the 1st Field text box contains the name of the first field in the database.) If you want to group the report on one or more fields, you enter the names of those fields in the 1st Field, 2nd Field, and 3rd Field text boxes.

Next, you select the New command from the Report menu to display a default report definition like the one shown in Figure 10-10 on the next page. Notice that the default report definition includes five bands, or rows: two Intr Page bands, a Record band, a Summ Inv # field, and a Summ Report band. Because the database is currently empty, the default report presents only those fields that contain cell formulas.

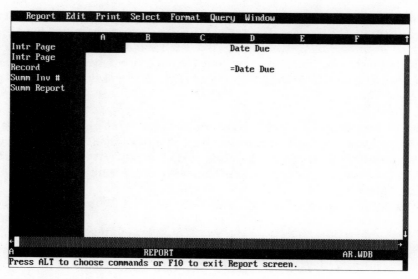

Figure 10-10.

After Works creates the default definition, you can either build your report from this default definition or use the Delete command on the Edit menu to erase the report definition so that you can start from scratch. Either way, you can use the Insert command on the Edit menu to add new bands to the report definition and the Delete command to remove existing bands. You can enter labels and formulas in the cells of the report definition to specify and arrange the contents of the report. You can also use the commands on the Format menu to modify the column widths and data formats. Finally, you can use the Layout command on the Print menu to set the margins for the report and to define a header and a footer for the report.

The INVOICELIST report

Let's begin by creating the INVOICELIST report. As mentioned earlier, this report simply lists the records in the AR database. It includes the Inv #, Inv Date, Net Amount, Date Due, Cust Name, and Cust PO # fields. The report contains a formula that computes the total of the values in the Net Amount field for the entire report.

To begin, select the Sort command from the Query menu to display the Sort dialog box shown in Figure 10-18 on page 266. Notice that Works enters the name of the first field in the database, Inv #, in the 1st Field text box. Because you want this report to be sorted on the Inv # field, simply check to see that the entry *Inv #* appears in the 1st Field text box and that the 2nd Field and 3rd Field boxes are empty. When you're finished, press Enter or choose OK.

Then, select New from the Report menu to display the default report definition, shown in Figure 10-10. Because this default definition is far more involved than the report definition we want to create, delete the contents of this new definition. To do this, simply highlight all five rows in the new definition and select Delete from the Edit menu.

Now, highlight the first row in the definition and select Insert from the Edit menu to display the Insert dialog box, shown in Figure 10-11. This box lists the different elements you can use in this report: Intr Report, Intr Page, and so on. To insert an Intr Page band, choose the Intr Page option and press Enter or choose OK.

Now you need to define the contents of the new band. To begin, press the Right Arrow key to move the cursor to column B and enter the label *Invoice*. Then, move the cursor to column C and type the label *Net*. Next, enter the label *Customer* in column F. To center these three labels, highlight them, select Style from the Format menu, choose the Center option, and press Enter or choose OK.

Next, highlight row 2 and select Insert from the Edit menu. When the Insert dialog box appears, choose Intr Page and press Enter or choose OK. Then, enter the label *Invoice* in column A of the new band, the label *Date* in column B, the label *Amount* in column C, the label *Date Due* in column D, the label *Customer Name* in column E, and the label *PO Number* in column F. To center these six labels, highlight them, select Style from the Format menu, choose Center, and press Enter or choose OK.

Now, highlight row 3 and select Insert from the Edit menu. To insert a Record band, choose Record from the Insert dialog box and press Enter or choose OK. Next, enter the formulas listed in the table in Figure 10-12 on the following page. First enter =*Inv #* in column A of the new band. Then, press the Right Arrow key to move the cursor to column B and enter the formula =*Inv Date*. Continue in this fashion—

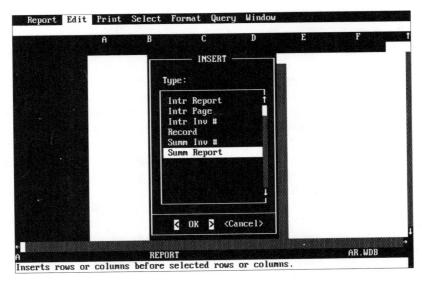

Figure 10-11.

Column	Formula
A	=Inv #
B	=Inv Date
C	=Net Amount
D	=Date Due
E	=Cust Name
F	=Cust PO #

Figure 10-12. Formulas for Record band.

entering a formula in each column across the row—until you have entered all the formulas in the list. After you enter the formula in column F, format that cell so that the results will appear right-aligned in the finished report. To do so, choose Style from the Format menu, choose Right, and then press Enter or choose OK. Because these formulas are in a Record band, Works prints them once for each record in the report. These formulas simply display the contents of the Inv #, Inv Date, Net Amount, Date Due, Cust Name, and Cust PO # fields for each record.

Now, press the Down Arrow key once to move the cursor to the next row in the definition (currently undefined). Then move the cursor to column C and enter a label consisting of two spaces followed by eight hyphens. When you make this entry, Works creates a new Summ Report band and inserts this new label into it. This demonstrates a useful technique you can use in other reports. Whenever you enter a formula or label in a row that you have not yet defined, Works creates a Summ Report band to hold the new entry.

Now, press the Down Arrow key once to move the cursor to the next row in the definition, and enter the formula *=SUM(Net Amount)*. Works creates a new Summ Report band and inserts this new formula into it. Because this formula is in a Summ Report band, Works prints it only once, at the end of the report. The formula computes the sum of the entries in the Net Amount field for the entire report.

Now, press the Down Arrow key again and enter a label consisting of two spaces followed by eight equal signs (========). Works creates yet another Summ Report band to incorporate the new label.

Now you need to change a series of column widths. To change the width of a column in a report, simply move the cursor to that column, select Width from the Format menu, type the new width, and press Enter or choose OK. The table in Figure 10-13 lists the widths of the columns in the INVOICELIST report.

Next, you need to change the formats of columns B, C, and D. To begin, highlight column B either by moving the cursor to any cell in column B and selecting Column from the Select menu or, if you have a mouse, by clicking on the letter B at the top of the column. Now, select Time/Date from the Format menu, choose the Month, Day, Year option, and press Enter or choose OK. This command assigns the MM/DD/YY format to column B.

Column	Width
A	8
B	9
C	11
D	9
E	25
F	10

Figure 10-13. *Column widths for the INVOICELIST report.*

Next, highlight column C, select Dollar from the Format menu, and press Enter or choose OK. This command assigns Dollar format with two decimal places to column C. Then, highlight column D, select Time/Date from the Format menu, choose the Month, Day, Year option, and press Enter or choose OK to assign the MM/DD/YY format to column D.

Next, use the Layout command to set the margins for the report and to define a header and a footer for the report. To do this, select Layout from the Print menu to display the Layout dialog box, shown in Figure 10-14 on the following page. Now, move to the Left Margin text box and type *0.5*. This replaces the original setting, *1.3"*, and sets the left margin of the printed report to one-half inch. Next, move to the Right Margin text box and type *0* to set the right margin to 0 inches.

Now move to the Header text box and enter the header definition

&lDate: &d &cINVOICE LISTING &rPage: &p

This definition tells Works to print a header with three parts: the label *Date:*, followed by the current date, at the left edge of the header line; the label *INVOICE LISTING* in the center of the header line; and the label *Page:*, followed by the current page number, at the right edge of the header line. Works prints the header on each page of the report.

After you enter the header definition, press the Tab key to move to the Footer text box and press the Del key to delete the existing footer definition. Then, press Enter or choose OK to save the changes you made to the Layout dialog box.

That's all there is to it! The report is now defined. Before you do anything else, select Report from the Report menu to display the dialog box shown in Figure 10-15 on the following page. Move to the Name text box and type the name *INVOICELIST*. Then, choose the Rename option to change the name of the report you just defined from Report1 to INVOICELIST. Now, select Exit Report from the Report menu to return to the AR database. Then, select Save from the File menu to save the database and the completed report.

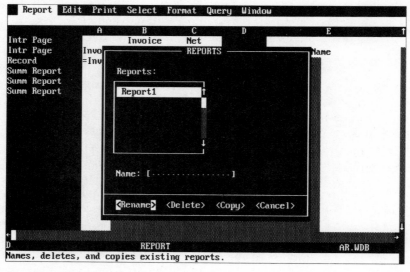

```
  Report  Edit  Print  Select  Format  Query  Window
                A      B      C       D              E           ↑
Intr Page            Invoice    Net
Intr Page    ┌──────────────────── LAYOUT ────────────────────┐
Record       │                                                │
Summ Repor   │  Top Margin:    [1"·····]   Page Length:  [11"·····]│
Summ Repor   │  Bottom Margin: [1"·····]   Page Width:   [8.5"····]│
Summ Repor   │  Left Margin:   [1.3"····]                          │
             │  Right Margin:  [1.2"····]   1st Page Number: [1····]│
             │                                                │
             │  Header: [·····································]  │
             │  Footer: [Page – &p·····························]  │
             │                                                │
             │  [ ] No Header on 1st Page  Header Margin: [0.5"····]│
             │  [ ] No Footer on 1st Page  Footer Margin: [0.5"····]│
             │                                                │
             │                        ◄ OK ► <Cancel>         │
             └────────────────────────────────────────────────┘
┌◄                                                            ↓
D                        REPORT                      AR.WDB
Specifies page size, margins, and headers.
```

Figure 10-14.

```
█ Report  Edit  Print  Select  Format  Query  Window
                A      B      C       D              E           ↑
Intr Page            Invoice    Net
Intr Page    Invo ┌──────────── REPORTS ────────────┐  Name
Record       =Inv │                                 │
Summ Report       │  Reports:                       │
Summ Report       │  ┌──────────────────────────┐↑  │
Summ Report       │  │ Report1                   │   │
                  │  │                           │   │
                  │  │                           │   │
                  │  │                           │   │
                  │  │                           │↓  │
                  │  └──────────────────────────┘   │
                  │                                 │
                  │  Name: [················]        │
                  │                                 │
                  │  ◄Rename► <Delete>  <Copy>  <Cancel> │
                  └─────────────────────────────────┘
┌◄                                                            ↓
D                        REPORT                      AR.WDB
Names, deletes, and copies existing reports.
```

Figure 10-15.

The AGING report

The AGING report includes the fields Inv #, Inv Date, Cust Name, Balance, 0-30 Days, 31-60 Days, 61-90 Days, and Over 90 Days. This report simply lists all the invoices, arranged by invoice number, and then classifies the balance of each by age. To create it, first select Sort from the Query menu. Be sure that the entry *Inv #* appears in the 1st Field text box and that the 2nd Field and 3rd Field boxes are empty. Then, press Enter or choose OK. This step tells Works to print the report in Inv # order. Next, select New from the Report menu. Works displays a default report definition, shown in Figure 10-10 on page 258. Because this default definition is unlike the report definition we want to create, delete the contents of this new definition. To do this, highlight all five rows in the new definition and select Delete from the Edit menu.

Now you're ready to define the report. To begin, highlight the first row in the report definition area and select Insert from the Edit menu. Selecting this command displays the Insert dialog box. When you see this box, choose the Intr Page option and press Enter or choose OK to insert an Intr Page band in the definition.

Now, enter the label *Invoice* in column A of the new band. Then, enter the label *Date* in column B, the label *Customer* in column C, the label *Balance* in column D, the label *Current* in column F, the label *31-60 Days* in column G, the label *61-90 Days* in column H, and the label *Over 90 Days* in column I. To center the labels in the first four columns, highlight the labels you entered in columns A through D, select Style from the Format menu, choose the Center option, and press Enter or choose OK.

Now, highlight row 2 and select Insert from the Edit menu. To insert a Record band into the report definition, choose Record from the Insert dialog box and press Enter or choose OK. Next, enter the formula *=Inv #* in column A of the new band. Then, press the Right Arrow key to move the cursor to column B and enter the formula *=Inv Date*. Next, move the cursor to column C and enter the formula *=Cust Name*. Continue in this way, entering the formula *=Balance* in column D, the formula *='0-30 Days'* in column F, the formula *='31-60 Days'* in column G, the formula *='61-90 Days'* in column H, and the formula *=Over 90 Days* in column I.

Because the field names 0-30 Days, 31-60 Days, and 61-90 Days all include a mathematical symbol (the minus sign), you have to enclose these field names in single quotes to use them in the formula. This same rule applies to other formulas you enter in columns F, G, and H, and to any other formulas that refer to field names that contain mathematical symbols (+, −, *, or /).

Because these formulas are in a Record band, Works calculates and prints them once for each record in the report. These formulas simply display the contents of the indicated fields for each record in AR.

The remaining rows are all Summ Report bands. As before, you can create these bands by simply entering formulas in undefined rows at the bottom of the report definition. To begin, press the Down Arrow key to move the cursor to the first blank row, and then enter labels consisting of two spaces followed by eight dashes in columns D, F, G, H, and I.

Now, move to the next row by pressing the Down Arrow key once more, move to column D, and enter the formula =SUM('31-60 Days'). Continue across the row in this way, entering the formula =SUM('31-60 Days') in column G, the formula =SUM('61-90 Days') in column H, and the formula =SUM(Over 90 Days) in column I. Once again, notice that you must enclose the field names that contain an operator (–) in single quotes. Because these formulas are in a Summ Report band, Works prints them only once, at the end of the report. These formulas compute the sum of the entries in the Net Amount field and the Balance field for the entire report.

Now, press the Down Arrow key to move to the next undefined row, and enter a label consisting of two spaces followed by eight equal signs in columns D, F, G, H, and I.

Now you need to change the widths of several columns in the report definition. The table in Figure 10-16 lists the widths of the columns in the AGING report.

Next, you need to change the formats of columns B, D, F, G, H, and I. To begin, highlight column B, select Time/Date from the Format menu, choose the Month, Day, Year option, and press Enter or choose OK. This command assigns the MM/DD/YY format to column B. Next, highlight column D, select Dollar from the Format menu, and press Enter or choose OK. This command assigns Dollar format with two decimal places to column C. Then, to assign the same format to columns F, G, H, and I, highlight those columns, select Dollar from the Format menu, and press Enter or choose OK. Figure 10-17 shows the report definition at this point.

Finally, use the Layout command to set the margins for the report and to define a header and a footer for the report. To do this, select Layout from the Print menu to display the Layout dialog box. Move to the Left Margin text box and type 0.5 to set the left margin of the printed report to one-half inch. Next, move to the Right Margin text box and type 0 to set the right margin to 0 inches. Then, if you have a wide-carriage printer, move the cursor to the Page Width text box and replace the default width, 8.5", with a new setting of 14". This setting tells Works to print the report on wide paper.

Column	Width
A	8
B	10
C	15
D	11
E	4
F	11
G	11
H	11
I	11

Figure 10-16. *Column widths for the AGING report.*

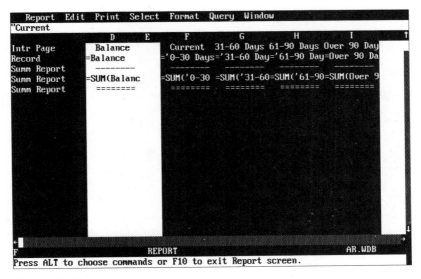

Figure 10-17.

Now, move to the Header text box and enter the header definition

```
&lDate: &d &cACCOUNTS RECEIVABLE AGING &rPage: &p
```

This definition tells Works to print a header with three parts: the label *Date:*, followed by the current date, at the left edge of the header line; the label *ACCOUNTS RECEIVABLE AGING* in the center; and the label *Page:*, followed by the current page number, at the right edge. Works prints the header on each page of the report.

After you enter the header definition, press the Tab key, move to the Footer text box and then press the Del key to delete the existing footer definition. Then, press Enter or choose OK to save the changes you made to the Layout dialog box.

Now you're ready to save the completed report definition. Before you do anything else, select Report from the Report menu to display the Report dialog box. Then, move to the Name text box, type the name *AGING*, and choose the Rename option. Next, select Exit Report from the Report menu to return to the AR database. Then, select Save from the File menu to save the database and the completed report.

The OVERDUE report

The next report, OVERDUE, lists only overdue invoices. It includes the fields Cust Name, Inv #, Net Amount, Balance, and Days Past Due. This report arranges records based on the entries in the Days Past Due and Balance fields.

To begin, choose Sort from the Query menu and enter the field name *Days Past Due* in the 1st Field text box and the field name *Balance* in the 2nd Field text box as shown in Figure 10-18 on the following page. Press Enter or choose OK to leave the dialog box.

Figure 10-18.

Next, select New from the Report menu. Works displays the default report definition. Because this default definition is unlike the report definition we want to create, delete the contents of this new definition. To do so, highlight all five rows in the new definition and select Delete from the Edit menu.

Now you're ready to define the report. To begin, highlight the first row in the definition and select Insert from the Edit menu to display the Insert dialog box. To insert an Intr Page band into the report definition, choose the Intr Page option and press Enter or choose OK.

Now you need to define the contents of the new band. To begin, press the Right Arrow key twice to move the cursor to column C and enter the label *Original*. Then, move the cursor to column E and type the label *Days*. To center these two labels, highlight them, select Style from the Format menu, choose the Center option, and press Enter or choose OK.

Next, highlight row 2 and select Insert from the Edit menu to display the Insert dialog box. To insert an Intr Page band, choose the Intr Page option and press Enter or choose OK. Then, enter the label *Customer* in column A of the new band, the label *Invoice* in column B, the label *Amount* in column C, the label *Balance* in column D, and the label *Overdue* in column E. Next, to center the labels you entered in columns A, B, C, D, and E, highlight them, select Style from the Format menu, choose the Center option, and press Enter or choose OK.

Now, highlight row 3, select the Insert command from the Edit menu, choose the Record option, and press Enter or choose OK. Next, enter the formula *=Cust Name* in column A of the new band. Then, press the Right Arrow key to move the cursor to column B and enter the formula *=Inv #*. Next, enter the formula *=Net Amount* in column C, the formula *=Balance* in column D, and the formula *=Days Past Due* in column E. Because these formulas are in a Record band, Works prints them once for each record in the report. These formulas simply display the contents of the indicated fields for each record in AR.WDB.

Next, highlight row 4, select Insert from the Edit menu, choose the Summ Report option, and press Enter or choose OK. Now, enter a label consisting of two spaces followed by eight hyphens in columns C and D. Of course, you could simply enter these labels in the first undefined row to create a new Summ Report band. Next, press the Down Arrow key, move the cursor to column B, and enter the label *Total:*. Works incorporates the label into a new Summ Report band.

Next, highlight row 5, select Insert from the Edit menu, choose the Summ Report option, and press Enter or choose OK. Then, move the cursor to column B and enter the label *Total:*. Now, move the cursor to column C and enter the formula *=SUM(Net Amount)*. Then, move to column D and enter the formula *=SUM(Balance)*. These formulas compute the sum of the entries in the Net Amount field and the Balance field for the entire report. Because they are in a Summ Report band, Works prints the results of these formulas only once, at the end of the report.

Next, press the Down Arrow key once to move to the next row, and enter a label consisting of two spaces followed by eight equal signs in columns C and D. Works inserts a Summ Report band into the report definition to hold the label.

Now, create another Summ Report band by moving the cursor to column B of the next row, and entering the label *Average:*. Now, enter the formula *=AVG(Net Amount)* in column C, the formula *=AVG(Balance)* in column D, and the formula *=AVG(Days Past Due)* in column E. These formulas compute the average of the entries in the Net Amount, Balance, and Days Past Due fields for the entire report. Because they are in a Summ Report band, Works prints the results of these formulas only once, at the end of the report.

Finally, create one last Summ Report band by entering labels consisting of two spaces followed by eight equal signs in columns C and D of the next row in the definition.

Now, you need to change the widths of columns A through E. The table in Figure 10-19 lists the widths of the columns in the OVERDUE report.

Column	Width
A	25
B	8
C	11
D	11
E	7

Figure 10-19. *Column widths for the OVERDUE report.*

Next, you need to change the formats of columns C, D, and E. To begin, highlight columns C and D, select Dollar from the Format menu, and press Enter or choose OK. This command assigns Dollar format with two decimal places to columns C and D. Then, highlight column E, select Fixed from the Format menu, type *0*, and press Enter or choose OK. Figure 10-20 shows the report definition at this point.

Last, use the Layout command to set the margins for the report and to define a header and a footer for the report. To do this, select Layout from the Print menu to display the Layout dialog box. Then, move to the Left Margin text box and type *0.5* to set the left margin of the printed report at one-half inch. Next, move to the Right Margin text box and type *0* to set the right margin to 0 inches.

Now, move to the Header text box and enter the header definition

&lDate: &d &cOVERDUE ACCOUNTS BY AGE AND AMOUNT &rPage: &p

This definition tells Works to print a header with three parts. On each page of the report, Works prints the label *Date:*, followed by the current date, at the left edge of the header line; the label *OVERDUE ACCOUNTS BY AGE AND AMOUNT* in the center; and the label *Page:*, followed by the current page number, at the right edge.

After you enter the header definition, press the Tab key to move to the Footer text box, and press the Del key to delete the existing footer definition. Then, press Enter or choose OK to save your changes to the Layout dialog box.

Now you're ready to save the completed report definition. Before you do anything else, select Report from the Report menu. When you see the Report dialog box, move to the Name text box and type the name *OVERDUE*. Then, choose Rename

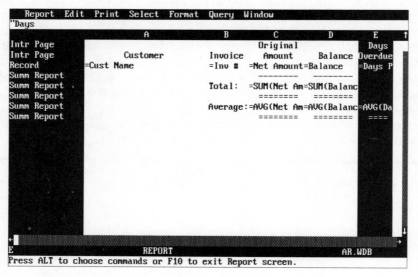

Figure 10-20.

to change the name of the report you just defined. Next, select Exit Report from the Report menu to return to the AR database, and select Save from the File menu to save the database and the completed report.

The CUSTLIST report

The fourth report, CUSTLIST, lists the customers with invoices in the database. The records in the report are arranged by customer name and include the fields Cust Name, Cust Address, Cust City, Cust State, Cust Zip, Cust Phone, and Balance. To create the report, first choose Sort from the Query menu, enter the field name *Cust Name* in the 1st Field text box, and delete the field name *Balance* from the 2nd Field text box. Then, press Enter or choose OK to leave the dialog box.

Next, select New from the Report menu to display a default report definition. Because this default definition is unlike the report definition we want to create, highlight all five rows in the new definition and select Delete from the Edit menu.

Now, highlight the first row in the report definition and select Insert from the Edit menu to display the Insert dialog box. To insert an Intr Page band into the report definition, choose the Intr Page option and press Enter or choose OK.

Next, enter the label *Customer* in column A of the new band. Then, enter the label *Address* in column B, the label *City* in column C, the label *ST* in column D, the label *Zip* in column E, the label *Phone* in column F, and the label *Balance* in column G. After you enter this last label, select Style from the Format menu, choose the Right option, and press Enter or choose OK. Then, move the cursor back to column E, select Style from the Format menu, choose the Center option, and press Enter or choose OK.

Next, highlight row 2 and select Insert from the Edit menu to display the Insert dialog box. To insert a Summ Cust Name band, choose the Summ Cust Name option and press Enter or choose OK. Next, enter the formula *=Cust Name* in column A of the new band, the formula *=Cust Address* in column B, the formula *=Cust City* in column C, the formula *=Cust State* in column D, the formula *=Cust Zip* in column E, the formula *=Cust Phone* in column F, and the formula *=SUM(Balance)* in column G. The formulas in columns A through F simply display the name, address, city, state, zip, and phone number of the current customer. The formulas in column G compute the balance of all the invoices for that customer. Because these formulas are in a Summ Cust Name band, Works prints them once for each Cust Name in the report.

Now, move the cursor to column G of the next band in the report definition and enter a label consisting of two spaces followed by eight hyphens. Works then inserts a Summ Report band to hold this new label.

Next, press the Down Arrow key once, move to column F, and enter the label *Total:*. Then, move to column G and enter the formula *=SUM(Balance)*. The formula computes the sum of the entries in the Balance field for the entire report. Because this formula is in a Summ Report band, Works prints it only once, at the end of the report.

Next, move the cursor to column G of the next row, and enter a label consisting of two spaces followed by eight equal signs. Works inserts another Summ Report row to include the new label.

Now you need to change the widths of the columns in the report definition as indicated by the table in Figure 10-21.

Next, change the format of column G to Dollar format with two decimal places. To do this, highlight column G, select Dollar from the Format menu, type 2, and press Enter or choose OK. Figure 10-22 shows the definition at this point.

Finally, use the Layout command to set the margins for the report and to define a header and a footer for the report. To do this, select Layout from the Print menu, move to the Left Margin text box, and type *0.5*. This change sets the left margin of the printed report to one-half inch. Next, move to the Right Margin text box and type *0* to set the right margin to 0 inches. Then, if you have a wide-carriage printer, move the cursor to the Page Width text box and replace the default width, 8.5", with a new setting of 14". This setting tells Works to print the report on wide paper.

Now move to the Header text box and enter the header definition

`&lDate: &d &cCUSTOMER LIST &rPage: &p`

This definition tells Works to print a header with three parts. On each page of the report, Works prints the label *Date:*, followed by the current date, at the left edge of the header line; the label *CUSTOMER LIST* in the center; and the label *Page:*, followed by the current page number, at the right edge.

After you enter the header definition, press the Tab key to move to the Footer text box, and press the Del key to delete the existing entry. Then, press Enter or choose OK to save your changes to the Layout dialog box.

Now you're ready to save the completed report definition. Before you do anything else, select Report from the Report menu. When you see the Report dialog box, move to the Name text box and type the name *CUSTLIST*. Then, choose the Rename option to change the name of the report you just defined. Next, select Exit

Column	Width
A	25
B	20
C	15
D	3
E	10
F	14
G	11

Figure 10-21. Column widths for the CUSTLIST report.

Figure 10-22.

Report from the Report menu to return to the AR database, and select Save from the
File menu to save the database and the completed report.

The OPENBYCUST report

The OPENBYCUST report lists the open invoices in the database by customer. It
is grouped by customer name and invoice number. It includes the fields Cust Name,
Inv #, Inv Date, Net Amount, Date Due, Balance, and Days Past Due.

To create the report, select Sort from the Query menu to display the Sort dialog
box. Because you want to group the OPENBYCUST report on the Cust Name and Inv
fields, enter the field name *Cust Name* in the 1st Field text box, enter *Inv #* in the 2nd
Field text box, and press Enter or choose OK.

Next, select New from the Report menu. As before, this action displays a default
report definition. Because this default definition is unlike the report definition we
want to create, highlight all six rows in the new definition and select Delete from the
Edit menu.

Next, select Sort from the Query menu to display the Sort dialog box. The 1st
Field text box retains the field name *Cust Name* you entered as you were creating the
CUSTLIST report. Because you want to group the OPENBYCUST report on the Cust
Name and Inv # fields, merely enter the field name *Inv #* in the 2nd Field text box
and press Enter or choose OK to leave the dialog box.

Now you're ready to define the report. To begin, highlight the first row in the
definition and select Insert from the Edit menu to display the Insert dialog box. To
insert an Intr Cust Name band into the report definition, choose the Intr Cust Name
option and press Enter or choose OK. Next, enter the label *Cust Name:* in column A of

the new band. Then, move the cursor to column B and enter the formula *=Cust Name.* The formula in column B simply displays the name of each customer before the group or records for that customer. Because these entries are in an Intr Cust Name band, Works prints them only once for each Cust Name in the report.

Next, highlight row 2 and select Insert from the Edit menu. To insert another Intr Cust Name band, choose the Intr Cust Name option from the Insert dialog box and press Enter or choose OK. Because you insert this band only for spacing, you need not enter anything in it. When you print the report, Works uses this band to place a blank line immediately before each Cust Name group.

Now highlight row 3, select Insert from the Edit menu, choose Intr Cust Name, and press Enter or choose OK. Next, enter the label *Original* in column C of the new band, the label *Current* in column E, and the label *Days* in column F. To right-align the labels in columns C and E, highlight columns C, D, and E in the new band, select Style from the Format menu, choose the Right option, and press Enter or choose OK. Next, highlight column F in the new band, select Style from the Format menu, choose the Center option, and press Enter or choose OK.

Now, highlight row 4, select the Insert command from the Edit menu, choose the Intr Cust Name option again, and press Enter or choose OK. Next, enter the label *Invoice* in column A of the new band, the label *Date* in column B, the label *Amount* in column C, the label *Date Due* in column D, the label *Balance* in column E, and the label *Past Due* in column F. After you enter this last label, highlight columns A through F in the new band, select Style from the Format menu, choose the Right option, and press Enter or choose OK. This command right-aligns the labels in columns A, B, C, D, E, and F.

Next, highlight row 5, select Insert from the Edit menu, choose the Record option, and press Enter or choose OK. Next, enter the formula *=Inv #* in column A of the new band, the formula *=Inv Date* in column B, the formula *=Net Amount* in column C, the formula *=Date Due* in column D, the formula *=Balance* in column E, and the formula *=Days Past Due* in column F. Because these formulas are in a Record band, Works prints them once for each record in the report.

Next, highlight row 6, select Insert from the Edit menu, choose the Summ Cust Name option, and press Enter or choose OK. Now, enter a label consisting of two spaces followed by eight hyphens in column E.

Now, highlight row 7, select Insert from the Edit menu, choose the Summ Cust Name option again, and press Enter or choose OK. Next, enter the label *Customer Total:* in column C of the new band and the formula *=SUM(Balance)* in column E. The formula in column E computes the sum of the Balance field entries for each Cust Name group. Because these entries are in a Summ Cust Name band, Works prints them only once for each different project in the report.

Next, move the cursor to column E of the eighth row and enter a label consisting of two spaces followed by eight hyphens. Works creates a Summ Report band to hold this new label. Now, press the Down Arrow key once, move to column C, and enter the label *Report Total:*. Again, Works creates a Summ Report band to hold this new label. Next, move the cursor to column E and enter the formula =*SUM(Balance)*. This formula computes the sum of the Balance field entries for the entire report. Because these entries are in a Summ Report band, Works prints them only once, at the end of the report.

Finally, press the Down Arrow key to move to column E of the next row, and enter a label consisting of two spaces followed by eight equal signs in column E of the new band. Works inserts another Summ Report band to include the new label.

Now, you need to change the widths of the columns in the report definition. The table in Figure 10-23 lists the widths of the columns in the OPENBYCUST report.

Next, change the format of columns B, C, D, E, and F. To begin, highlight column B, select Time/Date from the Format menu, choose the Month, Day, Year option, and press Enter or choose OK. This command assigns the MM/DD/YY format to column B. Next, highlight column C, select Dollar from the Format menu, and press Enter or choose OK to assign Dollar format with two decimal places to column C. Then, highlight column D, select Time/Date from the Format menu, choose the Month, Day, Year option, and press Enter or choose OK. Next, highlight column E, select Dollar from the Format menu, and press Enter or choose OK. Finally, select column F, select Fixed from the Format menu, type *0*, and press Enter or choose OK. This command assigns Fixed format with zero decimal places to column F. Figure 10-24 on the following page shows the definition at this point.

Last, use the Layout command to set the margins for the report and to define a header and a footer. To do this, select Layout from the Print menu to display the Layout dialog box. Move to the Left Margin text box and type *0.5* to set the left margin of the printed report to one-half inch. Next, move to the Right Margin text box and type *0* to set the right margin to 0 inches.

Now, move to the Header text box and enter the header definition

&lDate: &d &cOPEN ITEMS BY CUSTOMER &rPage: &p

This definition tells Works to print a header with three parts. On each page of the report, Works prints the label *Date:*, followed by the current date, at the left edge of the header line; the label *OPEN ITEMS BY CUSTOMER* in the center; and the label *Page:*, followed by the current page number, at the right edge.

Column	Width
A	10
B	10
C	11
D	10
E	11
F	8

Figure 10-23. *Column widths for the OPENBYCUST report.*

Figure 10-24.

After you enter the header definition, press the Tab key to move to the Footer text box, and press the Del key to delete the existing entry. Then, press Enter or choose OK to save your changes to the Layout dialog box.

Now you're ready to save the completed report definition. Before you do anything else, select Report from the Report menu. When you see the Report dialog box, move to the Name text box and type the name *OPENBYCUST*. Then, choose the Rename option to change the name of the report you just defined. Next, select Exit Report from the Report menu to return to the AR database. Then, select Save from the File menu to save the database and the completed report.

The STATEMENT report

The last report, STATEMENT, is a billing statement that includes the fields Cust Name, Cust Address, Cust City, Cust State, Cust Zip, Inv Date, Inv #, Cust PO #, Pmt1 Amnt, Pmt2 Amnt, and Balance. This report groups records on the Cust Name field.

To create the report, select Sort from the Query menu and verify that the field name *Cust Name* appears in the 1st Field text box and that the 2nd Field and 3rd Field text boxes are empty. Then, press Enter or choose OK to leave the dialog box.

Next, select New from the Report menu to display the default report definition (shown in Figure 10-10 on page 258). Because this default definition is unlike the report definition we want to create, delete the contents of this new definition. To do so, simply highlight all five rows in the new definition and select Delete from the Edit menu.

Now you're ready to define the report. Unlike the reports you've created so far, this report contains 14 Intr Cust Name bands at the top of the definition. To save time, we'll create these bands with just one command. To do this, position the cursor on any field of the first row, and press the Extend key ([F8]). Then, press the Down Arrow key 13 times and press Ctrl-[F8] to highlight the first 14 rows of the definition. Next, select Insert from the Edit menu to display the Insert dialog box, choose Intr Cust Name, and press Enter or choose OK. Works creates 14 blank Intr Cust Name bands in the report definition. Next, type the label *STATEMENT* in column D of row 1, the new band. After you make this entry, select Style from the Format menu, choose the Bold option, and press Enter or choose OK. This command causes Works to display the entry in column D in boldface. Because you made this entry in an Intr Cust Name band, Works prints it once for each different Cust Name in the report.

Because you want to use bands 2 and 3 for spacing, do not enter any information in them. When you print the report, Works uses these bands to place two blank lines before each Cust Name group.

Next, type the label *Date* in column A of row 4. Then, select Time/Date from the Format menu, select the Month, Day, Year option, and press Enter or choose OK. Because you made this entry in an Intr Cust Name band, Works prints it once for each different Cust Name in the report.

Before you actually print this report, you need to replace the label *Date* with the current date. Because Works doesn't allow you to enter NOW or DATE functions in a report definition, you have to enter the date manually.

Row 5 also provides spacing—do not insert any information in it. When you print the report, Works uses band 5 to place a blank line between the date and the address of each statement. Now, enter the formula *=Cust Name* in column A of row 6. The formula simply displays the name of each customer above the group for that customer. Because this formula is in an Intr Cust Name band, Works prints it only once for each Cust Name in the report.

Next, enter the formula *=Cust Address* in column A of row 7. The formula simply displays the address of each customer above the group for that customer. Because this formula is in an Intr Cust Name band, Works prints it only once for each Cust Name in the report.

Now, enter the formula *=Cust City* in column A of row 8, the formula *=Cust State* in column C, and the formula *=Cust Zip* in column D. These formulas print the city, state, and zip code of each customer above the group for that customer. Once again, because they are in an Intr Cust Name band, Works prints the results of these formulas only once for each Cust Name in the report.

It is unfortunate that we have to enter these three formulas in three separate cells. It would be better if we could use a formula like

```
=Cust City+", "+Cust State+"  "+Cust Zip
```

to link them together into a single cell. Works does not, however, support this kind of formula, so we have to be content with entering the formulas in separate cells.

The next three Intr Cust Name bands are intended for spacing only; you need not make any entries into these rows. When you print the report, Works uses these bands to place three blank lines between the address and the body of the statement.

Now you want to create the column headers for the statement. You'll begin by entering information in band 12. In column A, type two spaces and enter the label *Invoice*. Then, move to column B, type one space, and enter the label *Invoice*. Likewise, type one space in column C, followed by the label *Customer*. Enter the label *Original* in column D, the label *Payments* in column E, and the label *Current* in column F. After you enter the last label, highlight columns D, E, and F in the new band, select Style from the Format menu, choose the Right option, and press Enter or choose OK. This command right-aligns the labels in columns D, E, and F.

Next, you'll add labels in band 13. To begin, enter a label consisting of three spaces followed by *Date* in column A. Then, move to column B and type one space, followed by the label *Number*, and in column C, type one space and enter the label *PO Number*. Then, enter the label *Balance* in column D, the label *Applied* in column E, and the label *Balance* in column F. After you enter the last label, highlight columns D, E, and F in the new band, select Style from the Format menu, choose the Right option, and press Enter or choose OK.

Finally, in row 14, enter a label consisting of two spaces followed by eight hyphens in columns A, C, D, E, and F, and a label consisting of two spaces followed by six hyphens in column B.

Because these column header labels are all in Intr Cust Name bands, Works prints them once at the beginning of each Cust Name group.

Next, highlight row 15, and select Insert from the Edit menu to display the Insert dialog box. This time, choose the Record option, and press Enter or choose OK. Next, enter the formula *=Inv Date* in column A of the new band, the formula *=Inv #* in column B, the formula *=Cust PO #* in column C, the formula *=Net Amount* in column D, the formula *=Pmt1 Amnt+Pmt2 Amnt* in column E, and the formula *=Balance* in column F. The formulas in columns A, B, C, D, and F simply display the contents of the Inv Date, Inv #, Cust PO #, Net Amount, and Balance fields for each record in AR.WDB. The formula in column E, *=Pmt1 Amnt+Pmt2 Amnt*, adds the values in the Pmt1 Amnt and Pmt2 Amnt fields and displays the total—the total that has been paid against the invoice. Because all these formulas are in a Record band, Works prints them once for each record in the report.

The remaining eight rows of this report are Summ Cust Name bands. To create all these bands at once, press the Down Arrow key to place the cursor on row 16 and then press [F8]. Now, press the Down Arrow key seven times and press Ctrl-[F8] to highlight rows 16 through 23. Finally, select Insert from the Edit menu, choose Summ Cust Name, and then press Enter or choose OK to create eight new Summ Cust Name bands.

The first three Summ Cust Name bands are used to display balance totals for each customer. To set up these bands, first move the cursor to column F of band 16 and enter a label consisting of two spaces followed by eight hyphens. Next, move to column D of band 17 and enter the label *Total Amount Due:*. Then, in column F of the same band, enter the formula *=SUM(Balance)*. This formula computes the sum of the entries in the Balance field for each customer. Next, move the cursor to column F of band 18 and enter a label consisting of two spaces followed by eight equal signs. Because these entries are in Summ Cust Name bands, Works prints them only once for each customer, following the customer's Record band results.

You want to use the final four Summ Cust Name bands to print messages at the bottom of each customer's invoice and to insert a page break between invoices. To begin, skip band 19 and move the cursor to column A of band 20. Here, enter the label *Please submit a copy of this statement with your payment.* Now, press the Down Arrow key twice to move to column A of band 22, and enter the label *Thank you for your business!* Because bands 19 and 21 simply provide spacing, do not enter any information in either band.

Finally, move the cursor to the bottom of the report definition and highlight band 23. When the cursor is in place, select the Insert Page Break command from the Print menu. When you do this, the symbol >> appears next to the band name at the left edge of the screen. This symbol shows that Works has placed a manual page break in the report in this band. When you print the report, this band causes Works to advance to the top of a new page after it prints each invoice.

Now you need to make some formatting changes to the report. First, change the widths of the columns in the report definition to the widths shown in the table in Figure 10-25. Then, move the cursor to column C of the Record row; this cell contains the formula *= Cust PO #*. Choose Style from the Format menu, and then choose Right and press Enter or choose OK.

Next, change the format of columns A, D, E, and F. To begin, highlight column A, select Time/Date from the Format menu, choose the Month, Day, Year option, and press Enter or choose OK. Next, highlight columns D, E, and F, select Dollar from the Format menu, and press Enter or choose OK to assign these columns Dollar format with two decimal places. Figure 10-26 on the following page shows the definition at this point.

Column	Width
A	10
B	8
C	10
D	11
E	11
F	11

Figure 10-25. *Column widths for the STATEMENT report.*

Figure 10-26.

Finally, use the Layout command to set the margins for the report and to define a header and a footer for the report. To do this, select Layout from the Print menu to display the Layout dialog box. Then, move to the Left Margin text box and type *0.5* to set the left margin of the printed report to one-half inch. Next, move to the Right Margin text box and type *0* to set the right margin to 0 inches. Now, move to the Footer text box and press the Backspace key to delete the existing footer definition. This change means that the printed report has neither a header nor a footer. After you make your changes, press Enter or choose OK.

Now you're ready to save the completed report definition. Before you do anything else, select Report from the Report menu. When you see the Report dialog box, move to the Name text box and type the name *STATEMENT*. Then, choose the Rename option to change the name of the report you just defined. Next, select Exit Report from the Report menu to return to the AR database, and select Save from the File menu to save the database and the completed report.

USING THE TEMPLATE

After you create the AR database and the six associated reports, you can begin to use the template. To begin, simply record each invoice you write in the AR database. Then, from time to time, you can query, sort, and print reports and statements from the database.

Entering Data

When you first start to use the template, you will probably want to go back and enter any outstanding invoices that you have already written. Then, you'll begin recording new invoices in the database. Enter the information for each new invoice as soon as you write the invoice. That way, you don't lose or forget any invoices and your database remains up to date.

Each record in the AR database stores the information about one invoice. For the most part, the names of the fields explain the type of information you need to enter or the type of information computed by the formula for that field. You'll enter information in the Inv #, Inv Date, Net Amount, Pmt1 Date, Pmt1 Amnt, Pmt2 Date, Pmt2 Amnt, Cust PO #, Cust Name, Cust Address, Cust City, Cust State, Cust Zip, Cust Phone, and Comments fields.

The Inv # field stores the number of the invoice. The Inv Date field holds the date on which the invoice was written and the Net Amount field stores the original amount of the invoice. The Pmt1 Date, Pmt1 Amnt, Pmt2 Date, and Pmt2 Amnt fields record the date and amount of any payments that have been made against the invoice. The Cust PO # field holds the customer's purchase order number. The Cust Name, Cust Address, Cust City, Cust State, Cust Zip, and Cust Phone fields contain the name, address, and phone number of the customer from whom payment is due. The last field, Comments, holds any comments you want to make about a customer or an invoice.

The other fields contain formulas that compute the entry for that field. You won't make entries directly into these fields. The Date Due field contains a formula that computes the date on which payment is due. The Balance field contains a formula that computes the current balance by subtracting the values in the Pmt1 Amnt and Pmt2 Amnt fields from the values in the Net Amount field. The 0-30 Days, 31-60 Days, 61-90 Days, and Over 90 Days fields contains formulas that "age" the invoice into one of four categories: less than 31 days old, more than 30 days old but less than 61 days old, more than 60 days old but less than 91 days old, and over 90 days old. The Days Past Due field contains a formula that computes the actual number of days that have elapsed since the invoice's due date.

To begin making entries, open the AR database. (If you just created the template, skip this step.) To open the template, choose Open from the File menu. Then, if the file you want to open is not in the current directory, select the directory that contains the file from the Other Drives & Directories box and choose OK. Now, choose the name of the file from the list of files and press Enter or choose OK to open the file. If AR.WDB is already open, you can make it the active document by pulling down the Window menu and selecting its name. In either case, Works displays the Form screen for the empty database and positions the cursor in the first field (Inv #), as shown in Figure 10-2 on page 246.

After you open the database, use the View Form command on the Options menu to move into the Form screen. (If you already see the form on the screen, skip this step.) Figure 10-2 on page 246 shows the empty form. To enter information in a database through a form, position the cursor on the field in which you want to make an entry, type that entry, and press Enter or one of the direction keys. If you press Enter, Works stores the entry and keeps the cell pointer on that entry. If you press one of the arrow keys, Works stores the entry and moves the cursor to a new field.

As you enter records in the database, you will probably make a few mistakes. To modify an entry, move the cursor to it, press the Edit key ([F2]), make the change, and press Enter. To overwrite an entry, move the cursor to it, type the new entry, and then press Enter. To delete an entire record, use the Ctrl-PgUp or Ctrl-PgDn key combinations to display it, pull down the Edit menu, and select Delete. To insert a blank record above the current one, pull down the Edit menu and select Insert.

An example

To learn how this template works, enter the information shown in Figure 10-3 on page 247 in the AR database. First, however, let's take a minute to change your computer's system clock. Because several fields in the database refer to the system clock, the results in these fields for this example will be incorrect unless we reset the clock. Of course, you won't need to change the system date when you enter your own accounts receivable data in the database.

To reset the clock, select DOS from the File menu and then choose OK when you see the *About to run DOS* dialog box. Selecting this command temporarily moves you out of Works and into MS-DOS. (It is a good practice to save recent changes before using the DOS command.) Now, type *date 5/15/87* and press Enter to change your system clock date to May 15, 1987. Now, type *exit* and press Enter to return to Works.

After you finish working through the examples in this chapter, take a moment to reset the system clock to the current date. To reset the clock, select DOS from the File menu and then choose OK when you see the *About to run DOS* dialog box. Then, type *date*, followed by a blank space and then today's date in the format we used above, and press Enter. This command changes your system clock date to today's date. Now, type *exit* and press Enter to return to Works.

Entering the sample records

To enter records, begin by opening the AR.WDB database. If the List screen appears, select View Form from the Options menu to switch to the Form screen, on which you can examine one record at a time. (If the database contains data already, choose Insert from the Edit menu to begin with an empty form.) With the cursor in the Inv # field, type *10001* and press the Right Arrow key to store your entry. When you do, notice that Works computes values for those fields which contain calculated formulas. Now, type *1/2/87*, press the Right Arrow key, type *1234.56*, press the Right

Arrow key 13 times to move to the Cust Name field, type *XYZ, Inc.*, press the
Right Arrow key, type *32005*, press the Right Arrow key, type *55 W. Market St.*, press
the Right Arrow key, type *Louisville*, press the Right Arrow key, type *KY*, press the
Right Arrow key, type *40223*, press the Right Arrow key, type *(502) 896-3344*, and
press Enter. As you enter these values in the form, Works computes values for the
computed fields in the database. For instance, as soon as you enter the date *1/2/87* in
the Inv Date field, Works computes the value for the Date Due field, *2/1/87*, and displays that value in the form. As soon as you enter the value 1234.56 in the Net
Amount field, Works computes the values for the Balance, 0-30 Days, 31-60 Days,
61-90 Days, and Over 90 Days fields. Figure 10-27 shows the completed form.

After you enter XYZ, Inc.'s phone number in the Cust Phone field of the first
record, press the Right Arrow key to move the cursor to the first field of the second
record. At that point, you can enter the second record. To do this, type *10002* in the
Inv # field, press the Right Arrow key, type *1/5/87*, press the Right Arrow key, type
416, press the Right Arrow key three times to move to the Pmt1 Date field, type *2/3/87*,
press the Right Arrow key, type *416*, press the Right Arrow key nine times to move
the cursor to the Cust Name field, type *ABC Corp.*, press the Right Arrow key, type
123, press the Right Arrow key, type *123 Commerce Dr.*, press the Right Arrow key,
type *Louisville*, press the Right Arrow key, type *KY*, press the Right Arrow key, type
40202, press the Right Arrow key, type *(502) 452-1188*, and press Enter. Once again, as
you enter these values, Works computes values for the computed fields. Figure 10-28
on the following page shows the completed form. After you enter the second record,
enter the remaining 26 records in the same fashion.

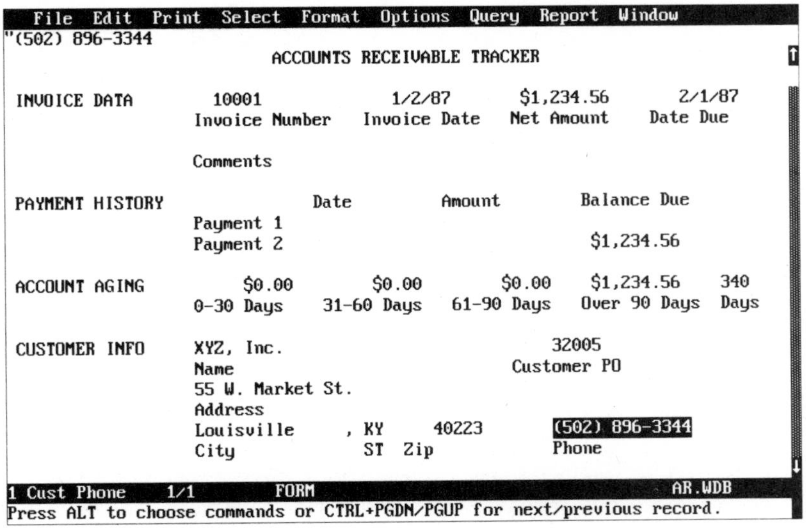

Figure 10-27.

```
 File  Edit  Print  Select  Format  Options  Query  Report  Window
"(502) 452-1188
                            ACCOUNTS RECEIVABLE TRACKER                       ↑

 INVOICE DATA       10002            1/5/87          $416.00         2/4/87
                    Invoice Number   Invoice Date   Net Amount     Date Due

                    Comments

 PAYMENT HISTORY                  Date         Amount        Balance Due
                    Payment 1     2/3/87       $416.00
                    Payment 2                                 $0.00

 ACCOUNT AGING       $0.00        $0.00        $0.00        $0.00       0
                    0-30 Days   31-60 Days   61-90 Days   Over 90 Days  Days

 CUSTOMER INFO      ABC Corp.                          123
                    Name                          Customer PO
                    123 Commerce Dr.
                    Address
                    Louisville    , KY      40202    (502) 452-1188
                    City          ST  Zip            Phone
                                                                             ↓
2 Cust Phone      2/2        FORM                           AR.WDB
Press ALT to choose commands or CTRL+PGDN/PGUP for next/previous record.
```

Figure 10-28.

Saving the database

After you enter the sample records in the database, save it. The first time you save the Accounts Receivable Tracker after you've entered records, you should save it under a new name. To do this, select Save As from the File menu. Then, if you want to save the file in a directory other than the current one, choose that directory from the Other Drives & Directories list box and choose OK. Next, type a new name and press Enter or choose OK. If you want to save the file in the current directory, simply type a name and press Enter or choose OK. Choose a name for the file that clearly identifies its contents, such as *AR1987.WDB* for your 1987 accounts receivable records. Always be sure to choose a name other than AR.WDB when you save the filled-in AR database for the first time. If you save a filled-in database under the same name as the original template, the filled-in version replaces the original version.

After you open the database, you can enter new records in it as you did in the example. You can also edit or even delete existing records. Always resave the database after you make any changes. After you save the database for the first time, you can use the Save command to save the database under the name you previously gave it.

To avoid memory capacity problems, "start over" with a fresh database every so often—usually at the beginning of a year. To do so, use the Open command to open the original, empty template and make any entries that apply to the new period. Then use the Save As command to save the database under a new name. The new name should clearly identify the contents of the file. For instance, you might save the file that contains the records for 1988 under the name AR1988.WDB.

Querying the Database

Queries are tools that let you select specific records, a subset of the records in a database. To do this, use the Define command on the Query menu to create a query form for your database. Then, enter selection conditions (criteria) in the query form that tell Works which records you want to select. Next, apply those criteria to the database. When you do this, Works displays only those records that match the stated criteria. If you then print the database, Works prints only the selected records.

When you want to view all the records in a database again, select Show All Records from the Query menu. To reapply the criteria, select Apply Query from the Query menu.

To define a second query for a database, select Define from the Query menu to enter the query form again. Then, if you want to change the criteria completely, select Delete from the Edit menu to delete any existing criteria and enter your new criteria in the form. To modify the existing criteria, you can edit the entries in the form or add additional criteria. When the query is ready, simply press [F10] or pull down the Edit menu and select Exit Query to activate it.

An example

You can query the AR1987 database in many interesting ways. For example, suppose you want to select only those records for the customer ABC Corp. To do this, select Define from the Query menu to display the query form for the database. The query form looks exactly like the entry form you created.

To have Works select only those records that have the entry *ABC Corp.* in the Cust Name field, enter that criterion in the query form. To do this, press the Right Arrow key until the cursor is in the Cust Name field, type *ABC Corp.*, and press Enter. Figure 10-29 on the following page shows the completed query.

To activate this selection condition, press [F10] or choose Exit Query from the Edit menu. When you do this, Works exits the Query definition screen and returns to the database. Instead of showing you all the records in that database, however, Works lets you look at only those records that have the entry *ABC Corp.* in the Cust Name field. If you are looking at the database in the Form screen, you'll see the first matching record in the database, as shown in Figure 10-30 on the following page. Notice the message *2/28* at the bottom of the screen. This message tells you that only 2 of the 28 records in the database were selected. If you press Ctrl-PgUp or Ctrl-PgDn to move from one record to the next, Works allows you to move only to matching records.

If you chose the List screen, the database looks like Figure 10-31 on page 285. As you can see, only the selected records are visible.

To view the entire database again, select Show All Records from the Query menu. Works then displays all the records in the database. On the Form screen, the message *28/28* appears at the bottom of the screen. On the list screen, Works displays all the records in the database.

```
 Edit  Window
"ABC Corp.
                        ACCOUNTS RECEIVABLE TRACKER

  INVOICE DATA
                   Invoice Number   Invoice Date   Net Amount    Date Due

                   Comments

  PAYMENT HISTORY              Date          Amount        Balance Due
                   Payment 1
                   Payment 2

  ACCOUNT AGING
                   0-30 Days    31-60 Days   61-90 Days   Over 90 Days   Days

  CUSTOMER INFO    ABC Corp.
                   Name                          Customer PO

                   Address

                   City           ST  Zip            Phone

1 Cust Name                 QUERY                            AR1987.WDB
Press ALT to choose commands or F10 to exit Query screen.
```

Figure 10-29.

```
  File  Edit  Print  Select  Format  Options  Query  Report  Window
10002
                        ACCOUNTS RECEIVABLE TRACKER

  INVOICE DATA      10002          1/5/87        $416.00      2/4/87
                   Invoice Number   Invoice Date   Net Amount    Date Due

                   Comments

  PAYMENT HISTORY              Date          Amount        Balance Due
                   Payment 1     2/3/87      $416.00
                   Payment 2                              $0.00

  ACCOUNT AGING     $0.00        $0.00        $0.00        $0.00      0
                   0-30 Days    31-60 Days   61-90 Days   Over 90 Days  Days

  CUSTOMER INFO    ABC Corp.                     123
                   Name                     Customer PO
                   123 Commerce Dr.
                   Address
                   Louisville    , KY      40202     (502) 452-1188
                   City           ST  Zip            Phone

2 Inv #      2/28      FORM                          AR1987.WDB
Press ALT to choose commands or CTRL+PGDN/PGUP for next/previous record.
```

Figure 10-30.

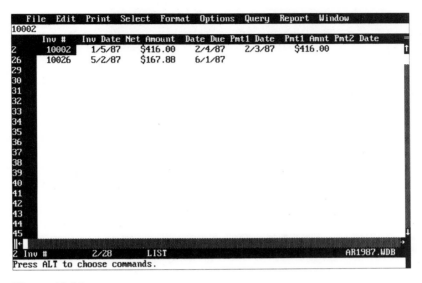

Figure 10-31.

Another example

Let's consider another example. Suppose you want to select only those records for invoices that have an outstanding balance. To begin, select Define from the Query menu to enter the query form again. Then, select Delete from the Edit menu to delete any existing criteria. Now, enter the value *>0.01* in the Balance field and press Enter. To activate this selection condition, simply press [F10] or pull down the Edit menu and select Exit Query. When you do this, Works exits the Query definition screen and returns to the database, where it lets you view only those records that have an entry greater than .01 in the Balance field. The reason you enter *>0.01* rather than simply *>0* is that the calculations used to determine the Balance value can produce fractional values less than one cent. Querying for a balance greater than one cent offsets this fact. On the Form screen, you see the first matching record, invoice number 10001. If you are viewing the List screen, you see a list like the one shown in Figure 10-32 on the following page. As you can see, only the selected records are visible.

To display the entire database again, choose Show All Records from the Query menu. When you do this, Works displays all the records in the database.

Of course, these examples are among the simplest queries you can create to select records from a Works database. For more information on the use of criteria, see pages 406–416 in the *Microsoft Works Reference.*

```
  File   Edit   Print   Select   Format   Options   Query   Report   Window
=Net Amount-Pmt1 Amnt-Pmt2 Amnt
       Net Amount   Date Due Pmt1 Date  Pmt1 Amnt Pmt2 Date  Pmt2 Amnt    Balance =
1      $1,234.56    2/1/87                                              $1,234.56 ↑
4        $415.76   2/14/87   2/15/87     $215.00   3/7/87    $200.00        $0.76
7        $872.55    3/1/87                                                $872.55
10       $109.52   3/10/87                                                $109.52
13     $1,234.56   3/26/87                                              $1,234.56
16       $700.43    4/7/87                                                $700.43
18       $916.00   4/19/87   4/17/87     $900.00                           $16.00
19       $494.34   4/21/87                                                $494.34
21       $377.80    5/7/87                                                $377.80
22       $165.75   5/16/87                                                $165.75
23     $2,100.00   5/22/87                                              $2,100.00
24     $1,467.33   5/25/87                                              $1,467.33
25       $210.55   5/30/87                                                $210.55
26       $167.88    6/1/87                                                $167.88
27       $944.44    6/6/87                                                $944.44
28       $744.00    6/9/87                                                $744.00
29
30
31
‖←                                                                              →
1 Balance          16/28       LIST                            AR1987.WDB
Press ALT to choose commands.
```

Figure 10-32.

Sorting Records

The Sort command on the Query menu allows you to arrange the records in a database so that the entries in one, two, or three fields are in ascending or descending order. Sorting arranges the database so that specific records are easier to locate.

The process is relatively simple. To begin, pull down the Query menu and select Sort to display a Sort dialog box. This box allows you to define as many as three Sort fields. To define the first Sort field for a database, move the cursor to the text box for the 1st Sort field, type the name of the field on which you want to sort the database, and select a sort order (either Ascend or Descend) for that field. When you choose OK, Works closes the Sort dialog box and sorts the database into the order you specified.

Works remembers the settings you enter in the Sort dialog box. After you specify a group of sort settings, those same settings reappear the next time you select the Sort command. To use those settings again, simply press Enter or choose OK. To use different settings, replace some or all of the current settings with new ones and delete any unneeded settings from the dialog box before you sort. To delete an unwanted entry, tab to the box that contains that entry and press the Del key.

Suppose, for example, you want to sort the AR1987 database into ascending order based on the entries in the Cust Name field. To do this, pull down the Query menu, select Sort, type *Cust Name* in the 1st Field text box, and select Ascend (if it is not selected already). Then, if there are entries in the 2nd Field and 3rd Field text boxes, delete those entries. Figure 10-33 shows the dialog box at this point. Finally, choose

OK or press Enter to sort the database. As you can see in Figure 10-34, Works arranges the records in the database in ascending order based on the entries in the Cust Name field. In effect, the database is now "grouped" by Cust Name.

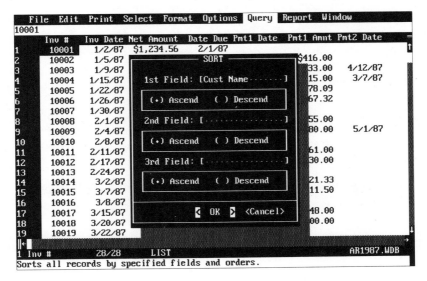

Figure 10-33.

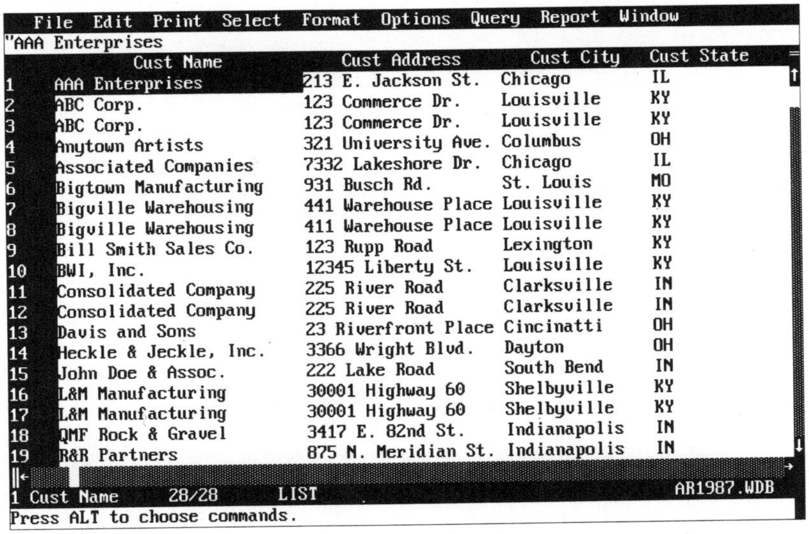

Figure 10-34.

Now suppose you want to sort the AR1987 database again so that the entries in each Cust Name group are arranged in descending order based on the entries in the Balance field. To do this, select Sort from the Query menu. When the Sort dialog box appears, the 1st Field text box still contains the entry *Cust Name*. Because you want to use this setting, you need not change or delete it. Instead, press the Tab key twice to move the cursor to the 2nd Field text box, type *Balance,* and then select Descend (if it is not selected already). Finally, press Enter or choose OK to sort the database. As you can see in Figure 10-35, Works arranges the records in the database in descending order based on the entries in the Cust Name field, and arranges the entries in each customer group by balance in descending order. (We've used the Split Screen command to place the Balance column next to the Cust Name column on the List screen.)

Once again, this simple example has barely scratched the surface of the potential ways you can sort a database. For more information on sorting, see pages 422–25 in the *Microsoft Works Reference.*

```
 File   Edit  Print  Select  Format  Options  Query  Report  Window
"AAA Enterprises
     Balance    ║      Cust Name     ║    Cust Address      Cust City    ═
1        $0.00  ║AAA Enterprises     ║213 E. Jackson St.  Chicago         ↑
2      $167.88  ║ABC Corp.           ║123 Commerce Dr.    Louisville
3        $0.00  ║ABC Corp.           ║123 Commerce Dr.    Louisville
4      $165.75  ║Anytown Artists     ║321 University Ave. Columbus
5        $0.00  ║Associated Companies║7332 Lakeshore Dr.  Chicago
6      $377.80  ║Bigtown Manufacturing║931 Busch Rd.      St. Louis
7      $494.34  ║Bigville Warehousing║411 Warehouse Place Louisville
8        $0.00  ║Bigville Warehousing║441 Warehouse Place Louisville
9        $0.00  ║Bill Smith Sales Co.║123 Rupp Road       Lexington
10     $744.00  ║BWI, Inc.           ║12345 Liberty St.   Louisville
11     $700.43  ║Consolidated Company║225 River Road      Clarksville
12       $0.00  ║Consolidated Company║225 River Road      Clarksville
13       $0.00  ║Davis and Sons      ║23 Riverfront Place Cincinatti
14       $0.00  ║Heckle & Jeckle, Inc.║3366 Wright Blvd.  Dayton
15       $0.00  ║John Doe & Assoc.   ║222 Lake Road       South Bend
16   $1,467.33  ║L&M Manufacturing   ║30001 Highway 60    Shelbyville
17       $0.76  ║L&M Manufacturing   ║30001 Highway 60    Shelbyville
18      $16.00  ║QMF Rock & Gravel   ║3417 E. 82nd St.    Indianapolis
19     $872.55  ║R&R Partners        ║875 N. Meridian St. Indianapolis  ↓
←                →║←                                                  →
1 Cust Name      28/28      LIST                        AR1987.WDB
Press ALT to choose commands.
```

Figure 10-35.

Printing the Reports

You can use the six reports you've created for the AR database to print the information from that database in a variety of ways. Printing database reports is a simple process. First, if you want to print only a subset of your records, use a query to select those records. Next, pull down the Report menu and select the report you want to print. Then, select Print Report from the Print menu and press Enter or choose Print to print the report.

To cancel the printing process before Works prints every label, simply press the Esc key. When you do, Works displays a dialog box that offers two options, labeled OK and Cancel. Choose OK to stop printing; choose Cancel to cancel the interruption and continue printing labels.

A simple example

Suppose, for example, you want to print a copy of the INVOICELIST report for the entire AR1987 database. To begin, select Show All Records from the Query menu to make sure that all the records are displayed. Then, pull down the Report menu. As you can see in Figure 10-36, this menu includes the names of all the reports you defined. Highlight the INVOICELIST report and press Enter.

Next, select Print Report from the Print menu to display the Print dialog box shown in Figure 10-37 on the following page. The first setting allows you to specify how many copies of the report you want Works to print. In most cases, one copy (the default setting) is sufficient. The second setting, Print Specific Pages, allows you to select the pages you want to print. For instance, you could use this option to tell Works to print only the first page of the report, or pages 1 through 5, or pages 3 and 4, or pages 1, 3, and 5. Usually, you skip this option when you are printing a database report. The third setting, Print to File, allows you to print the report to a text file instead of to your printer. To do this, select this option and specify the name of the file to which you want Works to print the report. The final setting, Print All But Record Rows, allows you to print only the Intr and Summ rows from the report definition. Once again, you rarely select this option.

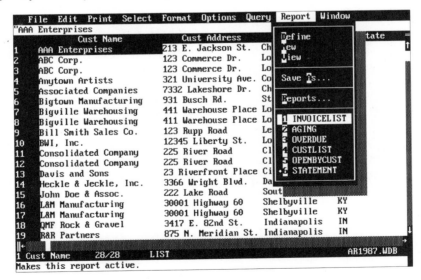

Figure 10-36.

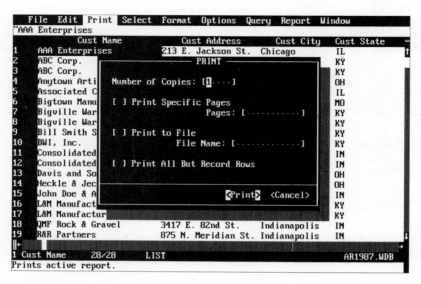

Figure 10-37.

After you adjust any settings you want to change in the Print dialog box, you can print the report. Be sure that your printer is properly connected to your computer and that it is turned on and online. Then, simply choose Print from the bottom of the Print dialog box to print the report, shown in Figure 10-38.

Printing selected records

When Works prints a database report, it extracts information from only the records that are selected at the time. If all the records are shown, the report includes every record in the database. If only certain records are shown, Works prints only those records.

To see how this works, suppose you want to print a copy of the AGING report for only those records in the sample AR1987 database that have a balance greater than $0.01. To begin, select Define from the Query menu to enter the query form. Then, select the Delete command from the Edit menu to delete any existing criteria. Now, enter the value >0.01 in the Balance field and press Enter. To activate this selection condition, simply press [F10] or pull down the Edit menu and select Exit Query. Works then exits the Query definition screen and returns to the database, where it lets you view only those records that have an entry greater than 0.01 in the Balance field. Figure 10-39 on page 292 shows these selected records on the List screen.

```
Date: 6/15/87                    INVOICE LISTING                          Page: 1


              Invoice      Net                                        Customer
    Invoice    Date      Amount    Due Date      Customer Name        PO Number
    10001     1/2/87   $1,234.56   2/1/87  XYZ, Inc.                    32005
    10002     1/5/87     $416.00   2/4/87  ABC Corp.                      123
    10003     1/9/87     $333.67   2/8/87  Consolidated Company
    10004    1/15/87     $415.76  2/14/87  L&M Manufacturing             5991
    10005    1/22/87   $1,278.09  2/21/87  AAA Enterprises               6672
    10006    1/26/87     $367.32  2/25/87  ZZZ Limited                   1234
    10007    1/30/87     $872.55   3/1/87  R&R Partners                    92
    10008     2/1/87      $55.00   3/3/87  Bigville Warehousing
    10009     2/4/87      $81.90   3/6/87  Bill Smith Sales Co.
    10010     2/8/87     $109.52  3/10/87  Williams, Jobs, & Lutz         445
    10011    2/11/87     $261.00  3/13/87  Associated Companies           712
    10012    2/17/87     $630.00  3/19/87  SmallTown Processing         A3442
    10013    2/24/87   $1,234.56  3/26/87  XYZ, Inc.                      145
    10014     3/2/87     $721.33   4/1/87  Rivertown Food Supply         8011
    10015     3/7/87     $911.50   4/6/87  Heckle & Jeckle, Inc.         7012
    10016     3/8/87     $700.43   4/7/87  Consolidated Company
    10017    3/15/87     $848.00  4/14/87  Davis and Sons                1001
    10018    3/20/87     $916.00  4/19/87  QMF Rock & Gravel             5176
    10019    3/22/87     $494.34  4/21/87  Bigville Warehousing          7794
    10020     4/2/87     $900.00   5/2/87  John Doe & Assoc.              904
    10021     4/7/87     $377.80   5/7/87  Bigtown Manufacturing        XY123
    10022    4/16/87     $165.75  5/16/87  Anytown Artists
    10023    4/22/87   $2,100.00  5/22/87  SmallTown Processing         A3510
    10024    4/25/87   $1,467.33  5/25/87  L&M Manufacturing             6044
    10025    4/30/87     $210.55  5/30/87  ZZZ Limited                   1677
    10026     5/2/87     $167.88   6/1/87  ABC Corp.                     3295
    10027     5/7/87     $944.44   6/6/87  XYZ, Inc.                      179
    10028    5/10/87     $744.00   6/9/87  BWI, Inc.                     3312
                        ---------
                       $18,959.28
                       =========
```

Figure 10-38.

Next, pull down the Report menu and select the AGING report. Then, select Print Report from the Print menu and double-check your paper and your printer. Because this report is wide, use 14-inch-wide paper, if possible. However, if you do not have a wide-carriage printer, you might be able to fit the report on standard-width paper by reducing the margins and by using the Font command on the Print menu to choose a compressed style and size of type. Now, choose Print from the bottom of the Print dialog box or press Enter to print the report. Figure 10-40 on the following page shows the printed report. Notice that it contains only the selected records from the database.

File Edit Print Select Format Options Query Report Window

10001

	Inv #	Inv Date	Net Amount	Date Due	Pmt1 Date	Pmt1 Amnt	Pmt2 Date
1	10001	1/2/87	$1,234.56	2/1/87			
4	10004	1/15/87	$415.76	2/14/87	2/15/87	$215.00	3/7/87
7	10007	1/30/87	$872.55	3/1/87			
10	10010	2/8/87	$109.52	3/10/87			
13	10013	2/24/87	$1,234.56	3/26/87			
16	10016	3/8/87	$700.43	4/7/87			
18	10018	3/20/87	$916.00	4/19/87	4/17/87	$900.00	
19	10019	3/22/87	$494.34	4/21/87			
21	10021	4/7/87	$377.80	5/7/87			
22	10022	4/16/87	$165.75	5/16/87			
23	10023	4/22/87	$2,100.00	5/22/87			
24	10024	4/25/87	$1,467.33	5/25/87			
25	10025	4/30/87	$210.55	5/30/87			
26	10026	5/2/87	$167.88	6/1/87			
27	10027	5/7/87	$944.44	6/6/87			
28	10028	5/10/87	$744.00	6/9/87			
29							
30							
31							

1 Inv # 16/28 LIST AR1987.WDB

Press ALT to choose commands.

Figure 10-39.

Date: 6/15/87 ACCOUNTS RECEIVABLE AGING Page: 1

Invoice	Date	Customer	Balance	Current	31-60 Days	61-90 Days	Over 90 Days
10001	1/2/87	XYZ, Inc.	$1,234.56	$0.00	$0.00	$0.00	$1,234.56
10004	1/15/87	L&M Manufacturing	$0.76	$0.00	$0.00	$0.00	$0.76
10007	1/30/87	R&R Partners	$872.55	$0.00	$0.00	$0.00	$872.55
10010	2/8/87	Williams, Jobs, & Lutz	$109.52	$0.00	$0.00	$0.00	$109.52
10013	2/24/87	XYZ, Inc.	$1,234.56	$0.00	$0.00	$1,234.56	$0.00
10016	3/8/87	Consolidated Company	$700.43	$0.00	$0.00	$700.43	$0.00
10018	3/20/87	QMF Rock & Gravel	$16.00	$0.00	$16.00	$0.00	$0.00
10019	3/22/87	Bigville Warehousing	$494.34	$0.00	$494.34	$0.00	$0.00
10021	4/7/87	Bigtown Manufacturing	$377.80	$0.00	$377.80	$0.00	$0.00
10022	4/16/87	Anytown Artists	$165.75	$0.00	$165.75	$0.00	$0.00
10023	4/22/87	SmallTown Processing	$2,100.00	$2,100.00	$0.00	$0.00	$0.00
10024	4/25/87	L&M Manufacturing	$1,467.33	$1,467.33	$0.00	$0.00	$0.00
10025	4/30/87	ZZZ Limited	$210.55	$210.55	$0.00	$0.00	$0.00
10026	5/2/87	ABC Corp.	$167.88	$167.88	$0.00	$0.00	$0.00
10027	5/7/87	XYZ, Inc.	$944.44	$944.44	$0.00	$0.00	$0.00
10028	5/10/87	BWI, Inc.	$744.00	$744.00	$0.00	$0.00	$0.00
			--------	--------	--------	--------	--------
			$10,840.47	$5,634.20	$1,053.89	$1,934.99	$2,217.39
			========	========	========	========	========

Figure 10-40.

Printing a grouped report

Now suppose that you want to print a CUSTLIST report. To begin, select Show All Records from the Query menu to be certain that all the records are selected. Then, pull down the Report menu and select the CUSTLIST report. Next, select Print Report from the Print menu to display the Print dialog box. Before you begin to print, place the proper kind of paper (8.5-inch-wide paper for this report) in your printer and align the paper in your printer so that the print head is on the first line of a new sheet. Then, be sure that your printer is properly connected to your computer and that it is turned on and online. Finally, choose Print to print the report.

Figure 10-41 shows the printed report. As you can see, the items in this report are grouped by the names of the customers. In fact, the report contains only one line for each customer. Works presents customer names in alphabetical order, and it computes and prints a total for the Balance field for each customer group and for the report as a whole.

```
Date: 6/15/87                        CUSTOMER LIST                              Page: 1


Customer               Address            City         ST    Zip   Phone            Balance
AAA Enterprises        213 E. Jackson St. Chicago      IL    60619 (312) 555-6519     $0.00
ABC Corp.              123 Commerce Dr.   Louisville   KY    40202 (502) 452-1188   $167.88
Anytown Artists        321 University Ave. Columbus    OH    43210 (614) 333-1256   $165.75
Associated Companies   7332 Lakeshore Dr. Chicago      IL    60601 (312) 521-0087     $0.00
Bigtown Manufacturing  931 Busch Rd.      St. Louis    MO    63121 (314) 555-7809   $377.80
Bigville Warehousing   411 Warehouse Place Louisville  KY    40011 (502) 566-1234   $494.34
Bill Smith Sales Co.   123 Rupp Road      Lexington    KY    40511 (606) 776-1556     $0.00
BWI, Inc.              12345 Liberty St.  Louisville   KY    40207 (502) 590-6930   $744.00
Consolidated Company   225 River Road     Clarksville  IN    47130 (812) 288-8899   $700.43
Davis and Sons         23 Riverfront Place Cincinatti  OH    45244 (513) 722-3988     $0.00
Heckle & Jeckle, Inc.  3366 Wright Blvd.  Dayton       OH    45435 (513) 431-6992     $0.00
John Doe & Assoc.      222 Lake Road      South Bend   IN    46615 (219) 382-8722     $0.00
L&M Manufacturing      30001 Highway 60   Shelbyville  KY    40065 (502) 456-6655 $1,468.09
QMF Rock & Gravel      3417 E. 82nd St.   IndianapolisIN     46321 (317) 844-7733    $16.00
R&R Partners           875 N. Meridian St. IndianapolisIN    46250 (317) 842-7162   $872.55
Rivertown Food Supply  123 Oak Street     Louisville   KY    40202 (502) 452-1848     $0.00
SmallTown Processing   777 Spring St.     New Albany   IN    47150 (812) 288-6611 $2,100.00
Williams, Jobs, & Lutz 266 Clark Road     Springfield  IL    62763 (217) 690-8333   $109.52
XYZ, Inc.              55 W. Market St.   Louisville   KY    40220 (502) 896-3344 $3,413.56
ZZZ Limited            901 Main Street    Louisville   KY    40018 (502) 377-8766   $210.55
                                                                      --------
                                                             Total:       $10,840.47
                                                                      ========
```

Figure 10-41.

Printing a grouped report for selected records only

Now suppose you want to print a copy of the OPENBYCUST report for only those records in the sample AR database that have an entry in the Balance field greater than $0.00. To begin, choose Define from the Query menu to enter the query form. Then, select Delete from the Edit menu to delete any existing criteria. Now, enter the condition *>0.01* in the Balance field and press Enter. To activate this selection condition, simply press [F10] or choose Exit Query from the Edit menu. When you do this, Works exits the Query definition screen and returns to the database, letting you view only those records that have an entry greater than 0.01 in the Balance field.

Next, pull down the Report menu and select the OPENBYCUST report. Then, choose Print Report from the Print menu, double-check your paper and your printer, and press Enter or choose Print from the bottom of the Print dialog box to print the report. Figure 10-42 shows the printed report. Notice that this report contains only the selected records from the database. Also notice that in this report, Works groups items by the entries in the Cust Name field and prints the name of each customer on a line above the group of records for that customer. Within each customer group, the records are further grouped by invoice number. Works computes and prints a total for the Balance field for each customer group and for the report as a whole.

MODIFICATIONS

You can make several interesting modifications to the AR database. For one thing, you might create more reports for the database. Creating these additional reports is no harder than creating the reports explained in this chapter. Simply select New from the Report menu, delete the default definition, insert bands into the definition, and make entries in the bands. You can probably conceive a great number of useful reports. Works, however, allows you to create a maximum of eight reports for a single database, so decide carefully which reports you want to include.

You might also choose to modify one or more of the reports we created for the template. You might add or delete fields, add additional statistics, or add or delete spacing bands. If your printer has the necessary capabilities, you might also use the Style command on the Format menu to boldface, underline, or italicize parts of a report.

If you find that your customers sometimes make more than two payments against a single invoice, you might want to add two new fields, Pmt3 Date and Pmt3 Amnt, to the database after the Pmt2 Date and Pmt2 Amnt fields. In these fields, enter the date and amount of the third payment made against any invoice. Assign the Pmt3 Date field MM/DD/YY format, and assign the Pmt3 Amnt field Dollar format with two decimal places. If you add these fields, you need to change the formula in the Balance field to

```
Net Amount-Pmt1 Amnt-Pmt2 Amnt-Pmt3 Amnt
```

You also need to rearrange the form to accommodate these new fields.

```
Date: 6/15/87                    OPEN ITEMS BY CUSTOMER                          Page: 1


Customer: ABC Corp.

                         Original                    Current   Days
       Invoice    Date     Amount   Due Date        Balance Past Due
       10026     5/2/87   $167.88    6/1/87         $167.88      14
                                                    --------
                       Customer Total:              $167.88
Customer: Anytown Artists

                         Original                    Current   Days
       Invoice    Date     Amount   Due Date        Balance Past Due
       10022    4/16/87   $165.75   5/16/87         $165.75      30
                                                    --------
                       Customer Total:              $165.75
Customer: Bigtown Manufacturing

                         Original                    Current   Days
       Invoice    Date     Amount   Due Date        Balance Past Due
       10021     4/7/87   $377.80    5/7/87         $377.80      39
                                                    --------
                       Customer Total:              $377.80
Customer: Bigville Warehousing

                         Original                    Current   Days
       Invoice    Date     Amount   Due Date        Balance Past Due
       10019    3/22/87   $494.34   4/21/87         $494.34      55
                                                    --------
                       Customer Total:              $494.34
Customer: BWI, Inc.

                         Original                    Current   Days
       Invoice    Date     Amount   Due Date        Balance Past Due
       10028    5/10/87   $744.00    6/9/87         $744.00       6
                                                    --------
                       Customer Total:              $744.00
Customer: Consolidated Company

                         Original                    Current   Days
       Invoice    Date     Amount   Due Date        Balance Past Due
       10016     3/8/87   $700.43    4/7/87         $700.43      69
                                                    --------
                       Customer Total:              $700.43
Customer: L&M Manufacturing

                         Original                    Current   Days
       Invoice    Date     Amount   Due Date        Balance Past Due
       10004    1/15/87   $415.76   2/14/87           $0.76     121
       10024    4/25/87 $1,467.33   5/25/87       $1,467.33      21
                                                    --------
                       Customer Total:            $1,468.09
```

Figure 10-42.   *(continued)*

Figure 10-42. Continued.

```
Date: 6/15/87                    OPEN ITEMS BY CUSTOMER                      Page: 2


Customer: QMF Rock & Gravel

                       Original                Current   Days
     Invoice    Date     Amount  Due Date      Balance Past Due
     10018    3/20/87   $916.00  4/19/87       $16.00     57
                                               --------
                  Customer Total:              $16.00
Customer: R&R Partners

                       Original                Current   Days
     Invoice    Date     Amount  Due Date      Balance Past Due
     10007    1/30/87   $872.55   3/1/87       $872.55    106
                                               --------
                  Customer Total:              $872.55
Customer: SmallTown Processing

                       Original                Current   Days
     Invoice    Date     Amount  Due Date      Balance Past Due
     10023    4/22/87 $2,100.00  5/22/87     $2,100.00     24
                                             ---------
                  Customer Total:            $2,100.00
Customer: Williams, Jobs, & Lutz

                       Original                Current   Days
     Invoice    Date     Amount  Due Date      Balance Past Due
     10010     2/8/87   $109.52  3/10/87       $109.52     97
                                               --------
                  Customer Total:              $109.52
Customer: XYZ, Inc.

                       Original                Current   Days
     Invoice    Date     Amount  Due Date      Balance Past Due
     10001     1/2/87 $1,234.56   2/1/87     $1,234.56    134
     10013    2/24/87 $1,234.56  3/26/87     $1,234.56     81
     10027     5/7/87   $944.44   6/6/87       $944.44      9
                                             ---------
                  Customer Total:            $3,413.56
Customer: ZZZ Limited

                       Original                Current   Days
     Invoice    Date     Amount  Due Date      Balance Past Due
     10025    4/30/87   $210.55  5/30/87       $210.55     16
                                               --------
                  Customer Total:              $210.55
                                               --------
                  Report Total:             $10,840.47
                                             =========
```

CONCLUSION

If you sell your goods or services on credit, you need a good way to track the money that your customers or clients owe you. In this chapter, you created a system you can use to track your accounts receivable. Along the way, you learned how to create, query, and sort databases, and how to create and use database reports.

The Profit and Loss Forecast

Does your business have a profit plan? A profit plan—a forecast of income and expenses for the coming year (or two)—is an indispensable management tool. It alerts you to potential problems with profitability and cash flow far enough in advance that you can take action to correct or avoid them. And it allows you to measure the actual performance of your business against your forecast performance.

The Profit and Loss Forecast makes it easy to build a profit plan for the coming year. The template for this spreadsheet is flexible enough to be used by almost any size business. Although it is fairly involved, it is also extremely useful. If you run a business, you ought to consider building and using this spreadsheet.

ABOUT THE TEMPLATE

Figure 11-1, which begins on the next page, shows the Profit and Loss Forecast with some sample information entered in it. As you can see, the template has only two areas, labeled INCOME STATEMENT and BALANCE SHEET. When you first create the template, column B contains no assumptions, and the formulas return either *0* or *ERR*.

As shown in Figure 11-2 on page 304, the top left portion of the Income Statement appears when you first load the spreadsheet. Altogether, it occupies the range A4:P51. In this area, you enter information about your company's income and expenses: sales, cost of goods sold, other income, operating expenses, taxes, and so on. Using this information, the formulas in row 50 of this area compute your company's net income for each month in the coming year.

	A	B	C	D	E	F	G
1	================================	=====================	=======	=======	=======	=======
2	PROFIT AND LOSS FORECAST	Assumptions		Jan	Feb	Mar	Apr
3	=========================	=====================	=======	=======	=======	=======
4	INCOME STATEMENT						
5	==
6	Sales						
7	Total Sales	1%	Growth Rate	$115,000	$116,150	$117,312	$118,485
8	Less: Returns/Credits	3%	of Sales	($3,450)	($3,485)	($3,519)	($3,555)
9				-------	-------	-------	-------
10	Net Sales			$111,550	$112,666	$113,792	$114,930
11							
12	Cost of Goods Sold	45%	of Sales	$51,750	$52,268	$52,790	$53,318
13				-------	-------	-------	-------
14	Gross Margin			$59,800	$60,398	$61,002	$61,612
15							
16	Other Income						
17	Interest Income	9.00%	Annual Rate	$0	$0	$0	$0
18	Earned on Cash over $50,000						
19	Other Income			$0	$0	$5,000	$0
20				-------	-------	-------	-------
21				$59,800	$60,398	$61,002	$61,632
22				-------	-------	-------	-------
23	Operating Expenses						
24	Salaries and Wages	1%	Growth Rate	$22,000	$22,220	$22,442	$22,667
25	Benefits	20.00%	of Salaries	$4,400	$4,444	$4,488	$4,533
26	Payroll Taxes	15.00%	of Salaries	$3,300	$3,333	$3,366	$3,400
27	Office Rent	0%	Growth Rate	$4,000	$4,000	$4,000	$4,000
28	Supplies	2%	Growth Rate	$650	$663	$676	$690
29	Postage	1%	Growth Rate	$1,500	$1,515	$1,530	$1,545
30	Telephone	1%	Growth Rate	$1,500	$1,515	$1,530	$1,545
31	Insurance	1%	Growth Rate	$50	$51	$51	$52
32	Dues and Subscriptions	1%	Growth Rate	$300	$303	$306	$309
33	Advertising and Promotion	0%	Growth Rate	$2,500	$2,500	$2,500	$2,500
34	Travel and Entertainment	1%	Growth Rate	$1,500	$1,515	$1,530	$1,545
35	Professional Fees	1%	Growth Rate	$500	$505	$510	$2,500
36	Maintenance	1%	Growth Rate	$500	$505	$510	$515
37	Equipment Rental	1%	Growth Rate	$100	$0	$0	$0
38	Depreciation	60	Months	$4,716	$4,883	$4,883	$4,883
39	Interest						
40	Short-Term Debt	8.00%		$433	$433	$433	$433
41	Long-Term Debt	10.00%		$1,250	$1,250	$1,250	$1,250
42	Other	1%	Growth Rate	$300	$303	$306	$309
43				-------	-------	-------	-------
44	Total Operating Expenses			$49,499	$49,938	$50,313	$52,677
45				-------	-------	-------	-------
46	Profit before Taxes			$10,301	$10,461	$10,689	$8,955
47							
48	Income Taxes			$1,545	$1,569	$1,603	$1,343
49				-------	-------	-------	-------
50	Net Income			$8,756	$8,891	$9,086	$7,612
51				=======	=======	=======	=======

Figure 11-1.

H	I	J	K	L	M	N	O	P
May	Jun	Jul	Aug	Sep	Oct	Nov	Dec	Total
$119,669	$120,866	$122,075	$123,296	$124,529	$125,774	$127,032	$128,302	$1,458,488
($3,590)	($3,626)	($3,662)	($3,699)	($3,736)	($3,773)	($3,811)	($3,849)	($43,755)
$116,079	$117,240	$118,413	$119,597	$120,793	$122,001	$123,221	$124,453	$1,414,733
$53,851	$54,390	$54,934	$55,483	$56,038	$56,598	$57,164	$57,736	$656,320
$62,228	$62,850	$63,479	$64,114	$64,755	$65,402	$66,056	$66,717	$758,414
$44	$21	$112	$197	$283	$183	$268	$354	$1,462
$0	$0	$0	$0	$0	$0	$0	$0	$0
$62,346	$62,945	$63,665	$64,384	$65,111	$65,653	$66,391	$67,138	$760,466
$22,893	$23,122	$23,353	$23,587	$23,823	$24,061	$24,302	$24,545	$279,015
$4,579	$4,624	$4,671	$4,717	$4,765	$4,812	$4,860	$4,909	$55,803
$3,434	$3,468	$3,503	$3,538	$3,573	$3,609	$3,645	$3,682	$41,852
$4,000	$4,000	$4,000	$4,000	$4,000	$4,000	$4,000	$4,000	$48,000
$704	$718	$732	$747	$762	$777	$792	$808	$8,718
$1,561	$1,577	$1,592	$1,608	$1,624	$1,641	$1,657	$1,674	$19,024
$1,561	$1,577	$1,592	$1,608	$1,624	$1,641	$1,657	$1,674	$19,024
$52	$53	$53	$54	$54	$55	$55	$56	$634
$312	$315	$318	$322	$325	$328	$331	$335	$3,805
$2,500	$2,500	$2,500	$2,500	$2,500	$2,500	$2,500	$2,500	$30,000
$1,561	$1,577	$1,592	$1,608	$1,624	$1,641	$1,657	$1,674	$19,024
$515	$520	$525	$531	$536	$541	$547	$552	$8,282
$520	$526	$531	$536	$541	$547	$552	$558	$6,341
$0	$0	$0	$0	$0	$0	$0	$0	$100
$4,883	$4,883	$4,883	$4,883	$4,883	$4,883	$4,883	$4,883	$58,429
$433	$333	$333	$333	$333	$166	$166	$166	$3,995
$1,250	$1,250	$1,250	$1,250	$1,250	$1,250	$1,250	$1,250	$15,000
$312	$315	$318	$322	$325	$328	$331	$335	$3,805
$51,070	$51,357	$51,748	$52,143	$52,542	$52,779	$53,186	$53,598	$620,851
$11,276	$11,588	$11,917	$12,240	$12,568	$12,875	$13,205	$13,540	$139,615
$2,819	$2,897	$4,052	$4,162	$4,273	$5,021	$5,150	$5,281	$39,715
$8,457	$8,691	$7,865	$8,079	$8,295	$7,853	$8,055	$8,259	$99,900

(continued)

Figure 11-1. Continued.

	A	B	C	D	E	F	G
52	==
53	BALANCE SHEET
54	==
55	Current Assets
56	Cash				$17,735	$19,882	$32,218	$42,770
57	Accounts Receivable	45	Days Sales	$165,032	$166,683	$168,350	$170,033
58	Inventory	30	Days CGS	$51,041	$51,551	$52,067	$52,587
59	Other			$0	$0	$0	$0
60				-------	-------	-------	-------
61	Total Current Assets			$233,808	$238,116	$252,635	$265,390
62	
63	Plant, Property, and Equipment
64	Leasehold Improvements			$26,000	$36,000	$36,000	$36,000
65	Furniture and Fixtures			$87,000	$87,000	$87,000	$87,000
66	Equipment			$125,000	$125,000	$100,000	$125,000
67	Office Equipment			$45,000	$45,000	$45,000	$45,000
68				-------	-------	-------	-------
69	Gross PP&E			$283,000	$293,000	$293,000	$293,000
70	Accumulated Depreciation	$70,750	Prior Balance	$75,466	$80,349	$65,232	$90,115
71				-------	-------	-------	-------
72	Net PP&E			$207,534	$212,651	$207,768	$202,885
73	
74	Other Fixed Assets			$0	$0	$0	$0
75				-------	-------	-------	-------
76	Total Assets			$441,342	$450,767	$460,403	$468,275
77				=======	=======	=======	=======
78	
79	Current Liabilities
80	Accounts Payable	30	Days CGS	$51,041	$51,551	$52,067	$52,587
81	Short-Term Debt			$65,000	$65,000	$65,000	$65,000
82	Income Taxes Payable			$1,545	$1,569	$1,603	$1,343
83	Accrued Expenses			$25,000	$25,000	$25,000	$25,000
84	Other			$0	$0	$0	$0
85				-------	-------	-------	-------
86	Total Current Liabilities			$142,586	$143,120	$143,670	$143,930
87	
88	Noncurrent Liabilities
89	Long-Term Debt			$150,000	$150,000	$150,000	$150,000
90	Other			$0	$0	$0	$0
91				-------	-------	-------	-------
92	Total Liabilities			$292,586	$293,120	$293,670	$293,930
93	
94	Common Stock			$50,000	$50,000	$50,000	$50,000
95	Retained Earnings	$90,000	Prior Balance	$98,756	$107,647	$116,733	$124,345
96				-------	-------	-------	-------
97	Total Liabilities and Equity			$441,342	$450,767	$460,403	$468,275
98				=======	=======	=======	=======

H	I	J	K	L	M	N	O	P
===								
===								
$55,886	$52,820	$64,989	$76,309	$87,829	$74,526	$85,789	$97,238	
$171,733	$173,451	$175,185	$176,937	$178,706	$180,494	$182,298	$184,121	
$53,113	$53,644	$54,181	$54,722	$55,270	$55,822	$56,381	$56,944	
$0	$0	$0	$0	$0	$0	$0	$0	
-------	-------	-------	-------	-------	-------	-------	-------	
$280,732	$279,915	$294,355	$307,968	$321,805	$310,842	$324,468	$338,303	
$36,000	$36,000	$36,000	$36,000	$36,000	$36,000	$36,000	$36,000	
$87,000	$87,000	$87,000	$87,000	$87,000	$87,000	$87,000	$87,000	
$125,000	$125,000	$125,000	$125,000	$125,000	$125,000	$125,000	$125,000	
$45,000	$45,000	$45,000	$45,000	$45,000	$45,000	$45,000	$45,000	
-------	-------	-------	-------	-------	-------	-------	-------	
$293,000	$293,000	$293,000	$293,000	$293,000	$293,000	$293,000	$293,000	
$94,998	$99,881	$104,764	$109,647	$114,530	$119,413	$124,296	$129,179	
-------	-------	-------	-------	-------	-------	-------	-------	
$198,002	$193,119	$188,236	$183,353	$178,470	$173,587	$168,704	$163,821	
$0	$0	$0	$0	$0	$0	$0	$0	
-------	-------	-------	-------	-------	-------	-------	-------	
$478,734	$473,034	$482,591	$491,321	$500,275	$484,429	$493,172	$502,124	
=======	=======	=======	=======	=======	=======	=======	=======	
$53,113	$53,644	$54,181	$54,722	$55,270	$55,822	$56,381	$56,944	
$65,000	$50,000	$50,000	$50,000	$50,000	$25,000	$25,000	$25,000	
$2,819	$2,897	$4,052	$4,162	$4,273	$5,021	$5,150	$5,281	
$25,000	$25,000	$25,000	$25,000	$25,000	$25,000	$25,000	$25,000	
$0	$0	$0	$0	$0	$0	$0	$0	
-------	-------	-------	-------	-------	-------	-------	-------	
$145,932	$131,541	$133,233	$133,884	$134,543	$110,843	$111,531	$112,225	
$150,000	$150,000	$150,000	$150,000	$150,000	$150,000	$150,000	$150,000	
$0	$0	$0	$0	$0	$0	$0	$0	
-------	-------	-------	-------	-------	-------	-------	-------	
$295,932	$281,541	$283,233	$283,884	$284,543	$260,843	$261,531	$262,225	
$50,000	$50,000	$50,000	$50,000	$50,000	$50,000	$50,000	$50,000	
$132,802	$141,493	$149,358	$157,437	$165,732	$173,586	$181,641	$189,900	
-------	-------	-------	-------	-------	-------	-------	-------	
$478,734	$473,034	$482,591	$491,321	$500,275	$484,429	$493,172	$502,124	
=======	=======	=======	=======	=======	=======	=======	=======	

```
 File  Edit  Print  Select  Format  Options  Chart  Window
═══════════════════════════════════════════════════════════
              A            B          C        D        E
1  ═══════════════════════════════════════════════════════════
2  PROFIT AND LOSS FORECAST       Assumptions     Jan     Feb
3  ═══════════════════════════════════════════════════════════
4  INCOME STATEMENT          ███████████
5  ═══════════════════════════════════════════════════════════
6  Sales
7    Total Sales             Growth Rate                  $0
8    Less: Returns/Credits   of Sales          $0         $0
9                                          _____  _____
10 Net Sales                                    $0         $0
11
12 Cost of Goods Sold        of Sales          $0         $0
13                                          _____  _____
14 Gross Margin                                 $0         $0
15
16 Other Income
17   Interest Income         Annual Rate       $0         $0
18     Earned on Cash over
19   Other Income                              $0         $0
20                                          _____  _____
B4                            CIRC                  BSINC.WKS
Press ALT to choose commands.
```

Figure 11-2.

The Balance Sheet uses your assumptions and the information recorded in the Income Statement to create a balance sheet for your company. This area occupies the range A53:O98. The formulas in row 76 compute the total value of your assets, and the formulas in row 92 compute the total value of your liabilities. The formulas in row 97 compute your total liabilities and equity by adding your liability and equity (common stock and retained earnings) accounts.

In column B, you'll enter a number of basic assumptions—such as your estimated monthly growth rate for sales and most of your expense categories, the number of days sales you expect to have in accounts receivable, the number of days cost of goods sold you expect to have in accounts payable, and so on. You'll also enter beginning balances for some accounts in column D. The template uses these assumptions to make a number of computations. For example, it uses the growth rate you enter in cell B7 and the January sales assumption you enter in cell D7 to compute estimated sales for February and succeeding months.

Most of the cells in columns D through O contain formulas that compute monthly values for your income, expense, or balance sheet accounts. Some of these formulas refer to the assumptions in column B; others make calculations based on values in other columns. A few cells will contain simple values that you enter manually to represent unusual income or expense items. Column P contains a series of SUM functions that compute the annual total for each row in the Income Statement.

CREATING THE TEMPLATE

To create the Profit and Loss Forecast, first choose New from the File menu if the New dialog box is not already displayed. Next, select Spreadsheet and choose the New button to create a new spreadsheet. Then, select Manual Calculation from the Options menu to speed up the process of creating the template. In the manual recalculation mode, Works does not recalculate all formulas each time you make an entry in the spreadsheet.

Now, change the default format for the spreadsheet from General to Dollar with zero decimal places. First, hold down the Shift and Ctrl keys and press [F8] to highlight the entire spreadsheet (or click with your mouse in the upper left margin of the spreadsheet). Next, select Dollar from the Format menu. When the Decimals dialog box appears, type *0* and then press Enter or choose OK.

Next, change the widths of some columns in the spreadsheet. To change the width of a column, position the cursor in that column, select Width from the Format menu, type the new column width, and press Enter or choose OK. The table in Figure 11-3 lists the columns you need to reformat and the new widths for each column.

After you change the widths of these columns, you're ready to make entries. To begin, enter the header labels in rows 1, 2, and 3. The double line in row 1, which spans columns A through P, is composed of equal signs (=). To enter each label in row 1, type a quotation mark (") followed by the proper number of equal signs (corresponding to the column width). For example, to enter the label in cell A1, move the cursor to cell A1, type a quotation mark, and then type a string of 26 equal signs. If you forget the quotation mark, Works tries to interpret the entry as a formula and displays the message *Error: Missing Operand*.

Next, enter the label *PROFIT AND LOSS FORECAST* in cell A2. Then, move the cursor across row 2 to column B and type seven spaces followed by the word *Assumptions* in cell B2. Now, enter the label *Jan* in cell D2. Continue to move across row 2 one cell at a time, entering the label *Feb* in cell E2, the label *Mar* in cell F2, and so on. When the cursor reaches cell P2, enter the label *Total*.

Next, enter a series of double-line labels in row 3. Be sure to type a leading quotation mark for each label. In cell A3, enter a series of 26 equal signs. The label in

Column	Width
A	26
B	9
C	14
P	11

Figure 11-3. *Column widths for the Profit and Loss Forecast.*

cell B3 consists of seven equal signs preceded by two spaces. Across the rest of the row, cell C3 requires 14 equal signs, the labels in cells D3 through O3, 7 equal signs, and the label in cell P3, 8 equal signs.

When all these labels are in place, right-align the ones in cells D2 through P3. To do this, highlight the range D2:P3, select Style from the Format menu, choose Right from the Style dialog box, and press Enter or choose OK.

The Income Statement

Now you're ready to begin defining the Income Statement. To begin, move the cursor to cell A4 and enter the label *INCOME STATEMENT*. Then, move the cursor to cell A1, highlight the range A1:P1, select Copy from the Edit menu, highlight cell A5, and press Enter. This step copies the double-line labels from row 1 to row 5.

To begin entering the row headers in column A, move the cursor to cell A6 and enter the label *Sales*. Then, move to cell A7 and enter a single space, followed by the label *Total Sales*. Next, move to cell A8 and enter the label *Less: Returns/Credits*, also preceded by a space. Continue in this fashion—moving down column A and entering labels—until all row headers for the Income Statement, shown in column A in Figure 11-1 on page 300, are in place.

Notice that some labels in column A are indented one space and others are indented two spaces from the left edge of column A. These indentions help to make the spreadsheet easier to read and understand. To indent a label, simply type the appropriate number of spaces before you type the label itself.

Now you need to enter a few labels in column C which identify the assumptions you will enter in column B. To begin, move the cursor to cell C7, type one space, and enter the label *Growth Rate*. (As you did with this label, precede all the labels in column C by a single space.) Then, move to cell C8 and enter the label *of Sales*. Next, enter the label *of Sales* in cell C12. Continue in this fashion—moving down column C and entering labels—until all the labels for column C in the Income Statement are in place.

Entering formulas

Now you're ready to enter formulas (and a few labels) in columns D and E in the Income Statement. The table in Figure 11-4 lists the formulas you enter in each cell in these columns in the Income Statement.

You can use the Fill Down command on the Edit menu to help you enter some of these formulas. Instead of entering each formula manually in a series of similar formulas, you can type only the first formula and then use the Fill Down command to create the others. For instance, instead of typing formulas in cells E27 through E37, you can enter the formula *=(1+$B27)*D27* in cell E27, highlight the range E27:E37, and select Fill Down from the Edit menu. Choosing this command copies the formula in cell E27 to cells E28 through E37.

Cell	Formula
E7	=(1+$B7)*D7
D8	=−$B8*D7
E8	=−$B8*E7
D10	=SUM(D7:D9)
E10	=SUM(E7:E9)
D12	=$B12*D7
E12	=$B12*D7
D14	=D10−D12
E14	=E10−E12
D17	=IF(ISERR(D56),0,IF(D56>$B18,INT($B17/12*(D56−$B18)),0))
E17	=IF(ISERR(E56),0,IF(E56>$B18,INT($B17/12*(E56−$B18)),0))
E19	=D19
D21	=D17+D19
E21	=E17+E19
E24	=(1+$B24)*D24
D25	=$B25*D24
E25	=$B25*E24
D26	=$B26*D24
E26	=$B26*E24
E27	=(1+$B27)*D27
E28	=(1+$B28)*D28
E29	=(1+$B29)*D29
E30	=(1+$B30)*D30
E31	=(1+$B31)*D31
E32	=(1+$B32)*D32
E33	=(1+$B33)*D33
E34	=(1+$B34)*D34
E35	=(1+$B35)*D35
E36	=(1+$B36)*D36
E37	=(1+$B37)*D37
D38	=INT(D68/$B38)
E38	=INT(E68/$B38)
D40	=INT($B40/12*D80)
E40	=INT($B40/12*D80)
D41	=INT($B41/12*D88)
E41	=INT($B41/12*E88)
E42	=(1+$B42)*D42
D44	=SUM(D24:D43)

Figure 11-4. *Formulas for columns D and E in the Income Statement.*   (continued)

Figure 11-4. *Continued.*

Cell	Formula
E44	=SUM(E24:E43)
D46	=D14–D44
E46	=E14–E44
D48	=D46*IF(SUM($D$46:D46)>335000,.34,IF(SUM($D$46:D46)>10000,0,.39, IF(SUM($D$46:D46)>75000,.34,IF(SUM($D$46:D46)>50000,.25, IF(SUM($D$46:D46)>0,.15,0)))))
E48	=E46*IF(SUM($D$46:E46)>335000,.34,IF(SUM($D$46:E46)>100000,.39, IF(SUM($D$46:E46)>75000,.34,IF(SUM($D$46:E46)>50000,.25, IF(SUM($D$46:E46)>0,.15,0)))))
D50	=D46–D48
E50	=E46–E48

About the formulas

Let's take a look at each formula in columns D and E. Some of these formulas subtract one value from another. For example, the formula in cell D50, *=D46–D48*, subtracts income tax for January (cell D48) from profit before taxes for January (cell D46). The formula in cell E50, *=E46–E48*, computes the same result for February. Other formulas add one value to another. For example, the formula in cell D21, *=D14+D17+D19*, adds net sales for January (cell D14) to interest income (cell D17) and other income (cell D19). Similarly, the formula in cell E44, *=SUM(E24:E43)*, computes total operating expenses for February by summing the values in the range E24:E43. (Because you have not yet entered any assumptions in the spreadsheet, these formulas, and the other formulas in this section, return 0 for now.)

The formulas in cells E7 and E24, in cells E27 through E37, and in cell E42 are all very similar. These formulas compute the February balance for each of a variety of accounts by multiplying the January balance for an account, in column D, by one plus the growth rate for that account, in column B. For example, the formula in cell E7, *=(1+$B7)*D7*, computes the February balance for total sales by multiplying the January balance for that account (cell D7) by one plus the estimated growth rate for total sales (cell B7).

Some formulas in these columns make computations based on other values in columns D and E and on assumptions in column B. For instance, the formula in cell D8, *=–$B8*D7*, computes returns/credits for January by negating the result of multiplying the returns/credit percentage assumption (cell B8) by the total sales value (cell D7). Similarly, the formula in cell D25, *=$B25*D24*, computes the benefits expense for January by multiplying the salaries and wages expense for January (cell D24) by the benefits percentage assumption (cell B25).

The formulas in rows 40 and 41 compute monthly interest expense on short-term and long-term debt. For example, the formula in cell D40, *=INT($B40/12*D80)*, computes short-term interest for January by dividing the short-term interest rate assumption (cell B40) by 12 (thus computing a monthly rate), multiplying that monthly rate by the short-term debt balance for January (which will be computed in cell D81), and then computing the integer of that result.

The formulas in cells D38 and E38 compute the depreciation expense for January and February. For example, the formula in cell E38 computes the depreciation expense for February by dividing the gross plant, property, and equipment balance for February (cell E68) by the assumed average lifespan of an asset (cell B38).

The formulas in cells D17 and E17 compute interest income for the months of January and February. These formulas refer to cell B17, in which you enter your estimate of the annual rate of interest you expect to earn on excess cash, and to cell B18, in which you enter a number that represents the cash balance above which your cash begins to earn interest. For example, look at the formula in cell E17

`=IF(ISERR(E56),0,IF(E56>$B18,INT($B17/12*(E56-$B18)),0))`

This formula says: If cell E56 (the cash balance for February) contains the value *ERR*, then return the value 0. Otherwise, if the value in cell E56 (the cash balance for February) is greater than the value in cell B18 (the balance above which your cash begins to earn interest), then divide the value in cell B17 (the annual rate of interest earned by excess cash) by 12 to compute a monthly rate, multiply that result by the difference between the value in cell E56 (the cash balance for February) and the value in cell B18 (the balance above which your cash begins to earn interest), and return the integer of that result. Finally, if the value in cell E56 (the cash balance for February) is not greater than the value in cell B18 (the balance above which your cash begins to earn interest), then return 0.

The formulas in cells D48 and E48 compute income tax expense for January and February. For example, the formula in cell E49 computes the estimated income tax expense for February

```
=E46*IF(SUM($D$46:E46)>335000,.34,IF(SUM($D$46:E46)>100000,.39,
IF(SUM($D$46:E46)>75000,.34,IF(SUM($D$46:E46)>50000,.25,
IF(SUM($D$46:E46)>0,.15,0)))))
```

This formula multiplies the profit before taxes for February (cell E46) by a percentage to arrive at the proper tax expense. The correct percentage is determined by a series of rather complicated IF functions. If the total profit before taxes through the month of February (the sum of the range D46:E46) is greater than $335,000, then the formula returns .34, or 34 percent; if the profit before taxes through February is greater than $100,000, the formula returns .39, or 39 percent; if the profit is greater than $75,000, the formula returns .34, or 34 percent; if the profit is greater than $50,000, the formula returns .25, or 25 percent; if the profit is greater than $0, the formula returns .15, or 15 percent; and if the profit is less than $0, the formula returns 0.

These formulas are based on the corporate tax rates for tax years beginning after June 30, 1987, under the Tax Reform Act of 1986. These formulas are designed for profit and loss forecasting purposes only. While they are accurate enough to be used for that purpose, they are not accurate enough for tax planning or for computing actual tax liability. In addition, be aware that tax laws and tax rates change often. While the rates used in these formulas were accurate when this book was published, they may not be accurate for later years.

Entering labels

In addition to entering the formulas in Figure 11-4 in columns D and E, enter a label consisting of two spaces followed by seven hyphens (-------) in the following cells in those columns: D9, E9, D13, E13, D20, E20, D22, E22, D43, E43, D45, E45, D49, and E49. These labels serve as "underlines" for columns of figures that you plan to add. To enter one of these labels, move the cursor to the appropriate cell, press the Spacebar twice, type seven hyphens, and press Enter. You can use the Fill Right and the Copy commands to help you enter these labels. Also, enter a label consisting of two spaces followed by seven equal signs (=======) in cells D51 and E51.

Copying the formulas

After you enter the formulas shown in Figure 11-4 in columns D and E of the Income Statement, copy these formulas from column E to columns F through O. To do this, highlight the range E6:O51 and select Fill Right from the Edit menu. Works copies the formulas and labels from column E to columns F, G, H, and so on through column O.

Let's look at the result of this Fill Right command. Notice that any reference to an assumption in column B in these formulas is mixed. That is, the column portion of the reference is fixed, but the row portion is relative. However, all references to cells in columns D and E are relative. For example, in the formula you entered in cell D38, =INT(D68/$B38), the reference to column B is a mixed reference, but the reference to cell D68 is relative. As a result, the references to cells in column B do not change when you use the Fill Right command to copy these formulas. However, the references to cells in columns D and E change so that each copy refers to a cell in its own column. For example, after the copy is complete, the formula in cell F38 is =INT(F68/$B38), the formula in cell G38 is =INT(G68/$B38), and so on.

The formulas in row 48 (which compute income tax) demonstrate an even more interesting use of absolute and relative references. The formula in cell E48 contains a number of SUM functions, each of which refers to the range $D$46:E46. Notice that the first cell of this range reference is absolute ($D$46), while the second cell is relative (E46). When you copy this formula across row 48, the first half of the range reference remains fixed on cell D46; the second half, however, changes to reflect the location of each copy. For example, the formula in cell F48 is

```
=F46*IF(SUM($D$46:F46)>335000,.34,IF(SUM($D$46:F46)>100000,.39,
IF(SUM($D$46:F46)>75000,.34,IF(SUM($D$46:F46)>50000,.25,
IF(SUM($D$46:F46)>0,.15,0))))
```

Notice that the first half of each range reference in this formula still refers to cell D46 but that the second half refers to cell F46. As you might expect, the SUM functions in the copy in cell G48 refer to the range $D$46:G46, the SUM functions in cell H48 refer to the range $D$46:H46, and so on.

The magic of this technique is that it lets us create a "running sum" in row 48. In other words, the SUM range for each formula in row 48 is one cell larger than the SUM range for the previous formula. As a result, each formula computes the tax based on the cumulative profit before tax through a certain point in the year: The formula in cell F48 computes taxes based on the cumulative profit before tax through February, the formula in cell G48 computes the tax based on the cumulative profit before tax through March, and so on.

You might think that the approach we used in building the Income Statement is inefficient—entering all the formulas in columns D and E and then using the Fill Right command to duplicate these formulas in columns F through O. In fact, it is the most efficient way to create a spreadsheet (or an area of a spreadsheet) in which each cell in each row contains the same basic formula. This approach is far more efficient than the next best alternative: entering and copying the formulas for each row separately. You'd probably be surprised at how many of your spreadsheets fit this pattern and at how much time you can save by building those spreadsheets using this approach. We'll use it again to build the Balance Sheet and to build the Business Cash Flow Forecast and the Personal Financial Plan in the next two chapters.

Formulas for column B

Now you need to enter a simple formula in several cells in column B in the Income Statement. To do this, move the cursor to cell B27 and enter the formula =B$24. This formula refers to cell B24, in which you'll enter a growth rate assumption for salaries and wages. Now, select Percent from the Format menu, type 2, and press Enter or choose OK to assign Percent format with two decimal places to cell B27.

Next, highlight the range B27:B37 and select Fill Down from the Edit menu to copy the formula from cell B27 into the other cells in the highlighted range. Because the reference to cell B24 in the formula in cell B27 is mixed (with the row portion absolute), each copy is identical to the original. For example, cell B28 contains the formula =B$24, cell B29 contains the formula =B$24, and so on.

After you make these copies, move the cursor to cell B37 and select Copy from the Edit menu. Then, move to cell B42 and press Enter to copy the formula from cell B37 to cell B42. Once again, because the formula in cell B37 contains an absolute row reference, the copy is identical to the original.

These formulas are designed to save you time when you actually use the spreadsheet. Because all these formulas refer to cell B24, the growth rate you enter in cell B24 is passed along to all the other cells. In other words, the growth rate for all these expenses is the same as the growth rate for salaries and wages. Of course, you can easily change the growth rate of an individual expense item by entering a different percentage in the appropriate cell in column B. But if most of your expenses are increasing at the same approximate rate, these formulas will keep you from having to enter a growth percentage for each expense.

Formulas for column P

Next, you need to enter a series of SUM functions in column P. Each formula sums the contents of columns D through O in one of the rows of the spreadsheet, creating a series of annual totals in column P. For example, cell P7 contains the formula =SUM(D7:O7), which sums the values in row 7. The table in Figure 11-5 shows the formulas that you should enter in the cells of column P.

Although you can enter each formula manually, you'll probably want to enter the formula in cell P7 and then use the Copy and Fill Down commands to copy it to all the other cells. To begin, enter the formula =SUM(D7:O7) in cell P7. Then, highlight the range P7:P8 and select Fill Down from the Edit menu to copy the formula to cell P8. Because the formula contains relative references, the formula in cell P8 is =SUM(D8:O8). Next, move the cursor to cell P7, select Copy from the Edit menu, highlight cell P10, and press Enter to copy the formula from cell P7 to cell P10. Now, select the Copy command again, highlight cell P12, and press Enter to copy the formula from cell P10 to cell P12. Continue in this way—entering selected formulas and using the Copy and Fill Down commands to create the others—until you've created all the formulas shown in Figure 11-5.

Cell	Formula
P7	=SUM(D7:O7)
P8	=SUM(D8:O8)
P10	=SUM(D10:O10)
P12	=SUM(D12:O12)
P14	=SUM(D14:O14)
P17	=SUM(D17:O17)
P19	=SUM(D19:O19)
P21	=SUM(D21:O21)
P24	=SUM(D24:O24)
P25	=SUM(D25:O25)
P26	=SUM(D26:O26)
P27	=SUM(D27:O27)
P28	=SUM(D28:O28)
P29	=SUM(D29:O29)
P30	=SUM(D30:O30)
P31	=SUM(D31:O31)
P32	=SUM(D32:O32)

Figure 11-5. *Formulas for column P in the Income Statement.*   (continued)

Figure 11-5. Continued.

Cell	Formula
P33	=SUM(D33:O33)
P34	=SUM(D34:O34)
P35	=SUM(D35:O35)
P36	=SUM(D36:O36)
P37	=SUM(D37:O37)
P38	=SUM(D38:O38)
P40	=SUM(D40:O40)
P41	=SUM(D41:O41)
P42	=SUM(D42:O42)
P44	=SUM(D44:O44)
P46	=SUM(D46:O46)
P48	=SUM(D48:O48)
P50	=SUM(D50:O50)

The Balance Sheet

Now you're ready to define the Balance Sheet. To begin, enter the label *BALANCE SHEET* in cell A53. Then, move the cursor to cell A1, highlight the range A1:P1, select Copy from the Edit menu, highlight cell A52, and press Enter. This step copies the double-line labels from row 1 to row 52. Then, without moving the cursor, select the Copy command again, highlight cell A54, and press Enter. This step copies the double-line labels from row 52 to row 54.

Now you're ready to enter the row headers in column A. Move the cursor to cell A55 and enter the label *Current Assets*. Then, move to cell A56 and enter the label *Cash*, preceded by a single space. Next, move to cell A57 and enter the label *Accounts Receivable*, also preceded by a space. Continue in this fashion—moving down column A and entering labels—until all the row headers shown in column A in the Balance Sheet in Figure 11-1 on page 302 are in place.

As in the Income Statement, some labels in column A in the Balance Sheet are indented one space to make the spreadsheet easier to read and understand. To indent a label, simply type a space before you begin typing the label itself.

Now you need to enter a few labels in column C. These labels identify the assumptions that you enter in column B. To begin, move the cursor to cell C57 and enter the label *Days Sales*, preceded by a single space. (Like this one, the other labels in column C use this single-space indention.) Now, move to cell C58 and enter the label *Days CGS*. Next, enter the label *Prior Balance* in cell C69, the label *Days CGS* in cell C79, and the label *Prior Balance* again in cell C94.

Entering formulas

Now you're ready to enter the formulas that define the Expenses area. The table in Figure 11-6 lists the formulas you enter in columns D and E in the Balance Sheet. As before, you can use the Fill Down command on the Edit menu to help you enter some formulas. Instead of entering each formula manually in a series of similar formulas, type only the first formula, and then use the Fill Down command to create the others.

Cell	Formula	Cell	Formula
D56	=D97−D57−D58−D59−D72−D74	E56	=E97−E57−E58−E59−E72−E74
D57	=INT(($B57/365)*D10*12)	E57	=INT(($B57/365)*E10*12)
D58	=INT($B58/365)*D12*12)	E58	=INT($B58/365)*E12*12)
		E59	=D59
D61	=SUM(D56:D60)	E61	=SUM(E56:E60)
		E64	=D64
		E65	=D65
		E66	=D66
		E67	=D67
D69	=SUM(D64:D68)	E69	=SUM(E64:E68)
D70	=B70+D38	E70	=D70+E38
D72	=D69−D70	E72	=E69−E70
		E74	=D74
D76	=D61+D72+D74	E76	=E61+E72+E74
D80	=INT(($B80/365)*D12*12)	E80	=INT(($B80/365)*E12*12)
		E81	=D81
		E82	=D82
		E83	=D83
		E84	=D84
D86	=SUM(D80:D85)	E86	=SUM(E80:E85)
		E89	=D89
		E90	=D90
D92	=D86+D89	E92	=E86+E89
		E94	=D94
D95	=B95+D50	E95	=D95+E50
D97	=D92+D94+D95	E97	=E92+E94+E95

Figure 11-6. *Formulas for columns D and E in the Balance Sheet.*

About the formulas

As in the Income Statement, many formulas in the Balance Sheet simply add or subtract a series of values. For example, the formula in cell D60 computes total current assets for January by summing the cash balance (cell D56), accounts receivable balance (cell D57), inventory balance (cell D58), and other current assets balance (cell D59) for that month. Similarly, the formula in cell D69 computes gross plant, property, and equipment for January by summing the range D64:D68. The formula in cell D72 computes net plant, property, and equipment for January by subtracting the accumulated depreciation balance for January (cell D70) from the gross plant, property, and equipment balance in cell D69. (Because you have not yet entered any assumptions in the spreadsheet, these formulas, and the other formulas in this area, return 0 for now.)

The formulas in row 56 compute the cash balance for January and February. For example, the formula in cell E56

`=E97-E57-E58-E59-E72-E74`

computes the cash balance for February by subtracting the February balances for accounts receivable (cell E57), inventory (cell E58), other current assets (cell E59), net plant, property, and equipment (cell E72), and other fixed assets (cell E74) from the total liabilities and equity balance (cell E97) for February. This formula might seem to offer an unnecessarily complicated way to compute the cash balance, but it has one important advantage: It guarantees that your balance sheet will balance. The formula makes the Cash account a "plug" account; that is, the cash balance is equal to total liabilities and equity minus all asset accounts except for the Cash account.

Other formulas in this area carry forward the assumptions from column D to columns E through O. For instance, the formula in cell E59 is *=D59*. The formula in cell E90 is *=D90*. Because the references in these formulas are relative, the references change when you copy the formulas to columns F through G. As a result, the formulas in columns F through P always refer to the cell in the previous column of the same row. The effect of these formulas is to pass the value in column D in each row across columns E through P.

The formulas in row 70 compute accumulated depreciation for the months of January and February. The accumulated depreciation balance in any month is simply the sum of the depreciation expense for that month and the prior month's accumulated depreciation balance (assuming that no assets were sold). The formulas in row 70 are just that simple. The formula in cell D70, *=B70+D38*, adds the depreciation expense for January (cell D38) to the beginning balance for accumulated depreciation that you enter in cell B70. The formula in cell E70 adds the depreciation expense for February (cell E38) to the accumulated depreciation balance for January (cell D70).

The formulas in row 95 use a similar approach to compute retained earnings for January and February. Retained earnings in any month are simply the sum of the net income for that month and the prior month's retained earnings. The formula in cell

D95, *=B95+D50*, adds net income for January (cell D50) to the beginning balance for retained earnings that you enter in cell B95. The formula in cell E95 adds net income for February (cell E50) to the retained earnings balance for January (cell D95).

The formulas in rows 57, 58, and 80 are all similar. These formulas use the assumptions you enter in cells B57, B58, and B80 to compute the accounts receivable, inventory, and accounts payable balances for January and February. For example, the formula in cell D57

`=INT(($B57/365)*D10*12)`

computes the accounts receivable balance for January. This formula assumes that the accounts receivable balance can be stated as a certain number of days worth of sales. It first divides the days sales assumption that you enter in cell B57 by 365 to compute the percentage of sales that should be in accounts receivable. Then, it multiplies that result by the monthly sales for January (cell D10) and by 12 to compute the accounts receivable balance for January. The formula in cell E57, *=INT(($B57/365)*E10*12)*, makes the same computation for February.

The formulas in row 58 compute the inventory balance. These formulas assume that inventory can be stated as a certain number of days worth of cost of goods sold. For example, the formula in cell D58 computes the inventory balance for January

`=INT(($B58/365)*D12*12)`

This formula first divides the *Days CGS* assumption that you enter in cell B58 by 365 to compute the percentage of cost of goods sold that should be in inventory. Then, it multiplies that result by the monthly cost of goods sold for January (cell D10) and by 12 to compute the inventory balance for January. The formula in cell E58 makes the same computation for February.

The formulas in row 80 compute the accounts payable balances for January and February. These formulas assume that accounts payable also can be stated as a certain number of days worth of cost of goods sold. For example, the formula in cell D80 computes the accounts payable balance for January

`=INT(($B80/365)*D12*12)`

This formula first divides the days cost of goods sold assumption that you enter in cell B80 by 365 to compute the percentage of cost of goods sold that should be in accounts payable. Then, it multiplies that result by the monthly cost of goods sold for January (cell D10) and by 12 to compute the accounts payable balance for January. The formula in cell E80 makes the same computation for February.

Notice that we have not entered a formula in every cell in column D in the Balance Sheet. For example, we left cell D59 blank, which would hold a value for the Other Current Assets account for January. In fact, we entered formulas only in cells whose value could be computed from other values in column D (in either the Balance Sheet or the Income Statement) or from assumptions entered in column B. Later in this chapter, you'll learn how to enter the values in the remaining rows manually.

Entering labels

In addition to entering the formulas in Figure 11-6 in columns D and E, enter a label consisting of two spaces followed by seven dashes in the following cells: D59, E59, D67, E67, D70, E70, D74, E74, D84, E84, D90, E90, D95, and E95. These labels serve as "underlines" for columns of figures that you plan to add. You can use the Copy command and the Fill Right command to help you enter these labels. Also, enter a label consisting of two spaces followed by seven equal signs in cells D76, E76, D97, and E97.

Copying the formulas

After you enter the formulas shown in Figure 11-6, copy these formulas from column E to columns F through O. To do this, highlight the range E56:O97 and select Fill Right from the Edit menu. Works copies the formulas and labels from column E to columns F, G, and so on through column O.

As stated previously, many formulas in column E of the Balance Sheet simply refer to the cell in column D in the same row. Because the references in those formulas are relative, when you copied the formulas to columns F through G, the references changed to reflect the new position of each copy. As a result, many of the formulas in columns F through P in the Balance Sheet of the template refer to the cell in the previous column of the same row. The effect of these formulas is to pass the value in column D in each row across columns E through P.

A few formulas in this section contain mixed references to cells in column B. For example, the formula in cell E57, *=INT(($B57/365)*E10*12)*, contains a mixed reference to cell B57. Because these references are absolute with respect to column B, the copies of the formulas across the spreadsheet also refer to column B. For example, the formula in cell F57, *=INT(($B57/365)*F10*12)*, contains the same mixed reference to cell B57.

Freezing Rows and Columns

As the last step in creating the template, freeze column A and rows 1, 2, and 3 onto the screen. This ensures that the appropriate row and column headers remain visible on the screen—even when the cursor is way off to the right or way down toward the bottom of the spreadsheet. To freeze column A and rows 1, 2, and 3, move the cursor to cell B4 and select Freeze Titles from the Options menu.

Saving the Template

That's it! Now, before you do anything else, save your work (or resave it, if you have been saving as you go along). To save the template for the first time, select Save As from the File menu. Then, if you want to save the file in a directory other than the current one, choose that directory from the Other Drives & Directories list box and choose OK. Next, type a name (such as *BSINC.WKS*) and press Enter or choose OK to

save the file. If you want to save the file in the current directory, simply type a filename and press Enter or choose OK. If you saved the template at an earlier stage,
simply select Save from the File menu to save it again.

USING THE TEMPLATE

After you create the Profit and Loss Forecast, you're ready to put it to work. To
begin, open the spreadsheet to which you saved the template. (If you just created the
template, skip this step.) To open the spreadsheet, choose Open from the File menu.
Then, change the current directory (if necessary) and either type the filename under
which you saved the template, including the extension (for example, *BSINC.WKS*), or
highlight the name of the template in the list, and press Enter or choose OK.

To begin using the template, you must enter a series of assumptions in columns B
and D. Next, you need to go back and enter values for any irregular accounts in the
appropriate cells. Then, you have to adjust any account that Works has calculated but
which you know will be different from the predicted amount. Finally, you need to
recalculate the spreadsheet.

Entering Assumptions

At this point, you're ready to enter some basic assumptions in columns B and D.
Some are percentages, others are dollar amounts, and others are numbers of days.
The spreadsheet uses these assumptions to make a variety of computations. For ex-
ample, the spreadsheet uses the annual sales growth rate assumption you enter in cell
B7 and the January sales assumption you enter in cell D7 as the basis for computing
sales in cells E7 through O7.

The table in Figure 11-7 explains each assumption. To enter each one, move the
cursor to the cell listed in the table and enter the appropriate value. Then, if necessary, use the Percent command or the Fixed command (from the Format menu) to
assign a format to the cell with the indicated number of decimal places. You can use
the sample spreadsheet in Figure 11-1 on page 302 to help you figure out how to enter
these assumptions. Remember, however, that you should enter your own assumptions in your spreadsheet—not the assumptions in the example.

The Income Statement and Balance Sheet you created in the template are generic.
For this reason, it is likely that the income statement and balance sheet for your company do not match those in the template exactly. Use your judgment to decide how
you should enter the information for your company in the generic financial statements in the template. You'll probably find that some items listed in Figure 11-7 don't
apply. If a particular account does not apply to you, leave the cell containing the
assumption for that account blank or enter a *0* in that cell. You can usually overcome
other discrepancies simply by combining less important or unusual items from your
company's financial statements into the accounts offered by the template. However,
you might find that you have to modify the structure of the Income Statement or the

Balance Sheet in the template to accommodate peculiarities in your company's financial statements. You will learn how to do that later in this chapter.

Cell	Assumption	Format, Decimal Places
B7	Annual sales growth rate	Percent, 0
D7	January sales	
B8	Returns/Credits as a percent of sales	Percent, 0
B12	Cost of goods sold as a percent of sales	Percent, 0
B17	Interest rate earned on excess cash	Percent, 2
B18	Cash balance required before interest can be earned	
B24	Annual salaries and wages growth rate	Percent, 0
D24	January salaries and wages expense	
B25	Benefits as a percentage of salaries and wages	Percent, 2
B26	Payroll taxes as a percentage of salaries and wages	Percent, 2
D27	January office rent expense	
D28	January supplies expense	
D29	January postage expense	
D30	January telephone expense	
D31	January insurance expense	
D32	January dues and subscriptions expense	
D33	January advertising and promotion expense	
D34	January travel and entertainment expense	
D35	January professional fees expense	
D36	January maintenance expense	
D37	January equipment rental expense	
B38	Average depreciable life of PP&E in months	
B40	Average annual interest rate on short-term debt	Percent, 2
B41	Average annual interest rate on long-term debt	Percent, 2
D42	January other operating expenses	
B57	Average days sales in accounts receivable	Fixed, 0
B58	Average days cost of goods sold in inventory	Fixed, 0
D59	January other current assets balance	
D64	January leasehold improvements balance	
D65	January furniture and fixtures balance	
D66	January equipment balance	
D67	January office equipment balance	
B70	December accumulated depreciation balance	
D74	January other current assets balance	

Figure 11-7. Assumptions to enter manually.   *(continued)*

Figure 11-7. Continued.

Cell	Assumption	Format, Decimal Places
B80	Average days cost of goods sold in accounts payable	Fixed, 0
D81	January short-term debt balance	
D82	January income taxes payable balance	
D83	January accrued expenses balance	
D84	January other current liabilities balance	
D89	January long-term debt balance	
D90	January other noncurrent liabilities balance	
D94	January common stock balance	
B95	December retained earnings balance	

The structure of this template illustrates an important guideline for creating new spreadsheets: Always make your assumptions explicit. Your assumptions include those fundamental values and percentages on which the formulas in the spreadsheet depend. Making those values explicit means that you enter them in cells by themselves instead of burying them in formulas. By following this guideline, you can more easily change your assumptions. You'll also find that your spreadsheet is easier to understand: Instead of trying to figure out the assumptions on which the spreadsheet is based, you can simply read those values from the spreadsheet itself.

Calculating the Spreadsheet

After you post all your assumptions, select Calculate Now from the Options menu or press the Calc key ([F9]) to update all the formulas in the spreadsheet. The carry-forward formulas carry the values from columns C and D to columns E through O. Other formulas compute balances for each account in the Income Statement and Balance Sheet. The SUM functions compute the totals for each row and for each month.

The Profit and Loss Forecast has one unusual characteristic that you need to keep in mind when you calculate: It contains a deliberate circular reference. A circular reference occurs when a formula in a spreadsheet refers to itself. For example, if you enter the formula *=A1* in cell A1, you create a circular reference. Similarly, if you enter the formula *=A2* in cell A1 and the formula *=A1* in cell A2, you create a circular reference. Why is it circular? Because the formula in cell A1 refers to cell A2, which contains a formula that refers to cell A1. In other words, cell A1 refers to itself by way of cell A2. Likewise, if you enter the formula *=A2+A3* in cell A1, the value *1000* in cell A2, and the formula *=.5*A1* in cell A3, you create another circular reference. This time the circular reference is the result of the formula in cell A1, which refers to cell A3, which contains a formula that refers to cell A1 again.

Circular references make it difficult for Works to calculate the spreadsheet. Some circular references simply cannot be resolved. Others can be resolved only by calculating the spreadsheet repeatedly. During each recalculation, Works gets a little closer to computing the right answer for all the formulas involved in the circular reference. After a certain number of calculations, all the formulas return the "correct" answer. This process of repeatedly calculating the spreadsheet is called iterative recalculation.

The circular reference in this spreadsheet results from the interest income calculations in row 17. These calculations refer to the cash balances in row 56. Recall that the cash balances are computed by subtracting the balances from a number of accounts—Accounts Receivable, Inventory, Other Current Assets, Net PP&E, and Other Fixed Assets—from the balance for Total Liabilities and Equity in row 97. Also recall that the Total Liabilities and Equity balance is the sum of other account balances—Total Liabilities in row 92, Common Stock in row 94, and Retained Earnings in row 95. Then, recall that retained earnings in any month are equal to the retained earnings from the prior month plus the net income from the current month (in row 50). Finally, realize that one component of net income in any month is the interest income earned in that month. In other words, the formulas in row 17 that compute interest income are dependent upon the formulas in row 56, which compute the cash balances for each month, and the formulas in row 56 are, in turn, dependent on the formulas in row 17 that compute interest income.

Fortunately, you can resolve this circular reference through iterative recalculation. For that reason, each time you recalculate this spreadsheet, press the Calc key ([F9]) or select Calculate Now from the Options menu at least eight times. Eight successive recalculations are almost always sufficient to resolve the circular reference completely. If you forget to calculate repeatedly, then the formulas in rows 17 and 56 might return incorrect results, and your net income and your total assets balance might be misstated. Be careful!

Changing Computed Balances

Now you need to adjust any accounts that Works calculated but which you know will be different from the predicted amount. These include income and expense items that vary slightly from month to month, accounts such as Other Income, Maintenance, Travel and Entertainment, Advertising and Promotion, and so on. It also includes items that are regular at one point in the year but which might change or even stop at another point. For example, suppose you know that in August you'll begin renting a small office in your building for $100 a month. You'll need to adjust the Other Income account in August and subsequent months to reflect this change. Similarly, you may sell or buy fixed assets at some point in the year, which will require you to adjust the PP&E and, perhaps, the Accumulated Depreciation accounts in the month of the purchase or sale.

To make a change to a calculated value, move the cursor to the cell that contains the value you need to change and enter a new value. For example, suppose you plan to reduce the balance in the Short-Term Debt account from $65,000 to $50,000 in June. To make this change, move the cursor to cell I81, which contains the Short-Term Debt balance for June, enter the value *50000*, and then press [F9].

Remember that we've entered formulas in many of the cells in the Income Statement and in the Balance Sheet that refer to the adjacent cell to the left. For example, cell J81 contains the formula *=I81*, cell K81 contains the formula *=J81*, and so on. This carry-forward technique comes in handy when you begin making changes like the ones explained in the previous paragraph. When you enter a value in a cell that contains a carry-forward formula, the value replaces the formula, changing the value of the cell. Then, the formula to the right of the cell in which you entered the value picks up that new value and passes it along through the spreadsheet. For instance, notice that cells J81, K81, L81, and so on in Figure 11-1 on page 303 all contain the value *$50,000*—the value we entered in cell I81. This occurs because each of these cells contains a carry-forward formula.

When you enter a value in a row that contains carry-forward formulas, Works carries that value forward until you enter another value in another cell in the row. When you enter another value, that value is passed across the row, until you enter another value, and so on. For example, suppose that you want to reduce the balance in the Short-Term Debt account again in October, this time to $25,000. Move the cursor to cell M81, enter the value *25000*, and then recalculate the spreadsheet. As shown in Figure 11-1, Works passes this new value along from cell M81 to cells N81 and O81.

Let's look at another example. Suppose you are renting a machine during January but stop renting it on the 31st of that month. To adjust the appropriate expense account, move the cursor to cell E37, which contains the February balance for the Equipment Rental account, enter the value *0*, and press the Calc key ([F9]).

Although the formulas in row 37 are not pure examples of the carry-forward technique, each refers to the cell one column to the left. For example, cell F37 contains the formula *=(1+$B37)*E37*, cell G37 contains the formula *=(1+$B37)*F37*, and so on. As a result, these formulas also carry forward any change you make. For instance, notice that cells F37, G37, H37, and so on in Figure 11-1 on pages 300–301 all display the value 0—the value entered in cell E37.

From time to time, you might sell or buy fixed assets. To record the purchase of an asset, increase the value of the PP&E account for the month in which the change occurred. For example, suppose that in February you plan to invest $10,000 in leasehold improvements. To record this change, move the cursor to cell E64, press the Edit key ([F2]), type *+10000*, and press Enter. This action changes the formula in cell E64 from *=D64* to *=D64+10000* and changes the balance in this account from *$26,000* to *$36,000*. In addition, because the formulas in row 64 are carry-forward formulas, Works passes this change through column O when you calculate the spreadsheet. If you look at Figure 11-1, which reflects this change, you see that cells E64, F64, G64, and so on on pages 302–303 all contain the value *$36,000*.

To record the sale of an asset, decrease the balance in both the PP&E and the Accumulated Depreciation accounts in the month of the sale. You might also need to make an entry in the Other Income account to reflect the gain or loss on the sale. For example, suppose that in March you plan to sell for $10,000 a truck that you originally purchased for $25,000. Suppose further that the truck has accumulated depreciation of $20,000. To record this sale, first move the cursor to cell F66, press the Edit key ([F2]), type –25000, and press Enter. This action changes the formula in cell E64 from =E66 to =E66–25000 and changes the balance in this account from $125,000 to $100,000. In addition, the carry-forward formulas in row 66 pass this change along through column O when you calculate the spreadsheet. Next, move the cursor to cell F70, press [F2], type –20000, and press Enter. This action changes the formula in cell F70 from =E70 to =E70–20000 and changes the balance in this account from $85,232 to $65,232. When you calculate the spreadsheet, Works passes this change through column O. Finally, to record the gain of $5,000 on this sale, move the cursor to cell F19 and enter the value 5000. Then, to prevent this value from being passed across row 19, move the cursor to cell G19 and enter the value 0.

Another change you probably need to make involves the growth percentages in cells B24, B27 through B37, and B42. Remember that these cells all contain formulas that refer to the growth rate assumption you entered in cell B24. For this reason, whatever value you enter in cell B24 also appears in all these other cells. For example, if you enter the growth rate 1 percent in cell B24, then that same rate appears in the other cells. Of course, it is likely that some expenses will increase more rapidly than others, and a few expenses may not increase at all. To account for these differences, adjust the growth rates of the inconsistent expense items: Simply enter a different percentage in the appropriate cell in column B.

For example, Figure 11-1 shows a growth rate of 0 percent for the Advertising and Promotion account. To make this change, we moved the cursor to cell B33 and entered the value 0. We made the same change to the growth rate for the Office Rent account. Likewise, we changed the growth rate for the Supplies account from 1 percent to 2 percent. To make this change, we entered the value .02 in cell B28.

In some cases, you need to change the balance in an account in one month without changing its balance in the following months. For example, suppose you know that you'll have to pay a $2,000 fee to your CPA firm in April for the preparation of your income tax. This additional expense will increase the April balance in your Professional Fees account to $2,500. In May, however, this balance will return to the predicted level: $515. To record this change, first move the cursor to cell G35, which contains the professional fees expense for April, and enter the value 2500. Then, move the cursor to cell H35 and enter the number 515 to replace the formula in cell H35 with the value 515. These two changes will create the desired effect: The professional fees expense for April becomes $2,500, but the change affects only the month of April. The balance in the Professional Fees account for May, June, July, and so on is unaffected by the change.

Saving and Printing

After you set up your forecast, save the spreadsheet to a new file. To do this, select Save As from the File menu. Then, if you want to save the file in a directory other than the current one, choose that directory from the Other Drives & Directories list box and choose OK. Next, type a new name for the spreadsheet, and press Enter or choose OK to save the file. If you want to save the file in the current directory, simply type a filename and press Enter or choose OK. Choose a name for the file that clearly identifies its contents—for example, *PL88.WKS* for your 1988 forecast.

Always be sure to save your filled-in Profit and Loss Forecast under a name other than the name you've used for the original, empty template. If you save a filled-in spreadsheet under the same name as the original template, the filled-in version replaces the original version.

To print the entire Profit and Loss Forecast, first choose Layout from the Print menu and change any print settings you want to change. For example, if you have a wide-carriage printer and plan to print this spreadsheet on 11-by-14-inch paper, you might want to change the Page Width setting from *8.5"* to *14"*. You might also want to change the Top, Bottom, Left, and Right margins and define a header and a footer. Next, you can choose Font from the Print menu to select the font you want Works to use to print the report. To squeeze the entire report onto one page, choose a relatively compressed font (such as Elite) and a small point size (such as 6 or 8). If you choose a proportional font, such as Times, the printed copy will lack proper alignment, and underlining, boldface, and so on will not work.

After you adjust the settings, select Print from the Print menu to display the Print dialog box. Adjust any settings in that box and then choose Print.

To print only a portion of the forecast, use the Set Print Area command on the Print menu to define the print area before you begin printing. To print only the Income Statement, for example, first highlight the range A1:P51 and select Set Print Area from the Print menu. Then, use the Layout and Font commands to make any necessary adjustments to the Works print settings. Finally, select Print from the Print menu and choose the Print button to print the selected range.

Using the Plan

After you recalculate the spreadsheet, review the result. Study the plan carefully so that you understand exactly what your financial condition will be at each point in the coming year. Is the monthly net income consistently negative? If so, you need to find a way to increase revenues or decrease expenses. Does the cash balance ever become negative? If so, you have to arrange for additional debt or equity financing to see you through the lean times. You'll also want to keep the tight spots in mind as unexpected expenses come to your attention, and, if necessary, modify your plans to avoid a problem. After you figure out how to solve your problems, make the appropriate changes to the spreadsheet and then recalculate the spreadsheet so that the effect of the changes becomes apparent.

At the end of each month, compare your actual financial statements to the forecast in the spreadsheet. Comparing your actual condition to the forecast helps you verify the accuracy of your estimates. If you find estimates that are either too high or too low, you can adjust them to be more in line with your actual activities. To adjust an income or expense item, move to the cell in the corresponding row and in the column for the current month, and enter the new estimate. The spreadsheet carries your change forward from that point to the end of the year. Similarly, if you acquire assets or incur liabilities that were not anticipated, adjust the appropriate accounts in the spreadsheet.

Adding Rows

As we mentioned earlier, the Profit and Loss Forecast includes a generic income statement and balance sheet. If necessary, you can modify the structure of the financial statements in the template to accommodate your company's specific needs. To do so, insert a blank row at the appropriate spot in the template: Highlight the row above which you want to add the new row, and select Insert from the Edit menu. If you want to add more than one row, highlight several rows and then select the Insert command. For each new row, enter a label in column A that defines the contents of the row, an assumption for the account in column B (if appropriate), and a label in column C that identifies the assumption. Next, enter a January balance assumption in column D or a formula that computes the January balance, a formula in column E that references the value in column D (if appropriate), and, if the new row is in the Income Statement, a formula in column P that totals the new account. Then, copy the formula from column D or column E to the remaining cells in the new row.

Finally, adjust any formulas in columns D through O in the Income Statement or Balance Sheet that are affected by the new account. Be careful! You will get inaccurate results—which can led to bad decisions—if you add an account and then forget to change the formulas that are affected by that account.

CONCLUSION

Every business needs a profit and loss forecast, or a profit plan. Without such a plan, it is difficult or impossible to predict what the future holds. As you have seen in this chapter, the Works Spreadsheet environment is an ideal tool for building a profit and loss forecast.

Projecting Cash Flow

If you run a business, you're concerned about cash flow. Everyone who runs a company worries about cash at one time or another. The problem—especially acute in new, growing companies—is usually that you lack sufficient cash to meet the payroll and other obligations.

To avoid cash flow problems, you need an accurate cash flow forecast, but getting one isn't as easy as it sounds. Your company's cash flow forecast must reflect a number of other factors that directly affect its cash requirements: sales, accounts receivable policies, purchasing policies, accounts payable terms, operating expenses, and interest rates.

The Business Cash Flow Forecast makes it easy to forecast your cash balances for the coming year. You enter your estimates for sales, cost of goods sold, operating expenses, purchases and sales of fixed assets, and debt service; the spreadsheet computes cash collection and disbursements and net cash receipts. The template includes a handy formula that assumes short-term debt when cash balances fall below a minimum debt level that you set and repays that debt when excess cash becomes available. The template is flexible enough to accommodate a small company or a multimillion-dollar business.

ABOUT THE TEMPLATE

Figure 12-1, which begins on the following page, shows the Business Cash Flow Forecast with some sample information entered in it. When you first create the template, most of the formulas will return values of 0. Others, such as those in row 38, will contain *100%*, and a few will return the message *ERR*. After you enter numbers in the input cells and recalculate, the spreadsheet will correct these values.

```
        A       B       C       D       E        F        G        H        I        J        K        L
1  =========================================================================================================
2  BUSINESS CASH FLOW FORECAST
3  =========================================================================================================
4  CASH RECEIPTS                              Oct      Nov      Dec      Jan      Feb      Mar      Apr      May
5  ==================================== ======  ======  ======  ======  ======  ======  ======  ======
6  Product 1                3.00% $55,720 $57,392 $59,113 $60,887 $75,000 $77,250 $79,568 $81,955
7  Product 2                5.00% $47,250 $49,613 $52,093 $54,698 $57,433 $60,304 $63,320 $66,485
8  Product 3                0.50% $65,383 $65,710 $66,038 $66,369 $66,701 $67,034 $67,369 $67,706
9  Product 4               -1.00% $45,556 $45,100 $44,649 $44,203 $43,761 $43,323 $42,890 $42,461
10 Product 5                3.00% $27,359 $28,180 $29,025 $29,896 $30,793 $31,717 $32,668 $33,648
11                                -------  -------  -------  -------  -------  -------  -------  -------
12 Total Sales                    $241,268 $245,994 $250,920 $256,052 $273,687 $279,628 $285,814 $292,255
13
14 Collections Schedule
15   Cash Sales                     25%      25%      25%      20%      20%      10%      10%      10%
16   30 Days                        15%      15%      15%      20%      20%      20%      20%      20%
17   60 Days                        45%      45%      45%      45%      45%      45%      45%      45%
18   90 Days                        15%      15%      15%      15%      15%      25%      25%      25%
19
20 Total Cash Collections                           $235,736 $255,761 $235,562 $246,074 $253,274
21                                                   ======= ======= ======= ======= =======
22
23 =========================================================================================================
24 COST OF GOODS SOLD                         Oct      Nov      Dec      Jan      Feb      Mar      Apr      May
25 ==================================== ======  ======  ======  ======  ======  ======  ======  ======
26 Product 1               45.00% $25,074 $25,826 $26,601 $27,399 $33,750 $34,763 $35,805 $36,880
27 Product 2               52.00% $24,570 $25,799 $27,088 $28,443 $29,865 $31,358 $32,926 $34,572
28 Product 3               40.00% $26,153 $26,284 $26,415 $26,547 $26,680 $26,814 $26,948 $27,082
29 Product 4               62.00% $28,245 $27,962 $27,683 $27,406 $27,132 $26,860 $26,592 $26,326
30 Product 5               25.00%  $6,840  $7,045  $7,256  $7,474  $7,698  $7,929  $8,167  $8,412
31                                -------  -------  -------  -------  -------  -------  -------  -------
32 Total Cost of Goods Sold       $110,882 $112,916 $115,044 $117,269 $125,125 $127,724 $130,438 $133,272
33
34 Purchasing Schedule
35   0 Days in Advance              10%      10%      10%      10%      10%      10%      10%      10%
36   30 Days in Advance             45%      45%      45%      45%      45%      45%      45%      45%
37   60 Days in Advance             30%      30%      30%      30%      30%      30%      30%      30%
38   90 Days in Advance             15%      15%      15%      15%      15%      15%      15%      15%
39
40 Total Purchases                $114,004 $117,011 $120,972 $125,916 $129,111 $131,886 $134,784 $137,810
41
42 Accounts Payable Schedule
43   Cash                           65%      65%      65%      65%      65%      65%      65%
44   30 Days                        25%      25%      25%      25%      25%      25%      25%
45   60 Days                        10%      10%      10%      10%      10%      10%      10%
46
47 Payment for Purchases (Cost of Goods Sold)      $123,789 $127,498 $130,595 $133,492 $136,461
48                                                 ======= ======= ======= ======= =======
49
50 =========================================================================================================
51 OPERATING EXPENSES                         Oct      Nov      Dec      Jan      Feb      Mar      Apr      May
52 ==================================== ======  ======  ======  ======  ======  ======  ======  ======
53 Total Operating Expenses  1.00%$115,000 $116,150 $117,312 $118,485 $119,669 $120,866 $122,075 $123,296
54
55 Accounts Payable Schedule
56   Cash                           65%      65%      65%      65%      65%      65%      65%
57   30 Days                        35%      35%      35%      35%      35%      35%      35%
58   60 Days                         0%       0%       0%       0%       0%       0%       0%
59
60 Payment for Purchases (Operating Expenses)      $118,074 $119,255 $120,447 $121,652 $122,868
61                                                 ======= ======= ======= ======= =======
62
63 =========================================================================================================
64 FIXED ASSETS                                               Jan      Feb      Mar      Apr      May
65 ==================================================== ======  ======  ======  ======  ======
66 Fixed Asset Purchases                                              $15,000
67 Fixed Asset Sales
68                                                  -------  -------  -------  -------  -------
69 Purchases of Fixed Assets                           $0       $0  $15,000       $0       $0
```

Figure 12-1.

```
         M        N        O        P        Q        R        S        T        U        V        W
========================================================================================================
========================================================================================================

        Jun      Jul      Aug      Sep      Oct      Nov      Dec     Total
       ======   ======   ======   ======   ======   ======   ======   =======
     $84,413  $86,946  $89,554  $92,241  $95,008  $97,858 $100,794 $1,021,471
     $69,810  $73,300  $76,965  $80,814  $84,854  $89,097  $93,552   $870,632
     $68,045  $68,385  $68,727  $69,070  $69,416  $69,763  $70,112   $818,695
     $42,037  $41,616  $41,200  $40,788  $40,380  $39,976  $39,577   $502,212
     $34,658  $35,697  $36,768  $37,871  $39,007  $40,178  $41,383   $424,284
     -------  -------  -------  -------  -------  -------  -------  --------
    $298,962 $305,944 $313,214 $320,784 $328,665 $336,872 $345,417 $3,637,294


        10%      10%      10%      10%      10%      10%      10%
        20%      20%      20%      20%      20%      20%      20%
        45%      45%      45%      45%      45%      45%      45%
        25%      25%      25%      25%      25%      25%      25%

    $286,871 $293,355 $300,107 $307,136 $314,456 $322,076 $330,011 $3,380,419
     ======   =======  =======  =======  =======  =======  =======  ========


        Jun      Jul      Aug      Sep      Oct      Nov      Dec     Total      Jan      Feb      Mar
       ======   ======   ======   ======   ======   ======   ======   =======   ======   ======   ======
     $37,986  $39,126  $40,299  $41,508  $42,753  $44,036  $45,357   $459,662
     $36,301  $38,116  $40,022  $42,023  $44,124  $46,330  $48,647   $452,728
     $27,218  $27,354  $27,491  $27,628  $27,766  $27,905  $28,045   $327,478
     $26,063  $25,802  $25,544  $25,289  $25,036  $24,785  $24,537   $311,372
      $8,664   $8,924   $9,192   $9,468   $9,752  $10,044  $10,346   $106,071
     -------  -------  -------  -------  -------  -------  -------  --------
    $136,232 $139,322 $142,548 $145,916 $149,431 $153,101 $156,932 $1,657,311 $160,858 $164,883 $169,008


        10%      10%      10%      10%      10%      10%      10%                 10%      10%      10%
        45%      45%      45%      45%      45%      45%      45%                 45%      45%      45%
        30%      30%      30%      30%      30%      30%      30%                 30%      30%      30%
        15%      15%      15%      15%      15%      15%      15%                 15%      15%      15%

    $140,970 $144,268 $147,712 $151,306 $155,047 $158,919 $162,896 $1,720,625


        65%      65%      65%      65%      65%      65%      65%
        25%      25%      25%      25%      25%      25%      25%
        10%      10%      10%      10%      10%      10%      10%

    $139,561 $142,798 $146,177 $149,704 $153,378 $157,190 $161,117 $1,701,761
     ======   =======  =======  =======  =======  =======  =======  =========


        Jun      Jul      Aug      Sep      Oct      Nov      Dec     Total
       ======   ======   ======   ======   ======   ======   ======   =======
    $124,529 $125,774 $127,032 $128,302 $129,585 $130,881 $132,190 $1,502,681


        65%      65%      65%      65%      65%      65%      65%
        35%      35%      35%      35%      35%      35%      35%
         0%       0%       0%       0%       0%       0%       0%

    $124,097 $125,338 $126,591 $127,857 $129,136 $130,427 $131,731 $1,497,474
     ======   =======  =======  =======  =======  =======  =======  =========


        Jun      Jul      Aug      Sep      Oct      Nov      Dec     Total
       ======   ======   ======   ======   ======   ======   ======   =======
             $50,000                                                  $65,000
                                                                          $0
     -------  -------  -------  -------  -------  -------  -------  --------
         $0  $50,000       $0       $0       $0       $0       $0   $65,000
```

(continued)

Figure 12-1. Continued.

	A	B	C	D	E	F	G	H	I	J	K	L
70												
71	Additions to Long-Term Debt											
72	Total New Debt											
73	Addition to Monthly Payment											
74								-------	-------	-------	-------	-------
75	Net Purchases of Fixed Assets							$0	$0	$15,000	$0	$0
76								=======	=======	=======	=======	=======
77												
78	==
79	DEBT SERVICE						Dec	Jan	Feb	Mar	Apr	May
80	==					======	======	======	======	======	======
81	Long-Term Debt											
82	Total Monthly Payment						$3,000	$3,000	$3,000	$3,000	$3,000	$3,000
83	Interest Rate						10.00%	10.00%	10.00%	10.00%	10.00%	10.00%
84	Interest Payments							$833	$815	$797	$779	$760
85	Principal Repayments							$2,167	$2,185	$2,203	$2,221	$2,240
86												
87												
88	Short-Term Debt											
89	Interest Rate						9.00%	9.00%	9.00%	9.00%	9.00%	9.00%
90	Interest Payments							$0	$0	$0	$200	$292
91								-------	-------	-------	-------	-------
92	Total Debt Service							$3,000	$3,000	$3,000	$3,200	$3,292
93								=======	=======	=======	=======	=======
94												
95	==
96	CASH FLOW SUMMARY							Jan	Feb	Mar	Apr	May
97	==							======	======	======	======	======
98	Cash Collections							$235,736	$255,761	$235,562	$246,074	$253,274
99	Other Cash Receipts											
100												
101	Cash Disbursements											
102	Payment for Inventory Purchases							$123,789	$127,498	$130,595	$133,492	$136,461
103	Payment for Operating Expenses							$118,074	$119,255	$120,447	$121,652	$122,868
104	Purchases of Fixed Assets							$0	$0	$15,000	$0	$0
105	Debt Service							$3,000	$3,000	$3,000	$3,200	$3,292
106	Income Tax Payments											
107	Other Disbursements											
108								-------	-------	-------	-------	-------
109	Total Cash Disbursements							$244,863	$249,753	$269,042	$258,344	$262,621
110								-------	-------	-------	-------	-------
111	Net Cash Generated by Operations							($9,128)	$6,008	($33,481)	($12,270)	($9,347)
112	Short-Term Borrowings/(Repayments)							$0	$0	$26,601	$12,270	$9,347
113								-------	-------	-------	-------	-------
114	Net Cash Flow							($9,128)	$6,008	($6,880)	$0	$0
115								=======	=======	=======	=======	=======
116												
117	==
118	ANALYSIS OF CASH REQUIREMENTS						Dec	Jan	Feb	Mar	Apr	May
119	==					======	======	======	======	======	======
120	Beginning Cash Balance							$125,000	$115,872	$121,880	$115,000	$115,000
121	Net Cash Generated by Operations							($9,128)	$6,008	($33,481)	($12,270)	($9,347)
122								-------	-------	-------	-------	-------
123	Cash Balance Before Borrowings							$115,872	$121,880	$88,399	$102,730	$105,653
124	Minimum Acceptable Cash Balance						$115,000	$115,000	$115,000	$115,000	$115,000	$115,000
125								-------	-------	-------	-------	-------
126	Cash Surplus/(Deficit)							$872	$6,880	($26,601)	($12,270)	($9,347)
127												
128	Current Short-Term Borrowings							$0	$0	$26,601	$12,270	$9,347
129								-------	-------	-------	-------	-------
130	Ending Cash Balance							$115,872	$121,880	$115,000	$115,000	$115,000
131								=======	=======	=======	=======	=======
132												
133	==
134	BALANCES						Dec	Jan	Feb	Mar	Apr	May
135	==					======	======	======	======	======	======
136	Assets											
137	Cash						$125,000	$115,872	$121,880	$115,000	$115,000	$115,000
138	Accounts Receivable						$65,000	$85,316	$103,242	$147,309	$187,049	$226,030
139	Inventory						$87,000	$95,647	$99,632	$103,794	$108,141	$112,679

M	N	O	P	Q	R	S	T	U	V	W
	$50,000						$50,000			
	$1,600						$1,600			
	-------	-------	-------	-------	-------	-------	--------			
$0	$0	$0	$0	$0	$0	$0	$15,000			
=======	=======	=======	=======	=======	=======	=======	========			

	Jun	Jul	Aug	Sep	Oct	Nov	Dec	Total
	======	======	======	======	======	======	======	=======
	$3,020	$3,020	$4,620	$4,620	$4,620	$4,620	$4,620	$44,140
	10.50%	10.50%	10.50%	10.50%	10.50%	10.50%	10.50%	
	$779	$759	$1,177	$1,147	$1,116	$1,086	$1,055	$11,102
	$2,241	$2,261	$3,443	$3,473	$3,504	$3,534	$3,565	$33,038
	9.00%	9.00%	9.00%	9.00%	9.00%	9.00%	9.00%	
	$362	$213	$48	$0	$0	$0	$0	$1,114
	-------	-------	-------	-------	-------	-------	-------	-------
	$3,382	$3,233	$4,668	$4,620	$4,620	$4,620	$4,620	$45,254
	=======	=======	=======	=======	=======	=======	=======	=========

	Jun	Jul	Aug	Sep	Oct	Nov	Dec	Total
	======	======	======	======	======	======	======	=======
	$286,871	$293,355	$300,107	$307,136	$314,456	$322,076	$330,011	$3,380,419
								$0
	$139,561	$142,798	$146,177	$149,704	$153,378	$157,190	$161,117	$1,701,761
	$124,097	$125,338	$126,591	$127,857	$129,136	$130,427	$131,731	$1,497,474
	$0	$0	$0	$0	$0	$0	$0	$15,000
	$3,382	$3,233	$4,668	$4,620	$4,620	$4,620	$4,620	$45,254
								$0
								$0
	-------	-------	-------	-------	-------	-------	-------	---------
	$267,040	$271,369	$277,436	$282,181	$287,134	$292,237	$297,468	$3,259,488
	-------	-------	-------	-------	-------	-------	-------	---------
	$19,831	$21,987	$22,671	$24,956	$27,322	$29,839	$32,543	$120,930
	($19,831)	($21,987)	($6,400)	$0	$0	$0	$0	$0
	-------	-------	-------	-------	-------	-------	-------	---------
	$0	$0	$16,271	$24,956	$27,322	$29,839	$32,543	$120,930
	=======	=======	=======	=======	=======	=======	=======	=========

	Jun	Jul	Aug	Sep	Oct	Nov	Dec
	======	======	======	======	======	======	======
	$115,000	$115,000	$115,000	$131,271	$156,226	$183,548	$213,387
	$19,831	$21,987	$22,671	$24,956	$27,322	$29,839	$32,543
	-------	-------	-------	-------	-------	-------	-------
	$134,831	$136,987	$137,671	$156,226	$183,548	$213,387	$245,930
	$115,000	$115,000	$115,000	$115,000	$115,000	$115,000	$115,000
	-------	-------	-------	-------	-------	-------	-------
	$19,831	$21,987	$22,671	$41,226	$68,548	$98,387	$130,930
	($19,831)	($21,987)	($6,400)	$0	$0	$0	$0
	-------	-------	-------	-------	-------	-------	-------
	$115,000	$115,000	$131,271	$156,226	$183,548	$213,387	$245,930
	=======	=======	=======	=======	=======	=======	=======

	Jun	Jul	Aug	Sep	Oct	Nov	Dec
	======	======	======	======	======	======	======
	$115,000	$115,000	$131,271	$156,226	$183,548	$213,387	$245,930
	$238,121	$250,710	$263,818	$277,465	$291,674	$306,470	$321,875
	$117,417	$122,363	$127,526	$132,917	$138,532	$144,350	$150,314

(continued)

Figure 12-1. Continued.

	A	B	C	D	E	F	G	H	I	J	K	L
140												
141	Liabilities											
142	Accounts Payable						$95,000	$97,537	$99,564	$101,274	$102,989	$104,765
143	Short-Term Debt						$0	$0	$0	$26,601	$38,870	$48,217
144							-------	-------	-------	-------	-------	-------
145	Net Working Capital						$182,000	$199,298	$225,191	$238,229	$268,331	$300,726
146							=======	=======	=======	=======	=======	=======
147												
148	Long-Term Debt						$100,000	$97,833	$95,649	$93,446	$91,224	$88,985
149							=======	=======	=======	=======	=======	=======

As you can see, the template has several distinct areas, labeled CASH RECEIPTS, COST OF GOODS SOLD, OPERATING EXPENSES, FIXED ASSETS, DEBT SERVICE, CASH FLOW SUMMARY, ANALYSIS OF CASH REQUIREMENTS, and BALANCES. The Cash Receipts area occupies the range A3:T22. The top left portion of the Cash Receipts area, shown in Figure 12-2, is displayed when you first load the spreadsheet. In this area, you enter information about your company's sales by product and about the pattern of collections of accounts receivable. This information allows the spreadsheet to compute the total cash collections for each month.

The Cost of Goods Sold area occupies the range A23:W49. In this area, you record your estimates of cost of goods sold by product for the coming year. You also use this area to schedule your expenses for cost of goods sold, and the payment schedule for those purchases. Figure 12-3 shows the upper left part of the Cost of Goods Sold area. The Operating Expenses area occupies the range A50:T62. Enter your estimates of monthly operating expenses and the payment schedule for those expenses in this area.

```
 File  Edit  Print  Select  Format  Options  Chart  Window
=========
        A        B        C        D        E        F        G        H    =
1   ========================================================================
2   BUSINESS CASH FLOW FORECAST
3   ========================================================================
4   CASH RECEIPTS                              Oct     Nov     Dec     Jan
5   ==========================================  ======  ======  ======  ======
6   Product 1                          3.00%  $55,720 $57,392 $59,113 $60,887
7   Product 2                          5.00%  $47,250 $49,613 $52,093 $54,698
8   Product 3                          0.50%  $65,383 $65,710 $66,038 $66,369
9   Product 4                         -1.00%  $45,556 $45,100 $44,649 $44,203
10  Product 5                          3.00%  $27,359 $28,180 $29,025 $29,896
11                                             ------- ------- ------- -------
12  Total Sales                               $241,268 $245,994 $250,920 $256,052
13
14  Collections Schedule
15    Cash Sales                                25%     25%     25%     20%
16    30 Days                                   15%     15%     15%     20%
17    60 Days                                   45%     45%     45%     45%
18    90 Days                                   15%     15%     15%     15%
19
||+
D1                                                           CASHPROJ.WKS
Press ALT to choose commands.
```

Figure 12-2.

M	N	O	P	Q	R	S	T	U	V	W
$106,605	$108,512	$110,487	$112,534	$114,652	$116,835	$119,072				
$28,387	$6,400	$0	$0	$0	$0	$0				
-------	-------	-------	-------	-------	-------	-------				
$335,546	$373,162	$412,128	$454,074	$499,103	$547,373	$599,048				
=======	=======	=======	=======	=======	=======	=======				
$86,743	$134,482	$131,039	$127,566	$124,062	$120,527	$116,962				
=======	=======	=======	=======	=======	=======	=======				

The next area, Fixed Assets, occupies the range A63:T77. In it, you enter your estimated purchases and sales of fixed assets, and your estimated additions to long-term debt. Enter your estimates of repayments of debt in the Debt Service area, which occupies the range A78:T94. Figure 12-4 on the following page shows the upper left corner of this area.

The Cash Flow Summary gives an overview of the cash inflows and outflows computed in other areas of the spreadsheet. It spans the range of cells A95:T116. Figure 12-5 on the following page shows the upper left corner of this area on the screen. In the Cash Flow Summary, row 98 computes total cash collections by month, row 109 computes total cash disbursements, and row 111 computes net cash generated by operations. The formulas in row 112 refer to cells in row 128 which, in turn, contain formulas that compute the amount of short-term borrowing required to maintain an acceptable cash balance. The formulas in row 114 then compute the net cash flow for each month, including short-term borrowing.

```
 File  Edit  Print  Select  Format  Options  Chart  Window
"=========
        A        B        C        D        E        F        G        H
23  =============================================================================
24  COST OF GOODS SOLD                       Oct      Nov      Dec      Jan
25  =============================================================================
26  Product 1                       45.00% $25,074  $25,826  $26,601  $27,399
27  Product 2                       52.00% $24,570  $25,799  $27,088  $28,443
28  Product 3                       40.00% $26,153  $26,284  $26,415  $26,547
29  Product 4                       62.00% $28,245  $27,962  $27,683  $27,406
30  Product 5                       25.00%  $6,840   $7,045   $7,256   $7,474
31                                          -------  -------  -------  -------
32  Total Cost of Goods Sold               $110,882 $112,916 $115,044 $117,269
33
34  Purchasing Schedule
35     0 Days in Advance                      10%      10%      10%      10%
36    30 Days in Advance                      45%      45%      45%      45%
37    60 Days in Advance                      30%      30%      30%      30%
38    90 Days in Advance                      15%      15%      15%      15%
39
40  Total Purchases                        $114,004 $117,011 $120,972 $125,916
41
||+                                                                         →
D23                                                              CASHPROJ.WKS
Press ALT to choose commands.
```

Figure 12-3.

```
 File  Edit  Print  Select  Format  Options  Chart  Window
"=========
         A       B       C       D       E       F       G       H
78 ==================================================================
79 DEBT SERVICE                                              Dec      Jan
80 ==================================================================
81 Long-Term Debt
82   Total Monthly Payment                                $3,000   $3,000
83     Interest Rate                                      10.00%   10.00%
84     Interest Payments                                            $833
85     Principal Repayments                                       $2,167
86
87
88 Short-Term Debt
89   Interest Rate                                         9.00%    9.00%
90   Interest Payments                                               $0
91                                                                -------
92 Total Debt Service                                             $3,000
93                                                                =======
94
95 ==================================================================
96 CASH FLOW SUMMARY                                                 Jan
||+                                                                   →
D78                                                          CASHPROJ.WKS
Press ALT to choose commands.
```

Figure 12-4.

```
 File  Edit  Print  Select  Format  Options  Chart  Window
"=========
         A       B       C       D       E       F       G       H
95 ==================================================================
96 CASH FLOW SUMMARY                                                 Jan
97 ==================================================================
98 Cash Collections                                              $235,736
99 Other Cash Receipts
100
101 Cash Disbursements
102   Payment for Inventory Purchases                             $123,789
103   Payment for Operating Expenses                              $118,074
104   Purchases of Fixed Assets                                        $0
105   Debt Service                                                  $3,000
106   Income Tax Payments
107   Other Disbursements
108                                                                -------
109 Total Cash Disbursements                                      $244,863
110                                                                -------
111 Net Cash Generated by Operations                              ($9,128)
112 Short-Term Borrowings/(Repayments)                                $0
113                                                                -------
||+                                                                   →
D95                                                          CASHPROJ.WKS
Press ALT to choose commands.
```

Figure 12-5.

The Analysis of Cash Requirements extends from cell A117 through cell S132. The formulas in this area compute the amount of short-term borrowing required to maintain an acceptable cash balance. Figure 12-6 shows the upper left corner of this area.

The last area of the spreadsheet, Balances, begins in cell A133. This area summarizes the balances in six key accounts: cash, accounts receivable, inventory, accounts payable, short-term debt, and long-term debt. The upper left corner of this area appears in Figure 12-7 on the following page.

In columns D, E, F, and G of this spreadsheet, you enter a number of basic assumptions—your beginning cash and accounts receivable balances, your combined accounts payable and short-term debt balance, and your estimated beginning interest rates. The spreadsheet uses these assumptions to make a variety of computations. For example, it uses the growth rates you enter in cells D6 through D10 to compute the monthly sales amounts in cells F6 to S10. Similarly, it uses the value you enter in cell G124 to to compute each month's additions to or repayments of short-term debt.

Most of the cells in columns H through S contain formulas. Some of these formulas refer to the assumptions in columns D through G; others make calculations based on values in other columns. A few cells in this region contain simple values that you enter manually. Column T contains a series of SUM functions that compute the annual total for each row in the spreadsheet.

```
 File  Edit  Print  Select  Format  Options  Chart  Window
"=========
       A        B        C        D        E        F        G        H       =
117 ====================================================================
118 ANALYSIS OF CASH REQUIREMENTS                              Dec      Jan
119 =================================================== ======   ======
120 Beginning Cash Balance                                          $125,000
121 Net Cash Generated by Operations                                 ($9,128)
122                                                                  --------
123 Cash Balance Before Borrowings                                  $115,872
124 Minimum Acceptable Cash Balance                        $115,000 $115,000
125                                                                  --------
126 Cash Surplus/(Deficit)                                              $872
127
128 Current Short-Term Borrowings                                        $0
129                                                                  --------
130 Ending Cash Balance                                             $115,872
131                                                                  =======
132
133 ==============================================================
134 BALANCES                                                   Dec      Jan
135 =================================================== ======   ======
||+|                                                                        |
D117                                                              CASHPROJ.WKS
Press ALT to choose commands.
```

Figure 12-6.

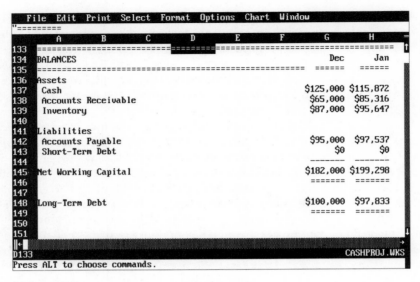

Figure 12-7.

CREATING THE TEMPLATE

To create the Business Cash Flow Forecast, first select Manual Calculation from the Options menu. Selecting this mode prevents Works from recalculating the spreadsheet each time you make an entry and so speeds up the process of creating the template considerably.

Next, change the default format for the spreadsheet from General to Dollar with zero decimal places. To do so, first highlight the entire spreadsheet by moving the cursor to cell A1 and selecting Row from the Select menu. This command selects every cell in row 1. Then, select Column from the Select menu. Because one cell in each column is already highlighted, choosing this command highlights every cell in the spreadsheet. (If you have a mouse, you can select the entire spreadsheet simply by clicking in the upper left corner of the spreadsheet—the area to the left of the letter A and just above the number 1.) Now, select Dollar from the Format menu. When the Decimals dialog box appears, type *0* and then press Enter or choose OK.

Next, change the width of columns A through S from 10 to 9 characters. First, highlight a range of cells that includes at least one cell in each of these columns. For instance, you might highlight the range A1:S1. Then, select Width from the Format menu, type the new width, *9*, and press Enter or choose OK. Next, change the width of column T from 10 to 11 characters. To do this, move the cursor to any cell in column T, select Width from the Format menu, type *11*, and press Enter or choose OK.

Now, give the cells in column D Percent format with two decimal places. To do so, highlight column D, select Percent from the Format menu, and press Enter to accept the default number of decimals. (Exactly how you highlight column D depends on whether you have a mouse. If you have a mouse, point to the letter D at the top of column D and click. If you don't have a mouse, move the cursor to any cell in column D and select Column from the Select menu.)

Entering Column and Row Headers

After you alter the column widths, you're ready to begin making entries. First, enter the header labels in rows 1, 2, and 3. The double lines in rows 1 and 3, which are composed of equal signs (=), span columns A through W. To create these double lines, you need to enter a label made up of a series of equal signs in each cell in row 1, and then copy those labels from row 1 to row 3. To enter each label in row 1, type a quotation mark (") followed by the proper number of equal signs. For example, move the cursor to cell A1 and type a quotation mark followed by a string of nine equal signs ("=========). If you forget the quotation mark, Works tries to interpret the entry as a formula and displays the message *Error: Missing Operand*.

After you enter a label in each cell in row 1, copy the labels from row 1 to row 3. To do this, highlight the range A1:W1, select Copy from the Edit menu, highlight cell A3, and press Enter.

Next, move the cursor to cell A2 and type *BUSINESS CASH FLOW FORECAST*. Then, move the cursor to cell A4 and enter the label *CASH RECEIPTS*. Now, move the cursor across row 4 to column E and enter the label *Oct*. Continue to move across row 4 one cell at a time, entering the label *Nov* in cell F4, the label *Dec* in cell G4, and so on. Finally, enter the label *Total* in cell T4.

Enter a series of double-line labels in row 5. The labels in cells A5, B5, C5, and D5 require nine equal signs ("=========). Those in cells E5 through S5 require only six ("======). For the label in cell T5, use seven equal signs ("=======).

When all these labels are in place, right-align the ones in cells E4 through T5. To do this, highlight the range E4:T5, select Style from the Format menu, and choose the Right option from the Style dialog box.

Now, you can use the header you created for the Cash Receipts area to create headers for the other sections as well. Simply copy the contents of rows 3, 4, and 5 to the appropriate locations in the spreadsheet, and then change the label *CASH RECEIPTS* to the appropriate section label. (You could create these headers from scratch, but why waste the effort?) To begin, highlight the range A3:T5 and select Copy from the Edit menu. Issuing this command causes the legend COPY to appear in the middle of the status bar at the bottom of the screen. Next, move the cursor to cell A23 (the upper left cell in the header for the Cost of Goods Sold area) and press Enter to complete the copy.

Now, use the newly copied header to create the header for the Operating Expenses area. Select Copy from the Edit menu, move the cursor to cell A50, and press Enter. Select the Copy command again, move the cursor to cell A63, and press Enter to create another copy of the header. Next, select the Copy command again, point to cell A78, and press Enter to copy the header again. Copy the header in this fashion three more times, positioning the cursor on cells A95, A117, and A133.

Now, you need to replace the label *CASH RECEIPTS* in each copy of the header with the appropriate label and to remove the labels *Oct, Nov,* and *Total* from those areas in which they don't apply. To begin, move the cursor to cell A134 and enter the label *BALANCES.* (Use the Ctrl-Up Arrow key sequence or the PgUp key to move quickly from one header to the next. If you have a mouse, use the scroll bar to move the cursor.) Now, highlight the range D134:F135 and select Fill Right from the Edit menu to "erase" the entries in cells E134, E135, F134, and F135 and replace them with copies of the entries from cells D134 and D135. Then, highlight the range T134:T135 and select Clear from the Edit menu to erase the labels in those cells.

Next, move to cell A118 and enter the label *ANALYSIS OF CASH REQUIRE-MENTS.* (Because the copied header in the range A23:T25 is already highlighted, you need not highlight it again before you select the Copy command.) Then, highlight the range D118:F119 and select Fill Right from the Edit menu. Next, highlight the range T118:T119 and select Clear from the Edit menu to erase the labels in those cells. Now, move to cell A96 and enter the label *CASH FLOW SUMMARY.* Then, highlight the range D96:G97 and select Fill Right from the Edit menu. Next, move to cell A79 and enter the label *DEBT SERVICE.* Then, highlight the range D79:F80 and select Fill Right from the Edit menu.

Now, move to cell A64 and enter the label *FIXED ASSETS.* Next, highlight the range D64:G65 and select Fill Right from the Edit menu. Then, move to cell A51 and enter the label *OPERATING EXPENSES.* Finally, move to cell A24 and enter the label *COST OF GOODS SOLD.* Now, highlight the range H23:J25, select Copy from the Edit menu, move to cell U23, and press Enter. This step copies the labels *Jan, Feb,* and *Mar* to cells U24 through W25.

Now you're ready to begin entering the row headers in column A. First, move the cursor to cell A6 and enter the label *Product 1.* Then, move to cell A7 and enter the label *Product 2.* Continue in this fashion—moving down column A and entering text—until all the row headers for column A shown in Figure 12-1, beginning on page 328, are in place.

Notice that some labels in column A are indented from the left edge of column A. These indentions help to make the template easier to read and understand. To indent a label, simply type the appropriate number of spaces before you type the label itself. For example, to indent the label Cash Sales one space, type a space, type the label *Cash Sales,* and press Enter.

Freezing Rows and Columns

After you enter all the row headers, freeze columns A, B, and C onto the screen to ensure that the appropriate labels in this column remain visible—even when the cursor is way off to the right in the spreadsheet. To freeze these columns, highlight column D and select Freeze Titles from the Options menu. From now on, columns A, B, and C remain visible on the screen.

The Cash Receipts Area

Now you're ready to enter formulas in columns E, F, G, and H. Begin by entering formulas for the Cash Receipts area in columns E, F, and H. The table in Figure 12-8 lists these formulas.

The Fill Down command on the Edit menu can help when you are entering a series of similar formulas. After you type the first formula, use the Fill Down command to create the others. For instance, instead of typing formulas in cells F7, F8, F9, and F10, enter the formula =E6*(1+$D6) in cell F6, highlight the range F6:F10, and select Fill Down from the Edit menu. Works copies the formula in cell F6 to cells F7, F8, F9, and F10. As it copies the formula, Works adjusts the references to cells E6 and D6 so that each copied formula references cells in the row it occupies.

Cell	Formula
F6	=E6*(1+$D6)
F7	=E7*(1+$D7)
F8	=E8*(1+$D8)
F9	=E9*(1+$D9)
F10	=E10*(1+$D10)
E12	=SUM(E6:E11)
F12	=SUM(F6:F11)
F15	=E15
F16	=E16
F17	=E17
E18	=1–SUM(E15:E17)
F18	=1–SUM(F15:F17)
H20	=E12*E18+F12*F17+G12*G16+H12*H15

Figure 12-8. Formulas for columns E, F, and H in the CASH RECEIPTS section.

About the formulas

The formulas in cells F6 through F10 are very similar to one another. Each formula computes the November sales for a product by multiplying the October sales for that product (in column E) by 1 plus the growth rate (from column D). (Because the cells in column D and E are currently empty, these formulas return the value 0.) For instance, the formula in cell F6, *=E6*(1+$D6)*, multiplies the October sales for Product 1, which you enter in cell E6, by 1 plus the Product 1 growth rate assumption you enter in cell D6. Notice that the references to the cells in column D are mixed references: absolute in respect to column D and relative in respect to the row. When you copy these formulas across the spreadsheet, the mixed references remain fixed.

The formulas in cells E12 and F12 compute total sales for the months of October and November. For example, the formula in cell E12, *=SUM(E6:E11)*, adds the values in cells E6, E7, E8, E9, E10, and E11. (These formulas return 0 until you enter your assumptions in columns D and E.)

The formulas in cells F15, F16, and F17 refer directly to the results of the formulas in column E. For instance, the formula in cell F15 is *=E15*. Because the references to column E in these formulas are relative, they change when you copy the formulas across the spreadsheet.

The formulas in cells E18 and F18 compute the percentage of October and November sales that will be collected in 90 days. These formulas use the following logic: The percentage of sales collected in 90 days is the difference between 100% of sales and the percentages that are paid for with cash, collected in 30 days, and collected in 60 days. The formula in cell E18 makes this computation by subtracting the sum of the range E15:E17 (which contains the percentages for cash sales, 30-day collections, and 60-day collections for October) from 1 (100%).

Because we used these formulas in cells E18 and F18, you never have to worry about whether the percentages in rows 15 through 18 total 100%. After you enter the percentages for cash sales, 30-day collections, and 60-day collections in rows 15, 16, and 17, the spreadsheet computes the 90-day collection percentage for you.

The formula in cell H20 computes the actual cash collections for the month of January. This formula is based on the following logic: Cash collections in January are equal to October sales (cell E12) times the percentage of October sales that were to be collected in 90 days (cell E18), plus November sales (cell F12) times the percentage of November sales that were to be collected in 60 days (cell F17), plus December sales (cell G12) times the percentage of December sales that were to be collected in 30 days (cell G16), plus January sales (cell H12) times the percentage of January sales that were to be paid for with cash (cell H15).

Entering labels

In addition to entering the formulas in Figure 12-8, enter "underlines" in cells E11 and F11 for the figures in columns E and F. To do this, first move the cursor to cell E11, enter a label consisting of one space followed by seven hyphens (-------), and press Enter. Then, repeat the process in cell F11. You also need to enter a similar label in cell H21. To enter this label, move the cursor to cell H21, press the Spacebar, type seven equal signs (=======), and press Enter.

Changing formats

After you enter the formulas and labels in this area, change the format of the range E15:S18 from Dollar to Percent with zero decimals. To make this change, highlight the range E15:S18, select Percent from the Format menu, type *0*, and press Enter.

Copying the formulas

The next step is to copy the formulas you entered to the other columns in the range. To begin, highlight the range F6:S18 and select Fill Right from the Edit menu. When you do this, Works copies the formulas and labels from column F to columns G through S. Now, highlight the range H20:S20 and select Fill Right from the Edit menu to copy the formula from cell H20 to cells I20, J20, and so on.

Let's take a minute to look at the result of the first Fill Right command. The formulas in cells F15, F16, F17, and F18 refer to the cell in column E in the same row. Because the references in those formulas are relative, they change as you copy the formulas across the spreadsheet to reflect the new position of each copy. In other words, cell G15 contains the formula *=F15*, cell H15 contains the formula *=G15*, and so on. The effect of these formulas is to pass the value in column E in each row across columns F through S. Because these formulas carry values forward from month to month, we call this use of formulas the "carry-forward technique." We'll look further at this technique when we begin to use the spreadsheet.

Similarly, the formulas in cells F6, F7, F8, F9, and F10 refer to the cells in columns D and E in the same row. The reference to the cell in column D is mixed (absolute with respect to column) and the reference to the cell in column E is relative. When you copy these formulas across the spreadsheet, the relative reference changes to reflect the new position of each copy, but the mixed reference does not change. In other words, cell G6 contains the formula *=F6*(1+$D6)*, cell H6 contains the formula *=G6*(1+$D6)*, and so on. Each formula returns a value that is equal to the value in the previous column times the sum of 1 and the value from column D.

The approach we used to building the Cash Receipts area might seem inefficient—entering all the formulas in columns E, F, and H and then using the Fill Right command to duplicate them to columns G through S. In fact, this is the most efficient way to create a spreadsheet (or a section of a spreadsheet) in which each cell in each row contains the same basic formula. This approach is far more efficient than the next best approach—entering and copying the formulas for each row separately. A surprising number of spreadsheets fit this pattern, and you can save considerable time and effort by building them using this approach. We'll use it again to build the other sections of this spreadsheet.

Saving your work

After you enter all the formulas shown in Figure 12-8 and copy them to columns G through S, take a moment to save the work you've done so far. Select Save As from the File menu. Then, if you want to save the file in a directory other than the current one, choose that directory from the Other Drives & Directories list box and choose OK. Next, type a name (such as *BUSCASH.WKS*), and press Enter or choose OK to save the file. If you want to save the file in the current directory, simply type a file-name and press Enter or choose OK.

Because this template is larger and more complex than some others in this book, you will spend more time creating it. By saving the spreadsheet from time to time as you build it, you avoid losing valuable time (in the event of a power failure or a similar problem).

The Cost of Goods Sold Area

Now, you're ready to enter the formulas that define the Cost of Goods Sold area. In fact, the Cost of Goods Sold area is very similar in structure to the Cash Receipts area you just created. The table in Figure 12-9 lists the formulas you enter in columns E, F, G, and H in the Cost of Goods Sold area. Once again, you can use the Fill Down command on the Edit menu to enter similar formulas more efficiently. Instead of manually entering each formula in a series of similar formulas, type only the first formula and then use the Fill Down command to create the others.

About the formulas

The formulas in cells E26 through F30 compute the cost of goods sold for October and November for each product by multiplying the sales values in cells E6 through F10 in the Cash Receipts area by the percentages in cells D26 through D30. For example, the formula in cell E26, *=E6*$D26*, multiplies the October sales for Product 1 (cell E6) by the cost of goods percentage for Product 1 (cell D26) to compute the October cost of goods sold for Product 1. (Because you have not yet entered your assumptions, these formulas, like those in the Cash Receipts area, return the value 0 for now.)

The formulas in cells F35, F36, and F37 refer to the assumptions you enter in cells E35, E36, and E37 regarding the purchasing schedule. For instance, the formula in cell F35 is *=E35*.

The formulas in cells E38 and F38 compute the percentages of October and November cost of goods sold that are purchased 90 days in advance. These formulas are similar to those in cells E18 and F18 in the Cash Receipts area. For example, the formula in cell E38 subtracts the sum of the range E35:E37 (which contains the percentages of cost of goods sold in October that are purchased 0, 30, and 60 days in advance) from 1 (100%). The result is the percentage of cost of goods sold purchased

Cell	Formula
E26	=E6*$D26
F26	=F6*$D26
E27	=E7*$D27
F27	=F7*$D27
E28	=E8*$D28
F28	=F8*$D28
E29	=E9*$D29
F29	=F9*$D29
E30	=E10*$D30
F30	=F10*$D30
E32	=SUM(E26:E31)
F32	=SUM(F26:F31)
F35	=E35
F36	=E36
F37	=E37
E38	=1−SUM(E35:E37)
F38	=1−SUM(F35:F37)
E40	=E35*E32+F36*F32+G37*G32+H38*H32
F40	=F35*F32+G36*G32+H37*H32+I38*I32
G43	=E43
G44	=F44
F45	=1−SUM(F43:F44)
G45	=1−SUM(G43:G44)
H47	=F45*F40+G44*G40+H43*H40

Figure 12-9. Formulas for columns E, F, G, and H in the Cost of Goods Sold area.

90 days in advance. Because we used these formulas in cells E38 and F38, you can expect the percentages in rows 35 through 38 to total 100%. You simply enter the percentages of cost of goods sold that you plan to purchase 0, 30, and 60 days in advance in rows 35, 36, and 37, and the spreadsheet computes the percentage to be purchased 90 days in advance.

The formulas in cells E40 and F40 compute the total purchases of cost of goods sold for the months of October and November. They are similar to the formulas that compute total monthly cash receipts. The formula in cell E40 is based on the following logic: Purchases in October are equal to October cost of goods sold (cell E32) times the percentage of October cost of goods sold that were to be purchased for cash (cell E35), plus November cost of goods sold (cell F32) times the percentage of November cost of goods sold that were to be purchased 30 days in advance (cell F36), plus December cost of goods sold (cell G32) times the percentage of December cost of goods sold that were to be purchased 60 days in advance (cell G37), plus January cost of goods sold (cell H32) times the percentage of January cost of goods sold that were to be purchased 90 days in advance (cell H38). After you enter the formula in cell E40, highlight the range E40:F40 and select Fill Right from the Edit menu to copy the formula to cell F40.

The formulas in cells G43, G44, F45, and G45 are similar to the formulas in cells F15, F16, F17, and F18 in the Cash Receipts area and cells F35, F36, F37, and F38 in the Cost of Goods Sold area. The formulas in cells G43 and G44 refer to the purchasing schedule assumptions you enter in cells E43 and E44. The formulas in cells F45 and G45 compute the percentage of November and December purchases you plan to pay for in 60 days. For example, the formula in cell F45 subtracts the sum of the range F43:F44 (which contains the percentages of November purchases paid for with cash or in 30 days) from 1 (100%). The result is the percentage of November purchases that you plan to pay for 60 days in the future.

The formula in cell H47 computes the total payments for cost of goods sold for the month of January. To find this total, the formula adds the November purchases (cell F40) times the percentage of November purchases payable in 60 days (cell F45), plus December purchases (cell G40) times the percentage of December purchases payable in 30 days (cell G44), plus January purchases (cell H40) times the percentage of January purchases to be made with cash (cell H43).

Entering labels

In addition to entering the formulas in Figure 12-9, enter a label consisting of one space followed by seven hyphens in cells E31 and F31. You can enter these labels manually, or you can use the Copy command to create this label by copying an existing, similar label. Next, enter a similar label consisting of a space followed by seven equal signs in cell H48 (or use the Copy command to create this label by copying an existing, similar label).

Changing formats

After you enter the formulas and labels in this section, change the format of the range E35:W38 from Dollar to Percent with zero decimal places. To make this change, highlight the range E35:W38, then select Percent from the Format menu, type 0, and press Enter.

Next, change the format of the range F43:S45 from Dollar to Percent with zero decimals: Highlight the range F43:S45, select Percent from the Format menu, type 0, and press Enter.

Copying the formulas

Your next step is to copy the formulas and labels from columns E, F, G, and H to the other columns in the Cost of Goods Sold area. To begin, highlight the range F26:S40 and select Fill Right from the Edit menu. Works copies the formulas and labels from column F to columns G through S. Next, highlight the range G43:S45 and select Fill Right from the Edit menu to copy the formulas from cells G43, G44, and G45 to columns H, I, J, and so on. Finally, highlight the range H47:S48 and select Fill Right from the Edit menu. Works copies the formula from cell H47 to cells I47, J47, K47, and so on.

Extending the formulas

Because each formula in row 40 which computes the total payments for cost of goods sold for each month refers to the cost of goods sold assumption for the following three months, you need to enter (or compute) the cost of goods sold for January, February, and March of the year following the year for which you are building a forecast. The spreadsheet uses the cost of goods sold for these months to compute purchases for October, November, and December in the previous year.

To create this part of the template, first move to cell U32 and enter the formula

`=S32*($S32/$R32)`

This formula estimates cost of goods sold for January by multiplying the cost of goods sold for December (in cell S32) by the ratio between the cost of goods sold in December (S32) and the cost of goods sold in November (R32). In effect, this formula assumes that cost of goods sold will increase by the same percentage between December and January by which it increased between November and December. Because cell R32 currently contains the value 0, the formula in cell U32 will return the message *ERR*.

Next, move the cursor to cell V32 and enter the formula *=U32*($S32/$R32)*. Then, select the range V32:W32 and select Fill Right from the Edit menu to copy the formula from cell V32 to cell W32. Again, the formula returns *ERR* because R32 currently contains a value of 0.

Now, move the cursor down to cell U35 and enter the formula =S35. This formula carries forward the percentage from cell S35 into cell U35. Next, select the range U35:U38 and select the Fill Down command from the Edit menu to copy the formula from cell U35 into cells U36, U37, and U38. Then move to cell V35 and enter the formula *=U35*. This formula carries forward the percentage from cell U35 into cell V35. Next, select the range V35:W38, select Fill Down from the Edit menu, and then select Fill Right from the Edit menu. These commands will copy the formula from cell V35 into the other cells in the selected range. Since the reference in cell V35 is a relative reference, it will change as it is copied into the other cells.

The Operating Expenses Area

Now you're ready to fill in the Operating Expenses area. To begin, move the cursor to cell F53 and enter the formula

`=E53*(1+$D53)`

This formula—which is similar to those in cells F6, F7, F8, F9, and F10 in the Cash Receipts area—sets the value of cell F53 (total operating expenses for November) equal to the value in cell E53 (total operating expenses for October) times 1 plus the monthly growth rate assumption in cell D53. (Because you have not yet entered any assumptions into the spreadsheet, these formulas, and the others in this area, return 0 for now.)

Next, move to cell G56 and enter the formula =F56. Then, move to cell G57 and enter the formula =F57. Now move to cell F58 and enter the formula

```
=1-SUM(F56:F57)
```

Highlight the range F58:G58 and use the Fill Right command to copy this formula into cell G58.

The formulas in cells G56, G57, F58, and G58 compute the percentages of operating expenses you expect to pay with cash, on 30-day terms, and on 60-day terms. The formulas in cells G56 and G57 refer to the assumptions you enter in cells F56 and F57. The formulas in cells F58 and G58 compute the percentage of November and December operating expenses payable in 60 days. These formulas are similar to the ones in cells F45 and G45 in the Cost of Goods Sold area.

Next, move the cursor to cell H60 and enter the formula

```
=F58*F53+G57*G53+H56*H53
```

This formula computes the total payments for operating expenses for the month of January. It finds this total by calculating November operating expenses (cell F53) times the percentage of November operating expenses payable in 60 days (cell F58), plus December operating expenses (cell G53) times the percentage of December operating expenses payable in 30 days (cell G57), plus January operating expenses (cell H53) times the percentage of January operating expenses to be purchased with cash (cell H56).

Next, enter a label consisting of one space followed by seven equal signs in cell H61. You can enter this label manually or copy an existing, similar label.

After you enter the formulas and labels in this section, change the format of the range F56:S58 from Dollar to Percent with zero decimals. To make this change, highlight the range F56:S58, select Percent from the Format menu, type 0, and press Enter.

Now, copy the formulas and labels from columns F, G, and H to the other columns in the Operating Expenses area. To begin, highlight the range F53:S53 and select Fill Right from the Edit menu. Works copies the formula from cell F53 to cells G53, H53, I53, and so on through column S. Next, highlight the range G56:S58 and select Fill Right from the Edit menu. This command copies the formula from cells G56, G57, and G58 to columns H, I, J, and so on. Finally, highlight the range H60:S61 and select Fill Right from the Edit menu to copy the formula from cell H60 to cells I60, J60, and so on.

The Fixed Assets Area

Now you're ready to fill in the Fixed Assets area. To begin, enter a label consisting of one space followed by seven hyphens in cells H68 and H74. Next, enter the formula =H66–H67 in cell H69, and enter the formula =H69–H72 in cell H75. Finally, move the cursor to cell H76 and enter a label consisting of a space followed by seven equal signs.

After you enter these labels and formulas in column H, use the Fill Right command to copy those formulas to the other cells in the Fixed Assets area. To do this, highlight the range H68:S76 and select the Fill Right command from the Edit menu. This command will copy the entries from column H to columns I through S in the Fixed Assets area.

The Debt Service Area

Now you're ready to create the Debt Service area. To begin, enter the formulas shown in the following table, Figure 12-10, in the indicated cells.

The formulas in this area compute several important values relating to long-term and short-term debt. The formula in cell H82 computes the long-term debt payment for January by adding the value in cell G73 (the addition to the monthly payment for December) to the value in cell G82 (the total monthly payment for December). The formula in cell H83, =G83, carries forward the value from cell G83 (the long-term debt interest rate for December). Because you haven't entered any assumptions in the spreadsheet, these formulas, and the others in this area, return 0 for now.

The formula in cell H84 computes the interest portion of the total long-term debt payment for January. This formula divides the interest rate in cell H83 by 12 to compute a monthly rate, then multiplies that rate by the long-term debt balance for December (cell G148). The formula in cell H85 subtracts the result from cell H84 from the total monthly payment in cell H82 to compute the principal portion of the total long-term debt payment for January.

Cell	Formula
H82	=G82+G73
H83	=G83
H84	=H83/12*G148
H85	=H82–H84
H89	=G89
H90	=H89/12*G143
H92	=H82+H90

Figure 12-10. Formulas for column H in the Debt Service area.

The formulas in cells H89 and H90 relate to short-term debt. The formula in cell H89, *=G89*, simply carries forward the short-term debt interest rate assumption from cell G89 to cell H89. The formula in cell H90 computes the interest portion of the short-term debt payment for January. This formula divides the interest rate in cell H89 by 12 to compute a monthly rate, then multiplies that rate by the short-term debt balance for December (cell G143).

The formula in cell H92, *=H82+H90*, sums the total long-term debt payment for January (cell H82) and the total short-term debt payment for January in cell H90 to compute the total debt service for January.

In addition to entering the formulas in Figure 12-10 in column H, enter a label consisting of one space followed by seven hyphens in cell H91. Then, enter a similar label (a space followed by seven equal signs) in cell H93.

Next, you need to change the format of the range G83:S83 from Dollar to Percent with two decimal places. To make this change, highlight the range G83:S83, select Percent from the Format menu, and press Enter to accept the default number of decimals. Next, change the format of the range G89:S89 from Dollar to Percent with two decimals: Highlight the range G89:S89, select Percent from the Format menu, and press Enter.

Now, copy these formulas in the Debt Service area from column H to columns I through S. To do so, highlight the range H82:S93 and select Fill Right from the Edit menu. Because the formulas in the range H82:H93 contain relative references, Works modifies those formulas as it copies them across the spreadsheet. For example, the formula in cell H82 is *=G82+G73*, so the formula Works copies in cell I82 is *=H82+H73*, the formula in J82 is *=I82+I73*, and so on.

The Cash Flow Summary

Now you're ready to enter the formulas that define the Cash Flow Summary. Most of the formulas in this area simply refer to cells in earlier sections. To begin, move to cell H98 and enter the formula *=H20*. This formula refers to cell H20, which contains a formula that computes total cash collections. Then, move to cell H102 and enter the formula *=H47*. (Because you have not yet entered any assumptions in the spreadsheet, this formula, and the others in this area, return the value 0 for now.) Cell H47 contains a formula that computes payments for purchases of cost of goods sold. Next, move the cursor to cell H103 and enter the formula *=H60*. This formula refers to cell H60, which contains a formula that computes payments for operating expenses. Now, enter the formula *=H75* in cell H104. The formula in cell H75 computes net purchases of fixed assets. Next, move the cursor to cell H105 and enter the formula *=H92*, which refers to the cell in the preceding area that computes total disbursements for debt service.

Next, enter a label of one space followed by seven hyphens in cell H108. (You can use the Copy command to create this label by copying an existing, similar label.) Then, move to cell H109 and enter the formula

=SUM(H102:H107)

This formula computes the total cash disbursements for January by summing the values in cells H102, H103, H104, H105, H106, and H107. Then, move the cursor to cell H110 and enter a label of one space followed by seven hyphens. (Again, you could create this label by copying a similar label.)

Now, move to cell H111 and enter the formula

=H98+H99-H109

This formula computes the net cash generated by operations by adding cash collections (cell H98) and other cash receipts (cell H99) for January, and then subtracting total cash disbursements (cell H109) for January.

Next, enter the formula *=H128* in cell H112. This formula refers to cell H128, which will contain a formula that computes the total short-term borrowing needed in January to maintain a minimum acceptable cash balance.

Finally, enter a label consisting of a space followed by seven hyphens in cell H113. (You can also create this label by copying an existing, similar label.) Then, move to cell H114 and enter the formula *=H111+H112*. This formula computes the net cash flow for January by adding the short-term borrowing for January to the net cash generated by operations. Next, move the cursor to cell H115 and enter a label consisting of one space followed by seven equal signs. (Once again, you could use the Copy command to create this label by copying a similar label.)

After you enter these formulas and labels in column H of the Cash Flow Summary, copy them from column H to columns I through S. To do so, highlight the range H98:S115 and select Fill Right from the Edit menu. Works copies the formulas and labels from column H to columns I, J, K, and so on through column S.

Because the formulas in column H in the Cash Flow Summary contain relative references, those references change as Works copies the formulas across the spreadsheet. For instance, cell H98 contains the formula *=H20*, cell I98 contains the formula *=I20*, cell J98 the formula *=J20*, and so on.

The Analysis of Cash Requirements

Next, you'll create the Analysis of Cash Requirements. The table in Figure 12-11 on the following page lists the formulas you enter in column H in this area.

For the most part, the formulas in this part of the template simply refer to the results of calculations that are performed elsewhere. For example, the formula in cell H120 refers to cell G137, which contains the cash balance at the end of December.

Cell	Formula
H120	=G137
H121	=H111
H123	=H120+H121
H124	=G124
H126	=H123–H124
H128	=IF(H126<0,–H126,IF(G143>0,IF(G143>H126,–H126,–G143),0))
H130	=H123+H128

Figure 12-11. Formulas for column H in the Analysis of Cash Requirements.

(Because you have not yet entered any assumptions in the spreadsheet, this formula, and the others in this area, return the value 0 for now.) Cell H121 refers to cell H111, which contains a formula that computes the net cash generated by operations in January. The formula in cell H123 simply sums the values in cells H120 and H121 to compute the cash balance before any short-term borrowing. The formula in cell H124 refers to the minimum cash balance assumption that you enter in cell G124. Cell H126 computes the cash surplus or deficit for January by subtracting the minimum acceptable balance (cell H124) from the cash balance before borrowing (cell H123).

The formula in cell H128 is the key formula in the entire template. This formula computes the amount of short-term debt, if any, that you must incur in January to maintain the minimum acceptable cash balance. This formula says: If the value in cell H126 is less than 0 (that is, if the value in cell H126 indicates a cash deficit in January), then borrow an amount equal to the deficit. Otherwise, if the short-term debt balance for December (cell G143) is greater than 0 (meaning that short-term debt was outstanding at the end of December), then repay either of two amounts: If the amount of debt outstanding at the end of December (cell G143) is greater than the cash surplus for January (cell H126), then repay an amount equal to the cash surplus in cell H126; otherwise, repay an amount equal to the total amount of debt outstanding at the end of December (cell G143). If the value in cell H126 is greater than 0 (meaning that you show a cash surplus for January), and if the value in cell G143 is not greater than 0 (meaning that there was no short-term debt outstanding at the end of December), then the formula returns a value of 0.

As you will see when we walk through a sample spreadsheet, this formula computes exactly the amount of borrowing that must occur in a period to maintain the established minimum cash balance. If you show a cash surplus in the period, the formula repays as much short-term debt as possible without violating the minimum cash balance. In essence, the entire template revolves around this formula. It is the "red flag" that shows you where you need extra cash and where you have spare cash to repay debt.

After you enter the formulas in Figure 12-11 in column H, enter underlines in cells H122, H125, and H129, and a double underline in cell H131. The underlines consist of one space followed by seven hyphens. The double underline in cell H131 consists of a space followed by seven equal signs. Enter these labels manually, or use the Copy command to create these labels by copying existing, similar labels.

After you enter these formulas and labels, copy them from column H to columns I through S. To do this, highlight the range H120:S131 and select Fill Right from the Edit menu. Works copies the formulas and labels from column H to columns I, J, K, and so on through column S.

Because the formulas in column H in the Analysis of Cash Requirements contain relative references, those references change as Works copies the formulas across the spreadsheet. For instance, cell H120 in this section contains the formula =G137, cell I120 contains the formula =H137, cell J120 the formula =I137, and so on.

The Balances Area

Now you're ready to enter the formulas for the Balances area, the last one in the template. The table in Figure 12-12 lists the formulas you enter in each cell in columns G and H in this section.

The formulas in these cells compute a series of balances for the month of January: cash, accounts receivable, inventory, accounts payable, short-term debt, and long-term debt. The formula in cell H137 computes the cash balance simply by referring to the ending cash balance in cell H130. Cell H138 computes the accounts receivable balance for January by adding the new sales for January (cell H12) to the prior month's accounts receivable balance (cell G138), and then subtracting the cash collections for January (cell H20) from that amount. The formula in cell H139 adds the total purchases for cost of goods sold for January (cell H40) to the prior month's inventory balance (cell G139), and then subtracts the actual cost of goods sold for January (cell H32) from that total to compute the inventory balance at the end of January. (Because

Cell	Formula
H137	=H130
H138	=G138+H12–H20
H139	=G139+H40–H32
H142	=G142+H40–H47+H53–H60
H143	=G143+H128
G145	=G137+G138+G139–G142–G143
H145	=H137+H138+H139–H142–H143
H148	=G148+H72–H85

Figure 12-12. Formulas for columns G and H in the Balances area.

you have not yet entered any assumptions in the spreadsheet, these formulas, and the others in this area, return the value 0 for now.)

Cell H142 adds the total purchases for cost of goods sold for January (cell H40) to the prior month's accounts payable balance (cell G142), subtracts the payments for cost of goods sold (cell H47) from that total, adds the total purchases of operating expenses for January (cell H53) to that result, and then subtracts the payments for operating expenses (H60) from that value. The result is the accounts payable balance for January. The formula in cell H143 computes the January balance for short-term debt by adding the current short-term borrowing for January (cell H128) to the December short-term balance (cell G143).

The formulas in cells G145 and H145 compute the company's net working capital for December and January. These formulas simply add the cash, accounts receivable, and inventory balances for the appropriate month and then subtract the accounts payable and short-term debt balances for those months.

Finally, the formula in cell H148 computes the January long-term debt balance. This formula adds the total new debt for January from cell H72 to the December long-term debt balance in cell G148, and then subtracts the long-term debt principal repayment for January in cell H85 from that result.

Next, enter a label consisting of one space followed by seven hyphens in cells G144 and H144. These labels serve as "underlines" for columns of figures that you plan to total. You can use the Copy command to help you enter these labels. Also, enter a label consisting of a space followed by seven equal signs in cells G149 and H149.

After you enter the formulas and labels in columns G and H of the Balances area, copy them from column H to columns I through S: Highlight the range H137:S149 and select Fill Right from the Edit menu.

Column T

Next, you need to enter a series of SUM functions in column T. Each formula sums the contents of columns H through S in one row of the spreadsheet, creating a series of annual totals in column T. For example, cell T6 will contain the formula *=SUM(H6:S6)*, which sums the values in row 6. The table in Figure 12-13 shows the formulas that you enter in the cells of column T.

Enter the formula in cell T6 and then use the Copy and Fill Down commands to copy it to all the other cells. To begin, enter the formula *=SUM(H6:S6)* in cell T6. Then, highlight the range T6:T10 and select Fill Down from the Edit menu. This step copies the formula from cell T6 to cells T7 through T10. Because the formula contains relative references, the formula in cell T7 is *=SUM(H7:S7)*, the formula in cell T8 is *=SUM(H8:S8)*, and so on. Now, highlight cell T10, select Copy from the Edit menu, move the cursor to cell T12, and press Enter to copy the formula from cell T10 to cell T12. Continue in this way—using the Copy and Fill Down commands to create the other formulas shown in the table.

Cell	Formula
T6	=SUM(H6:S6)
T7	=SUM(H7:S7)
T8	=SUM(H8:S8)
T9	=SUM(H9:S9)
T10	=SUM(H10:S10)
T12	=SUM(H12:S12)
T20	=SUM(H20:S20)
T26	=SUM(H26:S26)
T27	=SUM(H27:S27)
T28	=SUM(H28:S28)
T29	=SUM(H29:S29)
T30	=SUM(H30:S30)
T32	=SUM(H32:S32)
T40	=SUM(H40:S40)
T47	=SUM(H47:S47)
T53	=SUM(H53:S53)
T60	=SUM(H60:S60)
T66	=SUM(H66:S66)
T67	=SUM(H67:S67)
T69	=SUM(H69:S69)
T72	=SUM(H72:S72)
T73	=SUM(H73:S73)
T75	=SUM(H75:S75)
T82	=SUM(H82:S82)
T84	=SUM(H84:S84)
T85	=SUM(H85:S85)
T90	=SUM(H90:S90)
T92	=SUM(H92:S92)
T98	=SUM(H98:S98)
T99	=SUM(H99:S99)
T102	=SUM(H102:S102)
T103	=SUM(H103:S103)
T104	=SUM(H104:R104)
T105	=SUM(H105:S105)
T106	=SUM(H106:S106)
T107	=SUM(H107:S107)
T109	=SUM(H109:S109)
T111	=SUM(H111:S111)
T112	=SUM(H112:S112)
T114	=SUM(H114:S114)

Figure 12-13. *Formulas for column T.*

Next, enter underlines and double-underlines in some cells in column T. Enter a label (consisting of one space followed by eight hyphens) in cells T11, T31, T68, T74, T91, T108, T110, and T113 and a similar label (one space followed by eight equal signs) in cells T21, T48, T61, T76, T93, and T115. You can, of course, use the Copy command to help you enter these labels.

Saving the Template

After you create the last formula in column T, the template is finished. Save the spreadsheet immediately (or resave it, if you saved it as you went along). To save it for the first time, select Save As from the File menu. Then, if you want to save the file in a directory other than the current one, choose that directory from the Other Drives & Directories list box and choose OK. Next, type a name (such as *BUSCASH.WKS*), and press Enter or choose OK to save the file. If you want to save the file in the current directory, simply type a filename and press Enter or choose OK. If you saved the spreadsheet previously, save it again by choosing Save from the File menu.

USING THE TEMPLATE

After you create the Business Cash Flow Forecast, you're ready to put it to work. Begin by opening the spreadsheet. (If you just created the template, skip this step.) To do this, choose Open from the File menu. Now, if the file you want to open is not in the current directory, select the directory that contains the file from the Other Drives & Directories box and choose OK. Then, either type the filename under which you saved the template, including the extension (for example, *BUSCASH.WKS*), or highlight the name of the template in the list, and choose OK or press Enter. If the file you want to open is in the current directory, simply type or highlight the filename and then press Enter or choose OK.

To begin using the spreadsheet, enter a series of assumptions in columns D, E, F, and G. Then, go back and enter values for any irregular (non-repeating) items in appropriate cells. You also need to adjust any items that Works calculated for you but that you know will be different from the predicted amount. Finally, recalculate the spreadsheet.

Entering Assumptions

At this point, you're ready to enter some basic assumptions in columns D, E, F, and G. Some of these assumptions are percentages; others are dollar amounts. The template uses them to make a variety of computations. For example, the spreadsheet uses the growth-rate assumption you enter in cell D6 and the October sales assumption you enter in cell E6 to project sales for November and each subsequent month.

The table in Figure 12-14 explains each assumption you enter in columns D, E, F, and G. To enter these figures, move the cursor to the appropriate cell and enter the

Cell	Assumption
D6	Monthly sales growth rate for Product 1
E6	October sales for Product 1
D7	Monthly sales growth rate for Product 2
E7	October sales for Product 2
D8	Monthly sales growth rate for Product 3
E8	October sales for Product 3
D9	Monthly sales growth rate for Product 4
E9	October sales for Product 4
D10	Monthly sales growth rate for Product 5
E10	October sales for Product 5
E15	Percentage of October sales to be made for cash
E16	Percentage of October sales to be collected in 30 days
E17	Percentage of October sales to be collected in 60 days
D26	Cost of goods sold percentage for Product 1
D27	Cost of goods sold percentage for Product 2
D28	Cost of goods sold percentage for Product 3
D29	Cost of goods sold percentage for Product 4
D30	Cost of goods sold percentage for Product 5
E35	Percentage of October cost of goods sold to be purchased 0 days in advance
E36	Percentage of October cost of goods sold to be purchased 30 days in advance
E37	Percentage of October cost of goods sold to be purchased 60 days in advance
F43	Percentage of November purchases to be paid for with cash
F44	Percentage of November purchases to be paid for in 30 days
D53	Monthly growth rate for operating expenses
E53	Total October operating expenses
F56	Percentage of October operating expenses to be paid with cash
F57	Percentage of October operating expenses to be paid in 30 days
G82	Total monthly payment for long-term debt in December
G83	Average interest rate on long-term debt in December
G89	Average interest rate on short-term debt in December
G124	Minimum acceptable cash balance for December
G137	Cash balance at the end of December
G138	Accounts receivable balance at the end of December
G139	Inventory debt balance at the end of December
G142	Accounts payable balance at the end of December
G143	Short-term debt balance at the end of December
G148	Long-term debt balance at the end of December

Figure 12-14. Assumptions.

corresponding value. The sample spreadsheet in Figure 12-1 beginning on page 328 shows you how to enter these assumptions. Remember, however, to enter your own assumptions, not ours, in your spreadsheet.

Notice that the sample spreadsheet does not contain assumptions for every row. The Fixed Assets area, for example, contains no assumptions—the items in this area are not regular, or predictable, from month to month. For instance, you probably don't acquire major fixed assets every month. Figure 12-1 contains assumptions only for those items that are normally predictable. You need to enter the other assumptions manually. You'll learn how to do that in a few pages.

The structure of this template illustrates an excellent guideline for creating new spreadsheets: Always make your assumptions explicit. Doing so means that you enter your assumptions—the fundamental values and percentages on which the formulas in the spreadsheet depend—in cells by themselves instead of burying them in formulas. Making your assumptions explicit enables you to change them easily. It also makes the spreadsheet easier to understand—instead of trying to figure out the assumptions on which the spreadsheet are based, you can simply read them from the spreadsheet itself.

Entering Irregular Items

As we mentioned in the preceding section, the template cannot compute every item based on its limited set of assumptions. Some expenditures occur irregularly or infrequently—once a year or once a quarter. You have to enter this sort of item manually by moving the cursor to the cell at the intersection of the appropriate column (month) and row (account) and typing a number to represent the irregularly occurring item.

For example, row 66 in the template allows you to enter information about fixed asset purchases. In general, the entries in this account are irregular and variable. For this reason, the template does not require you to enter an assumption for this row. If you expect to purchase an asset, enter the amount of that receipt in the proper column of row 66. The sample spreadsheet shown in Figure 12-1 shows the value *$15,000* in cell J66. This number represents a fixed asset purchase of $15,000 in March of the coming year. To record this purchase, we moved the cursor to cell G66, typed the number *15000*, and pressed Enter.

The table in Figure 12-15 lists the accounts you have to define manually and the rows in which those accounts occur. Use this table as a guide as you enter your infrequent and irregular expenses in the spreadsheet. Keep in mind that you don't have to make an entry in every row. If a particular account does not apply to you, leave the corresponding row blank.

Row	Description	You Enter
66	Fixed Asset Purchases	Cash disbursements for purchases of fixed assets
67	Fixed Assets Sales	Cash received for sales of fixed assets
72	Total New Debt	Cash received as a result of new long-term debt
73	Addition to Monthly Payment	Additional monthly payment for new debt
99	Other Cash Receipts	Cash receipts not recorded elsewhere
106	Income Tax Payments	Cash disbursements for payments of income tax
107	Other Disbursements	Cash disbursements not recorded elsewhere

Figure 12-15. Irregular items.

Changing Regular Items

Next, you need to adjust any items that Works has calculated but which you know will be different from the predicted amount. This class of items includes receipts and disbursements that vary slightly from month to month or season to season, such as sales of products that are highly seasonal. It also includes items that are consistent much of the year but which change at a certain point. For example, you might plan a big advertising push for a product to boost its sales above the predicted levels for a couple of months.

To make a change to a calculated value, move the cursor to the cell that contains the value you need to change and enter a new value. In Figure 12-1 on page 359, for example, we changed the monthly sales in February for Product 1 in cell I6 to $75,000. To make this change, we simply moved the cursor to cell I6, typed *75000*, and pressed Enter. Similarly, notice we changed the percentages in cells H15 and H16 (which represent the percentages of January sales that will be paid for with cash and that will be collected in 30 days) from 25% and 15% to 20% and 20%. To make this change, we simply moved the cursor to cell H15, typed *.2*, and pressed Enter. Then, we moved the cursor down one cell, typed *.2* again, and pressed Enter.

Remember that many formulas in the spreadsheet refer to the adjacent cell to the left. For example, cell F6 contains the formula *=E6*(1+$D6)*, cell G6 contains the formula *=F6*(1+$D6)*, and so on. Similarly, cell F15 contains the formula *=E15*, cell G15 contains the formula *=F15*, and so on. This use of formulas, called the "carry-forward technique," comes in handy when you make changes such as those explained in the previous paragraph. When you enter a value in a cell that contains a carry-forward formula, the value replaces the formula and changes the value of the cell. Then, the formula to the right of the cell in which you entered the value picks up that new value and passes it along through the spreadsheet. In other words, the new value is carried forward through the spreadsheet. For instance, notice that cells I15 and I16 in Figure 12-1 both display the value 20%—the value we entered in cells H15 and H16.

This occurs because each of these cells contains a carry-forward formula. Likewise, notice that the value in cell J6, $77,250, is based on the value we entered in cell I6.

When you enter a value in a row, Works carries that value forward until you enter another value in the row. When you enter another value, Works passes that value along across the row until you enter another value, and so on. For example, notice that we changed the percentages in cells J15 and J16 (which represent the percentage of March sales to be paid for with cash and the percentage to be collected in 30 days) from 20% and 15% to 10% and 20%. To make this change, we moved the cursor to cell J15 and entered the value .1. Then, we moved the cursor down one cell and entered the value .2. Notice that the spreadsheet passed this new value along from cells J15 and J16 to cells K15 and K16, L15 and L16, and so on.

You can use these same techniques to adjust any values that the spreadsheet calculates. Of course, you don't have to make changes to every row. And note that any changes you make are carried forward only when you recalculate the spreadsheet. You'll do that in the next section.

Calculating the Spreadsheet

After you post all your assumptions, enter any irregular disbursements and receipts, and make any necessary changes to computed items, select Calculate Now from the Options menu or press the Calc key ([F9]) to calculate the spreadsheet. When you do this, Works updates all the formulas in the spreadsheet. The carry-forward formulas carry the values from columns D, E, F, and G to columns H through S. Other formulas compute such values as cash receipts for each month, cash disbursements for cost of goods sold and operating expenses, and short-term borrowing or repayments. The SUM functions compute the totals for each row and for each month.

Printing and Saving

After you set up your forecast, save the spreadsheet into a new file. To do this, select Save As from the File menu, type a new name for the spreadsheet, and press Enter or choose OK. Choose a name for the file that clearly identifies its contents— for example, BUDG88 for your 1988 forecast. To retrieve a file, select Open from the File menu, type the filename, and press Enter or choose OK.

Be sure to save your filled-in Business Cash Flow Forecast under a name other than the name you used for the original, empty template. If you save a filled-in spreadsheet under the same name as the original template, the filled-in version replaces the original version.

To print the entire Business Cash Flow Forecast, first choose Layout from the Print menu and change any print settings you want to fine-tune. For example, if you have a wide-carriage printer and plan to print this spreadsheet on 11-by-14-inch paper, you might want to change the Page Width setting from *8.5"* to *14"*. You might also want to change the Top, Bottom, Left, and Right margins, and define a header and a footer. Next, choose Font from the Print menu to select the style and size of type you want Works to use to print the report. (If you choose a proportional font, such as Times, the spreadsheet columns do not align properly in the printed copy, and underlining, boldface, and so on will not work.) If you want to squeeze the entire report onto one page, choose a relatively compressed font (such as Elite) and a small point size (such as 6 or 8).

After you adjust the layout, select Print from the Print menu to display the Print dialog box. Adjust any settings you want to change in that dialog box, and then choose Print to print the report.

To print only a portion of the forecast, first choose Set Print Area from the Print menu to define the area you want to print. To print only the Analysis of Cash Requirements, for example, highlight the range D117:S131 and select Set Print Area from the Print menu. (You need not highlight the titles in columns A, B, and C; Works routinely prints frozen titles.) Then, use the Layout and Font commands to make any needed adjustments to the Works print settings, select Print from the Print menu, and choose Print.

Using the Plan

After you recalculate the spreadsheet, review the result. Is the spreadsheet unrealistic? Is the monthly net sales figure consistently negative? Does the cash balance ever become negative? Is the balance in some other asset account negative? If so, you need to make a few adjustments. These might include changing the amount of a variable-expense estimate to avoid negative cash flows, changing the amount of a balance-sheet transfer to avoid negative cash or other asset balances, or creating a balance-sheet transfer to fund an unusual expenditure. After you make each adjustment, recalculate the spreadsheet to observe the effect of the transfer.

Now you can really begin to use the Business Cash Flow Forecast. The completed spreadsheet is your business financial plan, a tool you can use to measure your financial performance for the coming year. You should study the plan carefully so that you understand exactly what your condition will be at each point in the coming year. Are there any tight spots? Keep them in mind as unexpected expenses come to your attention. Are there any expenditures you want to make but which you currently cannot afford? Use the plan to develop a savings strategy that will make your business goals reachable.

At the end of each month, compare your actual disbursements and receipts to the estimates in the spreadsheet. Such comparisons help to verify the accuracy of your projections. If you find estimates that are inaccurate, adjust them to be more in line with your actual activities. To adjust a receipt or disbursement, move to the cell in the appropriate row and the column for the current month and enter the new estimate. The spreadsheet carries your change forward from that point to the end of the year.

MODIFICATIONS

Two modifications to the Business Cash Flow Forecast might better adapt it to your specific needs. First, you can add rows to the spreadsheet to hold new accounts. Second, you can create one or more charts from the data in the spreadsheet. The following sections show you how to make those changes.

Adding Products

We included only five products in the Cash Receipts and Cost of Goods Sold areas of the template. If your business has more than five products, you might be able to consolidate your products in some way to fit the existing template. If this won't work for you, however, you can insert additional rows in the spreadsheet.

To add a new product to the spreadsheet, highlight the row in the Cash Receipts area above which you want to add the new item and select Insert from the Edit menu. This step inserts a new, blank row into the spreadsheet. If you want to add more than one product, highlight several rows and select the Insert command. When the new row or rows are in place, enter labels in column A that define the contents of the rows, growth percentages in column D that define the anticipated growth rates for the new products, and October sales estimates in column E. Then, move the cursor over to column F and up one row so that it is on the November sales formula for the preceding product. Now, highlight that cell and the cells below it in the new row or rows and choose Fill Down from the Edit menu. Works copies the November sales formula to the new cells. Next, highlight the cells in columns F through S in the new rows and select Fill Right from the Edit menu to copy the formula from column F to the other columns. Finally, enter a SUM formula in column T of each new row to compute the annual sales totals.

For each new product you add in the Cash Receipts area, you need to add a row at the corresponding location in the Cost of Goods Sold area. (For example, insert a new product between Product 4 and Product 5 if you chose that location in the Cash Receipts area.) To do so, highlight the row above which you want to insert the new row (or multiple rows to insert multiple rows), choose Insert from the Edit menu, and press Enter or choose OK. Works inserts a new, blank row for each row you highlighted. Next, enter labels in column A that define the contents of the new rows and enter the cost of goods sold percentages in column D. Then, highlight the cells in columns E through T in the row above the new rows and select Fill Down from the Edit menu. Works copies the formulas that compute cost of goods sold for each month and the formula that computes total cost of goods sold for the new products.

The formulas in rows 12 and 32 include any products you add in the calculation of total sales and total cost of goods sold. Because these formulas use the SUM function, the range of summation expands when you add rows within the existing range.

Charting

Works lets you create one or more charts that display graphically the information in the Business Cash Flow Forecast. To create a chart from any information in the spreadsheet, highlight the range that contains that information and select New from the Chart menu. Then, select View from the Chart menu to view the chart. In addition, you can change the name of the chart, change its type, and enhance it with titles, legends, and other refinements.

For example, suppose you want to create a chart that illustrates the ending cash balance for each month. Highlight the range G137:S137 (which contains the ending cash balances) and select New from the Chart menu. Then, to place a series of legends on the x axis, highlight the range of month labels G134:S134 and choose X Series from the Data menu. Finally, choose View from the Chart menu in the Chart sublevel to display the chart shown in Figure 12-16. You can create as many as eight charts from the data in the Business Cash Flow Forecast.

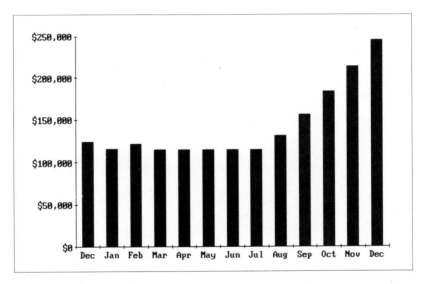

Figure 12-16.

CONCLUSION

Every business needs a cash flow forecast. Trying to run a business without a cash flow forecast is like trying to predict the weather without a barometer—you might be right from time to time, but it is hard to be consistently correct. As this template shows, the Spreadsheet environment in Works is an excellent tool for predicting cash flow. In almost any business, you can use the Business Cash Flow Forecast you built in this chapter to forecast cash flow and cash balances for the coming year.

Even if you don't use this template, you can employ some of the tricks and techniques you learned in building it in your own spreadsheets. You'll find that these techniques—including the carry-forward technique and the guideline for making your assumptions explicit—come in handy whenever you build a large or complex spreadsheet.

THIRTEEN

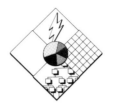

The Personal Financial Plan

Do you have a personal financial plan? If you are like millions of other Americans, you don't—but you should. Without a personal financial forecast, it is difficult or impossible to predict what the future holds for your personal finances. You won't be able to foresee cash crunches or predict the effect of unexpected expenditures on your financial condition. You risk running out of money when you need cash desperately or missing an investment opportunity that could make you a bundle.

The Spreadsheet environment in Microsoft Works is an ideal tool for creating a personal financial plan. The template described in this chapter, the Personal Financial Plan, uses a Works spreadsheet as the basis for a one-year personal income statement and balance sheet projection. Unless your situation is exceedingly complex, you can use this spreadsheet to forecast net income and cash balances for the upcoming year. For those of us with relatively simple financial situations, it is an ideal tool for creating a personal budget for the coming year.

The Personal Financial Plan also demonstrates several important techniques for building accurate and efficient spreadsheets. As you build this template, you'll learn an invaluable spreadsheet-building trick: the carry-forward technique. You'll also learn why you should always make your assumptions explicit, and you'll see how to go about doing that.

ABOUT THE TEMPLATE

Figure 13-1, which begins on the following page, shows the Personal Financial Plan with some sample information entered in it. Of course, when you first create the template, most of the cells will contain zeros rather than the numbers shown in the figure (D6:P215). As you can see, the template has several areas, labeled INCOME,

363

	A	B	C	D	E	F	G	H
1	==
2	PERSONAL FINANCIAL PLAN
3	==
4	INCOME				Jan	Feb	Mar	Apr	May
5	======================================			======	======	======	======	======
6	Salary 1			$50,000	$4,167	$4,167	$4,167	$4,167	$4,167
7	Withholdings
8	Federal Income Tax			$11,000	$917	$917	$917	$917	$917
9	State Income Tax			$2,000	$167	$167	$167	$167	$167
10	City Tax			$1,000	$83	$83	$83	$83	$83
11	FICA			7.05%	$294	$294	$294	$294	$294
12	Medical			$300	$25	$25	$25	$25	$25
13	Other			$0	$0	$0	$0	$0	$0
14					------	------	------	------	------
15	Total Withholdings				$1,485	$1,485	$1,485	$1,485	$1,485
16					------	------	------	------	------
17	Net Salary 1				$2,681	$2,681	$2,681	$2,681	$2,681
18					------	------	------	------	------
19	
20	Salary 2			$25,000	$2,083	$2,083	$2,083	$2,083	$2,083
21	Withholdings
22	Federal Income Tax			$1,250	$104	$104	$104	$104	$104
23	State Income Tax			$1,063	$89	$89	$89	$89	$89
24	City Tax			$500	$42	$42	$42	$42	$42
25	FICA			7.05%	$294	$294	$294	$294	$294
26	Medical			$0	$0	$0	$0	$0	$0
27	Other			$0	$0	$0	$0	$0	$0
28					------	------	------	------	------
29	Total Withholdings				$528	$528	$528	$528	$528
30					------	------	------	------	------
31	Net Salary 2				$1,555	$1,555	$1,555	$1,555	$1,555
32					------	------	------	------	------
33	Total Net Salary				$4,236	$4,236	$4,236	$4,236	$4,236
34	
35	Other Income
36	Interest				$6	$6	$192	$7	$8
37	Dividends				$0	$0	$75	$0	$0
38	Rent			$0	$0	$0	$0	$0	$0
39	Gifts
40	Other Income							$150
41					------	------	------	------	------
42	Total Other Income				$6	$6	$267	$157	$8
43					------	------	------	------	------
44	Total Income (Net of Withholdings)				$4,242	$4,243	$4,503	$4,394	$4,244
45					======	======	======	======	======
46	

Figure 13-1.

I	J	K	L	M	N	O	P
===							
===							
Jun	Jul	Aug	Sep	Oct	Nov	Dec	Total
======	======	======	======	======	======	======	======
$4,167	$4,167	$4,167	$4,167	$4,167	$4,167	$4,167	$50,000
$917	$917	$917	$917	$917	$917	$917	$11,000
$167	$167	$167	$167	$167	$167	$167	$2,000
$83	$83	$83	$83	$83	$83	$83	$1,000
$294	$294	$294	$294	$294	$294	$294	$3,525
$25	$25	$25	$25	$25	$25	$25	$300
$0	$0	$0	$0	$0	$0	$0	$0
------	------	------	------	------	------	------	------
$1,485	$1,485	$1,485	$1,485	$1,485	$1,485	$1,485	$17,825
------	------	------	------	------	------	------	------
$2,681	$2,681	$2,681	$2,681	$2,681	$2,681	$2,681	$32,175
------	------	------	------	------	------	------	------
$2,083	$2,083	$2,083	$2,083	$2,083	$2,083	$2,083	$25,000
$104	$104	$104	$104	$104	$104	$104	$1,250
$89	$89	$89	$89	$89	$89	$89	$1,063
$42	$42	$42	$42	$42	$42	$42	$500
$294	$294	$294	$294	$294	$294	$294	$3,525
$0	$0	$0	$0	$0	$0	$0	$0
$0	$0	$0	$0	$0	$0	$0	$0
------	------	------	------	------	------	------	------
$528	$528	$528	$528	$528	$528	$528	$6,338
------	------	------	------	------	------	------	------
$1,555	$1,555	$1,555	$1,555	$1,555	$1,555	$1,555	$18,662
------	------	------	------	------	------	------	------
$4,236	$4,236	$4,236	$4,236	$4,236	$4,236	$4,236	$50,837
$193	$9	$9	$195	$10	$11	$196	$842
$75	$0	$0	$75	$0	$0	$75	$300
$0	$0	$0	$0	$0	$0	$0	$0
							$0
							$150
------	------	------	------	------	------	------	------
$268	$9	$9	$270	$10	$11	$271	$1,292
------	------	------	------	------	------	------	------
$4,505	$4,245	$4,246	$4,506	$4,247	$4,247	$4,508	$52,129
======	======	======	======	======	======	======	======

(continued)

Figure 13-1. Continued.

	A	B	C	D	E	F	G	H
47	===
48	EXPENSES			Jan	Feb	Mar	Apr	May
49	===			======	======	======	======	======
50	Debt Service
51	Credit Cards		$10	$10	$10	$10	$25	$25
52	Interest		18.00%	$6	$6	$6	$10	$10
53	Principal			$4	$4	$4	$15	$15
54	
55	Personal Loan		$0	$0	$0	$0	$0	$0
56	Interest		0.00%	$0	$0	$0	$0	$0
57	Principal			$0	$0	$0	$0	$0
58	
59	Student Loan		$115	$115	$115	$115	$115	$115
60	Interest		7.00%	$34	$33	$33	$32	$32
61	Principal			$81	$82	$82	$83	$83
62	
63	Auto Loan #1		$275	$275	$275	$275	$275	$275
64	Interest		12.00%	$45	$43	$40	$38	$36
65	Principal			$230	$232	$235	$237	$239
66	
67	Auto Loan #2		$132	$132	$132	$132	$132	$132
68	Interest		13.00%	$87	$86	$86	$85	$85
69	Principal			$45	$46	$46	$47	$47
70	
71	Home Mortgage		$875	$875	$875	$875	$875	$875
72	Interest		9.50%	$783	$782	$781	$781	$780
73	Principal			$92	$93	$94	$94	$95
74	
75	Other Mortgage		$0	$0	$0	$0	$0	$0
76	Interest		0.00%	$0	$0	$0	$0	$0
77	Principal			$0	$0	$0	$0	$0
78				------	------	------	------	------
79	Total Debt Service			$1,407	$1,407	$1,407	$1,422	$1,422
80				------	------	------	------	------
81	Fixed Expenses
82	Tithe		10.00%	$424	$424	$450	$439	$424
83	Childcare		$525	$525	$525	$525	$525	$525
84	Homeowner's Expenses
85	Property Taxes					$975		
86	Homeowner's Insurance				$500			
87	Utilities
88	Gas and Electric		$200	$200	$200	$175	$150	$100
89	Water		$20	$20	$20	$20	$20	$20
90	Telephone		$50	$50	$50	$50	$50	$50
91	Food and Household Supplies		$300	$300	$300	$300	$300	$300
92	Insurance
93	Life Insurance
94	Automobile Insurance							$550
95	Other Medical Insurance
96				------	------	------	------	------
97	Total Fixed Expenses			$1,519	$2,019	$2,495	$1,484	$1,969
98				------	------	------	------	------

I	J	K	L	M	N	O	P
Jun	Jul	Aug	Sep	Oct	Nov	Dec	Total
$25	$25	$25	$25	$25	$25	$25	$255
$10	$10	$9	$9	$9	$9	$8	$102
$15	$15	$16	$16	$16	$16	$17	$153
$0	$0	$0	$0	$0	$0	$0	$0
$0	$0	$0	$0	$0	$0	$0	$0
$0	$0	$0	$0	$0	$0	$0	$0
$115	$115	$115	$115	$115	$115	$115	$1,380
$31	$31	$30	$30	$29	$29	$28	$374
$84	$84	$85	$85	$86	$86	$87	$1,006
$275	$275	$275	$275	$275	$275	$275	$3,300
$33	$31	$28	$26	$23	$21	$18	$383
$242	$244	$247	$249	$252	$254	$257	$2,917
$132	$132	$132	$132	$132	$132	$132	$1,584
$84	$84	$83	$83	$82	$82	$81	$1,006
$48	$48	$49	$49	$50	$50	$51	$578
$875	$875	$875	$875	$875	$875	$875	$10,500
$779	$778	$778	$777	$776	$775	$775	$9,346
$96	$97	$97	$98	$99	$100	$100	$1,154
$0	$0	$0	$0	$0	$0	$0	$0
$0	$0	$0	$0	$0	$0	$0	$0
$0	$0	$0	$0	$0	$0	$0	$0
------	------	------	------	------	------	------	------
$1,422	$1,422	$1,422	$1,422	$1,422	$1,422	$1,422	$17,019
------	------	------	------	------	------	------	------
$450	$425	$425	$451	$425	$425	$451	$5,213
$525	$525	$525	$525	$525	$525	$525	$6,300
$223		$318				$982	$2,498
	$500						$1,000
$100	$150	$150	$150	$150	$175	$200	$1,900
$20	$20	$20	$20	$20	$20	$20	$240
$50	$50	$50	$50	$50	$50	$50	$600
$300	$300	$300	$300	$300	$300	$300	$3,600
	$221						$221
			$300				$850
							$0
------	------	------	------	------	------	------	------
$1,668	$1,691	$2,288	$1,796	$1,470	$1,495	$2,528	$22,422
------	------	------	------	------	------	------	------

(continued)

Figure 13-1. Continued.

	A	B	C	D	E	F	G	H
99	Variable Expenses							
100	House Expenses							
101	Maintenance		$50	$50	$50	$50	$50	$50
102	Furniture					$300		
103	Improvements				$200			
104	Automobile Expenses							
105	Gasoline		$50	$50	$50	$50	$50	$50
106	Maintenance		$25	$25	$25	$25	$25	$25
107	Clothing Expenses							
108	New Clothing		$200	$200	$200	$200	$200	$200
109	Diapers		$48	$48	$48	$48	$48	$48
110	Cleaning		$43	$43	$43	$43	$43	$43
111	Medical Care							
112	Doctor's Bills		$25	$25	$25	$25	$25	$25
113	Prescription Drugs		$25	$25	$25	$25	$25	$25
114	Personal Expenses							
115	Athletic Club		$55	$55	$55	$55	$55	$55
116	Newspaper		$9	$9	$9	$9	$9	$9
117	Books and Magazines		$25	$25	$25	$25	$25	$25
118	Cable TV		$17	$17	$17	$17	$17	$17
119	Entertainment		$100	$100	$100	$100	$100	$100
120	Meals Out		$100	$100	$100	$100	$100	$100
121	Gifts					$100		
122	Vacation							$1,500
123	Haircuts			$87		$12		$12
124	Income Taxes							
125	Other Variable Expenses		$25	$25	$25	$25	$25	$25
126				------	------	------	------	------
127	Total Variable Expenses			$884	$997	$1,209	$797	$2,309
128				------	------	------	------	------
129	Total Expenses			$3,810	$4,423	$5,111	$3,703	$5,700
130				======	======	======	======	======
131								
132	==
133	RECAP			Jan	Feb	Mar	Apr	May
134	======================================			======	======	======	======	======
135	Total Income			$4,242	$4,243	$4,503	$4,394	$4,244
136	Total Expenses			($3,810)	($4,423)	($5,111)	($3,703)	($5,700)
137				------	------	------	------	------
138	Net Income/(Deficit)			$432	($180)	($608)	$690	($1,456)
139				======	======	======	======	======
140								

I	J	K	L	M	N	O	P
$50	$50	$50	$50	$50	$50	$50	$600
		$500		$200		$200	$1,200
$400						$600	$1,200
$50	$50	$50	$50	$50	$50	$50	$600
$25	$25	$25	$25	$25	$25	$25	$300
$200	$200	$200	$200	$200	$200	$200	$2,400
$48	$48	$48	$48	$48	$48	$48	$576
$43	$43	$43	$43	$43	$43	$43	$516
$25	$25	$25	$25	$25	$25	$25	$300
$25	$25	$25	$25	$25	$25	$25	$300
$55	$55	$55	$55	$55	$55	$55	$660
$9	$9	$9	$9	$9	$9	$9	$108
$25	$25	$25	$25	$25	$25	$25	$300
$17	$17	$17	$17	$17	$17	$17	$204
$100	$100	$100	$100	$100	$100	$100	$1,200
$100	$100	$100	$100	$100	$100	$100	$1,200
	$27			$100		$500	$727
					$250		$1,750
	$87		$12		$12		$222
($800)	($433)						($1,233)
$25	$25	$25	$25	$25	$25	$25	$300
------	------	------	------	------	------	------	------
$397	$478	$1,297	$809	$1,097	$1,059	$2,097	$13,430
------	------	------	------	------	------	------	------
$3,487	$3,591	$5,007	$4,027	$3,989	$3,976	$6,047	$52,871
======	======	======	======	======	======	======	======

Jun	Jul	Aug	Sep	Oct	Nov	Dec	Total
======	======	======	======	======	======	======	======
$4,505	$4,245	$4,246	$4,506	$4,247	$4,247	$4,508	$52,129
($3,487)	($3,591)	($5,007)	($4,027)	($3,989)	($3,976)	($6,047)	($52,871)
------	------	------	------	------	------	------	------
$1,017	$655	($761)	$479	$258	$271	($1,539)	($742)
======	======	======	======	======	======	======	======

(continued)

Figure 13-1. Continued.

	A	B	C	D	E	F	G	H
				Jan	Feb	Mar	Apr	May
141	===							
142	BALANCES			Jan	Feb	Mar	Apr	May
143	==================================			======	======	======	======	======
144	Cash			$7,114	$7,446	$7,166	$6,758	$7,348
145	Net Ordinary Income			$432	($180)	($608)	$690	($1,456)
146	Transfers (To)/From Savings			($100)	($100)	($100)	($100)	($100)
147	(Purchases)/Sales of Investments						$4,000	
148	Additions to IRA						($4,000)	
149	(Purchases)/Sales of Real Estate							
150	Purchases on Credit Cards					$300		
151				------	------	------	------	------
152	Ending Balance		$7,114	$7,446	$7,166	$6,758	$7,348	$5,792
153								
154	Savings Accounts			$1,350	$1,456	$1,562	$1,669	$1,776
155	Additions/(Subtractions)			$100	$100	$100	$100	$100
156	Interest Income		5.25%	$6	$6	$7	$7	$8
157				------	------	------	------	------
158	Ending Balance		$1,350	$1,456	$1,562	$1,669	$1,776	$1,884
159								
160	Marketable Securities			$14,600	$14,600	$14,600	$14,860	$10,860
161	Purchases/(Sales)						($4,000)	
162	Interest Income					$185		
163	Dividend Income					$75		
164				------	------	------	------	------
165	Ending Balance		$14,600	$14,600	$14,600	$14,860	$10,860	$10,860
166								
167	IRA			$8,000	$8,000	$8,000	$8,204	$12,204
168	Net Additions to IRA			$0	$0	$0	$4,000	$0
169	Interest/Dividends					$204		
170	Capital Gains/(Losses)							
171				------	------	------	------	------
172	Ending Balance		$8,000	$8,000	$8,000	$8,204	$12,204	$12,204
173								
174	House			$96,000	$96,240	$96,681	$96,922	$97,165
175	Appreciation		3.00%	$240	$241	$242	$242	$243
176	Improvements			$0	$200	$0	$0	$0
177				------	------	------	------	------
178	Ending Balance		$96,000	$96,240	$96,681	$96,922	$97,165	$97,408
179								
180	Other Real Estate			$0	$0	$0	$0	$0
181	Purchases/(Sales)			$0	$0	$0	$0	$0
182	Appreciation		0.00%	$0	$0	$0	$0	$0
183				------	------	------	------	------
184	Ending Balance		$0	$0	$0	$0	$0	$0
185								
186	Other Assets							
187	Automobile 1			$5,000	$4,867	$4,734	$4,601	$4,468
188	Depreciation		($133)	($133)	($133)	($133)	($133)	($133)
189				------	------	------	------	------
190	Ending Balance		$5,000	$4,867	$4,734	$4,601	$4,468	$4,335
191								

I	J	K	L	M	N	O	P
Jun	Jul	Aug	Sep	Oct	Nov	Dec	Total
======	======	======	======	======	======	======	======
$5,792	$6,709	$7,263	$6,403	$6,782	$6,940	$7,111	
$1,017	$655	($761)	$479	$258	$271	($1,539)	($742)
($100)	($100)	($100)	($100)	($100)	($100)	($100)	($1,200)
							$4,000
							($4,000)
							$0
							$300
------	------	------	------	------	------	------	
$6,709	$7,263	$6,403	$6,782	$6,940	$7,111	$5,472	
$1,884	$1,992	$2,101	$2,210	$2,320	$2,430	$2,541	
$100	$100	$100	$100	$100	$100	$100	$1,200
$8	$9	$9	$10	$10	$11	$11	$102
------	------	------	------	------	------	------	
$1,992	$2,101	$2,210	$2,320	$2,430	$2,541	$2,652	
$10,860	$11,120	$11,120	$11,120	$11,380	$11,380	$11,380	
							($4,000)
$185			$185			$185	$740
$75			$75			$75	$300
------	------	------	------	------	------	------	
$11,120	$11,120	$11,120	$11,380	$11,380	$11,380	$11,640	
$12,204	$12,504	$12,504	$12,504	$12,834	$12,834	$12,834	
$0	$0	$0	$0	$0	$0	$0	$4,000
$300			$330			$340	$1,174
							$0
------	------	------	------	------	------	------	
$12,504	$12,504	$12,504	$12,834	$12,834	$12,834	$13,174	
$97,408	$98,051	$98,296	$98,542	$98,788	$99,035	$99,283	
$244	$245	$246	$246	$247	$248	$248	$2,931
$400	$0	$0	$0	$0	$0	$600	$1,200
------	------	------	------	------	------	------	
$98,051	$98,296	$98,542	$98,788	$99,035	$99,283	$100,131	
$0	$0	$0	$0	$0	$0	$0	
$0	$0	$0	$0	$0	$0	$0	$0
$0	$0	$0	$0	$0	$0	$0	$0
------	------	------	------	------	------	------	
$0	$0	$0	$0	$0	$0	$0	
$4,335	$4,202	$4,069	$3,936	$3,803	$3,670	$3,537	
($133)	($133)	($133)	($133)	($133)	($133)	($133)	($1,596)
------	------	------	------	------	------	------	
$4,202	$4,069	$3,936	$3,803	$3,670	$3,537	$3,404	

(continued)

Figure 13-1. Continued.

	A	B	C	D	E	F	G	H
192	Automobile 2			$7,000	$6,845	$6,690	$6,535	$6,380
193	Depreciation		($155)	($155)	($155)	($155)	($155)	($155)
194			------	------	------	------	------	------
195	Ending Balance		$7,000	$6,845	$6,690	$6,535	$6,380	$6,225
196								
197	Personal Property		$20,000	$20,200	$20,400	$20,900	$21,100	$21,300
198				------	------	------	------	------
199	Total Other Assets			$31,912	$31,824	$32,036	$31,948	$31,860
200				------	------	------	------	------
201	Total Assets			$159,654	$159,832	$160,449	$161,301	$160,007
202				======	======	======	======	======
203	Liabilities							
204	Credit Cards		$400	$396	$392	$688	$673	$658
205	Personal Loan		$0	$0	$0	$0	$0	$0
206	Student Loan		$5,800	$5,719	$5,637	$5,555	$5,472	$5,389
207	Auto Loan #1		$4,500	$4,270	$4,038	$3,803	$3,566	$3,327
208	Auto Loan #2		$8,000	$7,955	$7,909	$7,863	$7,816	$7,768
209	Home Mortgage		$98,900	$98,808	$98,715	$98,622	$98,527	$98,432
210	Other Mortgage		$0	$0	$0	$0	$0	$0
211				------	------	------	------	------
212	Total Liabilities			$117,147	$116,691	$116,530	$116,055	$115,575
213	Net Worth			$42,507	$43,142	$43,919	$45,246	$44,432
214				------	------	------	------	------
215	Total Liabilities and Net Worth			$159,654	$159,832	$160,449	$161,301	$160,007
216				======	======	======	======	======

EXPENSES, RECAP, and BALANCES. The Income area occupies the range A5:P45. The top left portion of the Income area, shown in Figure 13-2 on page 374, appears when you first load the spreadsheet. In this area, you enter information about your income: salaries and wages (including details about withholdings), interest, dividends, rent, and so on.

The Expenses area occupies the range A48:P130. Figure 13-3 on page 374 shows the upper left part of this area. In the Expenses area, you record your estimates of expenditures for the coming year. It has three sections: Debt Service, Fixed Expenses, and Variable Expenses. In the Debt Service section, you estimate payments on your debts—credit card balances, student loans, car loans, mortgages, and so on. In the Fixed Expenses section, you forecast your other fixed expenses—child care, utilities, food, insurance, and other unavoidable expenses. The Variable Expenses section holds your estimates of variable expenses: furniture, gasoline, medical care, cleaning, and other expenses that are more or less discretionary.

The Recap area, which occupies the range A133:P139, simply summarizes Income and Expenses areas. The formulas in row 138 subtract total expenses from total income to compute your monthly net income or deficit.

I	J	K	L	M	N	O
$6,225	$6,070	$5,915	$5,760	$5,605	$5,450	$5,295
($155)	($155)	($155)	($155)	($155)	($155)	($155)
------	------	------	------	------	------	------
$6,070	$5,915	$5,760	$5,605	$5,450	$5,295	$5,140
$21,500	$21,700	$22,400	$22,600	$23,000	$23,200	$23,600
------	------	------	------	------	------	------
$31,772	$31,684	$32,096	$32,008	$32,120	$32,032	$32,144
------	------	------	------	------	------	------
$162,148	$162,969	$162,875	$164,112	$164,739	$165,181	$165,213
======	======	======	======	======	======	======
$643	$628	$612	$596	$580	$564	$547
$0	$0	$0	$0	$0	$0	$0
$5,306	$5,222	$5,137	$5,052	$4,967	$4,881	$4,794
$3,085	$2,841	$2,594	$2,345	$2,094	$1,840	$1,583
$7,721	$7,672	$7,623	$7,574	$7,524	$7,473	$7,422
$98,337	$98,240	$98,143	$98,045	$97,946	$97,846	$97,746
$0	$0	$0	$0	$0	$0	$0
------	------	------	------	------	------	------
$115,091	$114,603	$114,110	$113,613	$113,111	$112,604	$112,093
$47,057	$48,366	$48,765	$50,500	$51,629	$52,577	$53,120
------	------	------	------	------	------	------
$162,148	$162,969	$162,875	$164,112	$164,739	$165,181	$165,213
======	======	======	======	======	======	======

The last area, labeled BALANCES, is a simplified personal balance sheet. It computes the value of your assets—cash, savings, IRA accounts, house, personal property, and so on—and your liabilities—credit card balances, mortgages, car loans, and so on. This balance sheet occupies the range A142:O216. The formulas in row 201 compute the total value of your assets, and the formulas in row 212 compute the total value of your liabilities. The formulas in row 213 compute your net worth by subtracting your liabilities from your assets.

Your personal balance sheet is based on the information recorded in the Income and Expenses areas and on a number of basic assumptions that you enter in column C, such as your annual salary and your monthly mortgage and car loan payments. For example, the spreadsheet uses the annual salary assumption you enter in cell C6 as the basis for computing the monthly salary amounts in cells D6 to O6. Similarly, it uses the values you enter in cells C100 to C124 to compute monthly expenses.

Most of the cells in columns D through O contain formulas that compute the value of each income and expense account for each month. Some of these formulas refer to the assumptions in column C; others make calculations based on the values in other columns. In a few of these cells, you enter simple values that represent unusual income or expense items. Column P contains a series of SUM functions that compute the annual total for each row in the spreadsheet.

```
 File  Edit  Print  Select  Format  Options  Chart  Window
               A         B         C         D         E         F         G        =
1  =================================================================================↑
2  PERSONAL FINANCIAL PLAN
3  =================================================================================
4  INCOME                   ████████████            Jan       Feb       Mar       Apr
5  ==========================================      ======    ======    ======    ======
6  Salary 1                        $50,000       $4,167    $4,167    $4,167    $4,167
7   Withholdings
8    Federal Income Tax           $11,000         $917      $917      $917      $917
9    State Income Tax              $2,000         $167      $167      $167      $167
10   City Tax                      $1,000          $83       $83       $83       $83
11   FICA                           7.05%         $294      $294      $294      $294
12   Medical                         $300          $25       $25       $25       $25
13   Other                            $0           $0        $0        $0        $0
14                                               ------    ------    ------    ------
15   Total Withholdings                         $1,485    $1,485    $1,485    $1,485
16                                               ------    ------    ------    ------
17  Net Salary 1                                $2,681    $2,681    $2,681    $2,681
18                                               ------    ------    ------    ------
19                                                                                   ↓
║←█                                                                                →
B4                                                                        FAMILY.WKS
Press ALT to choose commands.
```

Figure 13-2.

```
 File  Edit  Print  Select  Format  Options  Chart  Window
               A         B         C         D         E         F         G        =
1  =================================================================================↑
2  PERSONAL FINANCIAL PLAN
3  =================================================================================
48 EXPENSES                 ████████████            Jan       Feb       Mar       Apr
49 ==========================================      ======    ======    ======    ======
50 Debt Service
51   Credit Cards                      $10          $10       $10       $10       $25
52    Interest                      18.00%           $6        $6        $6       $10
53    Principal                                      $4        $4        $4       $15
54
55   Personal Loan                      $0           $0        $0        $0        $0
56    Interest                       0.00%           $0        $0        $0        $0
57    Principal                                      $0        $0        $0        $0
58
59   Student Loan                     $115         $115      $115      $115      $115
60    Interest                       7.00%          $34       $33       $33       $32
61    Principal                                     $81       $82       $82       $83
62
63   Auto Loan #1                     $275         $275      $275      $275      $275   ↓
║←█                                                                                →
B48                                                                       FAMILY.WKS
Press ALT to choose commands.
```

Figure 13-3.

CREATING THE TEMPLATE

To create the Personal Financial Plan, first choose New from the Files menu if the New dialog box is not already on your screen. Then, choose Spreadsheet and press Enter or choose New to display a blank spreadsheet. Now, select Manual Calculation from the Options menu to prevent Works from recalculating the entire spreadsheet each time you make an entry.

Next, change the default format for the spreadsheet from General to Dollar with zero decimal places. To do so, first highlight the entire spreadsheet: Hold the Shift and Ctrl keys and press [F8]. When the entire spreadsheet is highlighted, select Dollar from the Format menu. When the Dollar dialog box appears, type 0 and then press Enter or choose OK.

Now, while the entire spreadsheet is still highlighted, change all the column widths: Choose Width from the Format menu, type the new width, 9, and press Enter or choose OK. Next, position the cursor on a cell in column A, choose Width from the Format menu, type 19, and press Enter or choose OK.

Entering Column and Row Headers

After you change the widths of these columns, you're ready to begin making entries. First, enter the header labels for the template in rows 1, 2, and 3. The double lines in rows 1 and 3 are composed of equal signs (=) that span columns A through P. To create these double lines, enter a label made up of a series of equal signs in each cell in row 1, and then copy that series of labels from row 1 to row 3. To enter each of the labels in row 1, type a quotation mark (") followed by the proper number of equal signs. For example, to enter the label in cell A1, move the cursor to cell A1, type a quotation mark, and then type a string of 19 equal signs. If you forget the quotation mark, Works tries to interpret the entry as a formula and displays the message *Error: Missing Operand*.

After you enter a label in each cell in row 1, you can copy the labels from row 1 to row 3. To do so, highlight the range A1:P1, select Copy from the Edit menu, highlight cell A3, and press Enter.

Now, move the cursor to cell A2 and type *PERSONAL FINANCIAL PLAN*. Next, move the cursor to cell A4 and enter the label *INCOME*. Then, move the cursor across row 4 to column D and enter the label *JAN*. Continue to move across row 4 one cell at a time, entering the label *FEB* in cell E4, the label *MAR* in cell F4, and so on. When the cursor reaches cell P4, enter the label *TOTAL*.

Now, move the cursor to row 5 and enter a series of broken double lines. Make the double-line label in cell A5 19 characters long. Make the labels in cells B5 and C5 9 characters long, and the labels in cells D5 through P5 6 characters each.

When all these labels are in place, right-align the ones in cells D4 through P5. To do this, highlight the range D4:P5, select Style from the Format menu, choose Right from the Style dialog box, and press Enter or choose OK.

Now, you can use the header you created for the Income area to create the headers for the other three areas. To do this, simply copy the contents of rows 3, 4, and 5 to the appropriate locations in the spreadsheet, then change the label *INCOME* to *EXPENSES*, *RECAP*, or *BALANCES*. (Of course, you could create these headers from scratch, but why waste the effort?)

To begin, highlight the range A3:P5 and select Copy from the Edit menu. Selecting this command causes the legend COPY to appear on the Status line at the bottom of the screen. When you see this legend, move the cursor to cell A47 (the upper left cell in the EXPENSES header) and press Enter.

Now, use the newly copied header to create the header for the Recap area. To do so, select Copy from the Edit menu, point to cell A132, and press Enter. (Because the copied header in the range A47:P49 is already highlighted, you don't have to highlight it before you select the Copy command.) Then select Copy again, point to cell A141, and press Enter to create another copy of the header.

To replace the label INCOME in each copy of the header, move the cursor to cell A142 and enter the label *BALANCES*; move to cell A133, enter the label *RECAP*; move the cursor to cell A48, and enter the label *EXPENSES*. (You can use Ctrl-Up Arrow to move quickly from one header to the next, or you can use PgUp. If you have a mouse, you can use the scroll bar to move the cursor.)

Now you're ready to begin entering the row headers in column A. To begin, move the cursor to cell A6 and enter the label *Salary 1*. Then, move to cell A7 and enter the label *Withholdings*, preceded by a single space. Next, move to cell A8 and enter the label *Federal Income Tax*, preceded by two spaces. Continue in this fashion— moving down column A and entering labels—until all the row headers shown in column A in Figure 13-1 are in place.

Notice that some labels in column A are indented one space, others two spaces, and yet others three spaces: These indentions help to make the spreadsheet easier to read and more understandable. To indent a label, type the appropriate number of spaces before you type the label itself.

Now, freeze column A and rows 1 through 3 to ensure that the appropriate labels remain visible on the screen—even when the cursor is far to the right or far down in the spreadsheet. To do this, position the cursor on cell B4 and choose Freeze Titles from the Options menu.

The Income Area

Now you're ready to begin entering formulas (and a few labels) in columns D and E. Begin by entering the formulas listed in the following table, Figure 13-4. As you can see, most of the formulas in column D refer to the assumptions you'll enter in column C. For instance, the formula in cell D6, =C6/12, divides the annual salary assumption you'll enter in cell C6 by 12 to compute a monthly salary. (Because the cells in column C are currently empty, these formulas return the value 0.) Some of these formulas sum other values in column D. For example, the formula in cell D17,

Cell	Formula	Cell	Formula
D6	=C6/12	E6	=D6
D8	=C8/12	E8	=D8
D9	=C9/12	E9	=D9
D10	=C10/12	E10	=D10
D11	=C11*D6	E11	=D11
D12	=C12/12	E12	=D12
D13	=C13/12	E13	=D13
D15	=SUM(D8:D14)	E15	=SUM(E8:E14)
D17	=D6−D15	E17	=E6−E15
D20	=C20/12	E20	=D20
D22	=C22/12	E22	=D22
D23	=C23/12	E23	=D23
D24	=C24/12	E24	=D24
D25	=D$6*$C25	E25	=D25
D26	=C26/12	E26	=D26
D27	=C27/12	E27	=D27
D29	=SUM(D22:D28)	E29	=SUM(E22:E28)
D31	=D20−D29	E31	=E20−E29
D33	=D17+D31	E33	=E17+E31
D36	=D156+D162	E36	=E156+E162
D37	=D163	E36	=E163
D38	=C38	E38	=D38
D42	=SUM(D36:D41)	E42	=SUM(E36:E41)
D44	=D33+D42	E44	=E33+E42

Figure 13-4. *Formulas for columns D and E in the Income area.*

=D6−D15, subtracts the value in cell D15 from the value in cell D6. The formulas in rows 36 and 37 refer to rows 156, 162, and 163 in the Balances area. (These formulas will return 0 until you complete that part of the template.) Most of the formulas in column E refer directly to the results of the formulas in column D. For instance, the formula in cell E6 is *=D6*.

You can use the Fill Down command on the Edit menu to help you enter some of these formulas. Instead of entering a series of similar formulas manually, type only the first formula and then use the Fill Down command to create the others. For instance, instead of typing formulas in cells D8, D9, and D10, enter the formula *=C8/12* in cell D8, highlight the range D8:D10, and select Fill Down from the Edit menu. Choosing this command copies the formula in cell D8 to cells D9 and D10. As it copies the formula, Works adjusts reference to cell C8 so that the copied formulas refer to cells C9 and C10.

In addition to entering the formulas in the table to columns D and E, enter a label consisting of two spaces followed by six hyphens (------) in the following cells in those columns: D14, E14, D16, E16, D18, E18, D28, E28, D30, E30, D32, E32, D41, E41, D43, and E43. These labels serve as "underlines" for columns of figures that you plan to add. To enter one of these labels, move the cursor to the appropriate cell, press the Spacebar twice, type six hyphens (------), and press Enter. You can use the Fill Right command and the Copy command to help you duplicate this label in other cells. Next, enter double-line labels in cells D45 and E45. To enter one of these labels, move the cursor to the appropriate cell, press the Spacebar twice, type six equal signs (======), and press Enter.

Copying the formulas

After you enter the formulas shown in the preceding table, copy the formulas and labels from column E to columns F through O. To do so, highlight the range E6:O45 and select Fill Right from the Edit menu. Works copies the formulas and labels from column E to columns F, G, H, and so on through column O. Figure 13-5 shows the upper left corner of the Income area after you copy these formulas.

Let's take a minute to look at the result of this Fill Right command. Most of the formulas in column E of the Income area simply refer to the cell in column D in the same row. (Of course, a few of these cells contain labels and a few contain formulas of a different kind.) Because the cell references in those formulas are relative, copying the formulas to other columns changes the references to reflect the new position of each copy. As a result, most of the formulas in columns F through O in the Income

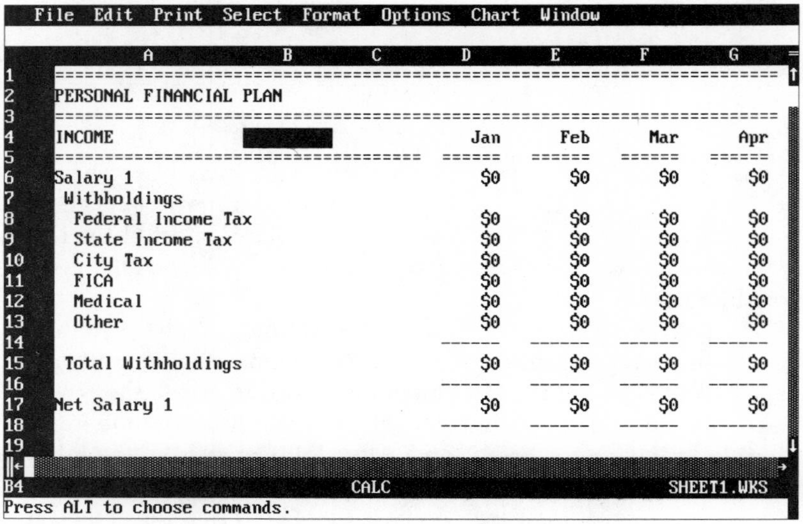

Figure 13-5.

area of the template reference the cell in the previous column of the same row. In other words, cell F6 contains the formula =E6, cell G6 contains the formula =F6, cell H6 the formula =G6, and so on.

These formulas pass the value in column D in each row across columns E through O. For example, notice that every cell in row 6 displays the same value calculated by the formula in cell D6. Because these formulas carry values forward from month to month in the spreadsheet, we call this use of formulas the "carry-forward technique." You'll learn more about this technique later as you read about using the spreadsheet.

The approach we used to build the Income area—entering all the formulas in columns D and E and then using the Fill Right command to duplicate those formulas into columns F through O—might seem inefficient. In fact, it is the most efficient way to create a spreadsheet (or an area of a spreadsheet) in which each cell in each row contains the same basic formula. This approach is far more efficient than the next best alternative: entering and copying the formulas for each row separately. You'd probably be surprised at how many of your spreadsheets fit this pattern and at how much time you can save by building those spreadsheets using this approach. We'll use it again to build the Expenses and Balances areas.

Saving your work

After you enter all the formulas shown in Figure 13-4 on page 377 and copy them to columns F through O, take a moment to save your work. To save the spreadsheet, select Save As from the File menu. Then, if you want to save the file in a directory other than the current one, choose that directory from the Other Drives & Directories list box and choose OK. Next, type a name (such as *FAMILY.WKS*) and press Enter or choose OK to save the file. If you want to save the file in the current directory, simply type a filename and press Enter or choose OK. Saving the partially completed template at this point protects your work from mishaps such as power failures or kicked-out electrical cords.

Because this template is larger and more complex than some others in this book, you'll invest more time in creating it. Save the template frequently as you build it to avoid losing valuable time.

The Expenses Area

After you enter the formulas for columns D and E in the Income area, you're ready to enter the formulas that define the Expenses area. To begin, move the cursor to cell D51 and enter the formula =C51. This formula sets the value of the cell D51, the monthly credit card payment for January, equal to the monthly payment assumption you will enter in cell C51. Next, move to cell D53 and enter the formula =D51–D52. This formula computes the monthly principal payment for January by subtracting the monthly interest payment (which we have not yet defined) from the total monthly payment (cell D51).

Now, you can use the Copy command to copy the formulas from D51 and D53 to the other cells in the Debt Service section. First, highlight the range D51:D53 and select Copy from the Edit menu. Then, point to cell D55 and press Enter to copy the formulas from cells D51 and D53 to cells D55 and D57. When the copy is completed, the range D55:D57 is highlighted. To make the next copy, select the Copy command again, point to cell D59, and press Enter. This command creates another copy of the formulas, this time in cells D59 and D61. Continue to copy the formulas in this way to cells D63 and D65, D67 and D69, D71 and D73, and D75 and D77.

Next, go back and create the formulas that calculate the interest for each different type of debt. Enter these formulas in cells D52, D56, D60, D64, D68, D72, and D76. The following table, Figure 13-6, lists the formulas you enter in these cells. Although these formulas are similar, and you might think you could create them by entering only one and then making copies, you must type each one individually.

Notice that each formula refers to a cell in column C—in which you'll enter an interest rate assumption—and to a cell in the Balances area of the template. Also notice that the references to the cells in column C are mixed references: absolute in respect to column C and relative in respect to the row. When you copy these formulas across the spreadsheet, Works retains the mixed references.

After you enter these formulas, move the cursor to cell D78 and enter a line of six hyphens preceded by two spaces. Then, with the cursor on cell D78, select Copy from the Edit menu, highlight cell D80, and press Enter. This command duplicates the dashed line from cell D78 to cell D80. Now, move to cell D79 and enter the formula

=D51+D55+D59+D63+D67+D71+D75

This formula sums the total monthly expenditures for each type of debt.

Now you're ready to enter the formulas that define the values in the Fixed Expenses and Variable Expenses sections. The table in Figure 13-7 lists the formulas you enter in column D in these sections. As you can see, most of these formulas simply refer to the value in the adjacent cell in column C. For instance, the formula in cell D83, =C83, refers to the value in cell C83. (Because the cells in column C are currently empty, these formulas return the value 0.)

Cell	Formula
D52	=$C52/12*C204
D56	=$C56/12*C205
D60	=$C60/12*C206
D64	=$C64/12*C207
D68	=$C68/12*C208
D72	=$C72/12*C209
D76	=$C76/12*C210

Figure 13-6. Formulas for column D in the Debt Service section of the Expenses area.

Cell	Formula
D82	=$C82*D44
D83	=C83
D88	=C88
D89	=C89
D90	=C90
D91	=C91
D97	=SUM(D82:D96)
D101	=C101
D105	=C105
D106	=C106
D108	=C108
D109	=C109
D110	=C110
D112	=C112
D113	=C113
D115	=C115
D116	=C116
D117	=C117
D118	=C118
D119	=C119
D120	=C120
D125	=C125
D127	=SUM(D100:D126)
D129	=D79+D97+D127

Figure 13-7. Formulas for column D in the Fixed Expenses and Variable Expenses sections of the Expenses area.

Once again, you can use the Fill Down command on the Edit menu to help you enter some of these formulas. Instead of entering manually each formula in a series of similar formulas, type only the first formula, and then use the Fill Down command to create the others.

In addition to entering the formulas in Figure 13-7 in column D, enter a label consisting of two spaces followed by six hyphens (------) in the following cells: D96, D98, D126, and D128. These labels serve as "underlines" for groups of figures that you plan to add. (You can use the Copy command to help you enter these labels.) In cell D130, enter a label consisting of six equal signs preceded by two spaces (======).

Now, you're ready to copy the formulas from column D to columns E through O. To do so, highlight the range D51:O130 and select Fill Right from the Edit menu.

Figure 13-8 shows the upper left corner of the Expenses area after you complete this part of the template.

As in the Income area, many formulas in the Expenses area simply carry forward the assumptions from column D into columns E through O. Other formulas, however, compute an expenditure for a particular month. For example, the formula in cell D52, *=$C52/12*C204*, computes credit card interest for the month of January. After you copy the formula, cell E52 contains a similar formula, *=$C52/12*D204*, which computes credit card interest for February. Cell F52 contains the formula *=$C52/12*E204*, which computes credit card interest for March. (Because the cells in column C are currently empty, these formulas all return the value 0.)

Notice that the reference to cell C52 in these formulas is constant; that is, it did not change as the formula was duplicated across row 52 from column D to columns E, F, G, and so on. The reference remains constant because the reference to column C in the formula is absolute, as indicated by the $ which precedes that part of the reference. This type of reference—in which the column or row portion of the reference is absolute and the other portion is relative—is called a mixed reference. The table in Figure 13-6 on page 380 contains a number of formulas that use mixed references to cells in column C. Notice that when Works copies those formulas, the references to column C remain fixed in every case.

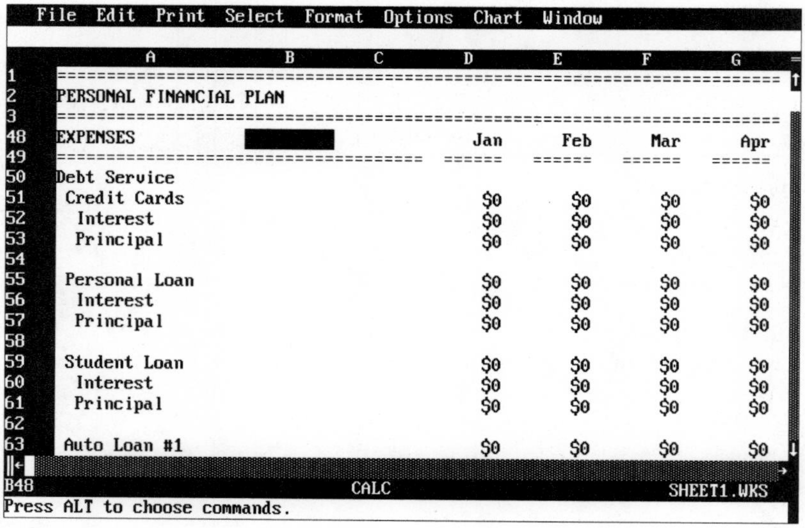

Figure 13-8.

The Recap Area

Now you're ready to enter the formulas that define the Recap area. To begin, move to cell D135 and enter the formula =D44. This formula refers to cell D44, which contains a formula that computes total income. Then, move to cell D136 and enter the formula =−D129. This formula refers to cell D129, which contains a formula that computes total expenses. Next, enter a label consisting of two spaces followed by six hyphens in cell D137. (You could also create this label by copying an existing, similar label.) Then move to cell D138 and enter the formula =D135+D136. This formula computes the monthly net income for January by subtracting total expenses from total income. Finally, move the cursor to cell D139 and enter a label consisting of two spaces followed by six equal signs. (Once again, you can copy a similar label.)

After you enter the formulas and the label in column D of the Recap area, copy them from column D to columns E through P. To make these copies, highlight the range D135:P139 and select the Fill Right command from the Edit menu. After Works copies the formulas, press the Calc key ([F9]) to recalculate the spreadsheet and update all the copied formulas. Figure 13-9 shows the left portion of the Recap area after you perform these steps.

Because the formulas in column D in the Recap area contain relative references, those references change as the formulas are copied across the spreadsheet. For instance, cell D135 in this area contains the formula =D44, cell E135 contains the formula =E44, cell F135 the formula =F44, and so on.

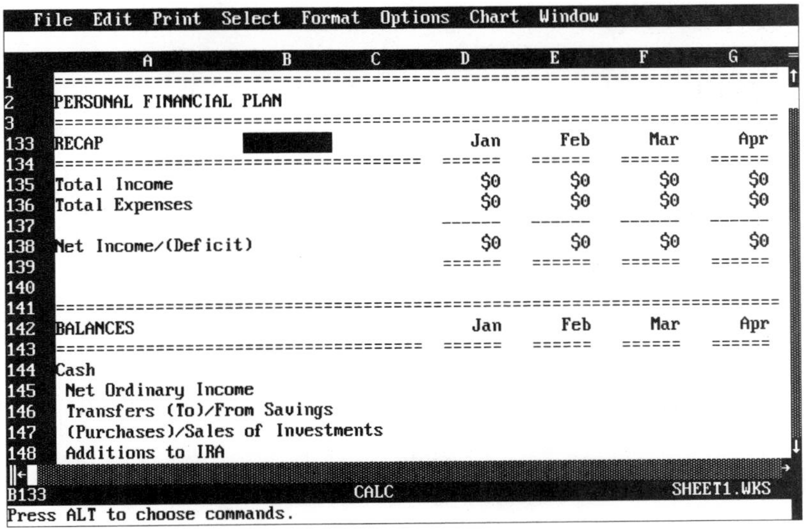

Figure 13-9.

The Balances Area

After you complete the Recap area, you're ready to enter the formulas for the last area of the template: the Balances area. The table in Figure 13-10 lists the formulas you enter in column D in this area. As before, you can use the Fill Down command on the Edit menu to help you enter some of these formulas.

Cell	Formula	Explanation
D144	=C152	Refers to prior month's ending cash balance assumption
D145	=D138	Refers to net income as calculated in cell D138
D152	=SUM(D144:D151)	Computes ending cash balance
D154	=C158	Refers to prior month's savings account ending balance assumption
D155	=−D146	Refers to transfers (to)/from savings entry in cell D146
D156	=$C156/12*C158	Computes monthly interest income from savings
D158	=SUM(D154:D157)	Computes ending savings account balance
D160	=C165	Refers to prior month's marketable securities ending assumption
D165	=SUM(D160:D164)	Computes ending marketable securities balance
D167	=C172	Refers to prior month's IRA ending balance assumption
D168	=−D148	Refers to additions to IRA entry in cell D148
D172	=SUM(D167:D171)	Computes ending IRA balance
D174	=C178	Refers to prior month's house ending value assumption
D175	=$C175/12*D174	Computes monthly appreciation of house
D176	=D103	Refers to improvements expenditure entry in cell D103
D178	=SUM(D174:D177)	Computes ending value of house
D180	=C184	Refers to prior month's other real estate ending value assumption
D181	=D149	Refers to purchases of real estate entry in cell D149
D182	=$C182/12*D180	Computes monthly appreciation of other real estate
D184	=SUM(D180:D183)	Computes ending value of other real estate
D187	=C190	Refers to prior month's auto 1 ending value assumption

Figure 13-10. Formulas for column D in the Balances area.   (continued)

Figure 13-10. Continued.

Cell	Formula	Explanation
D188	=C188	Refers to auto 1 depreciation assumption in cell C188
D190	=D187+D188	Computes ending value of automobile 1
D192	=C195	Refers to prior month's auto 2 ending value assumption
D193	=C193	Refers to auto 2 depreciation assumption in cell C193
D195	=D192+D193	Computes ending value of automobile 2
D197	=C197+D102+D108	Computes value of personal property: prior month's balance plus expenditures for furniture (D102) and clothing (D108)
D199	=D190+D195+D197	Computes total other assets
D201	=D152+D158+D165 +D172+D184+D199	Computes total assets
D204	=C204−D53+D150	Computes credit card balance: subtracts credit card balances (cell D53) from prior month's balance and adds current purchases on credit cards (cell D150)
D205	=C205−D57	Computes personal loan balance: subtracts repayment of personal loan (cell D57) from prior month's balance
D206	=C206−D61	Computes student loan balance: subtracts repayment of student loan (cell D61) from prior month's balance
D207	=C207−D65	Computes auto loan #1 balance: subtracts repayment of auto loan #1 (cell D65) from prior month's balance
D208	=C208−D69	Computes auto loan #2 balance: subtracts repayment of auto loan #2 (cell D69) from prior month's balance
D209	=C209−D73	Computes home mortgage balance: subtracts repayment of home mortgage (cell D73) from prior month's balance
D210	=C210−D77	Computes other mortgage balance: subtracts repayment of other mortgage (cell D77) from prior month's balance
D212	=SUM(D204:D211)	Computes total liabilities
D213	=D201−D212	Computes net worth: subtracts total liabilities (cell D212) from total assets
D215	=D212+D213	Computes total liabilities and net worth

386

Notice that we did not list a formula for every cell in column D in the Balances area. For example, we skipped cell D148, which would hold January additions to your IRA. In fact, we only entered formulas in cells whose value we could compute from other values in column D or from assumptions that you enter in column C. Typically, we can derive by formula only values in rows that will have regular, predictable activity. You must enter the values in other rows manually. You'll learn how later in this chapter.

After you enter the formulas from the preceding table, enter a label consisting of two spaces followed by six hyphens in each of the following cells: D151, D157, D164, D171, D177, D183, D189, D194, D198, D200, D211, and D214. These labels serve as "underlines" for columns of figures that you plan to add. You can use the Copy command to help you enter these labels. Next, enter a label consisting of two spaces followed by six equal signs in cells D202 and D216.

Now, copy the formulas and labels in the Balances area from column D to columns E through O. To make these copies, highlight the range D144:O216 and select Fill Right from the Edit menu. Figure 13-11 shows the upper left corner of the Balances area with these formulas in place.

As in the Income and Expenses areas, many formulas in the Balances area simply carry forward the assumptions from column D of a row into columns E through O in that row. Other formulas carry forward values from other rows. For example, the formulas in row 144 reference the entry in row 152 in the preceding column: Cell D144 contains the formula *=C152*, cell E144 contains the formula *=D152*, and so on. These formulas equate the beginning cash balance for one period with the ending

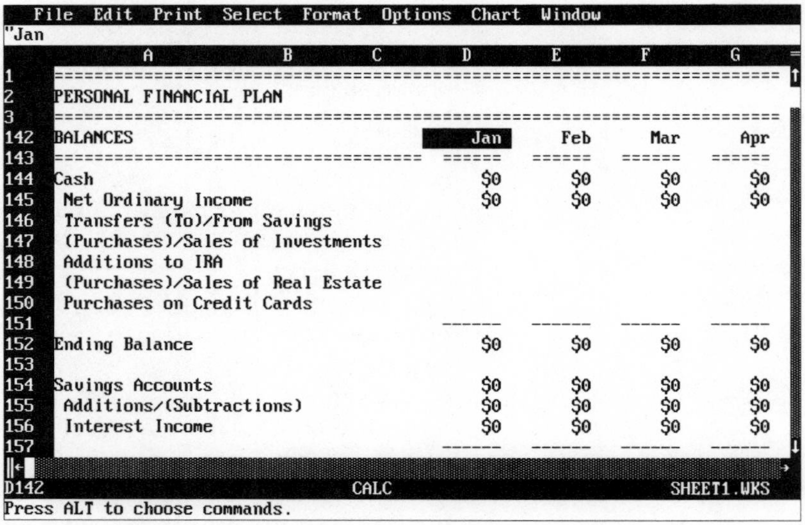

Figure 13-11.

cash balance for the previous period. The formulas in rows 154, 160, 167, 174, 180, 187, and 192 are similar to those in row 144. (Because the cells in column C are currently empty, all these formulas return the value 0.)

As in the Expenses area, other formulas in the Balances area make a simple computation. The formula in cell D156, for example, =$C156/12*C158, computes interest income from savings for the month of January. After you copy the formula, cell E156 contains a similar formula, =$C156/12*D158, which computes interest income from savings for February. Notice that the formula retains an absolute reference to column C as Works copies it across the spreadsheet.

The SUM Formulas

Next, enter a series of SUM functions in column P. Each formula sums the contents of columns D through O in one row of the spreadsheet, creating a series of annual totals in column P. For example, cell P6 will contain the formula =SUM(D6:O6), which sums the values in row 6. The table in Figure 13-12 shows the formulas you enter in column P.

You can, of course, enter each formula manually, but you'll probably want to enter the formula in cell D6 and then use the Copy command and the Fill Down command to copy it to the other cells. To begin, enter the formula =SUM(D6:O6) in cell P6. Then, position the cursor in cell P6. (It should already be there.) Select Copy from the Edit menu, highlight cell P8, and press Enter. This command copies the formula from cell P6 to cell P8. Because the formula contains relative references, the entry in cell P8 is =SUM(D8:O8). Now, select the range P8:P13 and select Fill Down from the Edit menu. Selecting this command copies the formula from cell P8 to cells P9 through P13.

Now, you can use the formulas in rows 6 through 13 to create the formulas in rows 20 through 27. Highlight the range P6:P13, select Copy from the Edit menu, highlight cell P20, and press Enter. This one command duplicates the formulas from cells P6 through P13 to the range P20:P27.

Continue in this way—entering selected formulas and using the Copy and Fill Down commands to create the others—to create the formulas listed in the table.

Cell	Formula	Cell	Formula
P6	=SUM(D6:O6)	P90	=SUM(D90:O90)
P8	=SUM(D8:O8)	P91	=SUM(D91:O91)
P9	=SUM(D9:O9)	P93	=SUM(D93:O93)
P10	=SUM(D10:O10)	P94	=SUM(D94:O94)
P11	=SUM(D11:O11)	P95	=SUM(D95:O95)
P12	=SUM(D12:O12)	P101	=SUM(D101:O101)
P13	=SUM(D13:O13)	P102	=SUM(D102:O102)

Figure 13-12. *Formulas for column P.*   *(continued)*

388

Figure 13-12. Continued.

Cell	Formula	Cell	Formula
P20	=SUM(D20:O20)	P103	=SUM(D103:O103)
P22	=SUM(D22:O22)	P105	=SUM(D105:O105)
P23	=SUM(D23:O23)	P106	=SUM(D106:O106)
P24	=SUM(D24:O24)	P108	=SUM(D108:O108)
P25	=SUM(D25:O25)	P109	=SUM(D109:O109)
P26	=SUM(D26:O26)	P110	=SUM(D110:O110)
P27	=SUM(D27:O27)	P112	=SUM(D112:O112)
P36	=SUM(D36:O36)	P113	=SUM(D113:O113)
P37	=SUM(D37:O37)	P115	=SUM(D115:O115)
P38	=SUM(D38:O38)	P116	=SUM(D116:O116)
P39	=SUM(D39:O39)	P117	=SUM(D117:O117)
P40	=SUM(D40:O40)	P118	=SUM(D118:O118)
P51	=SUM(D51:O51)	P119	=SUM(D119:O119)
P52	=SUM(D52:O52)	P120	=SUM(D120:O120)
P53	=SUM(D53:O53)	P121	=SUM(D121:O121)
P55	=SUM(D55:O55)	P122	=SUM(D122:O122)
P56	=SUM(D56:O56)	P123	=SUM(D123:O123)
P57	=SUM(D57:O57)	P124	=SUM(D124:O124)
P59	=SUM(D59:O59)	P125	=SUM(D125:O125)
P60	=SUM(D60:O60)	P145	=SUM(D145:O145)
P61	=SUM(D61:O61)	P146	=SUM(D146:O146)
P63	=SUM(D63:O63)	P147	=SUM(D147:O147)
P64	=SUM(D64:O64)	P148	=SUM(D148:O148)
P65	=SUM(D65:O65)	P149	=SUM(D149:O149)
P67	=SUM(D67:O67)	P150	=SUM(D150:O150)
P68	=SUM(D68:O68)	P155	=SUM(D155:O155)
P69	=SUM(D69:O69)	P156	=SUM(D156:O156)
P71	=SUM(D71:O71)	P161	=SUM(D161:O161)
P72	=SUM(D72:O72)	P162	=SUM(D162:O162)
P73	=SUM(D73:O73)	P163	=SUM(D163:O163)
P75	=SUM(D75:O75)	P168	=SUM(D168:O168)
P76	=SUM(D76:O76)	P169	=SUM(D169:O169)
P77	=SUM(D77:O77)	P170	=SUM(D170:O170)
P82	=SUM(D82:O82)	P175	=SUM(D175:O175)
P83	=SUM(D83:O83)	P176	=SUM(D176:O176)
P85	=SUM(D85:O85)	P181	=SUM(D181:O181)
P86	=SUM(D86:O86)	P182	=SUM(D182:O182)
P88	=SUM(D88:O88)	P188	=SUM(D188:O188)
P89	=SUM(D89:O89)	P193	=SUM(D193:O193)

Totals in Column P

To complete the template, create the formulas that compute totals for groups of sums in column P. To create these formulas, simply copy formulas you've already created in column O into column P. The table in Figure 13-13 lists the cells from which and to which you copy the formulas.

Let's look at one example. To create the first set of totals, first highlight the range O14:O18. Next, select Copy from the Edit menu, move the cursor to cell P14, and press Enter. Works copies the formulas and labels from the range O14:O18 to the range P14:P18. Because the formulas in the range O14:O18 contain relative references to cells in column O, the formulas in the copy are adjusted to refer to cells in column P. To recalculate the spreadsheet, press the Calc key ([F9]). Figure 13-14 shows this part of the spreadsheet after you perform these steps.

Copy from	Copy to
O14:O18	P14
O28:O33	P28
O41:O45	P41
O78:O80	P78
O96:O98	P96
O126:O130	P126

Figure 13-13. *Formulas from column O for column P.*

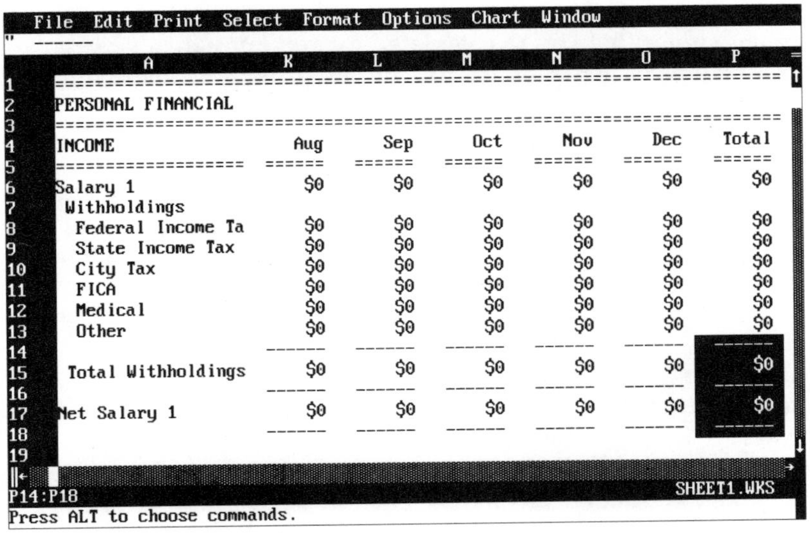

Figure 13-14.

Saving the Template

After you create the last formula in column P, the template is built. Before you do anything else, save the spreadsheet (or resave it, if you have been saving it routinely as you go along). To save the spreadsheet for the first time, select Save As from the File menu. Then, if you want to save the file in a directory other than the current one, choose that directory from the Other Drives & Directories list box and choose OK. Next, type a name (such as *FAMILY.WKS*), and press Enter or choose OK to save the file. If you want to save the file in the current directory, simply type a filename and press Enter or choose OK. If you've already saved the spreadsheet, save it again by selecting Save from the File menu.

USING THE SPREADSHEET

Now that you've created the Personal Financial Plan, you're ready to put it to work. To begin, you must open the spreadsheet. (If you just created the template, skip this step.) First, choose Open from the File menu. Next, if the file you want to open is not in the current directory, select the directory that contains the file from the Other Drives & Directories list box and choose OK. Then, either type the filename under which you saved the template, including the extension (for example, *FAMILY.WKS*), or highlight the name of the spreadsheet in the list, and press Enter or choose OK. If the file you want to open is in the current directory, simply type or highlight the filename and then press Enter or choose OK.

To begin using the spreadsheet, you need to enter a series of assumptions in column C. Then, go back and enter the value of any irregular (non-repeating) income or expense items in appropriate spots in the spreadsheet. You also have to adjust any income or expense items that Works calculated for you but which you know will be different from the predicted amount. Finally, you'll recalculate the spreadsheet.

Entering Assumptions

At this point, you're ready to enter some basic assumptions in column C. Some of these figures are percentages; others are dollar amounts. The spreadsheet uses your assumptions to make a variety of computations. For example, the spreadsheet uses the annual salary assumption you enter in cell C6 as the basis for computing the monthly salary amounts in cells D6 to O6. Similarly, the spreadsheet uses the values you enter in cells C100 to C124 to compute monthly expenses.

The table in Figure 13-15 explains the meaning of each assumption in column C. To enter these assumptions, move the cursor to the appropriate cell and enter the appropriate value. Then, if necessary, use the Percent command to assign the Percent format with two decimal places to the cell. The sample spreadsheet in Figure 13-1 beginning on page 364 shows you how to enter these assumptions. Remember, however, to enter your own assumptions in your spreadsheet—not those in the example.

Notice that we didn't enter assumptions for every expense category—many expenses are not regular, or predictable, from month to month. For example, you probably pay property taxes only once a year. We entered assumptions for those expenses that we think are predictable but did not enter assumptions for other expenses. You'll learn how to enter them manually later in the chapter.

If you are like most people, you won't need to enter a figure for every single assumption in the spreadsheet. If a particular account does not apply to you, leave the cell containing the corresponding assumption blank or enter a 0.

Cell	Assumption	Format, Decimal Places
C6	Annual dollar amount of salary 1	
C8	Estimated annual federal income tax withholding for salary 1	
C9	Estimated annual state income tax withholding for salary 1	
C10	Estimated annual city income tax withholding for salary 1 (if any)	
C11	FICA percentage for salary 1 (usually 7.05%)	Percent, 2
C12	Estimated annual medical insurance withholding for salary 1 (if any)	
C13	Estimated annual other withholding for salary 1 (if any)	
C20	Annual dollar amount of salary 2	
C22	Estimated annual federal income tax withholding for salary 2	
C23	Estimated annual state income tax withholding for salary 2	
C24	Estimated annual city income tax withholding for salary 2 (if any)	
C25	FICA percentage for salary 2 (usually 7.05%)	Percent, 2
C26	Estimated annual medical insurance withholding for salary 2 (if any)	
C27	Estimated annual other withholding for salary 2 (if any)	
C38	Estimated monthly rental income (if any)	
C51	Monthly payment on credit cards (if any)	
C52	Current annual interest rate on credit cards (if any)	Percent, 2
C55	Monthly payment on personal loan (if any)	
C56	Current annual interest rate on personal loan (if any)	Percent, 2
C59	Monthly payment on student loan (if any)	
C60	Current annual interest rate on student loan (if any)	Percent, 2
C63	Monthly payment on auto loan 1 (if any)	
C64	Current annual interest rate on auto loan 1 (if any)	Percent, 2
C67	Monthly payment on auto loan 2 (if any)	

Figure 13-15. *Basic assumptions for financial plan.*   *(continued)*

Figure 13-15. Continued.

Cell	Assumption	Format, Decimal Places
C68	Current annual interest rate on auto loan 2 (if any)	Percent, 2
C71	Monthly payment on home mortgage (if any)	
C72	Current annual interest rate on home mortgage (if any)	Percent, 2
C75	Monthly payment on other mortgage (if any)	
C76	Current annual interest rate on other mortgage (if any)	Percent, 2
C82	Percentage of total net income to tithe	Percent, 2
C83	Estimated monthly child care expense	
C88	Estimated monthly gas and electric expense	
C89	Estimated monthly water expense	
C90	Estimated monthly telephone expense	
C91	Estimated monthly food and household supplies expense	
C101	Estimated monthly house maintenance expense	
C105	Estimated monthly gasoline expense	
C106	Estimated monthly automobile maintenance expense	
C108	Estimated monthly clothing expense	
C109	Estimated monthly diapers expense	
C110	Estimated monthly clothes cleaning expense	
C112	Estimated monthly doctor's bills expense	
C113	Estimated monthly prescription drugs expense	
C115	Estimated monthly athletic club dues expense	
C116	Estimated monthly newspaper expense	
C117	Estimated monthly books and magazines expense	
C118	Estimated monthly cable TV expense	
C119	Estimated monthly entertainment expense	
C120	Estimated monthly meals out expense	
C125	Estimated monthly other variable expenses	
C152	Prior month's ending cash balance	
C156	Current annual interest rate earned by savings account (if any)	Percent, 2
C158	Prior month's ending savings account balance (if any)	
C165	Market value of marketable securities at end of prior month (if any)	
C172	Market value of IRA at end of prior month (if any)	
C175	Estimated annual percentage appreciation of house (if any)	Percent, 2
C178	Estimated market value of house at end of prior month (if any)	
C182	Estimated annual percentage appreciation of other real estate (if any)	Percent, 2

(continued)

Figure 13-15. Continued.

Cell	Assumption	Format, Decimal Places
C184	Estimated market value of other real estate at end of prior month (if any)	
C188	Estimated monthly depreciation (loss in resale value) of automobile 1	
C190	Estimated market value of automobile 1 at end of prior month (if any)	
C193	Estimated monthly depreciation (loss in resale value) of automobile 2	
C195	Estimated market value of automobile 2 at end of prior month (if any)	
C197	Estimated market value of personal property at end of prior month (if any)	
C204	Prior month's ending balance of all credit card accounts (if any)	
C205	Prior month's ending balance of all personal loans (if any)	
C206	Prior month's ending balance of all student loans (if any)	
C207	Prior month's ending balance of auto loan number 1 (if any)	
C208	Prior month's ending balance of auto loan number 2 (if any)	
C209	Prior month's ending balance of home mortgage (if any)	
C210	Prior month's ending balance of other mortgage (if any)	

The structure of this template illustrates an important guideline for creating new spreadsheets: Always make your assumptions—the fundamental values and percentages on which the formulas in the spreadsheet depend—explicit. That is, enter those assumptions in cells by themselves instead of burying them in formulas. Making your assumptions explicit enables you to change those assumptions more easily. It also makes the spreadsheet easier to understand—you don't have to figure out the assumptions on which the spreadsheet is based; you can simply read them from the spreadsheet itself.

Entering Irregular Items

As we mentioned a few pages ago, not every income and expense item can be computed by the spreadsheet. Some expenses and receipts occur irregularly or infrequently—once a year, for instance, or once a quarter. Others occur monthly but vary widely from month to month. You'll have to enter this sort of income or expense item manually. In other words, you must move to the cell at the intersection of the appropriate column (month) and row (account) and type a number representing that item.

For example, row 40 in the spreadsheet contains the Other Income account, intended for unusual income items that don't fit in any other account in this row. By definition, the entries in this account will be irregular and variable. For this reason, the template does not require you to enter an assumption for this row. If you expect to receive income in this category, enter the amount of that receipt in the proper column of row 40. In Figure 13-1 on page 364, we entered the value $150 in cell G40 in the sample spreadsheet. This number represents a special receipt of $150 in April of the coming year. To record this receipt, we moved the cursor to cell G40, typed the number *150*, and pressed Enter.

The table in Figure 13-16 lists the accounts that you have to define manually and the rows in which those accounts occur. Use this table as a guide as you enter your infrequent and irregular expenses in the spreadsheet. Keep in mind that you don't have to make an entry in every row. If a particular account does not apply to you, simply leave the corresponding row blank.

Row	Description	Enter
39	Gift Income	Gift income for each month (if any)
40	Other Income	Other income for each month (if any)
85	Property Taxes	Property taxes paid in each month (if any)
86	Homeowner's Insurance	Homeowner's insurance premium paid in each month (if any)
93	Life Insurance	Life insurance premium paid in each month (if any)
94	Auto Insurance	Automobile insurance premium paid in each month (if any)
95	Other Med Insurance	Other medical insurance premium paid in each month (if any)
102	Furniture	Furniture expenditures for each month (if any)
103	Improvements	Home improvements expenditures for each month (if any)
121	Gifts	Gift expenditures for each month (if any)
122	Vacation	Vacation expenditures for each month (if any)
123	Haircuts	Haircuts expenditures for each month (if any)
124	Income Taxes	Income Taxes expense for each month (if any)
150	Purchases on Credit	Amount of purchases made on credit cards (if any)

Figure 13-16. Irregular items in the financial plan.

Changing Regular Items

Now, you need to adjust any income or expense items that Works calculated but which you know will be different from the predicted amount. This class of items includes expenses and income items that vary slightly from month to month, such as your gas or electric bill. It also includes items that may be regular at one point in the year but which change or even stop at another point. Your FICA tax, for example, drops to 0 if you reach the annual limit.

To make a change to a calculated value, move the cursor to the cell that contains the value you need to change and enter a new value. For example, notice in Figure 13-1 that we changed the Credit Cards expenditure for April (cell G51) from $10 to $25. To make this change, we simply moved the cursor to cell G51, typed *25*, and pressed Enter. Similarly, notice that we changed the Gas and Electric expenditure for March (cell F88) from $200 to $175, the Gas and Electric expenditure for April (cell G88) to $150, and the Gas and Electric expenditure for May (cell H88) to $100. To make these changes, we simply moved the cursor to cell F88, typed *175*, pressed the Right Arrow key to move to cell G88, typed *150*, pressed the Right Arrow key to move to cell H88, typed *100*, and pressed Enter.

Remember that we entered formulas in many of the cells in the Income and Expenses areas that simply refer to the adjacent cell to the left. For example, cell D51 contains the formula =C51, cell E51 contains the formula =D51, and so on. We called this use of formulas the "carry-forward technique." The carry-forward technique comes in handy when you make changes such as the ones explained in the preceding paragraph. When you enter a value in a cell that contains a carry-forward formula, the value replaces the formula. Then, the formula to the right of the cell in which you entered the value picks up that new value and passes it along through the spreadsheet. In other words, the spreadsheet carries the new value forward. For instance, notice that cells H51, I51, J51, and so on in Figure 13-1 on pages 366 and 367 all display the value *25*—the value we entered in cell G51. This occurs because each of these cells contains a carry-forward formula. Likewise, notice that the value we entered in cell H88 has been carried forward into cell I88, which contains the formula =H88.

When you enter a value in a row, the spreadsheet formulas carry that value forward until you enter another value in another cell in the row. When you enter another value, the spreadsheet passes that value along across the row, and so on. For example, notice that cell J88 in Figure 13-1 contains the value $150. To make this change, we moved the cursor to cell J88 and entered the value $150. Notice that this new value was passed along from cell J88 to cells K88, L88, and M88. Cell N88 contains the value $175, and cell O88 the value $200.

The table in Figure 13-17 on the following page lists several rows and accounts that might be candidates for this kind of change. Of course, you don't have to make changes to each of these rows, and you might well need to make changes to rows that are not included in the table. Works does not carry your changes forward until you recalculate the spreadsheet. (You'll do that shortly.)

Row	Account
11	FICA Withholding (Salary 1)
13	Other Withholding (Salary 1)
25	FICA Withholding (Salary 2)
27	Other Withholding (Salary 2)
51	Credit Cards payment
88	Gas and Electric expense
89	Water expense
90	Telephone expense
101	House Maintenance expense
105	Gasoline expense
106	Automobile Maintenance expense
108	New Clothing expense
112	Doctor's Bill expense
113	Prescription Drugs expense
119	Entertainment expense

Figure 13-17. Regular accounts that are subject to change.

Making Balance Sheet Transfers

You have one final thing to do. Rows 146 to 149 allow you to record transfers between the Cash account and other asset accounts: Savings, Investments, IRA, and Real Estate. The table in Figure 13-18 describes the purpose of each row.

To record a transfer from Cash to one of these accounts (a reduction of cash and an increase in an investment), enter a negative number in the appropriate cell. For example, notice that we entered the value *–100* in each cell in row 146 in the sample spreadsheet in Figure 13-1 on pages 370–371. These negative numbers, indicated by parentheses in the spreadsheet, represent transfers from Cash to Savings. Similarly, notice that we entered the value *–4000* in cell G148 to represent a transfer from Cash to an IRA account.

Row	Description	Enter
146	Transfers (To)/From Savings	Amount transferred to/from savings each month
147	(Purchases)/Sales of Investments	Investments purchased or sold each month
148	Additions to IRA	Amount invested in IRA each month
149	(Purchases)/Sales of Real Estate	Real estate purchased or sold each month

Figure 13-18. Balance sheet transfers.

To record a transfer from an investment account to cash (an increase of cash and a reduction of one of the other accounts), enter a positive number in the appropriate cell. For example, the value $4,000 in cell G147 in Figure 13-1 represents a sale of an investment for $4,000 cash.

The spreadsheet passes any entry you make in one of these rows to another row in the Balances area. For example, each cell in row 155, Additions/(Subtractions) to Savings, refers to the corresponding cell in row 146: Cell D155 contains the formula =−D146, cell E155 contains the formula =−E146, and so on. If you enter a negative amount in any cell in row 146, the corresponding cell in row 155 displays the same number with a positive sign—an addition to savings. For instance, notice that cell D146 in Figure 13-1 contains the value −100, which appears in your spreadsheet as ($100), and cell D155 in that same spreadsheet displays the positive value $100. If you enter a positive number in any cell in row 146, the corresponding cell in row 155 displays the same number in parentheses.

Because the spreadsheet distributes the values you enter in rows 146 through 149 to the appropriate cells in the other parts of the Balances area, you don't have to post these transfers manually. Be careful, however, not to enter transfers that cause either the cash balance or one of the other asset balances to become negative.

Calculating the Spreadsheet

After you post all your assumptions, enter your irregular expenses and receipts, and make any necessary changes to regular items, select Calculate Now from the Options menu or press the Calc key ([F9]). The spreadsheet updates all its formulas: The carry-forward formulas pass the values from columns C and D to columns E through O; other formulas compute payroll withholding, interest income, and interest expense; and the SUM functions compute the totals for each row and for each month.

Now, review the result. Is the spreadsheet unrealistic? Is the monthly net income consistently negative? Does the cash balance ever become negative? Is the balance in some other asset account negative? If so, adjust your entries to correct the problem. You might change the amount of a variable expense estimate to avoid negative cash flows, reduce the amount of a balance sheet transfer to avoid negative cash or other asset balances, or create a balance sheet transfer to fund an unusual expenditure. After you make each adjustment, recalculate the spreadsheet so that the effect of the transfer becomes apparent.

Printing and Saving

After you set up your forecast, save the spreadsheet into a new file. To do this, select Save As from the File menu. If necessary, change the current directory; then type a new name for the spreadsheet and press Enter or choose OK. Choose a name that clearly identifies the file—for example, *BUDG88* for your 1988 forecast.

Be sure to save your filled-in Personal Financial Plan under a name other than the name you used for the original, empty template. If you save a filled-in spreadsheet under the same name as the original template, the filled-in version replaces the original.

To print the entire Personal Financial Plan, first choose Layout from the Print menu and replace any print settings you want to change. For example, if you have a wide-carriage printer and plan to print this spreadsheet onto 11-by-14-inch paper, you might want to change the Page Width setting from *8.5"* to *14"*. You might also want to change the Top, Bottom, Left, and Right margins, and define a header and a footer. Next, you can choose Font from the Print menu to select the style and size of type you want Works to use to print the report. (If you choose a proportional font, such as Times, then certain features such as underlining and boldface will not work.) If you want to squeeze the entire report onto one page, choose a relatively compressed font (such as Elite) and a small point size (such as 6 or 8).

After you adjust the layout, select Print from the Print menu to display the Print dialog box. Adjust any settings you want to change in that dialog box, and then choose Print to print the report.

To print only a portion of the financial plan, first choose Set Print Area from the Print menu to define the area you want to print. Then, use the Layout and Font commands to make any needed adjustments to the Works print settings, select Print from the Print menu, and choose Print.

Using the Plan

Now you can begin to use the Personal Financial Plan. The completed spreadsheet is your personal financial plan, a tool you can use to measure your financial performance for the coming year. Study the plan carefully to understand exactly what your condition will be at each point in the coming year. Are there any tight spots? Keep those in mind as unexpected expenses arise and, if necessary, modify your plans to avoid a problem. Will you need to consider any new investments during the year? The spreadsheet can give you the notice you need to plan for these investments in advance. Are there any expenditures you want to make but cannot currently afford? Use the financial plan to develop a savings strategy that will make your dream possible.

At the end of each month, sit down with your credit card receipts and check stubs and compare your actual expenditures to the estimates in the spreadsheet. Such a review helps you verify the accuracy of your estimates. If you find estimates that are either too high or too low, adjust them to be more in line with your actual activities. To adjust an income or expense item, move to the cell that falls in that row and in the column for the current month, and enter the new estimate. The spreadsheet carries your change forward from that point to the end of the year. If you cannot fit an expenditure into any of the defined accounts, you can add a new row to the spreadsheet. (You'll learn how to do that in the next section.)

MODIFICATIONS

Two modifications might make your Personal Financial Plan more useful. First, you can add rows to the spreadsheet to hold new accounts. Second, you can create one or more charts from the data in the spreadsheet. This section shows you how to make those changes.

Adding Rows

From time to time, you may need to add a row to the spreadsheet to hold a new income or expense account. For example, suppose your rich uncle dies and leaves you a trust fund that pays you $500 per month. To include this new income item in the spreadsheet, you need to add a row to the Other Income section. Or suppose you buy a boat or an airplane and need to add several rows to hold expense accounts for gasoline, maintenance, and other expenses relating to that purchase.

The process for adding a new income or expense item to the spreadsheet is simple: Highlight the row above which you want to add the new row and select Insert from the Edit menu. This step inserts a new, blank row into the spreadsheet. To add more than one row, highlight the number of rows you want to add and select the Insert command. When the new row or rows are in place, enter labels in column A that define the contents of the rows, assumptions in column C that identify the normal amount of the expenditures, and formulas in columns D through O that compute the monthly amounts. If the expense or income item you add is not regular, don't enter the assumptions and formulas; instead, enter the appropriate numbers in the cells of the new row.

After you insert and define the new row, be sure that its contents are being included in the formulas that compute total income, total expenses, and so forth. This step can be tricky, but it usually is not. The contents of any new rows you add between rows 36 and 41 in the Income area, or between rows 82 and 96 or rows 100 and 126 in the Expenses area, are added to the totals (currently) in rows 42, 97, or 127 because we used SUM formulas to compute these totals. Whenever you add a new row between the rows that define the range for a SUM function, the range expands to include those new rows.

If you add the new rows outside these ranges, you'll have a bit tougher time. In that event, you'll have to edit and correct the appropriate formulas to be sure that they pick up the new values. Adding a new form of debt or investment is particularly tricky. Making such a change to the spreadsheet might require adding rows in both the Balances area (to hold the new asset or liability) and either the Income area (in the case of an asset, to report income generated by that asset) or the Expenses area (to reflect interest paid on debt). Be careful! Study the spreadsheet shown in Figure 13-1 carefully before you undertake this kind of modification.

Charting

Works lets you create one or more charts that display the information in the Personal Financial Plan graphically. To create a chart, highlight the range of cells that contain the information you want to depict, select New from the Chart menu to create a new chart, and then select View to view the chart. You can change the name of the chart, change its type, and enhance it with titles, legends, and other things.

For example, suppose you want to create a chart that illustrates the ending cash balance for each month. To do this, highlight the range D152:O152 (which contains the ending cash balances) and select New from the Chart menu. Next, highlight the range D142:O142 and choose X-Series from the Data menu to add text along the x axis. Then, choose View from the Chart menu in the Chart sublevel to display the chart shown in Figure 13-19. You can create as many as eight charts from the data in your Personal Financial Plan.

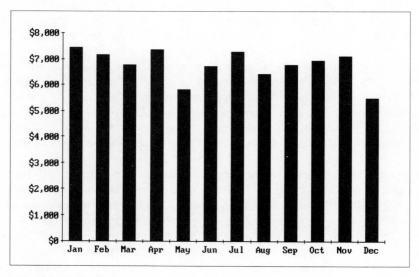

Figure 13-19.

CONCLUSION

Everyone needs a personal financial plan. Without one, you'll find it difficult or impossible to predict your financial future. As you have seen in this chapter, the Spreadsheet environment in Microsoft Works is the perfect tool for building personal financial plans. Unless your situation is exceedingly complex, you can use the Personal Financial Plan to forecast net income and cash balances for the year ahead.

Even if you don't use this spreadsheet, you can employ some of the tricks and techniques you learned in building it—including the carry-forward technique and the rule for always making your assumptions explicit. These techniques come in handy whenever you build a large or complex spreadsheet.

INDEX

DOUGLAS COBB

Douglas Cobb is president of The Cobb Group, Inc., a company that specializes in writing and publishing high-quality books, journals, and workbooks which support business software products. He is the coauthor of *Using 1-2-3*, perhaps the most successful computer book ever published. His most recent books published by Microsoft Press include the best-selling **EXCEL IN BUSINESS** and **DOUG COBB'S TIPS FOR MICROSOFT EXCEL**. In addition, Doug Cobb is a columnist for *PC Magazine*.

Other titles from Microsoft Press

RUNNING MS-DOS, 3rd edition

"This book is simply the definitive handbook of PC/MS-DOS...
written for both novices and experienced users."
BYTE magazine

A richly informative introduction to the MS-DOS and PC-DOS. Van Wolverton guides you through hands-on examples of PC- and MS-DOS commands and capabilities, illustrating not only how to enter the commands, but how PC- and MS-DOS respond. Wolverton explains how to work with files and directories on a floppy- or hard-disk system, how to effectively manage printers, monitors, and modems, how to automate frequently performed tasks with batch files, and much more. In addition, this book now features an expanded MS-DOS command reference with complete version-specific information and accompanying examples. Includes information on MS-DOS through version 3.3.
Van Wolverton, 496 pages, $22.95, softcover, Order Code 86-96262
$35.00, hardcover, Order Code 86-96270

SUPERCHARGING MS-DOS
The Microsoft Guide to High Performance Computing for the Experienced PC User

"Supercharging MS-DOS is a valuable addition to any PC user's
reference library. For advanced MS-DOS users and software
programmers it's a must."
Microtimes

When you're ready for more power, this sequel to RUNNING MS-DOS provides intermediate- to advanced-level tips on maximizing the power of MS-DOS. Control your screen and keyboard with ANSI.SYS; create, examine, or change any file; personalize your CONFIG.SYS file; and customize your menu system. Includes programs and dozens of valuable batch files.
Van Wolverton, 320 pages, $18.95, softcover, Order Code 86-95595

SUPERCHARGING MS-DOS is also available with a companion disk containing scores of batch files, script files, and programs from the book. Users will quickly learn how to create an interactive menu system, modify the system environment, and use the DEBUG function as well as other helpful utilities.
Supercharging MS-DOS Book/Disk Package, by Van Wolverton
320 pages, $34.95, softcover with one 5.25-inch disk, Order Code 86-96304

MANAGING YOUR MONEY WITH MANAGING YOUR MONEY

Includes information on the new tax laws! A valuable complement to Andrew Tobias's popular Managing Your Money software program. Included are strategies for managing your budget, evaluating your insurance needs, starting a personal investment portfolio, planning for your retirement or a child's education, and much more. Written for both IBM PC and Apple II users.
Jim Bartimo, 336 pages, $16.95, softcover, Order Code 86-95611

THE NEW WRITER

"Excellent, affordable guide to the art of writing on a computer...
Mitchell steers you clear of the rocks with sensible advice."
Computer Book Review

Discover how to write *well* with a computer and exploit its special features. Here are scores of techniques to help you revise and edit efficiently, avoid the common mistakes of computer writing, brainstorm on a computer, and use special computer tools such as idea processors, outliners, spell checkers, text analyzers, and indexers. If you use a computer in business or school, this book is guaranteed to make you a more powerful writer.
Joan P. Mitchell, 256 pages, $8.95, softcover, Order Code 86-95900

WORD PROCESSING POWER WITH MICROSOFT WORD, 2nd edition

*"Word owners should not be without Rinearson's book,
even if they read no more than a tenth of it."*
The New York Times

Here, from a Pulitzer Prize–winning author, is the most comprehensive, authoritative book on Microsoft Word. Includes special sections on style sheets, windows, creating personalized form letters, outlining with the glossary feature, and much more. The dozens of tested tips—many not included in the documentation—offer creative, timesaving ways to use Word in your work. Updated for version 3.1.
Peter Rinearson, 432 pages, $19.95, softcover, Order Code 86-95546

MICROSOFT WORD STYLE SHEETS BOOK/DISK PACKAGE

This book/disk package is a solid, timesaving value for Microsoft Word users. Style sheets—Word's innovative document formatting feature for IBM PCs and compatibles—are just a few keystrokes away with the help of this package. The accompanying 5.25-inch disk features more than one hundred ready-to-use style sheet templates, including models for correspondence, memos, newsletters, press releases, and résumés. This book/disk package is updated for version 4.0.
Peter Rinearson and JoAnne Woodcock
352 pages, $29.95, softcover with one 5.25-inch disk, Order Code 86-96320

FLIGHT SIMULATOR CO-PILOT

"...a must for all Flight Simulator devotees."
The New York Times

Master the Flight Simulator program and enjoy as you learn. Discover the fundamentals of flying "straight and level," climbing, descending, and turning, as well as some advanced maneuvers. Included are several exciting simulator trips using SubLOGIC's popular Scenery Disks. The perfect complement to Flight Simulator for the IBM PC and compatibles, the Commodore 64, Apple II, and Atari 800, XL, and XE computers.
Charles Gulick, 152 pages, $9.95, softcover, Order Code 86-95629

THE ALGORITHMIC IMAGE

"A well-written, thorough, and comprehensive celebration of a rapidly growing field."
PC World

A timely and artful look at the stunning accomplishments of the people in the computer graphics world. Science writer Robert Rivlin gives you the definitive history of the art and science of computer-generated graphics. Rivlin takes you inside the graphics scene at NASA's Jet Propulsion Laboratory, Lucasfilms, and the New York Institute of Technology, among others, and brings to light the technology that is changing the visual media in America. Packed with technological detail and scores of full-color photos. Voted best nonfiction book of 1987—Computer Press Association.
Robert Rivlin, 304 pages, $24.95, softcover, Order Code 86-95496

PROGRAMMERS AT WORK

*"This book is highly recommended—and as interesting a read
for the computerphobe as for the computerphile."*
PC Week

A collection of fascinating interviews with 19 of today's most notable programmers, including Jonathan Sachs (Lotus 1-2-3), Gary Kildall (CP/M), Bill Gates (BASIC), John Warnock (PostScript), and many others. Each interview examines the forces, the events, and the personality traits that have influenced the programmer's work.
Edited by Susan Lammers, 392 pages, $14.95, softcover, Order Code 86-95421

Available wherever fine books are sold, or place your credit card order by calling 1-800-638-3030. In Maryland, call collect 824-7300.

The manuscript for this book was prepared and submitted to Microsoft Press in electronic form. Text files were processed and formatted using Microsoft Word.

Cover design by Becker Design Associates
Interior text design by Darcie S. Furlan
Principal typographer: Ruth Pettis
Principal production artist: Peggy Herman

Text and display composition by Microsoft Press in Palatino, using the Magna composition system and the Linotronic 300 laser imagesetter.